Kansas City Jazz

Kansas City Jazz

From Ragtime to Bebop—A History

Frank Driggs and Chuck Haddix

OXFORD
UNIVERSITY PRESS

2005

OXFORD

UNIVERSITY PRESS

Oxford University Press, Inc., publishes works that further
Oxford University's objective of excellence
in research, scholarship, and education.

Oxford   New York
Auckland   Cape Town   Dar es Salaam   Hong Kong   Karachi
Kuala Lumpur   Madrid   Melbourne   Mexico City   Nairobi
New Delhi   Shanghai   Taipei   Toronto

With offices in
Argentina   Austria   Brazil   Chile   Czech Republic   France   Greece
Guatemala   Hungary   Italy   Japan   Poland   Portugal   Singapore
South Korea   Switzerland   Thailand   Turkey   Ukraine   Vietnam

Published by Oxford University Press, Inc.
198 Madison Avenue, New York, NY 10016
www.oup.com

Library of Congress Cataloging-in-Publication Data
Driggs, Frank.
Kansas City jazz : from ragtime to bebop / Frank Driggs and Chuck Haddix.
p. cm.
Notes: Includes bibliographical references and index.
Contents: Tales from Tom's town—Carrie's gone to Kansas City—
Get low-down blues—The territories—Blue devil blues—Moten's swing—
Until the real thing comes along—Roll 'em, Pete—Hootie's blues.
ISBN-13: 978-0-19-504767-7
ISBN-10: 0-19-504767-2
1. Jazz—Missouri—Kansas City—History and criticism.
I. Haddix, Chuck. II. Title.
ML3508.8.K37 D75 2005
781.65'09778'411—dc22
200463568

1 3 5 7 9 8 6 4 2
Printed in the United States of America
on acid-free paper

*For the late Richard Smith, who gave so much to this project,
and Joan Peyser, for everything you are. Much love.*

F. D.

*In fond memory of
Milton Morris, Dave E. Dexter, Jr., and the Honorable T. J. Pendergast,
who took me to the old town, inspired me to tell the story, and made it all happen.*

And for Terri Mac.

C. H.

Contents

Preface

THIS HISTORY OF KANSAS CITY JAZZ is decades in the making. In 1977, Frank Driggs entered into a contract with Oxford University Press to write a history of Kansas City Jazz. As the leading authority on Kansas City Jazz, he brought considerable resources to the project. Over the years, he had written extensively on the development of jazz in Kansas City and the Southwest, interviewed many of the musicians who created the tradition, and amassed a hefty collection of photos.

Driggs first heard the siren call of jazz while attending Princeton in the late 1940s. Listening to 78s of Jelly Roll Morton, King Oliver, Bunk Johnson, and other early New Orleans pioneers, Driggs fell under the spell of the music. After graduation, Driggs discovered Kansas City Jazz and began earnestly collecting 78 rpm discs of Bennie Moten, Count Basie, Jay McShann, and other Kansas City bands. Seeking long-out-of-print 78s, he became a regular fixture at Boris Rose's crowded studio in New York City on 15th Street east of the Third Avenue El. Rose, voluble and erudite, sold dubbed acetate discs of rare sides. More often than not, Driggs found himself standing elbow to elbow with the pale and gaunt avant-garde composer Alan Hovhaness.

Rose introduced Driggs to Marshall Stearns, whose Institute of Jazz Studies was running full blast out of his townhouse at 108 Waverly Place near Washington Square. Joining a dozen other acolytes, Driggs helped Stearns by teaching overflow adult education courses. On the side, Driggs interviewed Andy Kirk, Walter Page, Ed Lewis, and other veteran musicians from the Kansas City tradition who had settled in the New York area.

With Stearns's encouragement and financial help, Driggs went to Kansas City in October 1957 to gather more background and interviews. On the recommendation of trumpeter Ed Lewis, Driggs contacted Richard Smith, an official with the African American Musicians Union Local 627. The two hit it off, and Smith gave Driggs entrée into the tightly knit jazz community. Driggs spent the next two weeks interviewing musicians and enjoying nightly Jay McShann's Quintet at Johnny Baker's at 55th and Troost. Driggs came away from his visit more convinced of the significance of Kansas City Jazz.

From 1961 to 1967, Driggs worked with John Hammond at Columbia Records, producing the critically acclaimed Robert Johnson reissues. Back in Kansas City in the early 1970s to review a concert of college bands for Time-Life Records, Driggs met long-time bandleader Warren Durrett and conducted more interviews. In 1974, Driggs went to work for RCA-Victor, reviving its Bluebird label. After leaving RCA-Victor in 1977, Driggs wrote several chapters on Kansas City Jazz and submitted them to Sheldon Meyer at Oxford University Press. Meyer liked what he saw and gave Driggs a contract. However, after spending the summer writing, Driggs realized he couldn't complete the book without additional research.

For more than a decade, Driggs had collected photographs and memorabilia of jazz musicians, amassing a huge collection. By 1980, the collection had become a full-time business, keeping Driggs in New York, so he put the book aside until 1987 when he returned to Kansas City for the annual conference of the International Association of Jazz Record Collectors (IAJRC) at the invitation of Duncan Schiedt. Ken Posten, a former trumpet player and head of Kansas City's Jazz Commission, picked Driggs up at the airport and squired him around town. While in Kansas City, Driggs conducted more interviews and research. Driggs enlisted Posten to help with the local research, but he soon left Kansas City for a job with KOLN in Long Beach, California. Ironically, Chuck Haddix had crossed paths with Driggs at the IAJRC conference, but the two did not meet.

Around the same time Driggs signed with Oxford, Haddix embarked on his own research into Kansas City Jazz. While working in the record business, he became friends with Jay McShann, George Salisbury, Buddy Anderson, and numerous other musicians from the golden age of Kansas City Jazz. Haddix received a crash course in the history of Kansas City Jazz from legendary club owner and raconteur Milton Morris, at his namesake club on Main Street. Inspired by Morris's stories of the glory days of Kansas City Jazz, Haddix began to explore its history in earnest. In 1984, Haddix joined the staff of KCUR-FM, Kansas City's public radio station, as a jazz and blues producer. In 1987, he became the director of the Marr Sound Archives, a collection of historic sound recordings in the Miller Nichols Library at the University of Missouri–Kansas City. Dave E. Dexter, Jr., record producer, journalist, and the first to write about Kansas City Jazz, gave his collection to the sound archives in 1988. Becoming friends, Dexter encouraged Haddix to further research and write about Kansas City Jazz.

Driggs and Haddix first met in New York during the spring of 1994. After spending the afternoon comparing notes the two decided to complete the book together. Oxford issued a new contract in 1997, including Haddix as a co-author. Haddix then proceeded to collect additional interviews and systematically make copies of coverage of the bands, musicians, and others who created Kansas City Jazz style in microfilms of the *Kansas City Call, Kansas City Sun, Kansas City American, Kansas City Journal-Post, Kansas City Star, Down Beat, Metronome*, and other publications of the day. The information gleaned from the newspapers and periodicals was then organized into a timeline that chronicled in great detail the development of Kansas City Jazz, against the background of events unfolding nationally. Working together, with considerable back and forth between New York and Kansas City, Haddix and Driggs finally finished what is the first complete history of Kansas City Jazz.

Kansas City Jazz

Tell us a story, and don't let it be a lie.
Let it *mean* something if it's only one note.

Gene Ramey

Introduction

KANSAS CITY, MISSOURI, a cradle of jazz, along with New Orleans, Chicago, and New York, bred a distinct style of jazz that swiftly grew from ragtime to bebop. In 1921, James Scott published one of his last great rags, "Don't Jazz Me Rag (I'm Music)." Twenty years later, Charlie Parker composed "What Price Love," a bebop classic later renamed "Yardbird Suite." The golden age of Kansas City Jazz produced a legion of bands and soloists who changed the course of American music. Surprisingly, little scholarship has been devoted to the development of Kansas City Jazz.

Like Lerner and Lowe's Brigadoon, the celebrated mythical hamlet, Kansas City Jazz is an enigma, more myth than fact. Oral histories of musicians who created Kansas City jazz style relate epic tales of musical cutting contests and marathon battles of bands. Lacking context, these oral histories remain anecdotal, failing to trace the complete story of Kansas City Jazz. Generally, writers from either coast demurred spending extended stretches researching jazz in Kansas City, preferring to rely on second-hand sources. While the rise of the Kansas City jazz style and its contribution to the evolution of jazz nationally have been largely overlooked, the journey of jazz from New Orleans to New York has been well documented.

Jazz originated in New Orleans just after the turn of the century, the Creole offspring of an uneasy marriage of African-tribal and European-American musical traditions. An international port nestled on the banks of the Mississippi River, New Orleans cultivated a thriving sin industry, centered on Storyville, a city-sanctioned red-light district skirting the southwestern edge of the French Quarter. The bordellos and honky-tonks lining the narrow crowded streets of Storyville along with the dance halls scattered throughout the city provided steady work for Buddy Bolden, Louis Armstrong, Jelly Roll

Morton, Kid Ory, King Oliver, Sidney Bechet, and other first-generation New Orleans jazz greats. Free from convention, they jazzed up the standard repertoire of waltzes, ragtime, plantation songs, and popular standards with blue notes, vibrato, unevenly accented 4/4 rhythm, and countermelody, creating an uninhibited mode of musical expression that at the time was indelicately referred to as "gutbucket."

Shortly after its conception in Storyville, jazz spread across the country. Pianist Jelly Roll Morton, the self-proclaimed inventor of jazz, traveled widely from California to New York, heralding the arrival of the musical upstart. Bassist Bill Johnson led the first band to venture outside of New Orleans. After traveling across the Southwest with a brass band on a vaudeville circuit, Johnson stopped off in Los Angeles, where he formed the Creole Orchestra featuring his brother Dink on drums and cornetist Freddie Keppard. In 1917, the Original Dixieland Jazz Band, five white musicians from New Orleans, introduced the term jazz to the national vernacular with the wildly successful Victor recording "Dixie Jazz Band One-Step/Livery Stable Blues," recorded in New York. The closing of the Storyville district in November 1917 by the U.S. Navy hastened the exodus of New Orleans bands and musicians. New Orleans jazz, distinguished by collective improvisation from the front line featuring a cornet, trombone, and clarinet, evolved little beyond the original style but greatly influenced the development of jazz in other cities, particularly Chicago. With Storyville gone, a mass exodus of musicians journeyed north up the Mississippi and by railroad to Chicago and other northern cities.

Strategically situated on the southwestern shore of Lake Michigan near the confluence of rivers flowing west to the Mississippi River, Chicago brokered goods and services moving east and west on the national waterways. Chicago readily grew from a swampy wilderness outpost into a bustling center for transportation, commerce, manufacturing, and entertainment, becoming the nation's second largest city by 1900. Mayor Big Bill Thompson, a flamboyant, hard-drinking former Nebraska cowboy, first elected in 1915, encouraged the proliferation of cabarets and dance halls in the African American neighborhood surrounding State Street on the South Side. Protected by the Mayor's office, the clubs carried on business as usual after the enactment of Prohibition in January 1920. An astute politician, Thompson rewarded the loyalty and votes of African Americans with jobs in city government. Drawn by opportunity, African Americans from the Mississippi Delta to the Gulf Coast migrated to Chicago in droves. New Orleans jazz expatriates inspired the development of the Chicago style, which emphasized individual soloists and a freer rhythmic approach. At the center of this exciting new jazz was the extraordinary cornetist Louis Armstrong, jazz's first great soloist, whose Hot Five and Hot Seven groups revolutionized the jazz form.

Arriving in Chicago on the Panama Limited railroad with instruments in hand, King Oliver, Louis Armstrong, and other New Orleans jazz greats stepped up to steady engagements at Lincoln Gardens, De Luxe Café, Entertainer's Café, and other top night spots. The city remained segregated into a patchwork of ethnic neighborhoods, but African Americans and whites mingled freely in the black and tan clubs dotting the South Side, known as the "Stroll." Benny Goodman, Gene Krupa, Mezz Mezzrow, Jimmy McPartland, Frank Teschemacher, Bud Freeman, and other young white musicians idolized Oliver, Armstrong, Johnny Dodds, and other New Orleans musicians. Astute students of the New Orleans style, they added polished solos and rhythmic abandon, moving to an original Chicago sound. The sweep of a civic cleanup changed their musical direction. On the heels of a crackdown on the speakeasies in the mid-1920s, a host of Chicago musicians moved on to New York.

New York, the nation's largest metropolitan area, produced a number of outstanding big jazz bands, leading to the advent of arrangements orchestrating the sections and soloists that greatly enhanced jazz's popularity. New York served as the entertainment industry's hub. Film companies located on Long Island's Bay Shore captured the antics of the Keystone Cops and romantic escapades of Rudolph Valentino. In Manhattan, tunesmiths, hunched over pianos, frantically churned out catchy hits and sentimental favorites for the publishing houses lining West 28th Street between Broadway and Sixth Avenue, known as "Tin Pan Alley." Uptown in Harlem, W. C. Handy, the father of the blues, operated the Pace-Handy Music Company, the leading publisher of African American composers. Theatrical revues premiered the season's hit tunes in the stately theaters on Broadway before heading out on the vaudeville circuits crisscrossing the country. Shut out of Broadway, African American composers such as Eubie Blake, Noble Sissle, and James P. Johnson mounted their own grand productions at the Lafayette and other theaters in Harlem. "Shuffle Along," "Africana," and a string of touring African American revues gave audiences across the nation a glimpse of the exotic sophistication of Harlem, the nucleus of African American culture. Young writers and intellectuals like Langston Hughes flocked to Harlem, creating a renaissance of literature and music. At the time, the literature of the Harlem renaissance received little notice outside of the African American community, but the music created an international sensation.

Bandleader James Reese Europe pioneered New York's orchestral style of jazz. Europe, leading the Clef Club, a group of professional musicians and vocalists, presented a series of programs featuring ragtime, band favorites, and light classical selections at the Manhattan Casino, a spacious ballroom at 155th Street and Eighth Avenue. During World War I, then Lieutenant Europe led the legendary 369th Infantry "Hellfighter" band across France. Back in the states, Europe incorporated jazz into his sixty-piece brass band's repertoire and toured the country, until he was murdered by a deranged band member in 1919. Fletcher Henderson and Duke Ellington filled the void left by Europe's untimely death.

Pianist Fletcher Henderson hailed from a middle-class family in Georgia. Moving to New York in 1920, Henderson worked as a song plugger for Pace-Handy music before joining the staff of Black Swan records, a pioneering African American label. The phenomenal success of Mamie Smith's "Crazy Blues," recorded for the OKeh label in 1920, spawned a thriving race record industry that targeted African Americans. An in-demand session musician, Henderson became the accompanist of choice for Bessie Smith and a bevy of leading women blues shouters. Henderson fronted a series of small pickup ensembles, one of which evolved into a full-size orchestra by 1923. He carefully selected band members, recruiting Coleman Hawkins, a tenor saxophonist with a big dense tone, and Louis Armstrong as star soloists. Arranger Don Redman orchestrated the expansion of the band, voicing the sections to counterpoint Armstrong's fiery solos, creating for the first time a distinctive New York style of jazz. Henderson's recordings and long-run engagement at the grand Roseland Ballroom influenced the musical direction of orchestras across the country.

Before long, Duke Ellington eclipsed Henderson in popularity. Originally from Washington, D.C., Ellington arrived in New York in the spring of 1923 with novelty clarinetist Wilbur Sweatman's band. After initially failing to find a niche in New York, Ellington retreated to the comfort of his mother's home. Back in New York later that year, Ellington assumed leadership of the Washingtonians, a six-piece band that alternated between the Hollywood and Kentucky Clubs on Broadway. After moving uptown to the prestigious Cotton Club in 1927, Ellington expanded to a full-size band. A prolific composer, Ellington recorded for a wide variety of labels, evolving from his early "jungle music," inspired by the exotic decor of the Cotton Club, into a sophisticated orchestral expression of jazz. His music surpassed yet remained anchored in the New York tradition, and fostered a plethora of talented young jazz soloists. New York style continued to evolve from swing to bebop and beyond by absorbing musicians and bands from across the country, notably from Kansas City and the Midwest.

Influenced little by the other cradles of jazz, Kansas City spawned an original style. Bennie Moten and other early Kansas City bandleaders eclipsed the sway of New Orleans by voicing the brass and reed sections and crafting simple head arrangements, so-called because they were played from memory. Chicago's musicians union protected the jobs of local musicians by denying residency to visiting bands. Made unwelcome, Kansas City bands played only short stretches in Chicago, limiting interaction with local musicians. The arrival of Fletcher Henderson and Duke Ellington in Kansas City inspired Bennie Moten and Andy Kirk to create more polished arrangements and try their hand in New York. After initially emulating the New York bands, Kansas City bands led by Moten, Kirk, and later Count Basie transcended that influence to create a rawer, hard-swinging style of orchestral jazz. These so-called territory bands crisscrossed the region from Kansas and the Dakotas through the Southwest, especially Texas, and across the Mississippi, bringing a wide variety of jazz soloists, singers, and musical sounds.

Located in the heart of America, straddling the state line between Kansas and Missouri, Kansas City at first glance appears to be an unlikely location for the development of a unique jazz style. A frontier town hunkered down at the confluence of the Missouri and Kansas Rivers, Kansas City served as a crossroads for the great migration west, outfitting wagon trains headed west and brokering raw goods headed east. In 1869, Kansas City elbowed ahead of its nearest competitors to erect the first railroad bridge spanning the Missouri River. The already thriving river town became a major railway hub. After the Civil War, Kansas City became a business center for points north, south, east, and west. Commerce bred culture, and during the 1920s Kansas City blossomed into a cosmopolitan oasis of culture and entertainment, ranging from grand theaters and ballrooms to a thriving sin industry.

Kansas City's government, ruled from 1911 to 1939 by a Democratic political machine driven by Tom Pendergast, a burly Irishman with a twinkle in his eye, fostered the wanton nightlife rife with gambling, prostitution, and bootlegging. Twelfth Street, a tawdry string of taxi dance joints, bars, and gambling dens, stretched a mile east of downtown. The red-light district on 14th Street thrived in the shadow of city hall. Kansas City Jazz, a hardy hybrid, flourished in this immoderate environment. This is the story of Kansas City Jazz.

1

Tales from Tom's Town

ORIGINALLY A WILD-AND-WOOLY RIVER TOWN, established ahead of the great westward migration, Kansas City grew into a center of commerce and entertainment, becoming nationally known by the late 1930s as the "Paris of the Plains"—a comparison drawn, not for Kansas City's broad boulevards and fountains, but its immoderate nightlife and laissez-faire attitude. "Kansas City is more like Paris," syndicated columnist Westbrook Pegler observed. "The stuff is there, the gambling joints and the brothels, including among the latter a restaurant conducted in the imitation of that one in Paris, more haunted than the Louvre, where the waitresses wear nothing on before and a little less than half of that behind. But like Parisians, the people of Kansas City obviously believe that such things must be and, also like the Parisians, are proud of their own indifference."[1] Edward Morrow advised readers of the *Omaha World-Herald*, "[I]f you want to see some sin, forget Paris and go to Kansas City. With the possible exception of such renowned centers as Singapore and Port Said, Kansas City has the greatest sin industry in the world."[2] Ironically, the local government, run by a Democratic machine headed by Boss Tom Pendergast, fostered the vice and corruption. Kansas City Jazz flowered in this intemperate atmosphere. A stocky bull of a man with piercing blue eyes, Boss Tom dominated Kansas City and Missouri state politics from 1911 until his 1939 indictment for income tax evasion.

During the 1920s and 1930s, musicians from across the country flocked to Kansas City, drawn by the easy ambience and plentiful jobs in the dance halls and nightclubs sprinkled liberally between 12th and 18th Streets. Arriving in 1929, pianist Mary Lou Williams found Kansas City to be a "heavenly" place, with "music everywhere in the Negro section of town, and fifty or more cabarets rocking on 12th and 18th Streets. . . . Most of the night spots were run by politicians and hoodlums, and the town was wide open for drinking, gambling and pretty much every form of vice. Naturally, work was plentiful for musicians."[3]

Gambling dens, nightclubs, and taxi dance halls lined 12th Street, extending a mile east from the heart of downtown. Journalist Dave E. Dexter, Jr., estimated that one stretch of 12th Street "boasted as many as 20 illegal saloons and niteries in a single block."[4] The clubs ranged from rough, bucket-of-blood joints with sawdust on the floor and a stomp-down piano player, to elegant nightclubs, presenting elaborate floor shows accompanied by full bands. Club owners christened new clubs by giving a cab driver five dollars and the key to the front door with instructions to drive as far as he could and throw away the key.[5] "The clubs didn't close," recalled bandleader Jay McShann. "About 7:00 in the morning the cleanup man would come and all the guys at the bar would move out of the way. And the bartender would serve them at the table while the place got cleaned up. Then they would go back to the bar. The clubs went 24 hours a day."[6]

Downtown, at the Chesterfield Club on 9th Street, waitresses clad only in shoes and see-through cellophane aprons served up a businessmen's lunch. For adornment, they shaved their pubic hair in the shape of playing card pips. Briskly circulating among the tables crowded by cigar puffing politicos, businessmen, and shy high-school boys on a lark, the waitresses skillfully picked up tips without using their hands. The State Line Tavern on Southwest Boulevard sat astride the state boundary between Kansas and Missouri. A white line down the middle of the floor marked the border between the two states. When agents from one state raided the joint, customers just stepped across the line to the safety of the neighboring state. At Milton Morris's Hey Hay Club in the North End at 4th and Cherry, patrons sat on bales of hay in a converted barn decorated by corn shucks. Musicians decked out as work hands topped by red bandannas performed on a crude bandstand fashioned out of the flatbed of a hay wagon. During Prohibition, a hand-lettered cardboard sign posted behind the bar advertised twenty-five-cent whiskey shots and marijuana joints. Perched behind the bar, puffing on his signature cigar, owl-like Morris nonchalantly reasoned since both were illegal, "Why not?"[7]

At the Sunset Club situated on the southwest corner of 12th and Woodland, pianist Pete Johnson effortlessly rolled chorus after chorus of boogie-woogie, accompanying Big Joe Turner, apron clad, hollering the blues while dispensing drinks from behind the bar. The manager of the Sunset, Walter "Piney" Brown, a trim, dashing gambler well-known for his generosity to musicians, lorded over the nightly festivities upstairs, while number runners congregated in the basement, counting up the day's take and picking the lucky winners. "Piney was like a patron saint to all musicians," recalled saxophonist Eddie Barefield. "He used to take care of them. In fact, he was like a father to me. . . . Most all the playing and jamming happened at Piney's place. Piney was a man, he didn't care how much it cost; . . . if you needed money to pay your rent, he would give it to you and take you out and buy booze. He was a man you could always depend on for something if you needed it, as a musician."[8] In turn, musicians repaid Piney's generosity by lining up for the after-hours jam session at the Sunset. Often by sunrise, as many as fifteen musicians crowded the bandstand at the Sunset. Across the street, passersby gawked at sporting men in high-waisted gambler stripe pants intently shooting craps in the front window of the Lone Star. A short walk east, past a riot of neon signs and the clanging of trolleys lumbering down the center of the street, Count Basie and the Barons of Rhythm held court at the Reno Club, a nondescript storefront tucked away just a few blocks east of city hall. The weekly "Spook Breakfasts" at the Reno beginning at 4:00 Monday morning continued all day. Scores of musicians, instrument in hand, milled around in the alley behind the Reno, waiting to lock horns with tenor saxophonist Lester Young and other star soloists of the Basie band. The wildly popular early morning sessions sparked the famed tradition of "Blue Monday" parties. Musicians, not bound by state closing laws, gathered in clubs across the city in the wee hours of Monday morning, jamming until the people went home late the next day.

Gambling parlors scattered throughout the city offered action for high rollers and scratch gamblers alike. Local officials kicked off the horse-racing season on Memorial Day weekend at the Riverside Park Jockey Club, an illegal track operated by the Pendergast machine. Pendergast's crony, Judge Henry McElroy, the flinty city manager, gleefully cut the ribbon on opening day, an unofficial city holiday named in his honor.[9] Special streetcars and buses departed every few minutes from 7th and Grand, ferrying gamblers to the track located just north of the river, where they "invested" in their favorite nags, running seven races daily. On Memorial Day 1935, 17,000 spectators packed the stands.[10] The *Kansas City Journal-Post* splashed national race results across its front page. The cry "they're off in Texas" drifted across hotel lobbies, where racing windows stood shoulder to shoulder with courtesy desks. Bored matrons from the country club set, properly attired in stylish hats and white gloves, whiled away their afternoons lounging in bingo and tango parlors clustered around the busy intersection of 39th and Main. Policy writers swarmed the 18th and Vine area, stopping at each house as punctually as postmen. Slot machines vied for space with soda fountains on drugstore counters. City Manager McElroy dismissed complaints about the ready availability of one-arm bandits, stating flatly, "Nobody but a sucker would put a nickel, dime or quarter into a slot machine." As an afterthought, he added, "If the slot machine didn't get the sucker money something else would."[11]

The red-light district stretched blocks east from downtown on 14th Street. The brazen display of flesh in the large windows of the "dreary flats" lining 14th Street amazed journalist Edward Morrow. "In every window, upstairs and down, were women. Some knitted, some read, some sewed. Bright lights, in some cases bordering the windows, lighted the women's faces . . . when the cab drew near, the women dropped what they had in their hands, seized nickels and began to tap them furiously on the window pane."[12] Journalist Westbrook Pegler compared the sound of tapping on the windowpanes, accompanying his departing cab, to "hail."[13] Police Chief Otto Higgins defended the civic sanctioning of prostitution, explaining, "[W]hy, if you bother the girls you just push them into the back room. Then you don't know what's going on. This way we can maintain control over them."[14] Years later, President Harry Truman surprised club owner Milton Morris during a visit in the Oval Office by inquiring, right off the bat, after the welfare of the "whores on 14th Street."[15]

During Prohibition, liquor flowed freely in old Kaycee. Johnny Lazia, head of the North Side Democratic Club and an associate of Al Capone, lorded over an estimated $5 million-a-year bootlegging operation.[16] Dapper and soft spoken with wireless rim glasses that gave him the air of a clerk, Lazia exerted considerable control over the police department, hiring new recruits, and fielding phone calls at police headquarters. Journalist John Cameron Swayze recalled walking past "an alert waiter, attired in stiffly-starched white jacket, sitting primly in the front seat of a police car parked outside a 'speak' [speakeasy]. He was listening for calls on the police radio as the so-called officers of the law tarried at the bar within."[17] The climate of lawlessness gave safe haven to Harvey Bailey, the Barrow gang, and other gangsters on the lam. The Union Station Massacre established Kansas City's national notoriety for lawlessness.

On June 17, 1933, triggerman Verne Miller, bank robber Charles Arthur "Pretty Boy" Floyd, and Adam Richetti, a psychopathic alcoholic, converged on Union Station determined to free convicted bank robber Frank Nash, who was being escorted from Hot Springs, Arkansas, to the Federal Prison in Leavenworth, Kansas, by two FBI agents and an Oklahoma sheriff. Two Kansas City FBI agents and a pair of trusted local policemen met the law enforcement officers and Nash, as their Missouri-Pacific train pulled in the cavernous, limestone Union Station. Miller, Floyd, and Richetti got the drop on the lawmen, hastily loading Nash into a Chevrolet sedan parked right outside the arched entrance of the Station for the quick trip to Leavenworth. The ambush went awry, and when the smoke cleared, Nash, a federal agent, the Oklahoma sheriff, and two local policemen lay dead on the plaza in front of the bustling station. The national publicity ensuing from the bloody incident cemented Kansas City's reputation as a safe harbor for criminals. In the wake of the infamous Union Station Massacre, the national press designated Kansas City as the "Crime Capital" of the United States.[18]

THE TRADITION OF VICE AND LAWLESSNESS, as typified by the Union Station Massacre, stemmed from Kansas City's roots as a frontier town. Originally a humble wilderness settlement, in a forest of giant sycamores at the confluence

of the Kansas and Missouri Rivers, Kansas City, Missouri, quickly grew into a
bustling hub for transportation and business. In February 1831, Gabriel
Prudhomme purchased 271 acres of land, later known as Kansas City, for
$340. He farmed the fertile soil and operated a ferry from the natural rock
landing on the Missouri River. When he died later that year in a barroom
brawl, the land passed to his pregnant wife and six children. In July 1838, his
heirs auctioned off the land. When the guardian of the estate awarded the
land to a friend for a song, the courts, suspecting collusion, stepped in and
voided the sale. The following November, a corporation formed by fourteen
civic and business leaders purchased the land. After much discussion, they
decided to name the new burg the Town of Kansas after the Kansas Indians
who lived just west near the Kansas River.[19] The name proved an apt choice
considering the Kansas Indians' love of feasting, drinking, and gambling.[20]
Serving as a port of entry to the nation's westward expansion, Kansas City
prospered, selling goods to the forty-niners rushing to the gold fields of California and wagons of families lumbering westward across the Kansas Territory, a dusty prairie known as the Great American Desert, on the Santa Fe,
California, and Oregon Trails. Kansas City developed into a regional center
of commerce, moving furs and raw materials east and goods from river boats
to points west, south, and north. During the mid-1850s, road crews cleaved
the towering clay bluffs above the teeming river bottom, and the city moved
up the hill away from seasonal floods.

During the Civil War, border strife between Kansas free staters and southern sympathizers in Missouri engulfed Kansas City. Jay Hawkers from Kansas and Missouri Bushwhackers exchanged bloody raids across the state line,
wreaking havoc on the area surrounding Kansas City. Abolitionists led by
John Brown raided Missouri farms, liberating slaves. In retaliation, the Bushwhackers burned farms and terrorized towns just across the border in Kansas.
In August 1863, passions boiled over after four female relatives of southern
sympathizers, imprisoned in Kansas City by federal authorities, died when
their makeshift prison collapsed. Bushwhackers led by William Quantrill, a
former schoolteacher, descended on Lawrence, Kansas, fifty miles to the west,
slaughtered 150 men and boys, and then burned the town to the ground.
Four days later, Union Brigadier General Thomas Ewing issued his infamous
Order No. 11, commanding the displacement of all persons located outside
of a mile radius of union outposts in Jackson, Cass, and Bates Counties, bordering Kansas. Those who could prove their loyalty to the Union cause were
allowed to move to Union posts or Kansas. Twenty thousand residents who
refused to sign the loyalty oath fled east and south in a chaotic exodus, carrying what they could. The Union army then looted and destroyed their farms.[21]
Missouri's leading painter, George Caleb Bingham, commemorated the hor-
rific event in "Order No. 11," portraying aristocratic women begging Ewing
for mercy as the surrounding countryside burned. After the war, with little

love lost between local and federal authorities, Kansas City became a haven
for the James brothers and other outlaws. A boisterous frontier town, Kansas
City attracted scores of gamblers, con artists, and prostitutes intent on making a quick buck off the suckers heading west. The legions of vice engaged in
a running battle with the forces of reform, with vice ultimately prevailing in
the war for the soul of the city.

Sanctioned by the city fathers, gambling and prostitution grew into major
civic undertakings. In his history of the Pendergast machine, *Tom's Town*,
William Reddig recounted how gambling permeated the social fabric of Kansas City.

> The faro banks at Marble Hall and No. 3 Missouri Avenue were famous
> throughout the West. Scholarly gamblers like Canada Bill, who kept himself
> solvent betting on Webster's spelling and definition of words, and colorful
> plungers like Wild Bill Hickok, the two-gun marshal of Abilene, made the
> town their headquarters. Jesse James found relaxation in the gambling halls
> during periods when he lived incognito in Kansas City and was not molested.
> When they were not figuring on deals in lots, grain, hogs and cattle and other
> matters of commerce, the citizens exercised their financial genius at chuck-a-
> luck, faro, three-card monte, roulette, high five, keno, poker and, occasionally
> craps. They bet on horse races, dog fights, free-for-alls with rats, cock fights
> and in extremity, they played fly-loo. This last game called for rare judgement,
> the players placing their money on common houseflies and guessing which one
> would move first, in what direction and how far.[22]

Kansas City's notorious gaming parlors eventually caught the attention of
the Missouri state legislature. In 1881, the legislature, dominated by farmers,
pushed through the Johnson anti-gambling law, triggering a mild depression
in Kansas City's gambling industry. Reddig described how one indignant gambler met his demise in a grand gesture of objection.

> The Kansas City protest against this interference with freedom was registered
> in melodramatic fashion by Bob Potee, the elegant Virginia gentleman who
> was proprietor of the faro bank at No. 3 Missouri Avenue. Potee saw the Johnson
> law as the ominous dawn of a new era and decided he didn't want to be around
> to witness all the changes that were coming. One day he put on his high silk hat
> and gloves, picked up his gold-headed cane and took a walk down to the Mis-
> souri River. He kept walking majestically until the muddy waters swirled over
> his head. His body was recovered and the town staged an appropriate ceremony
> of farewell to a great man and his age. His funeral service was held in a Grand
> Avenue church and the Reverend Samuel Bookstaver Bell, a popular preacher
> of the day, delivered an impressive sermon over his casket. Literally, as in the
> words of the "Cowboy's Lament," six tall gamblers bore the casket into the
> church and carried it out for Bob Potee's last journey to his Virginia home.[23]

Unfortunately, Potee died in vain. Local authorities thumbed their noses at the state anti-gambling law, so the gaming continued unabated.

Prospectors flush from the Colorado gold fields and wealthy Texas cattlemen thronged to Kansas City's wealth of brothels, considered the finest in the Southwest. Annie Chambers's stately resort set the standard for other houses in the district. Located on the corner of 3rd and Wyandotte, the plain facade of the three-story brick building belied the opulence within. Patrons entering through massive metal doors framed by a portico supported by six bamboo columns encountered Chambers's name spelled out with blue tile in the colorful mosaic in the foyer floor. The letters A and C highlighted by red lights woven in the intricate brass filigree framed the entryway. A self-contained pleasure palace, the twenty-four-room estate lavishly decorated with gilt, marble, fine art, and massive mirrors featured a ballroom, barbershop, and wine tasting room. Miss Annie, a tall, handsome, dignified woman, cut a striking figure in the community. Local bankers eagerly lent her money, and the police department often helped at her parties, taking tickets and maintaining crowd control.

Cultured and well educated, Miss Annie instructed her girls on manners and ladylike behavior. "You should have seen some of them when they first came here," Miss Annie exclaimed. "Bless you, they looked worse than homely. They were down and out. I made them attractive. I bought them fine clothes. I showed them how to do their hair; I taught them manners. You wouldn't have known they were the same girls. It wasn't always the most beautiful girls who were the most popular. Manners and personality count more than looks, you know . . . I taught them manners and charm. The men who patronized my house demanded that. They wanted the girls to be feminine at all times."[24] Miss Annie's charges often wed clients, occasionally marrying into local high society. Like the booming city, Miss Annie, the other madams, and their girls all prospered, taking in an estimated one and a half million dollars a year.[25] Attracted by the thriving economy and tolerant atmosphere, waves of immigrants and first generation Americans flooded Kansas City.

The completion of the Hannibal Bridge in 1869, the first railroad bridge spanning the Missouri River, brought large populations of Irish, Germans, English, Canadians, Swedes, and African Americans to Kansas City. Hunkering down in the West Bottoms, they worked in the teeming stockyards, meatpacking houses, and railroad yards. Jim Pendergast, a big burly Irishman with a handlebar mustache, arrived in 1876 from St. Joseph, Missouri, located 70 miles upriver. Equipped with more ambition than means, Pendergast immediately found work as a smelter in an iron foundry. According to local lore, Pendergast's fortunes turned when his bet on a long shot at the horse-racing track paid off big. Big Jim prudently invested his winnings in a saloon, naming it Climax after the horse that arrived in the money. He expanded his operation in 1881, purchasing the American House, a combination saloon, boarding house, and hotel, strategically located near the bustling train station, Union Depot. Setting up shop among the battery of hustlers, gamblers, pimps, and whores surrounding the depot for blocks, Pendergast prospered.[26] A hale and well-met fellow, he acted as a banker, cashing payroll checks for his uncouth clientele. In turn, Big Jim relied on those he helped to deliver votes for the local Democratic party.[27]

In 1890, Pendergast expanded his sphere of influence, opening a second saloon at 508 Main Street, a block south of Market Square. The new saloon promptly became a popular gathering spot for businessmen, high-roller gamblers, lawyers, and politicians from city hall. While rubbing elbows with the elite, Pendergast continued cultivating his interests in the West Bottoms. In 1892, his unwashed constituents elected him alderman of the "bloody First Ward," known for settling political disputes with the business ends of pool cues and bare-knuckle brawls. Moving easily into his role as political boss, Pendergast delivered large blocs of votes for the Democratic party, monopolizing Kansas City politics. "I've got lots of friends," Pendergast bragged to a sympathetic journalist. "And, by the way, that's all there is to this boss business—friends. You can't coerce people into doing things for you—you can't make them vote for you. I never coerced anybody in my life. Whenever you see a man bulldozing anybody he doesn't last long. Still, I've been called a boss. All there is to it is having friends, doing things for people, and then later on they'll do things for you."[28] As Pendergast devoted more and more time to politics, he recruited his brothers and sisters to help run his businesses.

Jim's youngest brother Tom arrived in late 1894. Barrel-chested with a thick neck and jutting jaw, young Tom proved to be an astute student of saloon-keeping and politics. Tom, a whiz with numbers, helped keep the books for Jim's enterprises. Athletic and quick with his fists, he earned respect in the rough-and-tumble First Ward. A natural politician, Tom understood the spirit of compromise and mixed well with the crowd of politicos haunting the Main Street saloon. Impressed by his younger brother's promise, Jim groomed Tom to succeed him as boss, establishing a political dynasty.

AFTER BIG JIM'S DEATH IN 1911, Tom took charge of the family's businesses and political faction, known as the Goats, named after the numerous goats roaming the back yards of the Irish families recently settled on the West Bluff, a working-class neighborhood adjacent to the mansions on Quality Hill. The Goats' main political opposition, the Rabbits, headed by the wily Uncle Joe Shannon, dwelt over the hill in the southeast part of town. Shannon's followers were named after the rabbits that frolicked around O.K. Creek meandering through the nearby wooded valley. As William Reddig explained in *Tom's Town*, "In the heat of a campaign an opposition orator called the Pendergast partisans Goats after their numerous animal pets. Jim Pendergast liked goats and happily accepted them as a symbol of his faction's devotion to freedom and other liberal ideals. Leading his delegation on a march to a convention for a battle with the Shannon boys, he roared: 'When we come over the hill like goats, they'll run like rabbits.' When the contest was over the Goats had seized control of City Hall, ousting the Shannon men from their easy jobs."[29]

Tom immediately expanded the family's political influence and business interests, establishing the T. J. Pendergast Wholesale Liquor Company, and purchasing the Jefferson Hotel at 6th and Wyandotte.[30] A six-story brick European-style hotel, the Jefferson sported a smart cabaret in the basement. Entertainers strolled from table to table, singing torch songs, as sharply dressed waiters dashed among the tables serving food and drinks. A reporter, covering the cabaret's disregard of closing laws for the crusading *Kansas City Star*, painted a lurid portrait of the lively nightlife emanating from the basement of the Jefferson. "Cabaret entertainers wandered from table to table, singing sensuous songs. . . . Midnight passed and the crowd of underworld habitues became hilarious. At one o'clock, the hour required by law at which to stop selling liquor, the orgy was at its height. The hours passed and the waiters were busier than ever dispensing drinks, for the Jefferson hotel has police protection and is free to ignore the closing law, observed by other cabarets. Outside the cabaret, motor cars and taxis were lined against the curb and there was a babble of song and laughter in the grill in the basement."[31] Ironically, Pendergast rarely participated in the late-night revelry, preferring to retire early for a good night's sleep. Like his brother Jim, he favored betting on horses for entertainment. As a political boss, Pendergast worked tirelessly to advance the interests of saloons and the gaming industry. Pendergast held potential forces of reform in check by forming an uneasy alliance with local civic and business leaders from the affluent Ward Parkway area on the southwestern edge of Kansas City. For their part, social leaders generally shied away from politics, striving instead to elevate the rabble by supporting the performing arts. Setting an example, the local gentry flocked to the bright lights of Kansas City's theaters for opera, drama, minstrel shows, melodrama, and vaudeville.

From the beginning music played an important role in Kansas City's social life. Arriving in 1821, the first permanent white settlers, thirty-one French fur trappers led by Francois and Berenice Chouteau, brought music with them. Two of the trappers, the Rivard Brothers, played fiddles. According to Father Bernard Donnelly, the area's Catholic priest and first historian, during the winter months when the river froze, bringing traffic to a standstill, the community threw parties where old and young danced to music played by the fiddlers. Years later, Berenice Chouteau brought in the city's first piano from St. Louis on a keel boat with supplies for the trading post.[32] Over the next five tumultuous decades, the area of the first white settlement became Kansas City.

A railroad hub for the Midwest and points west, Kansas City attracted top artists and touring companies along with appreciative patrons to pack the theaters. Built in 1870, the grand Coates Opera House at 10th and Broadway presented leading opera companies and stars. Patrons slogged through the muddy unpaved streets to attend nightly performances. Built in 1883, the ornate Gillis Theater located on the prestigious corner of 5th and Main featured stage productions by national theater companies. Intricate woodcarvings and colorful frescos adorned the lobby of the Gillis. Inside the spacious auditorium, lace curtains veiled the boxes overlooking the broad stage. Opened in 1887, the Ninth Street Theater brought theater's plebeian cousin, vaudeville, to Kansas City audiences. By 1920, Kansas City sported nine grand theaters, complete with pit orchestras.[33] The host of musicians working in the theaters, saloons, and cabarets dotting Kansas City created a ready market for instruments and sheet music.

Music stores multiplied, growing from five in 1871 to two dozen by 1916. The Kansas City Talking Machine Company, J. W. Jenkins & Sons, Carl Hoffman, and other music companies, specializing in instruments, phonographs, and sheet music, soon branched out into music publishing. In 1897, Harriet Woodbury, the co-owner of the Kansas City Talking Machine Company along with her husband, published "The Letter Edged in Black" under the pseudonym Hattie Nevada. The sentimental southern ballad about the narrator receiving a letter edged in black bearing news of his mother's death became a national success, selling 300,000 copies at fifty cents each.[34] Inspired by the success of "The Letter Edged in Black," local music stores readily ventured into publishing, just in time to capitalize on the ragtime craze sweeping the nation.

In 1899, Carl Hoffman published Scott Joplin's "Original Rags." After a dispute with Hoffman over publishing credits to "Original Rags," Joplin switched to John Stark & Son of Sedalia, Missouri, for the publication of his renowned "Maple Leaf Rag."[35] The popularity of Charles L. Johnson's "Dill Pickles Rag," published by Hoffman in 1906, helped establish ragtime nationally. In 1916, J. W. Jenkins Music, a massive six-story music store located at 1013-15 Walnut, published Euday Bowman's "12th Street Rag." Cutting a deal to make the gamblers in the faro parlors in the old town proud, Jenkins paid Bowman a mere $50 for "12th Street Rag," one of the biggest ragtime sellers of all time.[36]

The easy availability of sheet music, musical instruments, and band orchestration books spawned a number of top-notch white dance bands, during the dawn of the "Jazz Age." Leading the way, the Eddie Kuhn Band, Paul Tremaine's Aristocrats of Rhythm, and the Coon-Sanders Original Night Hawk Orchestra further established Kansas City's national reputation as a music center.

Organized in 1917, the Eddie Kuhn Band brought Loren Dallas McMurray, the first in a long line of great Kansas City saxophone players, to national prominence. Pianist Kuhn, slim and dapper with aquiline features, began his career as a composer of popular songs and ragtime. J. W. Jenkins Music Company published his "Cornshucks Rag" (1908), "Some Pumpkins" (1908), and "Pickled Beets Rag" (1909). Building on his early publishing successes, Kuhn opened a full-service music shop at the busy intersection of 12th and Main. Kuhn formed his first band during World War I, when conscription depleted the ranks of local musicians, leaving musical contractors unable to fill engagements. Kuhn stepped in to fill the void, assembling a crack seven-piece band, specializing in dance music. Facing little competition, he garnered a lion's share of hotel and country club jobs throughout the Midwest. In early 1920, the band embarked on a tour of ballrooms, auditoriums, conventions, and a relatively new phenomenon, auto shows, a circuit leading to the East Coast. Operating in and out of New York City that summer and fall, the band recorded for the Pathé and Emerson labels. Kuhn, a better businessman than bandleader, deferred on the bandstand to saxophonist McMurray, the band's star soloist and defacto musical leader.

A child prodigy, Loren Dallas McMurray cut his musical teeth performing popular standards, marches, novelties, and light classics with his father's saxophone band in their hometown, McPherson, Kansas, located 200 miles southwest of Kansas City. McMurray left home in 1917, crisscrossing the Midwest with a concert band and male quartet on the Redpath-Horner Chautauqua circuit, based in Kansas City. Inspired by the popular lyceum societies in New England, Chautauquas were traveling troupes of entertainers, musicians, and elocutionists who delivered uplifting messages and brought entertainment and culture to small towns. At the end of the season McMurray settled down in Kansas City. He worked briefly with violinist Emil Chaquette's society orchestra before joining the newly formed Eddie Kuhn Band. McMurray, stout with a lantern jaw and slicked-back brown hair parted down the middle in the style of the day, readily established a reputation as an innovator and outstanding soloist. Clarinetist Cy Dewar remembered McMurray as "one of the finest hot men" in Kansas City and the "first . . . to play the A-flat alto, while everyone was playing the C melody, also the first to start the slap tongue vogue."[37] The tour with the Kuhn Band spread McMurray's fame far and wide.

A local newspaper in Springfield, Illinois, heralding a 1920 appearance of the Kuhn Band at an auto show, highly praised McMurray. "In these days of jazz music no orchestra is complete without the 'moan of the saxophone' and when one has once heard Loren McMurray, the general consensus of opinion is that his saxophone has the 'moanin'est' moan of them all. He discloses in his performance individual ideas which enables him to interpret all phases and styles of music. He has a wonderful personality, snap and dash, and brilliancy characterize Mr. McMurray's playing among all lovers of music."[38] Audiences marveled at McMurray's prodigious technique. Feeling his oats, McMurray confidently challenged saxophone virtuoso Rudy Wiedoeft in advertisements for the Kuhn band, immodestly billing himself as "McMurray who beats Wiedoeft on the saxaphone [*sic*]."³⁹ At the end of the tour, McMurray returned to Kansas City with the Kuhn band.

In June 1921, McMurray moved to New York, then the undisputed capital of the entertainment industry. An in-demand soloist, McMurray, in short order, worked with Bailey's Lucky Seven, Markel's Orchestra, Eddie Elkin's Orchestra, and the Society Orchestra before joining the Paul Whiteman Orchestra, then a rising dance band. A star soloist with the Whiteman band, McMurray led the Saxophone Sextette, featuring an array of saxophones ranging from the toy-like shrill soprano to the thundering bass, standing almost as tall as a man. A versatile soloist, moving easily between concert music and hot jazz, McMurray joined the front line of the Virginians, a small hot unit drawn from the larger Whiteman band. The C. G. Conn musical instrument company recognized McMurray's growing stature by featuring him along with a handful of top players in print advertisements, touting Conn saxophones as "The World's Best."⁴⁰

While working with Whiteman, McMurray freelanced around New York's busy recording scene, participating in five to twelve sessions a week for the Victor, Columbia, Emerson, Pathé, Gennett, OKeh, Cameo, Aeolian, and Brunswick labels. In the summer of 1922, McMurray made his debut as a leader during two recording sessions for the Gennett label. McMurray assembled a nine-piece group dubbed the California Thumpers, featuring trumpeter Phil Napolean and trombonist Miff Mole. The band recorded five selections, "Haunting Blues," "Just Because You're You," "That's Why, I Love You," "Oogie Oogie Wa Wa," and "Blue." McMurray's elegant solo on "Haunting Blues," spiced with flatted thirds and bent notes, illustrates his advanced technique and ideas. Shortly after the last Gennett session in September, the Victor Talking Machine Company offered McMurray a recording contract. Around the same time, Conn presented him with five gold-mounted saxophones for concert work. The opportunity to record for Victor and continued affiliation with Conn bode well for McMurray's career. Tragically, he did not live to fulfill his great promise.

A severe case of tonsillitis nipped McMurray's brilliant career in the bud. Despite the best efforts of a team of doctors, McMurray died on October 29, 1922, at the age of twenty-five. News of his death sent shock waves through the music community of Kansas City. The Rock Island Line train, bearing McMurray's casket home to McPherson, paused in Kansas City long enough for a 150-piece band, composed of friends and admirers, to salute his genius. McMurray's meteoric rise illuminated the path to success for Paul Tremaine's Aristocrats of Rhythm and the Coon-Sanders Original Night Hawk Orchestra.

A MUSICAL HYBRID, Paul Tremaine's Aristocrats of Rhythm specialized in orchestral arrangements of hymns. Born and bred on a sprawling cattle ranch near Canon City, Colorado, perched on the eastern slope of the Rocky Mountains near the mouth of the Royal Gorge, Tremaine learned music technique and theory from his father, Robert C. Tremaine, an accomplished multi-instrumentalist. A quick study, Tremaine mastered the saxophone and advanced music theory. Facing few musical opportunities in Colorado, Tremaine toured the Midwest before settling down in Kansas City in early August 1920. An accomplished soloist, Tremaine handily edged out the local competition and joined D. Ambert Haley's Orchestra, one of Kansas City's leading society bands. The rotund Haley, socially well connected and the business manager for the musicians union, fielded several bands under his banner for Kansas City's hotels, amusement parks, and country clubs. Haley retained a stable of top-notch musicians by paying well, sometimes as much as time and a half. Given ample musical latitude by Haley, band members formed smaller hot units. The Haley band "played as much jazz as any white group in Kansas City," reported saxophonist Floyd Estep. "We had several Dixie groups . . . at Fairyland Park, Haley had a big group in 1923, twelve pieces. We had two pianos and a good jazz group. Our outstanding sax men in the early years were Tremaine, McMurray, and myself."[41]

In 1922, Tremaine signed on as music director for radio station WHB's studio orchestra, led by Louis Forbstein. Radio bugs from coast to coast picked up WHB's 500-watt signal, introducing Tremaine to the national audience. In 1926, Tremaine struck out on his own, forming the ten-piece Aristocrats of Modern Music. Local dance fan Cliff Halliburton characterized Tremaine as "a musician of fine execution who liked to play solos out in front of his band. His father, Robert C. Tremaine, played cello, bass violin, and tuba with the band and also acted as its business manager. . . . The style of the group was set by Paul Tremaine and by pianist-arranger Charlie Bagby, who was a member of Phil Harris's orchestra in later years. They opened the Midland Theater in Kansas City early in 1926 and were presented mainly as a stage orchestra. . . . They played all kinds of music, including standard hymnal music arranged in a contemporary style, which went over very well. Banjoist Eddie Kilanoski made many of the band's jazz-style arrangements and wrote the tune 'Four Four Stomp,' which Victor recorded at the peak of their popularity."[42]

During 1927 and 1928, the Aristocrats of Modern Music barnstormed across Oklahoma, Michigan, Wisconsin, and Illinois, with summer engagements at the Crystal Palace Ballroom at Coloma, Michigan. The versatile sixteen-piece band, modeled after the Paul Whiteman Orchestra, featured a vocal trio singing hot and sweet selections, a saxophone octet, a violin sextet, a brass quintet, and a piano quartet. Tremaine's father, a savvy promoter, published a 5,000-run magazine, *A Tempo*, marketing the band to amusement park, ballrooms, and theater managers. From 1929 to 1930, the band played at Yoeng's Chinese Restaurant on Broadway in New York City and recorded for the Victor and Columbia labels. Tremaine's personal and professional fortunes declined following his father's death in 1930. Without the steady leadership of the elder Tremaine, the band slipped into obscurity, playing mostly at second-rate venues before disbanding.

The Coon-Sanders Original Night Hawk Orchestra, the most successful and influential of the early white bands to come out of Kansas City, achieved national recognition from its pioneering, late-night radio broadcasts. Hundreds of thousands of listeners tuned in to the nightly broadcasts over WDAF, establishing the Night Hawks' reputation nationally and making Kansas City a beacon of jazz across North America. The Night Hawks specialized in novelty tunes, popular songs, and hot jazz distinguished by close vocal harmonies, syncopation, instrumental solos, and spread voicing of the three-member saxophone section. Saxophonist Floyd Estep described the band's style as "dance music with a little jazz mixed in."[43] During the 1920s, the Night Hawks' popularity eclipsed the popular jazz bands of Jean Goldkette and Ben Bernie, and rivaled the "King of Jazz," Paul Whiteman. To their legions of fans across North America, the Night Hawks were the Pied Pipers of the "Jazz Age."

Carleton Coon and Joe Sanders first met by happenstance in the J. W. Jenkins Music store in downtown Kansas City in December 1918.[44] While making his way through the vast field of pianos spread across the ground floor of Jenkins, Coon came across then Corporal Sanders, intently auditioning new music for his army band, the Missouri Jazz Hounds. "On furlough, I dropped into Jenkins Music Company's sheet music department to try to get new songs for the Jazz Hounds," Sanders reminisced. "While playing a few songs, humming softly, I suddenly heard a voice join me. A lovely tenor quality proved to be possessed by Carleton A. Coon; a handsome and extremely personable man. We met and Coon said he would try to get the Union's permission to allow me to play a dance with him and a small band New Year's Eve."[45] With the approval of the musicians union in 1919 Sanders joined Coon and launched what turned out to be a wildly successful collaboration.

Carleton Coon—pudgy, gregarious, and self-assured with a mischievous grin—never met a stranger. Born in Rochester, Minnesota, Coon grew up in Lexington, Missouri, situated on a limestone bluff overlooking the Missouri River, sixty miles east of Kansas City. A bit of a rascal, Coon spent more time hanging out on the docks on the river with stevedores and warehousemen than helping at his father's hotel. Fascinated with music, Coon acquired a taste for work songs and spirituals from the African Americans laboring on the banks of the river. At their encouragement, he began playing bones, then graduated to drums.[46] Coon polished his technique by closely studying the cadet drummers in the brass bands at nearby Wentworth Military Academy. Moving with his family to Kansas City, Kansas, as a teenager, Coon led the sing-along segment at the Electric Theater. Affectionately known as "Coonie," he played around town with early bandleader Jack Riley, before establishing his own booking firm in the Gayety Theater Building.[47]

In contrast, Joseph L. Sanders was tall and strikingly handsome with sharply defined features. A natural athlete, he became known as the "old left-hander" after striking out twenty-seven batters in a regulation amateur baseball game in the Kansas City Athletic Club League. Proud, competitive, and quick tempered, Sanders had a tendency to alienate band members and club owners. Born in Thayer, Kansas, Sanders grew up in Belton, Missouri, a small town just south of Kansas City. A virtuoso, he became known locally as "Kansas City's Greatest Boy Pianist." Right before his senior year in high school, Sanders moved to Kansas City with his family. While attending Westport High School, he entertained on the sly at night in one of the roughest dives in town, the Blue Goose Café, accompanying female vocalists for tips. After graduating in 1914, Sanders performed vocal and piano recitals at local churches and halls. An accomplished vocalist, his range spanned two and a half octaves. Sanders toured on the Red Path, Affiliated, and Colt-Alber Circuits as a member of a vocal quartet, the United States Four, before being drafted in October 1918. While stationed at Camp Bowie near Fort Worth, Texas, he formed the Missouri Jazz Hounds, a four-piece ensemble that entertained officers and local society.

Following his discharge in the spring of 1919, Sanders returned to Kansas City and joined forces with Coon. The unlikely pair formed a small ensemble and booking company. Coon tended to business, while Sanders composed new tunes and wrote out arrangements of popular standards for the bands they booked. Sanders explained:

> Coonie and I got together and made our plans, he having arranged for my necessary Union affiliation. . . . We opened a booking office in the old Victor Building at 10th and Main and got under way. Coonie, being the older and having had several years of professional experience, contacted the best jobbing musicians available in town and we sent small units to various clubs, weddings and any function calling for dance music. In those days a four-piece outfit was considered a big band. Our small office became the rendezvous of the two top dancing clubs in town—The Raven Club and the Tiger Club. Our best unit played all the big dances for these two clubs, and the publicity gained started the Kansas City wave of popularity that was to be ours. The biggest dance annually was the Raven's Sunrise Dance. This started at midnight and continued to until six in the morning, at which time a truly excellent breakfast was served. Old Electric Park Pavilion was the setting for these unusual affairs.[48]

The band's celebrity rippled across midwestern social circles, creating new opportunities.

Later that year, the band received an invitation to play a grand society affair at the palatial estate of banker Earl Sinclair in Tulsa, Oklahoma. Before the party Sinclair's brother, Harry Sinclair, the head of Mammoth Oil Company, who later became a central figure in the Teapot Dome Scandal, kidnapped the band as a prank. Harry Sinclair's personal secretary lured the band on to his private train, ostensibly to play a pre-party engagement at a local country club. The opulence of Sinclair's private Pullman car dazzled Sanders.

> We were ushered into the most luxurious private car we had ever beheld, before or since. . . . Individually, we met a rugged pompous man who was Mr. Sinclair. He in turn asked us to meet his guest, Captain Archie Roosevelt. Affability personified, Mr. Sinclair asked us to be seated and make ourselves comfortable. He rang for Tom . . . a polished colored man who inquired our preference. The while, Mr. Sinclair and Capt. Roosevelt kept us busily engaged in conversation and the train sped on. We were so flattered that these great men sounded us out on our views, that we forgot the world and time. Mellowed a trifle by the excellent liqueurs and enthralled by the brilliance of our new friends, it was not until Tom appeared with the evening menu for the inspection of Mr. Sinclair, who adjusted his glasses and said, "Squab, Tom! Very good," that it began to dawn on us that since this extra party at the country club was a dinner party, it was odd in the extreme that preparations were being made for us to dine aboard the private car.[49]

Mr. Sinclair then confessed his real intention and invited the band to be his guest in New York. Without hesitating, the band agreed to accept his generosity. En route, the train stopped at a small town in Indiana. The local sheriff initially tried to break up the rolling celebration, then ended up joining the bacchanal headed for New York. The band and the sheriff lingered in New York for a week as the guests of Sinclair. Outfitted by Sinclair's tailor, they dined in the finest restaurants and stayed in the best hotels before returning home.

Later that year they expanded the band to eight pieces, forming the Coon-Sanders Novelty Orchestra.[50] The toast of the town, the band played three shows daily: a noon engagement at the Pompeiian Room in the Baltimore Hotel and a matinee with a vaudeville revue at the Newman Theater, followed by an evening date at the prestigious Plantation Grill in the lower level of the Hotel Muehlebach. In late March 1921, the band recorded four selections for the Columbia label, thus becoming the first band to record in Kansas City. The lone selection issued from the session, "Some Little Bird," rendered in the popular novelty style of the day, sold well locally, but failed to catch on nationally. Before long the emerging technology of radio introduced the band to the national audience.

In 1920, KDKA in East Pittsburgh, Pennsylvania, became the first radio station licensed by the government. The new phenomenon swiftly spread and transmitters were erected across the United States. Young "radio bugs," without the means to purchase commercially manufactured radios, constructed crystal radio sets out of oatmeal boxes, galena crystals, and thin strands of wires, referred to as "cat's whiskers," used to change frequencies. Using the springs of their metal beds for antennas and crude headphones, they tuned in late-night broadcasts beamed across the country by unregulated radio stations. Early radio stations, lacking networks to provide programming, relied on locally produced programs, which gave hometown entertainers and musicians the opportunity for broader exposure.

The Coon-Sanders band premiered on radio station WDAF, licensed to the *Kansas City Star*, on Sunday, November 26, 1922, as part of the stage show at the Newman Theater.[51] The next week, the band returned to the air waves featured on a nightly "midnight radio program" broadcast live over WDAF between 11:30 P.M. and 12:30 A.M. from the Plantation Grill in the Hotel Muehlebach. At the conclusion of the first broadcast, the engineer accidentally left on the microphone at the Plantation Grill. The announcer, Leo Fitzpatrick, later known as the "Merry Old Chief," inadvertently commented on air that "anyone who'd stay up this late to hear us would have to be a real night hawk."[52] The following week 5,000 listeners from Canada, Mexico, and thirty-one states in the United States responded by letter or telegraph, confirming they were indeed night hawks.[53]

Coon and Sanders seized the moment and changed the name of the band to the Coon-Sanders Original Night Hawk Orchestra. Sanders composed the theme song for the program, "Night Hawk Blues," inviting listeners to "tune right in on the radio, grab a telegram, and say hello." They also formed the first radio fan club, the Night Hawk Club. The Night Hawks issued cards and inducted new members on the air by reading their names and hometowns to the ceremonious clank of a cowbell. Listeners across the country wired their requests and appreciation. The Western Union and Postal Telegraph offices rushed the telegrams to the Grill to be read over the air. During the first year, over 37,000 listeners joined the club, known as "The Enemies of Sleep."[54] The late-night broadcasts, one of the first regular broadcasts by an organized band, attracted offers for engagements from across the country.

In the spring of 1924, the Night Hawks recorded for the Victor label in Chicago and opened a three-month engagement at the Lincoln Tavern, a roadhouse located four miles outside of Evanston, Illinois, owned by gangster Bugsy Moran. The year-long contract with Victor paid the band $200 per session with no royalties. In early April, the band recorded "Night Hawk Blues" and five other selections in Chicago, inaugurating a successful association that produced a steady stream of hits over the next eight years. The Night Hawks returned to the Chicago area the next month and premiered at the Lincoln Tavern. One night at the Tavern, Jules Stein, the owner of a fledgling booking agency with a paper-thin roster of bands, approached Coon and Sanders. Stein, a dapper, former optometrist and musician, lacked the venture capital necessary to build a stable of artists. Pulling Coon and Sanders aside, Stein offered to book the band on a midwestern tour. Admiring Stein's moxie, they agreed to let him book a four-week tour, starting on Labor Day. The tour succeeded on the strength of the Night Hawks' reputation, and Stein used his profits to establish the Music Corporation of America (MCA). With the Night Hawks aboard, Stein managed to sign other top-shelf bands, and MCA emerged as one of the leading booking agencies in the country. The Night Hawks became Stein's most important client, and Coon and Sanders moved the band's headquarters to Chicago.[55]

In October 1924, the Night Hawks opened at the Balloon Room in Chicago's stately Congress Hotel, broadcasting over KYW from midnight to 2:30 A.M. Chicagoans flocked to the Congress, adopting the Night Hawks as their own. Trombonist Rex Downing judged the Night Hawks to be "the number one band in Chicago as far as the dancing public was concerned, and as far as the young were concerned, we were number one straight across the country."[56] In September 1926, the Night Hawks moved to the Blackhawk Restaurant located on the corner of Wabash and Randolph. Freshly remodeled for the occasion, the Blackhawk immediately became the hottest nightspot in Chicago, especially for the young college crowd. Al Capone, a big fan of the Night Hawks, frequented the Blackhawk, lavishing $100 tips on the band. The band broadcast over WBBM for the first few years at the Blackhawk, and then switched to WGN, licensed to the *Chicago Tribune*, a media powerhouse. On Saturday nights the band held court at the program "Knights and Ladies of the Bath," so named because in those days most people bathed once a week— on Saturday night. Management, taking a cue for the "Night Hawk Frolic," installed Western Union and Postal Telegraph directly on the stage. So many requests and dedications came in that by the end of each broadcast a blizzard of paper covered the stage.

For three of the next four years, the Night Hawks maintained the Blackhawk as their winter headquarters.[57] During the summer of 1927, the Night Hawks toured the Midwest, traveling by train and caravan style in automobiles, with Coonie and Joe leading the way. The band spent the next three summers at the Dells, a supper club in Morton Grove, Illinois, owned by Al Capone. According to band member Rex Stout's wife, Florence, "[T]hey had a machine gun on the roof and 2 'hoods' patrolling the grounds."[58] During breaks band members played cards with Capone, their biggest fan and protector. Being from Kansas City, they felt perfectly at home sitting down for a friendly game of cards with one of the most notorious gangsters of the 1920s. When thugs robbed Coonie of his wallet and treasured diamond-studded pinky ring, Capone's henchmen located the culprits and returned the purloined wallet and ring with a note of apology.

In the fall of 1931, the band moved to New York and opened at the Terrace Room in the new Hotel New Yorker at 34th Street and Eighth Avenue. Bing Crosby, Russ Columbo, Guy Lombardo, Kate Smith, and a host of leading entertainers crowded the Terrace Room for the Night Hawks' debut.[59] Coon loved the nightlife of New York. After hours, he frequented the Cotton

Club and other nightclubs in Harlem, making friends with Cab Calloway, Duke Ellington, and other African American bandleaders. Coon and Calloway became friends and exchanged Christmas cards. Duke Ellington, a big fan, confessed to basing his classic "The Mooche" on the theme from the Night Hawks' recording "The Wail."

Sanders and other band members, less enamored of New York, yearned for the Midwest. Sanders grew to loathe New York as "a hideous nightmare, a cesspool of insincerity, a hotbed of double-crossers, a maze of 'angles.'"[60] Sanders expressed his antipathy for New York and homesickness in the composition "I Want to Go Home," recorded during the Night Hawks' last session for Victor on March 24, 1932. The same weariness weighing on the country from the Great Depression settled over the band. Sanders, naturally prone to melancholy, became increasingly morose and difficult to get along with. Excessive drinking turned Coon's happy-go-lucky nature into irresponsible behavior. The two drifted apart socially and professionally. Sanders considered leaving the band.

The Night Hawks returned to Chicago in early April 1932 for an engagement at the College Inn. Sanders, glad to be back in the Windy City, literally kissed the ground on arrival. Tragedy truncated his exuberance when on April 23, 1932, Coon entered the hospital in critical condition, stricken with blood poisoning from an abscessed tooth. Carleton Coon died on May 4, 1932. Coon's many friends and family staged one of the biggest funerals in Kansas City history, with the mournful procession stretching for miles. Sanders continued to lead the group for a short while as Joe Sanders' Night Hawk Orchestra, but the magic of the Coon-Sanders Original Night Hawk Orchestra ended with the death of Carleton Coon.[61]

In the end, Carleton Coon, Joe Sanders, Paul Tremaine, L. D. McMurray, and the other early white musicians received little credit for first establishing Kansas City's reputation as a jazz center. This was in part because, while these early white bands originated from Kansas City, they performed a more generic form of jazz in the vein of Paul Whiteman, Ben Bernie, and Jean Goldkette, not the western style that by the late 1920s distinguished Kansas City Jazz.

In 1941, journalist Dave E. Dexter, Jr., writing in *Down Beat*, pronounced Kansas City musically "strictly a colored town." With the exception of Joe Sanders, Paul Tremaine, and a few others, Dexter asserted, "[I]t is a peculiar fact that its sons are all colored."[62] His comments riled white Kansas City musicians and their relatives, but in the next issue of *Down Beat* he correctly insisted, "[F]or every white musician, ten colored ones have been developed."[63] As a native of Kansas City and the first to write about Kansas City Jazz in the *Kansas City Journal-Post*, *Metronome*, and *Down Beat*, Dexter's observations ring true. With few anomalies, Kansas City's distinctive jazz style originated in the African American community centered around the intersection of 18th and Vine—Kansas City's other downtown.

2

Carrie's Gone to Kansas City

Carrie's Gone to Kansas City,
She's Done Gone and I'm Going Too.

—John William "Blind" Boone, *Blind Boone's Southern
Rag Medley No. Two: Strains from the Flat Branch*, 1909

LIKE NEW YORK CITY'S HARLEM, Kansas City's 18th and Vine area developed
into a self-contained community. During the days of public segregation, the
intersection of 18th and Vine served as the hub of a bustling business and
entertainment district—the heart and soul of an African American community, bounded by Independence Avenue on the north, Troost Avenue on the
west, 27th Street on the south, and Benton Boulevard to the east. Baseball
legend and former Kansas City Monarch Buck O'Neil mused that racial segregation in Kansas City "was a horrible thing, but a bitter-sweet thing. We
owned the Street's Hotel. We owned Elnora's restaurant. The Kansas City
Monarchs were our team. The money we made in the community, stayed in
the community. When we traveled we spent money in other black communities and it came back when they came to Kansas City."[1]

Bandleader Andy Kirk, arriving in Kansas City from Oklahoma during the
summer of 1929, marveled at the large African American professional class.
"Blacks in the school systems, in business, in the professions. It was a revela-
tion to me," Kirk reported. "Kansas City was a regular Mecca for young blacks
from other parts of the country aspiring to higher things than janitor or chauf-
feur." Kirk found that African Americans in Kansas City "didn't care . . . they
had their own theaters and all types of black entertainment, their own clubs,
ballrooms, bars and grills, their own homes in residential areas, and their own
newspaper, the *Kansas City Call*. . . . In short, blacks in Kansas City had their

own everything, even their own baseball team, the Monarchs."[2] Born of necessity and reared by industry, the 18th and Vine area quickly grew from its humble beginnings into an urbane center for African American commerce, culture, and music.

Just after the turn of the nineteenth century, an African American preacher and his wife, the Reverend and Mrs. Sweeney, operated a truck farm in the 18th and Vine area. Eighteenth Street, then a rude, muddy country lane, traversed the tidy fields of corn, tomatoes, and bright green bell peppers. A walnut grove thrived in the area later to be intersected by Paseo Boulevard. By the late 1800s, thousands of African Americans had settled in the area, then known as the "Bowery."[3] In November 1909, the first moving picture theater for African Americans, the Star, opened in a wood-frame building at the northeast corner of 18th and Vine, forming the cornerstone of the new business district. The quarter grew quickly, and by 1915 dry goods stores, laundries, fish shops, bakeries, barbers, cobblers, tailors, restaurants, and all the businesses and services denied to the community downtown packed 18th Street east of Paseo Boulevard. Apartments and headquarters for social clubs perched on the second floor above the bustle of commerce below. The fragrant aroma of hickory smoke from Henry Perry's Barbeque pit at 19th and Highland wafted over the community. Streetcars rattled down the center of 18th Street, connecting the community to the rest of the city and jobs in packing plants, the railroads, and homes of the wealthy. Once established, the community grew swiftly and prospered.

The three-story red brick Lincoln building, located on the southeast corner of 18th and Vine, opened in 1921. Matlaw's, a men's fine clothing store, anchored the corner of the building. Dobbs hats, gleaming high-top shoes with white stitching lining the soles, box back coats, and crisp high-collar white shirts crowded the large rectangular windows on either side of the brightly lit entryway.[4] Owned by Jewish businessmen, Matlaw's allowed patrons to try on hats, shoes, and clothes, a simple courtesy refused at stores downtown. Lincoln Hall, a plain but popular dance hall catering to the younger set, occupied the top floor. Dentists, doctors, and attorneys populated the second floor. Up until the Great Depression, these college-educated professionals overwhelmingly supported the Republican party, putting them politically out of sync with the powerful Democratic machine in Kansas City. Consequently, the professional class wielded little power at city hall, but as men and women of "merit," they led the community by example. They enthusiastically supported classical music and opera, sponsoring performances by Roland Hayes, Marian Anderson, Paul Robeson, and other major stars of the day. In December 1917, Hayes attracted 7,000 concertgoers to Convention Hall in a benefit for African American soldiers stationed at Camp Funston, Kansas.[5] A cosmopolitan oasis, 18th and Vine became a cultural Mecca for African Americans from smaller burgs across the Midwest.

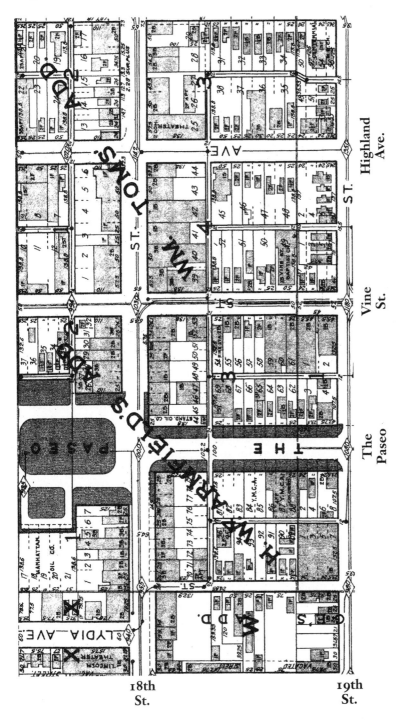

SOURCE: *Atlas of Kansas City, Mo., and environs, 1925* . . . (Tuttle-Ayers-Woodward Company). *Courtesy of the Kenneth J. LaBudde Department of Special Collections, Miller Nichols Library, University of Missouri–Kansas City.*

The elegant three-story brick Street Hotel that graced the northeast corner of 18th and Paseo was financed by funeral director T. B. Watkins and businessman R. S. Street. In May 1923, the *Kansas City Call* noted the Street fulfilled the "need for a properly equipped and properly managed hotel to house the transient and traveling public."[6] "The Street's," as it became affectionately known, provided African Americans shelter from white hostility they often encountered while traveling. Well appointed, the Street's boasted sixty rooms with hot and cold running water. The area's numerous social clubs packed the Rose Room, a fine dining room accommodating 300, and the Blue Room, a fashionable cabaret tucked in the rear, known as the place "to meet, to see, and to be seen." Seven years later, the Booker T. Washington Hotel opened right around the corner at 1821 Vine. Three stories, buff brick with terracotta trim, Booker T. offered sixty-two rooms, half with baths. Visiting musicians and entertainers favored the more affordable, modestly decorated Booker T., while Negro Baseball League players and other well-heeled travelers preferred to stay at the Street's.

The Kansas City Monarchs, the pride of the Negro Baseball Leagues, enjoyed the same esteem granted to ministers, doctors, dentists, and lawyers. Like their professional counterparts, team members adhered to a strict conduct code, seldom venturing into public without a suit and tie. Barnstorming across the country, they brought the community prestige and respect from New York, Chicago, St. Louis, Detroit, and other large African American centers. In February 1920, team owners from across the country established the National Negro League during a meeting at the YMCA located at 19th and Paseo in Kansas City, the westernmost city represented at the conference.

Ball players enjoyed the nightlife around 18th and Vine, partying alongside jazz musicians. "We traveled the same circuit as the musicians," Buck O'Neil explained. "They would see us at the park and we would see them at the clubs. At the [Subway Club], the musicians would jam all night and we'd be jamming with them."[7] At the Monarchs' spring homecoming dance, musicians entertained while baseball players mingled with the hometown fans. Pianist Julia Lee, one of Kansas City's most popular entertainers, married Frank Duncan, the catcher and long-time Monarchs manager. Like music, baseball gave African American youth, facing few other options, a shot at fame and fortune. Early sports writers affectionately referred to the Monarchs as the Kaysees. Later, Dave E. Dexter, Jr., and African American music journalists adapted the team's nickname and referred to Kansas City as Kaycee.[8]

The community supported a series of weekly newspapers: the *Rising Son* (1896–1907), *The Liberator* (1901–1903), *The Kansas City Sun* (1908–1924), and the *Kansas City American* (1928–1943). The *Kansas City Call*, established in 1919, continues publishing to this day.[9] On several occasions the community sustained two newspapers. During the late 1920s, competition for readers sparked a newspaper war between the *Kansas City Call* and the *Kansas City*

American, fueled by considerable animosity between the respective publishers, Chester A. Franklin and Felix H. Payne. A conservative Republican, Franklin set himself up as a pillar of the community, while Payne, a Democratic leader and well-known sporting man, openly operated speakeasies, policy wheels, and gambling dens. Franklin indignantly reported the frequent police raids on Payne's Eastside Musicians Club and editorialized on the evils of gambling and alcohol. Payne countered by alleging, on the front page of the *American*, that Franklin assaulted a woman in a fracas and banished his grandmother to the poor farm.[10] The weeklies published by Franklin, Payne, and others brought the community together with coverage of church news, sports, social events, and dances.

Social activities swirled around the Lincoln, Lyric, Dreamland, and other small dance halls in the 18th and Vine area. Kansas City's many social clubs, drawn together by profession or social status, staged regular weekly and special theme dances. The Portella Girls, a social club for teachers on the Kansas side, hosted a popular annual Thanksgiving breakfast dance. Under the watchful eye of ministers, dancers usually abided by the social decorum of the day that prohibited close physical contact between the sexes. Controversy arrived in the community with the introduction of the tango and other intimate dances. At the urging of local ministers, the self-appointed moral authority of the community, the Board of Public Welfare, briefly banned social dancing before rescinding the order in 1914. Ignoring the warnings of dire moral consequences, dancers at Lyric Hall mastered the tango, hesitation, waltz flirtation, schottische, and hesitation schottische. Small string ensembles, rendering popular standards and ragtime in precise time, accompanied the whirling dancers. Musically versatile, the early orchestras also performed in local theaters, adding mirth and drama to silent movies, stage plays, and vaudeville productions.

The Gem, Criteria, and other small theaters on 18th Street, unable to accommodate large vaudeville productions, offered second-run photoplays and modest theatrical productions. Whitney and Tutt's Smarter Set, Drake and Walker's Bombay Girls, Billy King, the Whitman Sisters, and other major attractions bypassed the 18th and Vine area for the majestic theaters downtown. The Orpheum, Grand, Gayety, and Auditorium Theaters made "arrangements for colored patrons," reserving a balcony or putting on a special "midnight ramble" show, but they also required African American patrons to use the back or side entrance.

The opening of the Lincoln Theatre in February 1920, ushered in larger vaudeville revues to 18th and Vine. Twisted pilasters, fluffy swags, curved shields, and other Baroque architectural motifs adorned Lincoln's tan terracotta facade, which occupied half a block west of Lydia on the north side of 18th Street. Seating 1,500 patrons, the Lincoln presented Paramount photoplays accompanied by the eight-piece Lincoln Orchestra. The *Kansas City Sun* hailed the opening of the "theatre beautiful" as a "distinct epoch in the social life of that large and ever-increasing number of our racial group who bitterly resent the discrimination and Jim-crowism practiced at down-town theatres."[11] The Lincoln, owned by Jewish businessmen but operated by African Americans, immediately established itself as the premiere movie house in the district. As a point of race pride, the Lincoln featured early Afri-can American films, such as Oscar Micheaux's *Within Our Gates* and *The Flames of Wrath*, a five-reel film produced locally by Mrs. Maria P. Williams, the secretary and treasurer of the Western Film Producing Company.

Later that summer, the Lincoln expanded its schedule to include stage plays and musical revues direct from Chicago and New York—a step up from the simple fare offered by smaller stages in the district but a far cry from the grand productions staged at downtown theaters. In early 1923, Lincoln joined the Theater Owners Booking Association (TOBA), bringing in national stars and grander productions. Established in Chattanooga, Tennessee, in 1920 with Milton Starr of the Bijou Theater in Nashville as President, the TOBA circuit swiftly grew into a string of eighty theaters, extending from the East Coast across the South and back across the Midwest. Kansas City, the farthest stop west, served as the turn-around point for the circuit. With the opening in October 1924 of the Ella D. Moore Theater in Dallas, owned by Chintz and Ella D. Moore, the TOBA stretched south, circulating musicians and entertainers between Kansas City and the southwestern territories.

The fast-paced shows traveling on the circuit spotlighted comedians, the-atrical revues, dancers, and blues shouters.[12] Fans adored the juvenile antics of Sunshine Sammy of "Our Gang" and Little Albert, who danced the Charles-ton on his knees. Former heavyweight champion Jack Johnson and other box-ers demonstrated their skills taking on local favorites. Not to be outdone by the theaters downtown, the TOBA featured the Lafayette Players from the Lafayette Theater in Harlem, stage shows like "Cotton Land," featuring James P. Johnson, and other refined productions. Sara Martin, Mamie Smith, Ida Cox, Bessie Smith, Clara Smith, Ma Rainey, and other blues shouters brought the house down nightly. Offering a little something for everybody, shows on the TOBA circuit packed theaters across the country.

To some musicians and entertainers traveling under the auspices of the Theater Owners Booking Association, the acronym TOBA meant "Tough on Black Asses." Clarence E. Muse, a veteran performer and producer on the circuit, bitterly complained, "[E]ach and every year just about this time when the colored artist has returned to New York, Chicago, Washington, from over the TOBA, broke and hungry and those who are trapped in parts un-known, the colored newspapers throughout the country receive official pro-cess sheets from the TOBA, stating in big broad headlines 'TOBA promises big season for actors, better shows, better railroad jumps, big salaries that are sure' and a lot of rot." Muse charged: "If an act fails to show they pay and pay dearly, even more than the contract will earn."[13] Entertainers more resigned to their fate affectionately referred to it as TOBY time, and enjoyed the opportunity to travel the country. Many musicians and entertainers on the circuit liked the urban sophistication of the 18th and Vine area and made their homes in Kansas City. New arrivals swelled the ranks of the local African American Musician's Union.

Established in 1917, the Colored Musicians Union Local 627, affiliated with the American Federation of Musicians, initially included twenty-five members and sponsored a fourteen-piece orchestra for social events, promenades, and theaters. The union was founded by musicians who played music primarily as an avocation, but it quickly grew into an organization of professionals. By 1919, Local 627 fielded three concert bands for a Labor Day parade. The next year members established an official headquarters on 18th Street. The union operated as a clearinghouse for engagements, a social center, and a vehicle for grievances against unfair practices by booking agents and band leaders. Affiliated with the national American Federation of Musicians, members touring the country enjoyed the same considerations as their white counterparts. The jazz style pioneered by the members of Local 627 developed along original lines influenced by, yet unique from, the traditions of New Orleans, Chicago, and New York. The distinctiveness of Kansas City Jazz originated from its roots in ragtime, blues, and band music.

CONCERT PIANIST JOHN WILLIAM "BLIND" BOONE and ragtime professors Euday Bowman and James Scott strongly influenced the development of the Kansas City jazz style. Blind Boone, the first great African American pianist and composer to crop up in Missouri, bridged the folk and ragtime traditions, performing mainly spirituals, plantation songs, and classical music, while occasionally putting "the cookies on the lower shelf where everyone can reach them," playing "Dixie" and other popular standards in "ragged time."[14] Boone's mother, Rachel, formerly a slave owned by descendants of Daniel Boone, served as a cook and washerwoman at a Union Army encampment near Miami, Missouri. According to Dr. O. H. Simpson, Rachel's long-time employer, Boone's father, a German bandleader with the Union Army, abandoned the family.[15] As a baby, Boone developed a "brain fever," and in keeping with medical practice of the day, a doctor surgically removed Boone's eyes to relieve pressure on his brain, then sewed his eyelids shut. An eternal optimist, Boone later observed how his loss of vision heightened his hearing and other senses.[16] A plump, pleasant child prodigy with perfect pitch, Boone could recall note for note any piece after hearing it one time.

After falling prey to several unscrupulous managers, Boone and his mother entered into a management agreement with John Lange, Jr., a contractor in Columbia, Missouri. Born into slavery to a French Creole father and slave mother, Lange served in the household of his owner James Shannon, the second president of the Missouri State University. Industrious, Lange found time to help out in his father's butcher shop. Light-skinned, sporting long drooping mutton-chop sideburns and closely cropped hair, Lange prospered after the Civil War by building roads in Boone County surrounding Columbia. Lange and Boone formed a fast friendship and partnership, organizing the Blind Boone Concert Company in 1880. In the early days, the two traveled by wagon-hauling Boone's massive piano from town to town. Later, when female vocalists came aboard, the concert company traveled by rail, selling out concert halls and churches across the country. Lange moved to Kansas City in 1897, and bought a spacious three-story limestone house, with cut-glass windows and crystal chandeliers, on the eastern edge of the town. Boone and Lange maintained the concert company's home base in Kansas City until Lange's death in 1916 in an automobile accident.

The Blind Boone Concert Company performed spirituals, concert music, and Boone's own compositions inspired by earlier folk forms he heard as a child in the Missouri Valley. One of his better known compositions, "Marshfield Tornado," composed in 1880, so accurately recreated the sound of a tornado that it panicked the concertgoers of Marshfield, Missouri, who thought they were undergoing another twister.[17] His masterpiece, *Blind Boone's Southern Rag Medley No. Two: Strains from the Flat Branch*, contains traces of jazz and blues, including one of the first instances of a published walking bass line.[18] Boone's development of the walking bass line provided the rhythmic foundation for boogie-woogie piano, and ultimately enabled Kansas City bands to move from traditional 2/4 beat rhythm dominated by the tuba to a more fluid 4/4 rhythm driven by the double bass. Walter Page, a member of the Blue Devils, Bennie Moten's Kansas City Orchestra, and the Count Basie Orchestra, used the walking bass line as a means to revolutionize the rhythm section, developing a hard-swinging style that became the hallmark of Kansas City Jazz. In 1929, two years after Boone's death, Kansas Citians, by popular vote, renamed the former Rialto Theater on the southeast corner of 18th and Highland the Boone Theater in his memory.

EUDAY BOWMAN, a hulk of a man with broad shoulders and large hands, hailed from Fort Worth, Texas, but made his musical mark in Kansas City. His ragtime compositions "Petticoat Lane," "Kansas City Blues," "11th Street Rag," "12th Street Rag," and "13th Street Rag" mapped the geography while capturing the élan of his adopted hometown. Bowman fled home as a youth, arriving in Kansas City in 1897. A self-taught pianist with an engaging grin, Bowman charmed his way into a regular slot with several small ragtime ensembles. Legend has it that Bowman found the inspiration for the three-over-four pattern of "12th Street Rag" in the trio of balls adorning the numerous pawnshops lining 12th Street east of Main Street. One day while standing at the bustling intersection of 12th and Main with Raggedy Ed, a friend from Fort Worth considering opening a pawnshop, Bowman promised, "If you get rich on those three balls. I'll write a piece on three notes to make myself rich."[19] On the spot he composed "12th Street Rag," modeling the three-over-four pattern after the three balls, clustered like golden grapes on the front of the pawnshops. Back in Fort Worth, Bowman continued playing the new song, but did not copyright it until 1915. Put off by a Dallas publisher, Bowman returned to Kansas City, and sold the rights to the Jenkins Music Company. An instant hit for its syncopation, catchy melody, and novelty appeal, "12th Street Rag" took the nation by storm. In 1919, Jenkins published a dotted rhythm version, marketed as a "fox trot arrangement."[20] Favored by early Kansas City bands, the song bridged the ragtime and jazz traditions. After Kansas City's Bennie Moten band recorded his version for the Victor label in 1927, "12th Street Rag" went on to become the most enduring hit from the ragtime era.

JAMES SCOTT, known as the "Little Professor" for his slight build and retiring manner, moved from Carthage, Missouri, to Kansas City, Kansas, in 1920.[21] Arriving just after the peak of ragtime, Scott brought a considerable reputation as a composer. Scott Joplin's publisher John Stark and Son Music Company published Scott's best-known compositions: "Frog Legs Rag" (1906), "Kansas City Rag" (1907), and "Grace and Beauty Rag" (1907). Considered to be one of the "big three" ragtime composers, along with Scott Joplin and Joseph Lamb, Scott composed "denser" and more difficult to perform rags than those of his contemporaries.[22] Scott's cousin Patsy Thomas recalled how "he never talked about music, just wrote, wrote, wrote and played it for anyone who would listen. He wrote music as fluently as writing a letter, humming and writing all at the same time." Thomas added that, when Scott played, "he sat at the piano with the left leg wrapped around the stool, and his body kept very still, no bouncing with the rhythm."[23] A familiar figure in the community, Scott often accompanied another cousin, Ada Brown, a vaudevillian with a voice to match her considerable girth. An accomplished arranger, Scott directed the orchestras at the Panama, Lincoln, and Eblon Theaters. Working under Scott's baton in the fourteen-piece Lincoln Orchestra, jazz musicians honed their reading skills while performing in an orchestral setting. One of his last rags, ironically given the title "Don't Jazz Me Rag (I'm Music)" (1921) by publisher Stark, anticipated the style of jazz bands during the 1920s.[24]

AS IN OTHER AGRICULTURAL REGIONS, Missouri's blues tradition evolved from work songs and field hollers. Blues pioneer Gertrude "Ma" Rainey first heard the blues around 1902 in a small Missouri town. Touring with a tent show, Rainey met a young woman who sang a poignant song about a man who left her. Enchanted, Rainey learned the song and used it as an encore.[25] African Americans migrating from rural areas brought the blues to 18th and Vine.

Writer Langston Hughes distinctly remembered first encountering the blues on Independence Avenue while living in Kansas City with his mother around 1914.[26] Blues shouters preached the gospel on sidewalks, attracting temporary street-corner congregations. As a young man, Big Joe Turner accompanied a blind blues shouter making his rounds. "I'd stay with him all day and we'd cover the town. He stopped on corners and sang and I passed the tin cup," Turner recollected. "We went into restaurants too, and when I was old enough I sang along. I made up words—blues words—to go along with his guitar music, and later, when I was singing with a band, I could sing for two or three hours straight and never repeat a lyric. Those blind blues singers would make quite a bit of change during the day, and they'd pay me fifty cents. I did that off and on for two or three years." Turner often sat in on impromptu sessions with street-corner jug bands. "I sang a lot on the streets, me and a bunch of the boys," Turner reported. "They played gaspipes with one end covered and an old banjo and big crock water jugs. They blew across the mouth of those jugs and made that bass sound to keep the beat."[27]

The blues in Kansas City assumed a more urban style with the arrival of the great women blues shouters. Mamie Smith's debut at the Century Theater in June 1921 created a sensation, commanding top dollar at the box office. Box seats sold for $2.75 and orchestra seats $2.20—roughly five times the going rate for vaudeville shows. During her six-day engagement, Smith and Her Jazz Hounds broke all attendance records. African Americans crammed the balcony, while white society, enthralled by the blues, bought blocks of tickets on the main floor. Impressed by the stock of local musicians, Smith persuaded young saxophonist Coleman Hawkins, a member of the theater orchestra, to join her band. Smith's pioneering 1920 blues recording "Crazy Blues" on the OKeh label inspired a thriving blues record trade.

Cashing in on the blues craze, confectioneries, shining parlors, and furniture stores in the 18th and Vine area stocked blues records as a sideline. The Winston Holmes Music Company, established in April 1920 at 18th and Highland, easily cornered the race record market. Holmes, a wiry scrapper with a flair for showmanship, boxed as a youth in the lightweight division as the Black Pearl under the management of "Birdlegs" Collins and toured the country with "The Smart Set," a popular revue staged by Bert Williams and George Walker.[28] Settling down in Kansas City in 1915, Holmes worked as a shop supervisor for the Starr Piano Company, repairing pianos and phonographs. In 1917, he mounted an unsuccessful bid for alderman of the Tenth Ward, running as an independent sponsored by the National Council of Colored Workers. A fervent follower of Marcus Garvey, Holmes proudly touted his shop as the "only Negro music house in town." The broad windows stretching across the front of his well-stocked music store displayed the latest phonographs, pianos, radios, and records. Holmes leveraged his contacts in the phonograph industry to win regional distribution rights for the Gennett, Black

Swan, Columbia, Paramount, OKeh, and other fledgling race labels. The clarion call of the blues blaring from the Victrola in front of Holmes's shop echoed up and down the canyon of 18th Street. Quite naturally, blues became a staple of Kansas City bands. From the beginning, the structure and feel of the blues formed the foundation of Kansas City jazz style.

Bennie Moten and other early Kansas City jazz musicians came of age musically playing in concert bands sponsored by the Elks and other fraternal organizations. The community enthusiastically supported a Ladies Band led by female trumpeter Josie Williams. The band, dressed in crisp uniforms, marched down 18th Street, with the saxophone section leading the way. Beginning in 1919, Dan Blackburn's municipal band played a popular summer series sponsored by the city. Originally from Louisiana, Blackburn began his career at the age of twelve with a brass band marching alongside German-Americans. He moved to Kansas in 1894 and joined the Midland Band, and organized the Knights Templar Band in 1915. Blackburn, a founding member of Local 627, obtained the sanction from the national union granting members of the local union the same rights as their white counterparts. Slim and intense, Blackburn formed a thirty-piece Municipal Band that included top players in the union.

Decked out in white captain's uniforms, the Municipal Band's Sunday night concerts, staged in Parade Park at 17th and Paseo, attracted upward of 6,000 people per performance and brought together all segments of the community. The *Kansas City Call* reported how concertgoers forgot their cares and the oppressive heat of Kansas City in July:

> They sat on newspapers and they lay on blankets which they had brought along to keep off the chiggers. Some of them had taken camp chairs with them. Others had hauled heavy kitchen chairs and dining room chairs to insure their comfort during the evening. Mama, papa, junior and sister were all there. Whole families grouped themselves together and chatted while the music played. Men in overalls rubbed elbows with other men who were nattily turned out in white linen suits or white shirts and white flannel trousers. The band played "Dangerous Blues" and the crowd swayed in sympathetic rhythm. Miss Randall sang "Humming to Myself" and her audience tapped an appreciative collective foot and hummed to itself. Cares were forgotten. Worries were put away. The heat no longer mattered. The sturdy trees on the hill and the soft black night formed a dreamy background for the happy throng. It was "Sunday evening out" and the band was playing a lazy soothing benediction.[29]

Children eager to jump on the concert bandwagon got a boost from local music studios. Professor Charles T. Watts, Clyde Leroy Glass, and other early music educators operated private conservatories that offered lessons for all level of study. Watts, dignified with a frock coat and high-stiff collar shirt, gave music lessons covering the latest ragtime hits as well as the classics in his home. "I went to Charles T. Watts Conservatory of Music to be a fiddler," bandleader Clarence Love reported. "Most every kid from my age on down that played took private lessons. My mother paid a dollar a lesson. . . . He had the job as supervisor of music of the public schools (we weren't integrated back then), all the black schools. . . . At the last of the year he'd combine all the schools together and we'd have a big concert, [with] marches."[30] Glass, an accomplished concert pianist trained at the New England Conservatory of Music, opened his studio in 1918. Pensive and cultured, Glass eschewed teaching ragtime and popular standards to concentrate on the classics. The studios operated by Watts, Glass, and other educators gave students the command of their instruments required for advanced studies at Lincoln High School, Western University, and the University of Kansas at Lawrence. Outside of the Horner Institute, a music conservatory in Kansas City, students had few opportunities for advanced studies in Missouri. At the time, the University of Missouri at Columbia, located in the heart of "Little Dixie," denied entrance to African Americans.

Major N. Clark Smith, "America's Greatest Colored Bandmaster," the director of the music programs at Western University (1914–1916) and Lincoln High (1916–1922), further polished the students by drilling them on theory and performance. "He was the music program at Lincoln," stressed bandleader Harlan Leonard. He had "a vivid and commanding personality. He was short, chubby, gruff, military in bearing, wore glasses and was never seen without his full uniform and decorations. His language was rather rough and occasionally shocking to the few young ladies who were taking music classes, though never offensive. Major Smith simply ran a tight ship. . . . He drilled the Lincoln marching bands until they were the best in the area, some said the best of their kind in the Middle West."[31] A strict disciplinarian, Smith frequently reprimanded students with the business end of his ruler. Saxophonist Williams Saunders regretted the day he forgot the elements of music when called on in class. Smith commanded him to the front of the room and put his head on a desk. Striking Saunders on the head with his ruler, Smith reminded him that "music is melody, BOOM! harmony. BOOM! and rhythm. BOOM!" Smith further instructed Saunders to "go home and tell your mammy I hit you." Saunders never forgot the lesson. Decades later, he simply stated, "I know what music is."[32]

Smith arrived at Lincoln well equipped to develop the music and military programs. Born in 1877 at Fort Leavenworth, Kansas, Smith attended the Army Service School and studied music with German bandmaster Professor H. E. Gungle. An ambitious youth, Smith spent his summers working for publisher Carl Hoffman. In 1891, Smith began his military career, serving as a trumpeter at Fort Sill, Oklahoma. Two years later, he moved to Wichita, Kansas, where he married and organized YMCA and pickaninny bands.[33] While leading a band at the 1893 Chicago World's Fair, Smith joined the Lyon and

Healy music company for which he organized bands and choruses. After a year of service, Smith left Lyon and Healy to form the Smith Jubilee Music Company, one of the nation's first African American publishing companies. Smith served as bandmaster for the Eighth Illinois Infantry for four years, touring Cuba during the Spanish-American War. In 1898, Smith led a pickaninny band from Kansas City on an eighteen-month tour of Europe and the Pacific, ending with an appearance at the Paris Exposition. Traveling across the Pacific, Smith, an early ethnomusicologist, gathered native songs, later incorporating the themes into his own compositions.

Back in the United States, Smith attended Chicago Musical College, graduating in 1905 with a Bachelor of Science in music. Two years later, Booker T. Washington recruited Smith as Commandant of Cadets at Tuskegee Institute in Alabama, a vocational school and college for African Americans. Smith formed the Tuskegee Cadet Marching Band, an orchestra and glee club. Smith and Washington, a matched pair, willful with strong opinions, frequently locked horns. Smith, high-strung, took offense at Washington's frequent criticism of the band. Taking a break from Washington, Smith spent summers touring with the concert band and along the way raising funds for the institute. The band traveled across the nation by Pullman car, bypassing local Jim Crow restrictions.[34] By the summer of 1913, a deep rift developed between Washington and Smith over the direction of the band. In a May 26 letter Washington admonished Smith for "not making more of the plantation melodies in connection with the band music." Clark tersely replied in a letter dated June 13, "I am discouraged by the way the Tuskegee authorities write to me. . . . It is rather embarrassing to have authorities dictate to me about their own structure, as to its merits good or bad, when they know absolutely nothing about it. I repeat: I hope you will give me more encouragement rather than discouragement, as I do not expect it of you."[35] In July, the Tuskegee Band, led by Smith, performed at the cavernous Convention Hall in Kansas City for the National Elks Convention. At the beginning of the fall semester, Smith abruptly resigned from Tuskegee and returned to Wichita, Kansas. In 1914, then Captain Smith joined the military department at Western University, a historic institution affiliated with the A.M.E. Church built on the site in Quindaro where abolitionist John Brown ferried slaves to freedom in Kansas.

The no-nonsense Smith promptly implemented military discipline and training for the choir and bands. Smith built bridges to the surrounding community, bringing together the choruses of Western University and Allen Chapel. That summer Smith led the band at Lincoln Electric Park, Kansas City's first African American amusement park. Denied access to Electric Park, Kansas City's glittering amusement park, African Americans established their own Lincoln Electric Park on the edge of the community at 19th and Woodland. Featuring a theater seating 700, a dance pavilion with a hardwood maple floor, an ornate merry-go-round, and the Big Eli Ferris Wheel, Lincoln Park mirrored its larger white counterpart. Couples promenaded on the plank walk-way fronting concession row, stepping lightly to the refrain of Smith's concert band. Once established in the community, Smith's projects became more am-bitious. In June 1916, Smith organized a sixty-piece band and a two-hundred-member chorus for the annual National Negro Business League conference. That fall, Smith joined the faculty of Lincoln High School, a move prompted by Western University's chronic financial problems. Lincoln needed a band-master and military instructor. Smith fit the bill for both positions.

Smith quickly advanced both programs by organizing drills three days a week and music instruction the other two. At the start of the school year, only five members of the band could play their instruments. By the year's end, all thirty members of the band had mastered Smith's challenging repertoire of spirituals and classical standards. Expanding the music program, Smith fielded a thirty-member girl's glee club, a twenty-four-member boy's glee club, and a fifteen-piece orchestra. Smith introduced Walter Page, a member of the 1916 orchestra, to the double bass, commanding him one day to "pick up the bass Pagey."[36] In the photo of the orchestra in the 1917 Lincoln yearbook, the *Lincolnian*, Page cradles his upright bass with his left hand resting on the top of the body and his right hand resting slightly lower on the right side of the bass with his two middle fingers extended toward the strings, indicating he plucked as well as bowed the bass.

Smith did not teach jazz but tacitly approved of his students' interest out-side of the classroom. "Major N. Clark Smith often let Walter [Page] take the bass home at night 'to get some practice,'" commented underclassman Jasper Allen. "It was only by accident of course, that some dance would be going on and Walter would 'just happen' to be called on to play with the band there. Well, he always had more spending money than the rest of us."[37] A descrip-tion of music program activities in the 1919 *Lincolnian* concluded with an addendum praising Walter Page's jazz orchestra: "lastly, I must not forget Page's jazz orchestra that furnishes music during the lunch period. It is some orchestra. I say it is!"[38] In 1922, Smith publicly embraced jazz by making "a plea for the catchy type of music made famous by Lieutenant Europe in France, and commonly called jazz" at a memorial service held in Chicago for James Reese Europe.[39] Later that year Smith moved to Chicago, where he orga-nized Pullman Porter singing groups and taught at Wendell Phillips High School.[40]

The music education program established by Watts, Glass, and Smith equipped students with a polished command of their instruments and a broad understanding of music theory, and in the process created confident soloists and accomplished section players. Walter Page, Thamon Hayes, Julia Lee, Harlan Leonard, Leroy Maxey, Lamar Wright, Jasper Allen, DePriest Wheeler, and other first-generation Kansas City jazz musicians learned their craft under Smith. The program Smith founded at Lincoln benefited generations of students under the leadership of his successors, composer William Dawson and Alonzo Lewis. One of the greatest improvisers of jazz, Charlie Parker, proudly took to the field as a member of the Lincoln High School band, marching and blowing his alto saxophone. Rooted in the ragtime, blues, and concert band traditions, nurtured in the 18th and Vine area, Kansas City Jazz grew into a hardy hybrid.

3

Get Low-Down Blues

"Stop that ragtime.
Let's get real lowdown."

—Bennie Moten's Kansas City Orchestra,
"Get Low-Down Blues," 1928

JAZZ ARRIVED AT THE CORNER of 18th and Vine one hot, dusty afternoon in July 1917. While playing a ballyhoo on 18th Street, a unit from Drake and Walker's Big Musical Production engaged the band from the Billy King tent show in an exchange of jazz licks.[1] Covering the musical street brawl for the *Kansas City Sun*, Charles Starks observed:

> There was the sound of rivalry as well as revelry last Monday night when Drake and Walker's six-piece band of jazz experts were playing down in the old 1500 block on 18th street. Drake has some soft toned cunning and sensational artists who run a close second in harmony and easily out jazz all jazzers in stirring and catchy syncopations. They had just finished a dissecting treatment of the "Blues" intermingling such popular stuff as "Yaaka Hula, Hicky Dula" and "My Mother's Rosary" played first in pianissimo and then in its loud opposite, such as seemingly only black musicians can do, when who should come thundering up the avenue but a delegation from Billy Kling's [King's]! The Jazz aggregation, however, discovered the attack in due time and entrenched themselves in readiness so that when the enemy were in their midst they vociferously let go a volley of shot that fairly rained on the invaders. There was a terrible interchange of vehement artillery fire for about two minutes between the opposing forces. Trombone and cornet vying while the big bass drums spoke above the din of battle in thrilling sounds.

Starks, an aspiring poet, wrapped up his account of the musical battle by comparing the "valiant six" from Drake and Walker's band to Kipling's "Noble Six Hundred of old."[2] Jazz quickly became the rage in Kansas City, spawning small ensembles led by Dave Lewis, Paul Banks, George E. Lee, and Bennie Moten.

Originally from Chicago, saxophonist Dave Lewis fronted the Jazz Boys, one of the city's earliest bands. Organized in 1917, the seven-piece band alternated between Lyric Hall and the McHugh Dance Academy, a spacious white-only dance hall at 15th and Troost. Short and stocky with a receding hairline, Lewis gave up his band in 1920 after losing the engagement at the Dance Academy. The manager of the Academy, impressed by a band featuring two saxophones playing at downtown theater, asked Lewis to add another saxophone. When Lewis declined, not wanting to split the band's meager take with another member, the manager fired the band. Discouraged, Lewis disbanded and returned to Chicago. Although short-lived, the Lewis band gave a number of outstanding young players their first professional break. Walter Page began his career with the Lewis band while still in high school. After the breakup of the band, drummer Leroy Maxey and trombonist DePriest Wheeler found fame as members of the Cotton Club Orchestra in New York.

The Paul Banks band also served as a training ground for up-and-coming young musicians on their way to better things. Trumpeter Ed Lewis, bandleader "Jap" Allen, and other promising young players got their first break in the ranks of the Banks band. Trim with protruding ears and slicked-back hair, Paul Banks established his musical career just before World War I, playing drums with the Western Imperial Brass Band and pianist Andy Miller at Emanon Hall in Kansas City, Kansas. Switching to piano, Banks toured the Midwest with minstrel and road shows. Back in Kansas City, he studied with Charles T. Watts and Clyde Glass before he organized a six-piece band. Banks recalled scant competition in Kansas City at the time. "The only other band I can remember which was organized before mine was one led by Walter Brown," Banks recounted. "He [Brown] was playing violin and had Lloyd Moody on trombone and Scrap Harris on piano . . . Bennie Moten was at the McHugh Dancing Academy at 15th and Paseo, and they were called the B. B. and D. then. Bennie Moten on piano, Dude Langford on drums, and Bailey Hancock on vocals. That was around 1918 when three pieces could draw a crowd. George E. Lee was singing around town, but hadn't gotten a band organized yet."[3] Banks persevered, but his full-time job in the Armour meatpacking plant thwarted his career as a bandleader. Unable to work nightly or tour regionally, the Banks band suffered a constant turnover of personnel. Forced to rely on young players who quickly moved on, the Banks band rarely rivaled the more professional Lee and Moten bands.

George Ewing Lee, tall and dashing with a broad toothy grin, hailed from a long line of professional musicians. He reportedly owned a violin made in

1717 and passed down through four generations of George E. Lees.[4] Just after the turn of the century, Lee's family moved from Boonville, Missouri, to Kansas City. Lee carried on the family musical tradition, playing cello and violin with his father's string band while still in grade school. During World War I he served in the army, entertaining troops in France with an orchestra and vocal quartet. A powerful vocalist and multi-instrumentalist, Lee specialized in the slap-tongue technique on saxophone, more for show than virtuosity. Discharged in 1919, Lee formed a quartet with his sister Julia, a plump, masterful, left-handed pianist blessed with a pleasant contralto voice and a sunny disposition.

The George E. Lee Singing Novelty Orchestra entertained dancers at Lyric and Lincoln Halls, performing "all the latest song hits." Lee's stentorian tenor vocals rose above the din of the band, carrying for blocks. As a child, bandleader Clarence Love first heard the clarion call of jazz in Lee's vocals ringing out of the open window of Lyric Hall one hot summer evening. "In those days, now, there was no air conditioning, so the dance hall . . . would have its windows open," Love recalled. "And ol' George'd be up there singin' and playin' and we kids would be out in the middle of the street dancin'. He really inspired me to have a dance band."[5]

Lee's broad smile and on-stage charisma masked his caddish ways and imperious treatment of band members off the bandstand.

A shameless womanizer, Lee's romantic escapades often ended with the bandleader two steps ahead of a spurned sweetheart. A spendthrift, he flaunted his prized Cord with gold spoke wheels, orchid body, and canary yellow fenders, while paying band members below scale. Adding insult to injury, Lee readily fined band members over minor infractions. His domineering personality stifled creativity and held back the band musically, which in turn caused a constant turnover of personnel. "He [Lee] changed men so many times, man, half of Kansas City was on there [in the band]," alto saxophonist Herman Walder reflected. "He used to call himself a big shot: he'd fine his sister. He was pretty overbearing. . . . He was a different kind of cat altogether from Bennie Moten."[6]

BENNIE MOTEN was known as an astute bandleader and businessman who generously rewarded band members by paying them well above scale and encouraging their creativity. Diminutive, portly, and reserved with a moon face topped by a tassel of smartly creased plastered-down hair, Moten preferred managing rather than fronting the band. Bandleader Jesse Stone said Moten "had to spend so much time taking care of business. He would work on the door and watch the ticket office and all that sort of stuff, and the band would be playing without a piano."[7] Although frequently absent from the bandstand, Moten inspired loyalty from band members with his generosity and steady management, creating a stable organization. The Moten band quickly became the leading local band and then the first African American band from Kansas City to break out nationally.

Born and bred in the 18th and Vine area, Benjamin Moten learned the basics of music from his mother at the massive upright piano in the parlor of their home.[8] Advancing quickly, he studied with Charles T. Watts and pianist Thomas "Scrap" Harris, a former student of Scott Joplin. Doubling on baritone horn, Moten joined a juvenile concert band led by Dan Blackburn in 1906. He attended Lincoln High School but before graduating left to pursue a music career.[9] While freelancing in the clubs around 18th and Vine, Moten swiftly established a reputation as a solid ragtime pianist and hustler true to his word. In 1918, Moten formed the B. B. and D. Orchestra with drummer Dude Langford and Bailey Hancock, a well-liked vocalist, specializing in blues and popular tunes. Langford, a sprightly rascal fond of drinking and gambling, recalled first meeting Moten, "playing around town, little old joints here, some of 'em just little fronts, a bar and a gambling room in the back." They drew the name B. B. and D. from the first initial of their first names. Privately they referred to themselves as "Big, Black and Dirty."[10]

Langford clearly recalled the band's debut at the Labor Temple right after Christmas 1918. "We had big placards made up, in great big letters, would put 'em all up in windows and things for our dances." Langford detailed:

Now we got cold feet, 'cause a streetcar strike was on [it was] snowing, cold. . . . Now it was so bad we were scared to go up in the hall, and we didn't have no money to pay Mr. Ringling [the owner]. In those days you could get dago red, dago wine. . . . We went over there and got that wine, got a little nerve [to] go on up there to the dance. A few people are standing outside, and say, "Look here, these people must be fools to come out on a night like this." But the dance hall is so nice, big nice dance floor. . . . We went on in. Took the elevator on up to the second floor, and still was kinda shaky but that wine kept us going. We had one of them [attendance counters] you press like that, to count people. We had a fellow would press that thing every time a couple would come on in, and at one time we had twenty-three hundred on the floor. . . . [T]hings was on in them days. That place was packed, you couldn't get in, the first floor and the second floor. . . . I'll tell you we was blowed, knocked us out. Got about seventy or eighty dollar apiece."[11]

Seizing the opportunity, Moten and Langford established the Labor Temple as their home base. Moten and Langford steadily expanded their sphere of influence, playing for white dancers at McHugh's Dance Academy and social events in the community. The two prospered, investing in Peerless and Chalmers automobiles.

While the footloose Langford caroused in clubs on 18th Street, Moten shouldered the responsibility for booking and promoting the band and in the process forged strong ties to leading fraternal and social clubs in the community.

In late March 1920, Moten played the part of Two Gun Johnson in the Elks' gala stage presentation "Rocky Gulch Frontier Days." The next month, the B. B. and D. presided over a benefit dance for the YWCA at the Labor Temple sponsored by the Beau Brummel Club, a social club for college-educated professionals. In July 1921, the band performed for the Grand Jubilee Welcome, honoring Jack Johnson, the former world heavyweight boxing champion, at the Auditorium Theater. Kansas City fans gave a hero's welcome to Johnson, who was just released from the federal penitentiary at Leavenworth after serving time for violating the Mann Act, an act of Congress prohibiting the transportation of women across state lines for immoral purposes.

At the end of 1921, Moten assumed full leadership of the band when Langford dropped out to freelance in the string of cabarets on 18th Street. Replacing Langford with William "Bill" Tall from the Lee band, Moten shrewdly controlled bookings at the Labor Temple for his new aggregation: the B. B. and B. Jazz Masters. Under Moten's solid leadership, the band reaped prestigious engagements. In April 1922, the Jazz Masters played for the annual fashion show at the Labor Temple. The social affair of the season, the fashion show and dance benefited Wheatley-Provident Hospital, the only African American hospital in Kansas City. The event exceeded all expectations with 2,400 patrons flocking to the gala. Buoyed by the success of the fashion show, Moten formed the first band bearing his name, Bennie Moten's Jazz Orchestra. An advertisement in the *Call* touted the band as "singing and playing all the latest hits of the season."[12]

Moten carefully crafted his band, drawing from top local talent. Raiding the Lee band again, Moten brought aboard George "Sam" Tall on banjo. Woodrow "Woody" Walder, a tall, light-skinned showman, joined the front line, singing in a froglike voice and buzzing the mouthpiece of his clarinet, creating a kazoo-like sound. A multi-instrumentalist, Walder doubled on tenor saxophone. Cornetist Lamar Wright, an accomplished soloist with a bright tone, came to the band fresh out of Lincoln High School. Stout with a shy gap-tooth grin, Wright guided the front line through tricky passages. Moten found a kindred soul in trombonist Thamon Hayes, a yeoman soloist, who lent a hand managing the band. An alumnus of Lincoln High, Hayes began his professional career playing classical music with W. G. Melford's Second Regimental Band. Known for his mellow beat, drummer William Hall provided a firm rhythmic foundation for the new band. For special occasions, Moten supplemented the core group with Bailey Hancock, violinist Roland Bruce, and other rising soloists.

In March 1923, the Moten band made its radio debut over WHB, a 500-watt station licensed to Sweeney School of Automobile-Tractor-Aviation. Like WDAF, WHB's signal, under favorable atmospheric conditions, carried to Canada and Cuba. Charles A. Starks, covering the band's radio debut for the *Kansas City Sun*, proudly reported:

It was the first time that a real representative colored orchestra was heard and the impression was great. . . . [H]ere was an aggregation of "All Star Jazzers," with Roland Bruce, violinist; Woody Walder, clarinetist; and Eli Logan, saxophonist, standing out boldly in the features. Bruce's violin solo, "Love Will Find A Way," was superbly rendered. After playing this number with the fine appreciation of a virtuoso, he furnished the "bugs" with jazz whimsicality of the same which relieved a strong background of beauty. Woody, with his clarinet, cleaned up in his speciality [*sic*], when the famous "St. Louis Blues" were played and Eli Logan's saxophone work was keen. Bennie Moten was distinctly successful in the role of director and presider over the wonderful Grand piano at his disposal. His accompaniment of Bruce's solo was pleasingly correct. Bill Hall, the peppery trap drummer, took "Running Wild" seriously enough to actually run wild—but was always on time with stick or cymbal. His rolls and crashes were pointed and enlivening. Thamon Hayes, trombonist, and Lamar Wright, cornetist, contributed their share of melody and syncopation. . . . Bailey Hancock, the ace tenor, sang three numbers with telling effect—"Bert Williams to the Land of Laughs and Smiles," "Carolina in the Morning" and "Da Da Strain," by special request.[13]

Station management, barraged by listener requests, brought the band back the next week. Capitalizing on the broadcasts, Moten proudly billed the band as Bennie Moten's Radio Orchestra.

LIKE RADIO, THE RECORDING INDUSTRY rarely featured African American bands. The two major record labels, Victor and Columbia, instead concentrated on recording jubilee quartets and novelty acts, more palatable to white tastes. Black Swan, OKeh, Paramount, Gennett, and a number of small independent record companies filled the void, issuing so-called race records catering specifically to African Americans. After initially recording mostly blues shouters and sermons, the labels cashed in on the jazz craze sweeping the nation in the early 1920s. Ironically, "Livery Stable Blues," recorded in 1917 by the white Original Dixieland Jazz Band, sparked the national jazz mania. Given the opportunity, African American bands took the lead. In 1921, Fletcher Henderson made his first recordings for the Black Swan label. During spring 1923, King Oliver's Creole Jazz Band, featuring Louis Armstrong, initiated successful associations with the Gennett and OKeh labels. A few months later, Jelly Roll Morton joined Oliver in the roster of Gennett. The race labels, aggressively vying for new acts, dispatched artist and repertoire agents across the country to sign undiscovered artists. Record-store owners in the know steered the A & R men to local talent. In Kansas City, Winston Holmes cut himself in on a piece of the action by facilitating recording sessions for the OKeh and Paramount labels, before launching his own Meritt label.

From the founding of his music company, Holmes fancied himself as a promoter, sponsoring local appearances by Marcus Garvey and blues singer

Trixie Smith. A former entertainer and amateur musician, Holmes naturally gravitated to the recording industry. In December 1922, Holmes negotiated with OKeh to record Trixie Smith, accompanied by the George E. Lee band. Unfortunately for Holmes, Smith, who previously recorded for Black Swan, proved to be an unreliable performer. The *Kansas City Call* reported a much heralded performance by Smith, promoted by Holmes at the Auditorium Theater, ended abruptly after the local orchestra, hired for the date, refused to work with her, "owing to her very peculiar and eccentric manner of getting her songs over."[14] Holmes dropped Smith from the session, and Julia Lee stepped in as the featured vocalist for the first recordings of Kansas City Jazz, "Waco Blues" and "Just Wait Until I'm Gone," recorded in Chicago in June 1923.

Although OKeh rejected the two tracks, an undeterred Holmes arranged a second session that featured vocalists Ada Brown and Mary Bradford accompanied by Bennie Moten's Kansas City Orchestra. Ada Brown, pear shaped and gregarious with a resounding contralto voice, grew up in Kansas City, Kansas. A seasoned entertainer, Brown began her career in 1910, with Bob Mott's Pekin Theater in Chicago. She then toured abroad, playing clubs in Berlin and Paris.[15] Returning home in March 1923, Brown joined Bennie Moten at the Panama Cabaret, a small upscale club catering to entertainers and musicians, located near 18th and Forest. Originally from Detroit, Mary Bradford arrived in Kansas City from Chicago's Sunset Café in July 1923. A petite, versatile entertainer with curly locks, Bradford worked briefly with Dude Langford and His Jazz Hounds at the Entertainer's Cabaret before joining the Moten band at the Panama. Holmes, acting as a liaison, set up an audition for Moten, Brown, and Bradford with Ralph S. Peer, a director of recording for OKeh. Born in Kansas City, Peer grew up working in his father's sewing machine store that sold records and phonographs on the side. A pioneer in the race music field, Peer, baby faced and well-groomed, supervised the recording of Mamie Smith's smash hit "Crazy Blues." Swiftly building OKeh's roster, Peer canvassed the country signing blues and country artists. While in Atlanta in June 1923, Peer recorded one of the first big country hits—Fiddlin' John Carson's "A Little Old Cabin Down the Lane." Stopping off in Kansas City, Peer auditioned Brown, Bradford, and the Moten band in the back room of Holmes's music store. Pleased, on the spot he signed both vocalists and the band to a one shot deal.[16]

Holmes accompanied the two vocalists and the Moten band to the Consolidated Music Company in Chicago to personally manage the session, in mid-October. Peer and Holmes stuck to OKeh's hit formula, recording Bradford and Brown performing blues numbers backed by the Moten band. Mary Bradford recorded "Chattanooga Blues," "Selma 'Bama Blues," and "Waco Texas Blues," a holdover from the first session. Ada Brown waxed "Ill Nature Blues," "Break O' Day Blues," and "Evil Mama Blues," the most successful recording from the session. Brown's strong delivery underscores the pure bucket of blood sentiment of "Evil Mama Blues." Drawing on a popular but lethal blues theme, Brown blames her no-good man for turning her from a "sweet lovin' mama" into an "evil mama" intent on revenge and armed with a "good and sharp" razor.[17]

The two selections recorded by the Moten band—"Elephant's Wobble" and "Crawdad Blues"—capture the band in musical transition. Lamar Wright, supported by the rhythm section and followed closely by Walder on clarinet, introduces the jaunty, syncopated theme of "Elephant's Wobble," leading to solo turns by Hayes, Walder, and George Tall on banjo. The ensemble restates the theme in the out chorus, then falls out, letting Wright wrap up with a soaring solitary coda statement reminiscent of a bugler. Collectively, the ensemble embraces the form and feel of jazz, but the soloists echo earlier conventions. Hayes's and Wright's execution retains a clipped military inflection, influenced by the brass band tradition. George Tall's prominent banjo solos, inspired by Vess Ossman, harken back to the minstrel era. Loosening up for "Crawdad Blues," the soloists aptly express the blues in an orchestral context. Wright sets the tone of "Crawdad Blues" with a string of flattened 3rd blue notes, underscoring the strong feeling of the blues. Inspired by Wright's lead, Hayes follows with a confident slurred trombone solo, which bolsters the blue mood. Walder rises to the occasion in the codetta following the out chorus, smearing up from two flatted 3rds to a major 3rd.

The OKeh sessions introduced Bradford, Jones, the Moten band, and—by association Kansas City Jazz—to the national audience. Realizing the significance of the occasion, Moten billed his band as the Kansas City Orchestra. Working together in the studio, Peer and Moten established an easy rapport that laid the groundwork for future sessions. Immediately after the session, Bradford, Brown, Holmes, and the Moten band posed for a group publicity shot. Tellingly, Holmes positioned himself in the center of the photo with Bradford and Brown on either side, surrounded by the band members. Once back in Kansas City, Holmes immodestly took full credit for the session, telling a *Kansas City Sun* reporter "it was solely through his efforts that negotiations were successfully completed by the trip."[18] He further bragged that the technology to make records would be in place in Kansas City within two months. Not content with producing recording sessions, Holmes dreamed of establishing Kansas City as a recording center.

Satisfied with the results of the session, OKeh promptly released "Elephant's Wobble" and "Crawdad Blues" by Bennie Moten's Kansas City Orchestra; "Break O' Day Blues" and "Evil Mama Blues" by Ada Brown; and "Chattanooga Blues" and "Selma 'Bama Blues" by Mary H. Bradford. In late November, a half-page advertisement in the *Kansas City Call* celebrated the releases by "Kansas City's Own Race Artists" recording in the "famous Kansas City style."[19] The advertisement, dominated by oversized photos of Bennie Moten,

Ada Brown, and Mary Bradford, listed eighteen local establishments selling the records, prominently mentioning the Winston Holmes Music Company.

Encouraged by his recent triumph, Holmes shopped his latest find, Lottie Beaman, a rotund contralto he nicknamed the "Kansas City Butterball," to OKeh and the Artophone Company. In January 1924, Beaman auditioned for both labels at Holmes's music company. Brushing aside Holmes's hard sell, the label representatives passed on Beaman. The next month, Holmes hosted a gathering of 350 OKeh territorial dealers, four representatives from OKeh, and an executive with Paramount. Moten's band and Mary Bradford entertained the group, performing "Theta's Got the Blues" and "Tulsa Blues." During the meeting, Beaman signed with Paramount and Moten struck a deal with Peer to record again for OKeh. Playing both ends against the middle, Holmes established a reputation as a regional power broker in the race-record industry.[20]

In early March 1924, Holmes ushered Beaman as well as twins Miles and Millus Pruett to Chicago where they recorded "Regular Man Blues," "Red River Blues," and "Honey Blues" for the Paramount label. Miles's steady rhythm guitar and Millus's banjo frills embellish Beaman's otherwise plain vocal delivery. Dazzled by the twins' virtuosity, the producer for Paramount pressed them into service for two additional sessions accompanying Ida Cox and Ma Rainey. Before leaving Chicago, Holmes and his entourage celebrated at Ma Rainey's home with Clara Smith, Edmonia Henderson, and other mainstays of the Paramount label.

While Holmes dallied with Paramount, his affiliation with Moten and OKeh came to an end. Peer and Moten forged their own partnership and cut Holmes out of the action. In turn, Holmes omitted mention of Moten's OKeh recordings in his weekly advertisements in the *Kansas City Call*. Holmes's gesture made little difference to Moten, who at the time was busily pursuing new business interests. In late March, Moten took over management of the Paseo Dancing Academy at 15th and Paseo. Known as "The Finest Hall in the West," Paseo Hall comfortably accommodated 2,200 dancers. Music and gaiety poured out of the large windows surrounding the hall to entice passersby at the busy intersection. Entering through the double doors on 15th Street, patrons purchased tickets at the box office window on the left. Staircases flanking the entrance to the ballroom on either side led to the balcony, where music lovers watched nattily dressed dancers two-stepping across the gleaming wood floor. A huge mirrored ball, suspended from the ceiling, presided over the festivities.

Moten featured his band on Thursday and Sunday nights and rented the hall to social clubs and fraternal groups on other nights for $50. Adding to the merriment, Moten gave away souvenir caps, canes, and horns as door prizes. Paseo Hall readily became the social center of the district, hosting theme dances for social clubs and huge holiday celebrations for the entire community. Needing a bigger sound to fill the hall, Moten expanded the band to eight pieces, adding Harry Cooper on cornet and Harlan Quentin Leonard on alto saxophone. Originally from Butler, Missouri, Leonard studied under Major N. Clark Smith and William Dawson at Lincoln High School.[21] An earnest student, he took private lessons from saxophonist Paul Tremaine. After graduating from Lincoln High School in 1923, Leonard studied math and engineering in junior college. A dedicated family man, Leonard worked with George E. Lee on the side. Dreamy eyed with broad angular features, Leonard shied away from solos, preferring to bolster the newly formed reed section. By creating reed and brass sections, Moten stepped away from the standard New Orleans jazz configuration and toward the creation of an original Kansas City jazz style.[22]

The next recording session for OKeh, held in early December 1924 in St. Louis, revealed Moten's new musical direction. The recordings retain strains of the principle influences on Kansas City Jazz—ragtime, blues, and band music—yet contain embryonic elements that came to distinguish the Kansas City style: four-to-the-bar rhythm, the use of head arrangements, and tight ensemble work in support of the soloists. The session was a hurried affair. The band left Kansas City on Sunday at midnight and spent only six hours in the studio on Monday before returning home. According to Harlan Leonard, band members collectively improvised in the studio around head arrangements memorized from sketched introductions.[23] The loose head arrangements allowed ample room for solo flights and interaction between sections, which gave the recordings a spontaneity lacking in the first session.

The ragged syncopation of the rhythm section accentuates the catchy melody of "South," composed by Thamon Hayes for the session. The two cornets play the same rhythm in a harmony line, revealing an increased harmonic sophistication. The four-to-the-bar rhythm of "Vine Street Blues" lays the foundation for the soloists buttressed by close ensemble work. Leonard contributes a well-executed gravel-tone alto saxophone solo before joining Walder playing double time in the out chorus. Introducing the theme of "Tulsa Blues," Moten sets the rhythmic mood between swing and straight eighth notes, with the ensemble echoing the pattern. Following a jaunty ragtime piano introduction by Moten, "Goofy Dust" features tight ensemble work with musical breaks showcasing brief solos. Accentuated breaks enhance the textured ensemble work of "Baby Dear." All of the selections recorded in the OKeh session became staples in the Moten band book.

As OKeh readied Moten's St. Louis recordings for issue, Winston Holmes released the first record on his newly-established Meritt label: "Cabbage Head Blues" and "City of the Dead" by Sylvester and Lena Kimbrough with Paul Banks Kansas Trio. The Kansas City Call reported that Holmes became "inspired to make records after seeing how the Caucasian concerns were trying to control the race market."[24] By naming his label Meritt, Holmes engaged in one-upmanship with Peer and OKeh. While "Okay" indicates only acceptable, "Merit" connotes excellence. Holmes's choice of Meritt reflected the

belief of middle-class African Americans that they had to be better than average and lead lives of merit to attain equality. Tragically, the technical limita-
tions of his studio and the lack of national distribution undermined Holmes's
aspiration for excellence.

Holmes made good on his promise to establish a recording studio locally,
recording the wax masters in the back room of his music company. Accompanying Lena and Sylvester Kimbrough, the Paul Banks Kansas Trio featured
Banks's brother Clifford Banks on clarinet and Simon Hoe on a single-string
violin of his own construction. Lena Kimbrough, joined by Hoe sawing away
on his invention and Clifford Banks squawking on clarinet, warbles her way
through "City of the Dead," a bloody tale of murder and suicide. Her brother
Sylvester, a dentist by profession, joins Kimbrough for "Cabbage Head Blues,"
a novelty blues duet in the vein of Butter Beans and Susie.[25] With no pressing
plants in the Midwest, Holmes sent the masters to Bridgeport, Connecticut,
for manufacture by Columbia Records.

The pressings met industry standard, but the poorly recorded wax masters
supplied by Holmes compounded the coarseness of the performance and undermined the quality of the record. The purple Meritt label featured two
roughly rendered jester-like theatrical masks representing drama and comedy
with distinct African American features facing each other, separated by "Meritt"
in gold letters with two eighth notes superimposed vertically over the "M."
"Winston Holmes Music Co. Kansas City Mo." blazoned in gold capital letters across the bottom of the label identified the source of the recording.
Incorrectly bragging that the Meritt recordings were the "first phonograph
records ever made in Kansas City," Holmes pledged to set up the equipment
necessary to manufacture the discs locally for his next release.[26]

During the next three years Holmes issued five more discs, ranging from
blues, sermons, and spirituals to stomp-down jazz. In April 1925, Holmes
recorded Hattie McDaniels, a rotund comedienne and entertainer with bulging eyes. Well on her way up, McDaniels, billed as the "Female Bert Williams," received rave reviews and standing ovations in theaters across the
Midwest. The *Kansas City Call* celebrated McDaniels as a "song bird par excellence and also a comedienne de luxe [who] has received special notice in
the press wherever she has appeared."[27] While in town for a series of dates
with the George Morrison band, McDaniels recorded "Quittin' My Man
Today" and "Brown-Skin Baby Doll." Wrapping up her tour with Morrison
in the spring of 1926, McDaniels joined a revue headlined by Butterbeans
and Susie on the TOBA circuit. McDaniels promoted her Meritt recordings
as she traveled the country, but to no avail. Lacking national distribution,
Holmes failed to capitalize on McDaniels's growing popularity.[28]

Holmes missed a second opportunity to establish the Meritt label nationally
with his third release, a pair of sermons by the Reverend J. C. Burnett, "The
Down Fall of Nebuchadnezzar" and "I've Even Heard of Thee." A native of

Downtown Kansas City in the 1920s. *Driggs Collection.*

Major N. Clark Smith (seated). A bandmaster and composer, Smith taught music in high schools in Kansas City, Chicago, and St. Louis. He then returned to Kansas City, where he died in 1935. *Driggs Collection.*

Coon-Sanders Novelty Orchestra, Kansas City, 1920. *Left to right*: Carleton Coon, drums/vocals/co-founder; Carl Nocatero, trombone; Hal McClain, alto sax; Harry Silverstone, violin; Joe Sanders, piano/vocals/co-founder; Harold Thiell, C melody sax; Bob Norfleet, banjo; Clyde Hendrick, trumpet. Debuting in 1920, Coon-Sanders relied mainly on novelty work. Their long run at the Muehlebach Hotel coupled with regular broadcasts over WDAF eventually brought them to Chicago's Congress Hotel in 1924. *Courtesy Duncan Schiedt.*

Loren D. McMurray (1897–1922), alto, C melody, and baritone sax, 1922. McMurray was the first star from Kansas City whose fame extended elsewhere. In New York he recorded regularly and was featured with half-a-dozen major names of the day. His untimely death in New York in 1922 was a great loss. *Driggs Collection.*

Dave Lewis Jazz Boys, Troost Dancing Academy, Kansas City, Missouri, 1920.
Left to right: Leroy Maxey, drums; Depriest Wheeler, trombone; unidentified,
banjo; Lawrence Denton, clarinet; Dude Knox, piano; unidentified, violin; Dave
Lewis, alto sax, leader. A Chicago musician, Lewis held down the best-paying
job in Kansas City in 1920, only to lose it when he refused to hire a second
saxophonist. Maxey and Wheeler became stars with Cab Calloway a decade later.
Courtesy Local 627, A.F.M.

Lena and Sylvester Kimbrough, accompanied by Paul Banks Kansas Trio, 1924. *Left to right*: Clifton Banks, alto sax; Winston M. W. Holmes, clarinet; Lena Kimbrough, vocals; Paul Banks, leader/piano; Sylvester Kimbrough, vocals. Paul Banks was probably the oldest bandleader. He worked steadily, keeping a day job at the Armour meat-packing company. He kept working into the late 1940s. *Courtesy Paul Bank; Driggs Collection.*

George E. Lee Singing Novelty Orchestra, Kansas City, 1924. Lee came out of the army in 1919 with a powerful singing voice. Together with his talented piano playing sister, Julia, they remained popular until the Depression. This early group featured the outstanding trombonist Thurston "Sox" Moppins. *Courtesy Charles Goodwin; Driggs Collection.*

Coon-Sanders Nighthawks, Congress Hotel, Chicago, c. 1924–25. *Left to right*: John Thiell, tenor sax; Carleton Coon, drums; Floyd Estep, first alto sax; Joe Sanders, piano/vocals; Harold Thiell, alto sax; Hank Jones, banjo; Joe Richolson, trumpet; Pop Estep, tuba; Rex Downing, trombone. The Coon-Sanders band became extremely popular at the Muehlebach Hotel through radio broadcasts. They became the first Kansas City band to achieve national popularity. *Courtesy Johnny Coon; Driggs Collection.*

Paul Tremaine played an outstanding saxophone with Louis Forbstein and D. Ambert Haley and did staff work at WDAF before forming his big band in 1926. He became popular playing spirituals and achieved national recognition by 1928. *Driggs Collection.*

Members of Kansas City's famed Black Musicians Union, Local 627 A.F.M., line up in front of their headquarters, 1823 Highland Avenue, prior to the Battle of Bands, May 4, 1930. The bands of Bennie Moten, George E. Lee, Paul Banks, and several lesser units are shown. *Included in photograph*: Budd Johnson (*7th from left*), Jesse Stone (*9th from left*), Henri Woode (*11th from left*), Eddie Durham (*14th from left*), Harlan Leonard (*16th from left*), Bus Moten (*18th from left*), Bennie Moten (*21st from left*), Jimmy Rushing (*22nd from left*), Count Basie (*23rd from left*). *Courtesy Local 627, A.F.M.*

Phil Baxter's Orchestra, El Torreon Ballroom (31st and Gillham), Kansas City, 1929. Baxter, pianist and composer, came to Kansas City in 1926 with his quintet, the Texas Tommies, to open the Submarine Ballroom. Expanded to twelve men, Baxter's became the house band at the New El Torreon Ballroom in 1927. *Courtesy Thurman Rotroff; Driggs Collection.*

Exterior of Pla-Mor Ballroom. This was the city's best-known ballroom. It featured the best black and white bands. *Driggs Collection.*

Pla-Mor Ballroom, Kansas City, 1920s. The Pla-Mor lasted from 1927 until 1957, although the best musicians said they preferred the El Torreon because it had a warmer sound. *Driggs Collection.*

Fairyland Park, Kansas City, 1930s. Fairyland Park was the main outdoor venue for the summer season in the 1930s—for Bennie Moten, Andy Kirk, Harlan Leonard, and Jay McShann and nationally known bands on tour. *Driggs Collection.*

Jap Allen's Cotton Club Orchestra, later known as the Cotton Pickers, Kansas City, 1930. *Left to right*: Joe Keyes, trumpet; Ben Webster, tenor sax; Jim Daddy Walker, guitar; Clyde Hart, piano/arranger; Slim Moore, trombone; Raymond Howell, drums; Jap Allen, bass/leader; Eddie "Orange" White, trumpet; Al Denny, alto sax; O. C. Wynne, vocals; Booker Pittman, alto sax/clarinet; Durwood "Dee" Stewart, trumpet. This band, modeled after McKinney's Cotton Pickers, was the hottest band in town during the 1930s, with extended engagements in Tulsa, Oklahoma City, Sioux Falls, and Sioux City, as well as in Kansas City. In 1931 Blanche Calloway raided the band, taking six key players, thereby breaking them up. Allen reorganized in St. Louis, but was not successful. *Driggs Collection.*

Walter Page Blue Devils, Ritz Ballroom, Oklahoma City, 1931. *Left to right*: Hot
Lips Page, trumpet; Leroy "Snake" White, trumpet; Walter Page, bass; James
Simpson, trumpet; Druie Bess, trombone; A. G. Godley, drums; Reuben Lynch,
banjo; Charlie Washington, piano; Reuben Roddy, tenor sax; Ernie Williams,
director/vocals; Theodore Ross, first alto sax; Buster Smith, alto sax/clarinet,
arranger. The Blue Devils, considered to be the most musical band of the time,
arrived in Kansas City to play the White Horse Tavern in 1928. One by one,
Bennie Moten hired away Hot Lips Page, Count Basie, and Jimmy Rushing. Even
Walter Page himself later had few options and joined Moten in 1931. *Courtesy
Druie Bess; Driggs Collection.*

Thamon Hayes's Kansas City Skyrockets, Fairyland Park, Kansas City, Summer 1932. *Left to right*: Harlan Leonard, first alto sax; Vic Dickenson, trombone; Herman Walder, third alto sax, clarinet; Thamon Hayes, lead trombone; Woody Walder, tenor sax/clarinet; Richard Smith, third trumpet; Booker Washington, second trumpet; Ed Lewis, first trumpet; Charles "Crook" Goodwin, banjo/vocals; Baby Lovett, drums; Vernon Page, bass/tuba; Jesse Stone, piano/arranger/conductor. The Hayes band became the best band in Kansas City for two years, 1932 and 1933, securing the best jobs and having the best *esprit du corps*, until a location job at a major new nightclub in Chicago was denied them by James Caesar-Petrillo in 1933. Thomas Hayes gave up, left music, and took a day job. Harlan Leonard took over. *Courtesy Ed Lewis; Driggs Collection.*

Bennie Moten's Kansas City Orchestra, Pearl Theater, Philadelphia, 1931. *Left to right*: Hot Lips Page, trumpet; Willie McWashington, drums; Ed Lewis, first trumpet; Thamon Hayes, trombone; Woody Walder, tenor sax, clarinet; Eddie Durham, trombone, guitar/arranger; Count Basie, piano/arranger; Jimmy Rushing, vocals; Leroy Berry, banjo, guitar; Harlan Leonard, first alto sax; Bennie Moten, piano, vocals; Vernon Page, tuba; Booker Washington, trumpet; Jack Washington, alto and baritone sax; Bus Moten, director, accordion. Not long after this photo was taken, Basie and Eddie Durham convinced Bennie Moten to hire new men and change the style of the band to be more competitive with the Eastern bands. *Driggs Collection.*

Johnny Lazia, the Al Capone of Kansas City. He was supposed to keep Kansas City safe from outside gangsters. The Union Station Massacre of 1933 cost him his life. *From the Goin' to Kansas City Collection, The Kansas City Star Company and the Kansas City Museum.*

Alabama, Burnett worked the tent circuit across Texas, Louisiana, and Mississippi preaching for the Greater Progressive Baptist Church and selling records along the way. In the fall of 1926, Burnett signed a contract with Columbia Records while still obligated to Meritt. Holmes responded by filing a lawsuit in federal court against Columbia. Legally outgunned, Holmes lost his suit and Burnett to Columbia.

Trying to duplicate the success of the Burnett recording, Holmes released two more sacred recordings by local religious figures in early 1927. The Reverend H. C. Gatewood, a storefront preacher joined by the Faithful Singers, preached sermons in song on "Regeneration" and "The Well of Salvation." Sanctified vocalists from the Church of God in Christ, Sisters Anna Grinstead and Ora Miller, accompanied by pianist Sister Florestine Gibson, delivered spirited holy roller performances on "Calvary" and "Don't Forget the Family Prayer." By recording local religious figures, who did not tour, Holmes further limited the already niche market for sacred recordings. The two releases sold modestly in Kansas City, mostly to church members, but failed to catch on even regionally.

Seeking broader appeal, Holmes recorded George E. Lee and His Novelty Singing Orchestra. After being rejected by OKeh, Lee regrouped, pulling together a band of talented soloists. Lee recruited big-tone trumpeter Sam Utterback, who was trim with a thin face and pointed chin, from the pit orchestra at the Avalon Theater. Thurston "Sox" Maupins, the leading local trombonist, joined Lee from Laura Rucker's band at Elmer Bean's nightclub. Clarence "Tweety" Taylor led the front line, performing on an arsenal of saxophones. Gangly with large eyes nestled under a protruding forehead, Taylor moved easily across the full array of saxophones, ranging from the soprano to baritone. Newcomer Clint Weaver on baritone horn and veteran drummer Abie Price joined Julia Lee in the rhythm section. With his rival Moten releasing new recordings, Lee jumped at the opportunity to get back in the studio.

Released in the spring of 1927, "Down Home Syncopated Blues" and "Meritt Stomp" capture the rocking back beat and unfettered execution of Lee's undisciplined aggregation. "Down Home Syncopated Blues," a blatant remake of "Royal Garden Blues," showcases George's forceful vocals, punctuated by Maupins's trombone exclamations. Wrapping things up neatly, Julia joins George for a vocal duet on the out chorus. The loosely improvised "Meritt Stomp" highlights solos by Maupins, Utterback, and Taylor, topped with Julia Lee's rollicking barrelhouse turn at the piano. The Lee recording sold well locally, but marked the swan song for the Meritt label. Financially strapped by increasing competition from other music stores on 18th Street, Holmes soon folded the Meritt label.[29] In the end, Holmes, unable to compete with larger race labels, failed to realize his dream of establishing his Meritt label nationally.

While Holmes struggled to get the Meritt label off the ground, the Moten band rose nationally, boosted by recordings for the OKeh and Victor labels. After parting ways with Holmes, Moten and Peer arranged a third session for OKeh. Expanding the band for the session, Moten added Vernon Page on tuba, who gave the rhythm section a fuller, more buoyant sound. William "Bill" Little, an experienced showman, joined as conductor and featured vocalist. Originally from Muskogee, Oklahoma, the affable Little traveled on the Chautauqua circuit with George R. Garner's Quartet before moving to Kansas City. Little, handsome and with a fine tenor voice, fronted the band while operating a combination shine parlor and musician's and messenger service on the side with Moten. LaForest Dent replaced George Tall on banjo. Dent's crisp ringing banjo technique sharpened the band's rhythmic attack and freed Moten to step out as a soloist. The new rhythmic foundation better supported the soloists and interplay between the sections and brought the group's ensemble closer to parity with jazz bands nationally.

In mid-May, Peer hauled a portable recording unit to Kansas City and recorded seven new selections in two days. The sessions show a significant improvement in the band's rhythm section, solo execution, and ensemble expression. After a vamp introduction by the sections, vocalist Little delivers a lively performance on "She's Sweeter Than Sugar," a popular number written by Moten and Hayes. For "South Street Blues" the band constructs a simple structure of well-spaced solos, sandwiched between an introduction and conclusion by the ensemble. The intonation of Walder's clarinet solo leaves much to be desired, but Hayes's trombone solo shows an increasingly sophisticated technique. Feeling his oats, Hayes contributes a wah-wah solo to the next selection, "Sister Honky Tonk." The ensemble collectively carries the lively melody of "As I Like It" without solo breaks. Lamar Wright, the band's star soloist, shines on "Things Seem So Blue to Me," illuminated by Hayes and the reed section alternately playing counterpoint. On "18th Street Strut," the ensemble introduces a snappily repeated theme, echoed and embellished by Wright's muted cornet, Hayes's staid trombone, and Walder's crying wah-wah clarinet in the middle section. In the final selection recorded, "Kater Street Rag," the band returns to its roots in the ragtime tradition. Taking a rare solo, Moten's 32-bar ragtime-flavored solo reveals an assured two-fisted pianist. Shortly after the session, Peer left OKeh, breaking Moten's link to the label.

The OKeh recordings advanced Moten's reputation nationally, but the band could not capitalize on the success and tour because there were no booking agencies that linked ballrooms and theaters across the country into a circuit. Content to be a big fish in a little pond for the time being, Moten spent 1925 and 1926 playing at Paseo Hall, the Labor Temple, and other venues in the 18th and Vine area. During the summers, the eight-piece Moten band divided its time between Monday night cruises aboard the "John Heckman," a massive three-deck steamer cruising the Missouri River, and the dance pavilion at Liberty Park, an African American amusement park and summer resort near Raytown, just east of Kansas City. Modeled after Fairyland Park, a white-only amusement resort at 79th and Prospect, Liberty Park featured a crystal pool and beach that accommodated 3,000 swimmers, the Dreamland Dance Pavilion, with a hardwood dance floor holding 300 couples, and a boisterous midway with a merry-go-round, miniature train, merry mix-up, and other carnival rides.

Following the 1926 summer season at Liberty Park, Moten brought the band up to nine pieces. LaForest Dent switched to alto and baritone saxophone when George Tall returned to banjo. Dent's move brought the saxophone section up to three members, the standard for full-size jazz bands. Sharp young percussionist Willie McWashington replaced Willie Hall on drums, adding a textured sheen to the rhythm section. With a wealth of local engagements and musicians clamoring to join the band, Moten formed a second unit, Bennie Moten Number 2. Moten continued playing piano with the original band, but he increasingly devoted more of his time to booking and managing both organizations. Fielding two bands, Moten dominated nightlife at 18th and Vine and received little competition from George E. Lee, who fronted a smaller, less accomplished band. Ironically, the Paul Banks band, with a sweeter sound, fared better than Moten with white downtown audiences.

During the fall of 1926, Paul Banks and the Maceo Birch Revue breached the Jim Crow line with a series of midnight ramble shows at the Newman Theater. Although theater management still denied entrance to African American patrons, the *Kansas City Call* praised the breakthrough: "[I]t has become quite the thing for colored acts to be booked at this theatre for shows each Sat. night."[30] Moten soon followed Banks and Birch into regular rotation at the Newman. According to the *Call*, Banks "played to equal honors" with Moten's band during a battle of the bands at the Newman Theater in late November 1926.[31] Banks felt his band bested the Moten unit. "Bennie Moten and my band were on the same stage at 11th and Main," Banks said. "There was just one piano, so we'd each play a number and applause would determine the winner. We were supposed to play three numbers each, and unknown to each other, we both chose 'Tiger Rag' as our final number. My bunch liked to stand up when they got hot and the wa-wa mutes and all we won the contest that night."[32] Bank's victory turned out to be pyrrhic. Moten soon edged him out of the regular engagement at the Newman. The midnight rambles at the Newman opened to new vistas in the white community for Moten, Banks, and other African American bands from the 18th and Vine area—just a brief streetcar ride away but socially a world apart.

MOTEN REACHED FAR BEYOND 18th Street by cultivating his contacts in the national white entertainment industry. Dropped by OKeh after the third session, Moten auditioned for the Victor label in Chicago in mid-December

1926. Ralph Peer, recently employed by Victor, made arrangements for the sessions. With Peer on staff, Victor jumped into the race market with both feet. Over two days in the studio, the band cooked up a roots gumbo of stomps, blues, shuffles spiced with hot jazz ensemble breaks, and solos, the kind of stomp-down fare favored by the dancers at Paseo Hall. Covering the audition, the *Kansas City Call* erroneously declared Moten "the first colored orchestra to record popular numbers and the second to record anything for the Victor Co., who just recently decided to feature the colored musicians."[33] Ironically, Peer ended up listing Moten alongside the Coon-Sanders band and other leading white bands in the Victor catalogue.

In a letter from New York on January 22, 1927, Peer praised the quality of Moten's recordings, ranking them with the work of top Victor artists. "Your records have just come through and I am mighty glad to tell you that they are the best you have ever made," Peer wrote. "I have interested one of our Musical Directors and, after listening very carefully to the records, he agrees with me that your work is good enough to justify listing in the white list along with Olsen, Whiteman, Coon-Sanders, etc. In Chicago, I told you of this possibility but really felt that you did not stand a very good chance. Your constant rehearsals and hard work during the past years have given the band an unusual style and for the first time, I hear a colored band which is always in tune." Peer concluded by urging Moten to sign an exclusive contract with Victor, "to put the proposition over with the record committee, I must be able to guarantee Victor exclusive rights to use your name. This seems fair enough as they will spend many thousand dollars in publicity.... The Record committee meets in Camden [New Jersey] next Monday and Tuesday and in order to get action, I will have to know that you presume that everything will be satisfactory but request that you wire me to that effect. These chances only come once and I want to be certain that I am free to go ahead."[34] Acting on Peer's recommendation, Moten readily signed with Victor. Peer had more than a passing interest in Moten's success. Victor's in-house publishing firm, Southern Music Company, headed by Peer, published Moten's compositions.

The Moten band returned to Kansas City in mid-February 1927 to a double bill with Fletcher Henderson at Paseo Hall. Henderson set the standard for other African American bands. Taking a break from a long-term engagement at the Roseland Ballroom in New York, Henderson toured the Midwest with stops in Detroit, Chicago, Cleveland, and St. Louis before arriving in Kansas City. The first Eastern big band to play in the 18th and Vine area, Henderson's sharp arrangements astounded the dance fans huddling around the bandstand at Paseo Hall. Inspired by Henderson's polished style that was distinguished by sharp section work, Moten began moving away from the stomp-down Kansas City style to a more refined mode of orchestral expression in anticipation of the band's scheduled Eastern debut later that year.

Victor released the Moten band's new recordings nationally in March 1927. Moten and Thamon Hayes capitalized on their association with Victor and opened a music store on 18th Street, a block west of the Winston Holmes Music Company. The Moten Hayes Music shop stocked Victor, Columbia, OKeh, and Paramount recordings, sheet music, and a wide array of phonographs. Joining a phalanx of music stores on 18th Street, the Moten Hayes operation thrived, giving Holmes stiff competition. By 1928, the volume of the phonographs promoting records on the sidewalks in front of record stores on 18th Street rose to such a volume that Roy Wilkins, the editor of the *Kansas City Call*, protested in an editorial about the cacophony ringing up and down 18th Street. Wilkins singled out one store in particular, "which persist in blues and sermons from preachers no one has ever heard of and on subjects one cannot find in the Bible. These sermons consist mostly of moanings and groanings and hysterical, unintelligible yelling."[35] Fighting off stiff competition from Moten and Hayes, Holmes continued promoting the sermons on his Meritt label and, despite Wilkins's complaints, cranked up the volume on 18th Street. Down the street, Hayes, quiet and unassuming, more at home behind a counter than on the bandstand, ran the music shop while Moten tended to the band.

During early summer 1927, Moten expanded the band to eleven pieces, adding Jack Washington on baritone saxophone and trumpeter Ed Lewis. Originally from Kansas City, Kansas, Washington began his career with Paul Banks before traveling the Midwest with Jesse Stone and the Blues Serenaders. Slight in stature, Washington delivered a big full sound that anchored the four-member saxophone section. Stocky Ed Lewis, the son of a well-known brass band musician, worked with pianists Jerry Westbrook, Paul Banks, and Laura Rucker before embarking on the TOBA circuit in early 1927. Back home after hitting a few rough spots on the road, Lewis tried out for the Moten band. Lewis' mother, Moten's cousin, smoothed the way for the audition. Playing Fletcher Henderson's "Stampede" from memory, Lewis won the tryout and joined Lamar Wright in the brass section. Lewis enjoyed the band's camaraderie and admired Moten's generosity. "The thing I liked about that band in those days was that it was a commonwealth band," Lewis accounted. "Bennie got double for being the leader, but everything else was split right down the middle . . . to this day, there hasn't been a squarer leader in the game than Bennie Moten. . . . I made my first records with the band soon after I joined them. They had recorded before and the older guys in the band, Lamar Wright, Woody Walder and Harlan Leonard used to tease us new guys by putting their fat recording checks on the music racks saying these were the only kind of notes they knew of."[36]

Eager to get back in the studio, the Moten band returned to Chicago for a second Victor recording session in early June 1927. The band recorded eight selections over two days. Guided by the highly orchestrated melodic style of

Fletcher Henderson, the Moten band changed musical course for the sessions. Buoyed by the rhythm section marking exact time, the soloists and sections traded off carrying the melody. Not breaking entirely with the Kansas City sound, the rhythm section laid down a pulsating Western beat, while the soloists challenged each other. "Part of the rhythm section would accent the second and fourth beats while the other part of it would place the emphasis on the first and third," bandleader Jap Allen explained. "Moten's boys also got a kick out of the old challenging or, as it is sometimes called, chasing each other. We always said challenging because that's what it was. Usually it started in rehearsals or when the boys were sitting around getting ideas. One guy would kick it off with a few bars and then someone else would pick it up and try to play it better. Then they would get going back and forth trying to cut each other, with the second man picking up the first man's challenge. . . . Moten's recording of 'Pass Out Lightly' . . . was challenging practically all the way through. The . . . recording was cut by time to just a few bars of each 'flight,' such as Woodie [Woody] Walder's tenor sax getting a challenge from Jack Washington's baritone horn, while Ed Lewis on muted trumpet got as much as he could handle from Lamar Wright on open trumpet."[37] Lewis's rich tone provided the perfect foil for Wright's piercing flights into the upper register.

A couple of months later, the band suffered a setback with the departure of Wright, the star soloist and most musically accomplished member. Parting amicably from the Moten band, Wright joined the famed Cotton Club Orchestra at 142nd and Lenox Avenue in Harlem. Ironically, although based in New York, most members of the Cotton Club Orchestra came from Missouri. Wright attended Lincoln High School with the manager and baritone horn player James "Smitty" Smith, drummer Leroy Maxey, and trombonist DePriest Wheeler. While not originally from Kansas City, the other trumpet player, Harry Cooper, worked for a short while with Wright in the Bennie Moten Orchestra. Another Kansas Citian, saxophonist Eli Logan, known for progressive ideas, played with the band until his untimely death in 1925. R. Q. Dickerson, trumpet; Earres Prince, piano; Charley Stamps, banjo; and other members hailed from St. Louis, Missouri. These musicians from Missouri helped the Cotton Club become a fashionable gathering spot for society and celebrities, long before the arrival of Duke Ellington, whose name later became synonymous with the club.

In New York, Wright found himself in heady surroundings. The orchestra played the Roxy, Earl Carroll's Madison Square Garden, the Columbia Theater, and other venues Wright claimed to "never even dreamed of ever seeing."[38] Taking a break from the Cotton Club in early 1928, the Orchestra joined Earl Dancer's Broadway revue "Africana," starring Ethel Waters. The sixty-member original Broadway cast traveled in its own train, playing major white theaters from the East Coast across the Midwest. After closing at the

Adelphi Theater in Chicago in early April 1928, "Africana" arrived in Kansas City for a week-long engagement at the Shubert Theater. To guarantee a packed house nightly, the Shubert reserved the first balcony and four-fifths of the upper balcony for African Americans. Still in her salad days, Ethel Waters received top billing, but the Cotton Club Orchestra merited favorable mention. The *Kansas City Call* toasted "the famous Cotton Club orchestra fresh from a brilliant triumph in the East where they created interest among music lovers by thousands."[39]

As the Cotton Club Orchestra worked its way west, the Moten band took the East by storm. Following Wright's departure for New York, Moten hired trumpeter Paul Webster for the band's premier on the East Coast. The band left Kansas City in late December 1927, embarking on a nine-month tour across the Midwest and to upstate New York. Supported by Victor, the band played major white ballrooms, hotels, and proms, traveling on the same circuit as Paul Whiteman, Guy Lombardo, and Ted Weems. In Buffalo, New York, Moten's men began a month-long series of engagements, alternating between the Arcadia and Paradise Ballrooms. Taking a break from Buffalo, the band played proms at Hobart College in Geneva, New York, and the Niagara University in Niagara Falls, New York. Pausing in Niagara Falls, the band spent a week at the exclusive Niagara Country Club. Back in Buffalo, the band settled into a month-long engagement in the dining room of the grand Statler Hotel, broadcasting over WOR. The band reportedly "packed continuously" the elite 20th Century Club before returning for a two-week engagement at the Arcadia Ballroom. Moving on to Rochester, New York, the band opened at the Sagamore Roof Garden for a two-week engagement. The band then returned to Buffalo for a second two-week stand at the Paradise Ballroom before finishing the busy summer season at the Pier Ballroom at the Celeron amusement park in Jamestown, New York.[40] The local press in Jamestown noted the Moten band's strong draw: "[T]he Pier Ballroom is proving immensely popular these warm evenings, not only because of Bennie Moten's Victor recording orchestra, the best colored dance band in the country, but also because the big pavilion is cool and comfortable even for dancing. . . . Moten's organization itself is capable of drawing a crowd wherever it plays. . . . Not only do they furnish music as only colored artists can, but they present several of their own compositions that have made enormous record sales."[41]

Wrapping up the eastern tour on a note of triumph, the band played a round of engagements at Roseland Gardens, Lafayette Theater, and Savoy Ballroom in Harlem. In keeping with Moten's philosophy of playing to the audience, the band moved comfortably between white audiences in upstate New York and African American audiences in Harlem. "Bennie had that old Boston beat which young and old alike had no trouble with," Leroy Berry explained. "The older people always came up to us and complimented us. We never played too fast and never too slow. We tried to study what the public liked and we gave it to them. Bennie was like that. Anytime we'd start a number too fast, he'd bring us right back down again. He pounded it into our heads that we weren't playing for ourselves but for the people who paid to dance, and he proved it all the time."[42] Harlem audiences, hungry for something different, loved the band's distinctive rhythmically accented style. "The people never heard anything like it," Ed Lewis observed. "It really upset New York, and from that time on we were known as the international band. Before that we were just known as a Midwestern band."[43]

Before heading back to Kansas City in early September 1928, the band recorded again for the Victor label in Camden, New Jersey. The recordings, with one exception, reflect Moten's desire to cater to his newfound white audience. The rhythm section, dominated by the banjo and drums, laid down a bouncing beat that even the squarest dancer could follow. The solos were measured and understated, with none of the flair found in the recordings of Henderson or Ellington. A fresh version of the old war horse "South" and the band's theme song, "Its Hard to Laugh or Smile," proved to be the most notable recordings from the session. The updated version of "South" became the band's most enduring hit, remaining in-print long after any other recordings from the session. The label rejected the vocal version of "It's Hard to Laugh or Smile," featuring James Taylor, in favor of the instrumental rendition. Victor rejected two of the three vocals by Taylor, a better band conductor than vocalist. "Get Low-Down Blues" best represents the sound of the band, playing hot for dancers in Harlem or 18th and Vine. Interrupting the ragtime piano introduction, Ed Lewis admonishes Moten to "Stop that ragtime. Let's get real lowdown." The mood of the piece then downshifts into a pure gut-bucket blues, with a lazy scat vocal chorus, leading to hot solos by Woody Walder, Jack Washington, and Ed Lewis. Jack Washington's growling baritone saxophone dips into the low register gutter, truly getting "lowdown."

On the way out of town, Moten generously rewarded band members for the Victor sessions. "Bennie got a check for $5,020," Ed Lewis accounted. "Bennie always wanted to please the guys and he cashed the check, but he wouldn't pay anybody until we were all on the train and had been under way a little while. We had a whole pullman to ourselves, and once we got rolling, Bennie announced pay day and pulled out all that money and split it right down the middle. Boy, that seemed like all the money in the world then!"[44]

Returning to Kansas City in glory, the Moten band celebrated with a grand homecoming dance at Paseo Hall in mid-September 1928. A reviewer for the *Kansas City Call* noted the band's "improvement in style that encore after encore was necessary to satisfy the huge crowd. James 'Tiny' Taylor was more than well received in the song numbers, and his unique style of orchestral direction excited much comment. And when Thaymon [Thamon] Hayes sang 'Ramona' to the muted accompaniment of soft brasses and whispering reed instruments, a distinct ripple of approbation stirred the crowd to heavy applause. A new way of playing the popular 'Coquette' song also pleased the crowd, and when 'Tiny' Taylor, Woody Walder, and Leroy 'Buck' Berry featured 'Mississippi Mud' it became plain why Moten's orchestra played in some of the best places in the East."[45] The band's change in musical direction stemmed from new arrangements of standards Moten purchased from Benny Carter and Duke Ellington in New York. Ironically, the hometown crowd preferred the old style, but applauded wildly, calling the band back for encore after encore out of respect and admiration for Moten.

AT THE DAWN OF THE JAZZ AGE AFTER WORLD WAR I, the United States became dance crazy. The loosening of the nation's moral fabric lifted hemlines and restrictions on public contact between the sexes. Tin Pan Alley songwriters churned out a wealth of danceable popular songs jazzed up by dance bands. African American composers and dancers, defying convention, created the Charleston, Black Bottom, and other wild dances that became the vogue for liberated young white women known as flappers. Ballrooms opened in cities across the country to meet the demand of the dance-hungry public. The grand lady of them all, the Roseland Ballroom in New York, opened in 1919, the refined Graystone Ballroom in Detroit made its debut in 1922, and the immense Aragon Ballroom in Chicago threw its doors open in 1926 to 4,000 dance enthusiasts.[46] In Kansas City, the Pla-Mor and El Torreon Ballrooms opened just a few months apart in late 1927. Moten expanded his local sphere of influence, playing for fans at Paseo Hall during the week and white dancers at the newly opened Pla-Mor and El Torreon ballrooms on the weekends. Located in mid-town, the Pla-Mor and its main competitor the El Torreon joined the circuit of elegant ballrooms opening in cities across the country. The Pla-Mor, a sprawling entertainment complex occupying several blocks on the west side of Main at 32nd Street, boasted a bowling alley on the ground floor, a spacious ballroom upstairs, and a mammoth indoor ice hockey arena around back. The Pla-Mor's "million dollar ballroom" opened with great fanfare on Thanksgiving evening in 1927. The *Kansas City Times* lavishly praised the immense ballroom's elegance: "Entrance was under a brilliant electric sign. Once past the door, wall decorations of freehand painting attracted attention. Rich carpet gave an impression of luxuriousness. Up a flight of steps and down a hall past the women's cloak room the eye followed vivid hunting and jungle scenes of the modern motif. Velour tapestries were admired particularly by the women. In the two women's rest rooms imported Italian furniture was another feature. The ball room and mezzanine were decorated in a more strictly patterned manner. Here the lighting brilliance demanded the first and lasting attention. Ceiling fixtures of beaded glass chains suspended bowl-shaped, with variable colors glowing through them, vied with tinted lamps casting full and toned colors across the floor from the walls."[47] The ballroom's spring-loaded 14,000-square-foot dance floor easily accommodated 3,000 dancers.

Popular bandleader Jean Goldkette managed the ballroom and booked the bands. A one-man musical franchise, Goldkette fielded several orchestras under his banner and headed a music service company, based in the Graystone Ballroom. Although primarily a dance band, the Goldkette band featured Bix Beiderbecke, Frankie Trumbauer, Joe Venuti, Tommy Dorsey, and other early jazz greats over the years. More of a businessman than bandleader, Goldkette normally declined to perform with the band, but he made a guest appearance opening night at the Pla-Mor. Pianist and composer Hoagy Carmichael, trim with an ever-present cigarette dangling from his bottom lip, soon joined the sixteen-piece Goldkette band at the Pla-Mor bringing his snappy new instrumental "Star Dust."[48] Sporting a sophisticated ambience and the elegant Goldkette Orchestra, the Pla-Mor immediately became the toast of the town.

The El Torreon Ballroom opened the next month, giving the Pla-Mor stiff competition. Comparing the two ballrooms, Floyd Estep, saxophonist for Coon-Sanders, said "the El Torreon was a warmer place, the Pla-Mor was kind of cold, more formal."[49] The El Torreon, located on the southeast corner of 31st Street and Gillham Road, just a short stroll east from the Pla-Mor, occupied the top floor of a squat two-story brick terra-cotta-trimmed building. Stylishly decorated in a Spanish Mission motif, the El Torreon sported a balcony on three sides overlooking the massive dance floor that could hold 2,000 dancers. An enormous crystal ball adorned with 100,000 mirrors suspended from the ceiling illuminated the teeming crowd swaying on the dance floor. The *Journal Post* reported the El Torreon's "dominant theme" floated high above the dancers' heads in "an azure, star studded ceiling . . . a cleverly executed cloud effect furnishing most of the effect."[50] The ethereal effect of the twinkling stars and clouds floating across the expansive vaulted ceiling inspired the El Torreon's motto, "where the clouds roll by."

Rolling out the big guns, the management brought the Coon-Sanders Original Night Hawk Orchestra back from Chicago for the gala opening celebration. Fans gave Coon and Sanders, returning after a three-year absence, a tumultuous welcome. A legion of admirers greeted their arrival at Union Station with a parade, stretching from Union Station to the Kansas City Athletic Club, an exclusive gentleman's club at 9th and Baltimore. The Night Hawks played a week-long engagement at the Pantages Theater, breaking all attendance records, before opening the El Torreon on a double bill with the house band, Phil Baxter and the El Torreon Orchestra.

Although not as charismatic or musically sophisticated as Coon and Sanders, Baxter had established a loyal following as the house band at the Submarine Ballroom before moving over to the El Torreon. Lanky with a pencil-thin mustache and dark slicked-back hair, Phil Baxter grew up in Rural Shade, Texas. As a youth, he learned to play piano by ear, accompanying silent movies at a local nickelodeon. After a stint in the Navy serving alongside Paul Whiteman during World War I, Baxter launched his career as a bandleader. Baxter and His Texas Tommies cut dashing figures, mounting the bandstand decked out in chaps, neckerchiefs, and ten-gallon hats. Unable to read music, Baxter and the band played popular standards from memory and collectively improvised hot jazz. Overcoming his musical handicap by hiring pianists to write out the musical notation, Baxter dabbled in songwriting, privately publishing "Gambler Blues," which was later published by Mills Music as "St. James Infirmary" without due credit. In September 1926, Baxter and the Texas Tommies rode into Kansas City, opening at the Submarine dance hall, located below street level at 31st Street and Prospect Avenue. The band clicked with Kansas City audiences, and helped the owner of the Submarine, Thomas O. Bright, fund the spacious El Torreon. Preparing for the opening, Baxter discarded the cowboy garb in favor of tuxedos, expanded the band to fourteen pieces, and composed the new ballroom's theme song, "El Torreon," played to kick off and conclude each night of dancing.

Opening night, 3,000 fans flocked to the El Torreon. The crowd laid back during Baxter's set, then went wild, surging forward when the Night Hawks hit the stage. After christening the El Torreon with a week-long engagement, playing nightly to packed houses, the Night Hawks resumed to touring the Midwest. The Baxter band remained a regular fixture at the El Torreon, establishing the new ballroom as the hot spot for the younger dance set. Competing with the Pla-Mor, the El Torreon featured two bands nightly. Baxter graciously shared the spotlight with Moten, Lee, and other local bands along with national African American bands. The Pla-Mor soon followed suit, establishing Kansas City as a lucrative stop on the emerging national band circuit. Fletcher Henderson, Duke Ellington, Louis Armstrong, and other leading bands played weekend engagements for white audiences at the El Torreon or Pla-Mor, followed with Monday night dates to appreciative crowds at Paseo Hall. The bounty of jobs in ballrooms, dance halls, and clubs drew the attention of the great territorial bands of the Southwest. Hungry for new opportunities, bands and musicians from Texas, Oklahoma, and Colorado migrated to Kansas City in droves, bringing inventive musical ideas that became absorbed into the Kansas City tradition and in the process helped create a new style of jazz.

4

The Territories

WALTER PAGE'S BLUE DEVILS and the legion of other bands barnstorming across the West were referred to as territorial bands in recognition of the vast areas they toured. Based in larger cities, some little more than dusty, overgrown frontier towns scattered across the plains, the bands staked out the western United States into immense territories. Bandleaders vigilantly protected their turf against claim-jumpers. "You had your own territory to play in and you didn't play anywhere else unless you got permission from the leading band in that territory," Ed Lewis explained. "Around Oklahoma City, Wichita, Kansas, and places like that, Walter Page's Blue Devils was the leading band. If Bennie Moten wanted to play dates in that territory, he had to get in touch with Walter Page."[1] Musical gunslingers, they settled territorial disputes in the spirit of the Wild West, shooting it out in battles of the bands. Walter Page boasted, "I cut both George E. Lee and Jesse Stone. . . . I was boss of that territory."[2]

During the 1920s and 1930s, well over one hundred bands worked the territories. Bassist Gene Ramey marveled at the number of bands based in Texas alone. "In those days, everywhere you looked there was bands," Ramey recounted. "There must've been eight to ten bands in San Antonio, and we knew four or five in Houston. There must've been twenty bands in Dallas and Ft. Worth. . . . So, the bands spread out all over."[3] The bands varied in sophistication from rugged musical rounders like Gene Coy's Happy Black Aces, Boots and His Buddies, Ben Smith's Blue Syncopators, and Edgar Battle's Dixie Stompers, to sleek full-size orchestras such as the George Morrison Orchestra, the Alphonso Trent Orchestra, Jesse Stone's Blues Serenaders, Walter Page's Blue Devils, and T Holder's Dark Clouds of Joy, which later became Andy Kirk and His Twelve Clouds of Joy. Sweeping across the range,

hell-bent for leather on dusty back roads, the bands played roadhouses, hotels, ballrooms, outdoor amusement parks, jitney dances, and in some cases
on hastily built stages in open fields illuminated by automobile headlights.

Traveling caravan style in sedans, often with band members hanging on to
fenders and doorposts for dear life, the territorial bands ranged north to Minneapolis and the Dakotas, south to New Orleans, west to Denver, and east to
Missouri. The bands deftly navigated the broad musical landscape. In the
Dakotas, Nebraska, and other states in the northern leg of the territories ruled
by Lawrence Welk, audiences demanded polkas, schottisches, and waltzes,
refusing to dance to anything else. The roughnecks crowding the roadhouses
strewn across Texas, Oklahoma, and Arkansas insisted on hoe-downs and
stomp-down western style. Fans crowding the dance halls in New Orleans
and Kansas City liked their music hot, preferring stomps, breakdowns, gut-
bucket blues, and torrid jazz. Band members crafted custom arrangements for
specific regions, establishing a tradition of orchestration. "We [the Blue Dev-
ils] played waltzes and sweet music up in Saginaw [Michigan], [for] people up
there," alto saxophonist Buster Smith related. "Had some tunes that sounded
like Guy Lombardo. Even in South Dakota, they liked sweet music and we
had to play a lot of that. I had to write a whole repertoire of music to go along
with it."[4] The heft of the multiple band books carried by the Blues Devils'
amazed bandleader Jesse Stone, a prolific composer and arranger in his own
right. "They [the Blue Devils] were just sharper, cleaner, more powerful, and
they had more material, which was an upset to us because we had five arrangers, including myself," Stone noted. "How could anybody have more material
than we had? We had a book about that thick, you know, all arrangements.
These guys came in with three books. Three books the same thickness."[5]

Usually operating as "commonwealth bands," members divided profits
evenly after expenses and democratically voted on business decisions. Blue
Devils' vocalist Jimmy Rushing fondly recalled the communal spirit shared
among band members. "We weren't making money, but we were all friends,"
Rushing observed. "If one of the boys needed money—like his wife needed
coal or had to pay the gas bill—we'd take the amount necessary out of the
gross, give it to him, and send him home and split the leavings among the rest
of us. Everybody was paid equal down to the leader."[6] Equally sharing good
and bad times inspired fierce loyalty among band members. Count Basie, looking back on his career with the Blue Devils, proudly declared, "once a Blue
Devil, always a Blue Devil."[7]

Kansas City, ripe with plum jobs and immoderate nightlife, became a favored stop on the territorial band circuit. Bennie Moten and George E. Lee,
eager to establish their own circuit, readily swapped territories with Walter
Page, Andy Kirk, and other bandleaders from the Southwest. This free flow
of bands and musicians from the Southwest strengthened and enhanced Kansas City's jazz tradition. The ranks of the Musicians Protective Union Local

627 swelled from 87 members in 1927 to 347 by May 1930.[8] Moten and Lee refined and expanded their bands, adding top players from the Southwest. New arrivals brought solo virtuosity, a tradition of musical arrangement allowing for a greater degree of orchestral sophistication along with a rhythmic shift from the 2/4 stomp-down style to a more fluid 4/4 rhythm, enriching Kansas City jazz style.

The influence of the territorial bands on the development of Kansas City Jazz began modestly with the arrival in 1923 of the George Morrison Orchestra, a precursor to the territorial tradition.[9] Hailing from Denver, Colorado, George Morrison fronted a concert band specializing in highly orchestrated popular tunes, classical, spirituals, blues, novelties, and camp songs. Band member Andy Kirk described the Morrison band as "a society band, but they had a beat and for that reason he was the leader in the field. There weren't many Negroes in Denver then, only six thousand out of a total population of three hundred thousand," Kirk added. "The best jobs in town were the country club, the city amusement park and private lawn parties when the white people wanted live music for entertainment. We'd play the colored dances too, but there weren't enough of them to keep you busy all the time."[10] A disciplinarian, Morrison held band members to lofty standards, requiring them to perform every day, for pay or charity. From early on, Morrison's band spawned a string of polished, disciplined musicians including entertainer and vocalist Hattie McDaniels and future bandleaders Andy Kirk and Jimmie Lunceford.

Originally from Fayette, Missouri, George Morrison grew up in a large musical family.[11] His father, the champion fiddler of Howard County, Missouri, died when Morrison was two years old. At first reluctant to follow in his father's footsteps, Morrison shunned the violin in favor of the guitar. As a youth, Morrison studied with his mother, an accomplished pianist while playing in the family's eight-piece string orchestra. Just after the turn of the century, Morrison's family moved to Boulder, Colorado, nestled on the eastern slope of the Rocky Mountains, thirty miles north of Denver. Morrison supported himself working odd jobs and performing with the Morrison Brothers Band in the rustic mining camps just to the west of Boulder. Tall and stocky with a round face, Morrison switched to violin while studying at the University of Colorado. After graduation, he moved to Denver and led a string trio at the elegant Albany Hotel. Popular with the well-heeled set at the Albany, the group grew to eleven pieces during the next year. Branching out, the Morrison band toured regionally.

In 1919, the Morrison band launched a tour of the United States and England. Well-received abroad, the band became one of the first American dance bands to play for English royalty. In 1920, while playing in New York at the Carlton Terrace Ballroom on 100th and Broadway, the Morrison band recorded "Pip-Pip, Toot-Toot, Goodbye-ee," "Royal Garden Blues," and "I

Know Why" for the Columbia label. Working both sides of the street, Morrison recorded two test recordings for the Victor label: "Royal Garden Blues" and "Jean." Victor declined to issue the tests, but Columbia released "I Know Why" by Morrison's Jazz Orchestra backed by "Somehow," featuring popular white bandleader Ted Lewis and his Jazz Band, a rare pairing on disc of an African American and white band.

In 1923, the Morrison band embarked on a second tour, billed as the "Greatest Negro Orchestra in the World." The band's May debut at Lincoln Hall created a stir among Kansas City dance fans, more accustomed to the crude stomp-down blues style of Moten and Lee. In April 1925, the Morrison band returned to Kansas City for an engagement at the Pantages Theater. While in town, Morrison presented a classical music program followed by dance music at the Labor Temple for fans in the 18th and Vine area.[12] By popular demand, Morrison performed an encore engagement the following week at the Rialto Theater at 18th and Highland. Hattie McDaniels's talent and personality boosted the success of Morrison's 1925 tour. A versatile entertainer with flawless comedic timing, McDaniels's acclaim with the Morrison band launched her career that swiftly soared from vaudeville to Hollywood.[13] Similarly, Andy Kirk rose from the ranks of the Morrison band to national acclaim on his own.

Had things worked out differently, Andy Kirk might never have emerged as a bandleader. Tall and dashing, but unassuming, he shunned the limelight and preferred to stay in the background, anchoring the rhythm section on bass horn. Originally from Newport, Kentucky, Kirk moved to Denver as a child to live with his aunt after the death of his mother.[14] He learned to read music in grade school, singing in a choir directed by Wilberforce Whiteman, supervisor of music for the Denver school system and father of famed bandleader Paul Whiteman. Pursuing his interest in instrumental music, Kirk bought a tenor saxophone and taught himself how to play. Yearning for a bigger sound, Kirk then mastered the tuba and baritone saxophone.

During World War I, Kirk worked as a mail carrier while moonlighting with the Morrison band. In 1919, he left government service to become a full-time member of the Morrison organization. A jack of all trades, Kirk performed with the full band and led smaller Morrison-sponsored units for casual engagements. During the summer of 1925, Kirk fronted a Morrison auxiliary band at the fashionable Lantern Club in Estes Park, Colorado. Kirk left the Morrison band in early fall 1925, and joined Stewart Hall's band at the Moonlight Ranch, a roadhouse on the outskirts of Denver. While working at the rough-and-tumble ranch, Kirk came into contact with the jazz bands just beginning to circulate through Denver. "There were a number of musicians who came through Denver on tour with bands like Fred Waring's Pennsylvanians, Ben Bernie's band and those type of outfits, but I didn't hear any real jazz until Gene Coy and His Happy Black Aces came through," Kirk revealed.

"They had a real beat and upset the town. From that time on I kept my ear open for music like that. Then Jelly Roll Morton came through as a single and I liked his style. In fact, he influenced me a great deal rhythmically."[15]

In 1926, Kirk moved to Chicago accompanied by alto saxophonist Alvin "Fats" Wall, a fellow former member of the George Morrison Orchestra. Kirk struggled to establish himself, but only managed to hustle up a few casuals with the Society Syncopators, a local dance band. With time on his hands, Kirk regularly attended the Vendome Theater, in the heart of the "Black Belt" on South State Street, absorbing the sophisticated style of the Erskine Tate Orchestra that featured Earl "Fatha" Hines and Louis Armstrong, fresh from the Dreamland Cafe. Unable to break into the Chicago scene, Wall left for Dallas to join a group being organized by T Holder, a talented trumpet soloist with a big open tone. Kirk shortly followed suit.

Terrence "T" Holder became well known for his ability to quickly assemble a band—a talent born from his unreliability and dubious business practices. Holder's financial shenanigans undermined his effectiveness as a leader, and caused his ouster from his own band on several occasions. Balding with a broad smashed nose and lantern jaw, Holder made his professional debut with Ida Cox at the Dreamland Theater in his hometown, Muskogee, Oklahoma.[16] Cox's music director Fletcher Henderson, forced to hastily patch together a band from local musicians, hired Holder sight unseen. Henderson found Holder not up to the task and soon dismissed him. Retreating to the woodshed, an undeterred Holder mastered the basics of music and polished his style.

During the mid-1920s, Holder joined the Alphonso Trent Orchestra, then the leading band in the territories. Based in the Adolphus Hotel in Dallas, the Trent band broadcast nightly over WFAA. With little competition on the airwaves, the broadcasts covered the Midwest as far north as Canada. These pioneering broadcasts, among the first regular broadcasts by an African American band, readily established Trent's reputation throughout the South and Midwest. Holder joined the band at the Adolphus as top soloist and business manager, responsible for distributing the payroll. Band members soon found their trust in Holder misplaced. Shortly after Holder took over as business manager, the owner of the Adolphus gave each band member a $25 a week raise. Instead of passing the money on to the rightful recipients, Holder kept the raise a secret and pocketed the money for his own use. When Holder bought a new Buick, Snub Mosely and other band members became suspicious of his sudden wealth. "We told Trent to go down and see what was happening, maybe the man gave us a raise," Mosley explained. "Sure enough Trent spoke to him [the owner] and said, 'it was about time for us to have a raise' . . . and he [the owner] said, 'I just gave you a raise about four or five months ago.'"[17] The incident ended Holder's job as business manager and prompted his departure from Trent. Having built up a following at the Adolphus, Holder formed his own band.

A booking agent christened Holder's band the Dark Clouds of Joy, but Andy Kirk recalled the band's early engagements as anything but heavenly. "We were working every night in a blood-and-thunder place called the Ozarks," Kirk divulged. "It was just outside of town, a typical roadhouse, lots of bloody fights every night." A hard-swinging unit, Holder's band featured crack soloists. "Outside of Alphonso Trent's band ours [the Holder band] was the most popular in Texas at that time. We had some terrific men in that band," Kirk added. "Big Jim [Lawson] and T on trumpets were two of the best jazzmen and the sweetest musicians I ever heard in my life, and when they used to play duets they'd break up any dance. Those two could play the prettiest waltzes too. . . . Eddie Durham's cousin Allen was on trombone, and we had a terrific alto player, Alvin 'Fats' Wall."[18]

In 1927, the Dark Clouds of Joy moved to Tulsa and joined the roster of the Southwest Amusement Corporation. The leading booking agency in the territories, Southwest operated the Winter Garden and Spring Lake Park in Oklahoma City, along with the Crystal City Park and Louvre Ballroom in Tulsa. The Dark Clouds of Joy worked steadily year round, switching venues every three months. At the Louvre, the band played for jitney dances, so called because each Friday night the management held a drawing for a new Ford, commonly known as a jitney. Men queued up to pay a nickel a dance, with the women milling around the ballroom. Since the men paid on a per-dance basis, management encouraged the band to perform truncated versions of popular standards, waltzes, and two-steps. Kirk and other band members began writing arrangements to make the music more interesting. "During those years we were just starting to write out arrangements, because playing for jitney dances as we were then, there wasn't any call for them," Kirk disclosed. "The idea then was to get the dancers on and off the floor. Two choruses was an arrangement then. To get around that, we'd make up an introduction that served as a bridge for the next chorus following, and we'd always make up a different ending for the same number."[19]

With secure, long-term engagements and arrangers on staff to orchestrate the change, Holder expanded the band to full size.[20] Vocalist Billy Massey, fair-skinned, dapper, and somewhat contrary, fronted the band, crooning ballads in the popular style of the day. Holder recruited Claude Williams, a trim, talented violinist and guitarist from Muskogee with a penchant for gambling. A steady rhythm player and tireless improviser, Williams preferred the solo spotlight to marking time in the rhythm section. Saxophonist John Williams, who came aboard in late August 1928, brought the reed section up to three members. A dark-skinned, bespectacled rounder, Williams arrived from Memphis, where he led his own band that featured his teenage bride Mary Lou, a powerful, gifted pianist, then known as Mary.[21] While John checked out the Holder band, Mary Lou stayed behind in Memphis to finish out the band's commitments. An independent woman, experienced beyond her years, Mary Lou assumed the helm of her husband's band without missing a beat.

MARY LOU WILLIAMS, the second daughter of an unwed mother, learned to fend for herself as a child growing up in Atlanta.[22] During World War I, her family joined the great migration north, moving to Pittsburgh. A child prodigy with instant recall, she learned spirituals, marches, ragtime, blues, and jazz from phonograph records and the player piano in the parlor of her home. While regularly entertaining at picnics and dances for neighbors and society, she became known as the "little piano girl of East Liberty."[23] Petite with large dreamy eyes, a shy smile and an independent streak, Williams began her professional career in her early teens, touring on the TOBA circuit with the Buzzin' "Sparrow" Harris and His Hits and Bits revue. Mary Lou's future husband, John Williams, joined the Harris Revue in Cincinnati. Confident and persuasive, Williams wooed the reluctant Mary Lou, eventually winning her over.

John and Mary Lou became stranded in Kansas City in early August 1924, when Hits and Bits folded after wrapping up an engagement at the Lincoln Theater. Eager to get back on the vaudeville circuit, they put together a band and joined a revue led by the dance team of Seymour and Jeanette Jones touring on the Keith-Orpheum wheel. On the road, Mary Lou met many jazz greats. In New York, she played with members of the Duke Ellington band at the Lincoln Theater and charmed Fats Waller, reproducing his music note for note. In contrast, Jelly Roll Morton did not take kindly to his precocious young student. "Mr. Jelly Lord was a more frightening proposition," Williams observed. "He was considered a big deal then, and he had me scared. . . . Indicating I should park my hips on the stool, Jelly gave over the piano and I got started on my favorite Morton piece, 'The Pearls.' Almost immediately I was stopped and reprimanded, told the right way to phrase it. I played it the way Jelly told me, and when I had it to his satisfaction, I slipped in one of my own tunes. This made no difference. I was soon stopped and told: 'Now that passage should be phrased like this.' . . . Any minute I was expecting to get up off the floor because I had played his 'Pearls' wrong. That's how they trained you in those days (half those chorus girls had black eyes!), and Morton had a reputation of being a demanding taskmaster."[24] After mastering the styles of Waller, Morton, James P. Johnson, and other early piano greats, Mary Lou developed a harmonically and rhythmically adventurous style all her own.

The troupe disbanded in mid-tour when Seymour Jones fell gravely ill. John and Mary Lou went to John's hometown, Memphis, where they married in November 1926. Following Seymour's death, a short while later, the two briefly reunited with Jeanette Jones in an attempt to keep the band together, but to no avail.[25] John and Mary Lou regrouped, taking over a small ensemble back in Memphis. A fast-talking hustler, John organized the first African American musician's union in Memphis, significantly increasing members' wages. Even at the higher scale, John's take as a bandleader could not match T Holder's generous offer of $60 per week to join the Dark Clouds of Joy. John left for Oklahoma to join the Holder band, leaving Mary Lou, then seventeen years old, to wrap up the band's obligations and move the household.

Mary Lou hired Jimmy Lunceford to replace John in the reed section for the band's remaining dates, then headed for Oklahoma City. "I worked off the outstanding engagements, then set out to join John in Oklahoma City, 700 hard miles away. He had left our Chevrolet for me to make the journey in, and with John's mother and a friend I hit the highway," Mary Lou recounted. "The Chev wasn't much of a 'short' to look at. It looked like a red bath-tub in fact, but ran like one of those streamlined trains on the Pennsylvania Railroad, and was the craziest for wear and tear. Unfortunately, we had miles of dirt and turtle-back roads to travel, and these excuses for highways were studded with sharp stones. To top all, it was August and hot as a young girl's dojiee. Every 40 or 50 miles we stopped to change tires or clean out the carburetor. As my passengers were non-fixers, I was in sole command. We got along somehow, and after what seemed like weeks of blow-outs and fuel trouble we fell into Oklahoma City."[26]

Arriving in the wee hours of the morning, Mary Lou stayed up all night anticipating the band's rehearsal the next morning. The band's showmanship and style exceeded her expectations. "I thought them the handsomest bunch of intellectuals I had seen so far" Williams judged. "They looked like collegians, all had beautiful brown complexions and wore sharp beige suits to match. Going out, they sported yellow raincoats with the instrument each man played illustrated on the back. Most came from good families, and their manners were perfect. I could hardly wait to hear the music. As I suspected, it was out of the ordinary. They had a novel arrangement of 'Casey Jones' featuring Claude Williams, who was strong on both guitar and violin. Tenorman Lawrence 'Slim' Freeman supplied the show stuff by playing bass clarinet while lying on his back. For the rest, they played jazz numbers and the better commercial things. They were all reading like mad and I had to admit it was a good and different orchestra: smooth showmanship . . . coupled with musical ability."[27] Band members quickly dashed Williams's hope of joining the band. Instead, she found herself relegated to the role of band wife, working odd jobs—at one point driving a hearse while playing music for her own pleasure.

In late December 1928, Holder's fiscal irresponsibility triggered his ouster from the band. Holder's financial sleight of hand had been a sore point with band members for some time. When confronted by Kirk and others about his financial transgressions, Holder merely shrugged and promised with a wry grin, "Aw, shucks fellas, I'll try harder next time."[28] During Christmas, Holder abruptly left for Dallas to reconcile with his estranged wife. Disappearing without explanation, Holder took the payroll, much to the dismay of band members. Tempers flared, but cooler heads prevailed, and band members dissuaded trumpeter Chester Clark from tracking down and shooting Holder. During an emergency band meeting, angry members voted Holder out of his own band. John Williams recalled he and other band members "waited to buy our wives Christmas presents and all and he's [Holder] gone with all the money.

So we fired him . . . and because Andy [Kirk] was the oldest and most settled, we voted to let Andy lead the band and that's how Andy got the band."[29]

Initially reluctant to take on the responsibility, Kirk coaxed Holder back into the band, but having broken faith with band members one too many times, he did not last long. The manager of the ballroom, Mr. Falkenberg, insisted Kirk take over leadership of the band or lose the engagement. Kirk reluctantly agreed, and all but three members stayed on. Gene Prince eased into Holder's chair in the trumpet section. Saxophonist John Harrington joined from the George Morrison band, replacing Theodore Ross on alto saxophone, and former Blue Devils drummer Ed "Crackshot" McNeil succeeded Stumpy Jones. Kirk resented the racial implications of Dark Clouds of Joy, so he shortened the band's name to the Clouds of Joy. Flourishing under Kirk's steady leadership, the band played leading venues across Oklahoma on the newly expanded Southwest Amusement Corporation circuit. Inspired by the George Morrison and the Erskine Tate band, Kirk cultivated a polished sophisticated style suited to white audiences on the circuit. The change in musical direction steered the band to new vistas.

In the summer of 1929, following a fortuitous encounter with George E. Lee, Kirk moved the band's headquarters to Kansas City. En route to an engagement in Oklahoma City, Lee had stopped by to check out the Kirk band. Favorably impressed by the refined style of the Clouds of Joy, Lee recommended the band to Bennet Stydham, the manager of the Pla-Mor Ballroom in Kansas City. Stydham, facing stiff competition from the Alabamians featuring Cab Calloway at the El Torreon, needed a sharp African American band from out of town to draw wayward dancers back to the Pla-Mor. Arriving in Tulsa the next day, Stydham auditioned and hired the Clouds of Joy on the spot for an extended engagement at the Pla-Mor.

As his former band rapidly rose in regional ranking, Holder's career plummeted. After leaving the Dark Clouds of Joy, Holder formed an alliance with bandleader Jesse Stone. Like Holder, Stone had recently suffered a setback, leading to the decline of his band, the Blues Serenaders. Stone joined forces with Holder at the North Dallas Club, assembling a band from the remnants of the Blues Serenaders, young local players, and musicians cast off from Holder's split with the Dark Clouds of Joy. Hoping to capitalize on his former association with the Dark Clouds of Joy, Holder christened his new band the Eleven Clouds of Joy. In early spring 1929, the band ventured out into the territories. Stopping off in Kansas City, the Eleven Clouds of Joy played for a Mother's Day dance at Paseo Hall. A few weeks later, Holder returned to Kansas City as a solo, featured with Chauncey Downs's Rinky Dinks for a big Decoration Day dance at Paseo Hall. Advertisements touted Holder as a former bandleader "reputed to have had the best band in the south."[30] Once again, band members ousted Holder from his own band because of his continued financial chicanery. Looking back on his brief association with Holder, Jesse Stone observed, "[H]e wasn't honest."[31]

Ultimately, Stone had little more success as a bandleader than Holder, but his failure as a leader stemmed from a lack of business acumen rather than dishonesty. Engrossed in composing, arranging, and mentoring musicians, Stone simply did not take care of business. The first great arranger and composer in the territorial band tradition, Stone easily assembled and trained outstanding bands, but without the help of a strong business manager he failed to keep them together.

JESSE STONE GREW UP in an extended musical family on a farm just outside of Atchison, Kansas, located sixty miles west of Kansas City.[32] A natural entertainer with angular features and crooked smile, Stone toured as a child with his uncle's minstrel show, Brown's Tennessee Minstrels. The show traveled through Wisconsin, northern Illinois, and the Dakotas. "We had a dog act," Stone recalled, "They were all cocker spaniels. Of course they had been trained to do the routine without me, but it looked as though I was a trainer with short pants. . . . I had a whip like those guys do in circuses and they would get up on these little boxes and they would roll over and do flips and all that kind of stuff, but they knew the routine. . . . I did comedy," Stone added. "The last thing was all the boys, all the males on the show were supposed to be working the farm or something like that, we'd all be layin' down asleep. The man comes in and finds us asleep, and one at a time he beats us over the behind, and it would just be a slapstick, a loud sound. Each one has a different line, like a gag he says as he runs off the stage. That was the closing scene and everybody came in after that."[33]

For economy's sake, members of the troupe doubled as musicians and entertainers, with Stone's father on drums and his uncle on trombone, in the band accompanying the stage show. Between acts, Stone paid close attention to the band. "They had a thing called 'Drummer Boy,' back there in those days and they had another thing called 'Sliding Sam,' it was a trombone solo." Stone reported. "There were two violins, trumpet, trombone, piano, bass horn, drums. . . . One night they would feature my uncle (on trombone) in the pit, the next night they would feature my father on drums. . . . They could read music at that time, but they didn't know the definition of an arrangement. They knew it was handwritten music and even when I came up in school they called it 'homemade music. . . .'"[34] Inspired by the band, Stone started playing the family's piano on the sly.

Stone continued his music studies after moving to Kansas City to live with his grandmother and attend elementary school. An eager student, Stone learned theory, harmony, and taught himself the rudiments of arranging. He began his professional career while still in high school, playing casuals and dances with a small ensemble led by violinist George Bell. Young Coleman Hawkins, then a cellist, wanted to join the band, but balked, feeling his chosen instrument ill suited for a dance band. Switching instruments, Hawkins mastered the C melody saxophone and joined alto saxophonist George Tyas in the group's front line. In early spring 1922, Hawkins and George Bell left the group to join Mamie Smith's Jazz Hounds. Smith tried to enlist Stone as an arranger for her band, but he declined, and formed his own band.

Forced to start from scratch, Stone gathered together a group of unseasoned musicians he informally tutored in high school. Stone explained, "[I]f a guy just had the inclination to play, I was willing to coach, teach and develop him."[35] Unable to afford a proper rehearsal space, Stone drilled his young charges in a local pool hall. After rehearsing and playing around Kansas City for a year, Stone and the Blues Serenaders launched a tour of western Missouri. Inexperienced as a bandleader, Stone neglected to string together enough engagements to carry the band financially.

While stranded in St. Joseph, Missouri, a chance encounter by Stone saved the band. By serendipity, Stone met Frank J. Rock, a wealthy undertaker and radio trailblazer. "We were starving and there was a guy who was building a broadcasting station in a little store," Stone confided. "I happened to be walking around there looking for something to do . . . and I saw this guy in there and all I saw were wires. . . . I decided to go in, I said, 'What are you making?' Because there were no radios then, he said, 'It's an invention that plays music on the air. You send it out and people who have radios at home . . . can sit and listen to the music.' I said, 'You should want a band . . . I got a band.' He said he could pay about five dollars a day. I thought it was pretty good. Five dollars for the whole band. I had eighteen [eight] pieces."[36] The two hit it off, and Rock hired the band to broadcast daily. A flood of favorable telegrams swayed Rock to assume management of the band. He generously bankrolled the band, advancing Stone $2,000 for new instruments and uniforms. Shopping hurriedly, band members forgot to buy new shoes to match their outfits. The group's first publicity photo, long treasured by band members, captured them in their new tuxedos wearing old hobnail boots.

Stone and the Blues Serenaders thrived under Rock's solid guidance. "Rock was sort of a mastermind," Stone recollected. "We'd play all kinds of things. We played theaters. We did stage presentations. We did concerts, fairs, and colleges. We played proms. . . . We liked dances the best. There was a closer contact with the people. We saw their reaction and we'd get fired up when they'd get fired up and we'd get along with them."[37] Capitalizing on a steady stream of well-paying engagements, Stone refined and expanded the band by adding trombonist Druie Bess, trumpeter Eddie Tompkins, and other more experienced musicians. Band members doubled on instruments other than their own, which made the stage show even more impressive. All the various configurations required special arrangements, ably supplied by Stone.

Rock helped Stone develop the band book by contacting national publishing houses and record companies for complimentary copies of the latest sheet music and recordings. Stone kept the band's repertoire current by creating fresh arrangements of new releases. Stone modeled the band's orchestral style after his idol Fletcher Henderson. Fashioning the band's stage show, Stone drew from earlier vaudeville and minstrel traditions. The combination of orchestral excellence and stage antics made the Blues Serenaders an unqualified success in the Midwest and western territories. "We packed them in," Stone declared. "We played against the best MCA [Music Corporation of America] bands in the business and we played them down, because we had such a versatile band. We could entertain. We had a dance team in the band. We had a quartet in the band. A glee club. We had three comedians. We could do any kind of skits. The guys used to put on women's clothes. . . . We could do at least ten or twelve weeks of shows without doing the same thing over. . . . We had four arrangers in the band beside myself . . . and I'm standing up in front of the band directing, acting, singing. . . . I would sit down and play (piano) and sing, but I would do a lot of Cab Calloway–style jumping and dancing. I did the splits. . . . We had the strongest band out in the West."[38]

Stone and the Blues Serenaders returned to Kansas City from the West in late March 1926 for a week-long engagement at the Pantages Theater, followed by a series of dances at Paseo Hall. Stone encroached on Moten and Lee's headquarters, challenging their supremacy in the Midwest. Stone's defiance sparked two orchestra contests, pitting the Blues Serenaders against the Lee and Moten bands respectively at Paseo Hall. These clashes marked the beginning of the great orchestra wars. Spirited affairs, usually staged more for the take at the box office than for blood or honor, battle of the bands drew the audience into the fray. Paseo Hall sported two bandstands at either end of the broad burnished dance floor. Trading sets, the bands musically one-upped each other, goaded on by the dancers whirling like tops between the two bandstands. At the conclusion of the festivities, often lasting to daylight, the audience judged the winner with a chorus of caterwauls, stomping, and clapping, echoing for blocks surrounding the hall.

Moten and Lee held the home-court advantage, but they were hard pressed to stay the Blues Serenaders. The *Kansas City Call* hailed the battle between Stone and Lee in late December 1926 as "a bloodless battle of songs and music."[39] Playing up the rivalry, Lee stated that he "has heard them [the Blues Serenaders] play and he admits that they are going to be hard to beat."[40] Lee barely managed to keep the "bacon in Kansas City," according to the *Kansas City Call*. "[F]or a time the orchestras were neck and neck, and it was hard to decide between them. But way late George and his boys forged to the front and were never headed."[41] In the end, Lee's on-stage charisma won the day, not the quality of his seven-piece band that lacked the finesse and tightness of Stone's ten-piece aggregation.

In early February 1927, the Blues Serenaders battled the Moten band at Paseo Hall. Stone publicly upped the ante of the contest with a $500 side bet. The wager, published in the *Kansas City Call*, would have raised eyebrows and the interest of the law in more modest towns, but in Kansas City it merely added to the spectacle. The hype associated with the event succeeded. The *Kansas City Call* reported, "[T]he largest crowd that ever attended an entertainment in Kansas City stormed the doors of Paseo Recreation Hall," with hundreds of fans being turned away.[42] The Blues Serenaders carried the day and made Kansas City a regular stop on their circuit.

After touring the Pantages Circuit across the Southwest to Los Angeles, they returned to the Midwest and recorded for the OKeh label in St. Louis.[43] To Stone's dismay, OKeh rejected "In Susi's Basement," favored by the dancers at Paseo Hall, and "Shufflin' Blues." Instead, they issued two selections: a richly textured "Starvation Blues" and a joyous, tightly orchestrated remake of "Tiger Rag" called "Boot To Boot," which illustrated Stone's genius as an arranger and composer and brilliantly showcased the band's sections and soloists. Taking "Starvation Blues" at a languid tempo, the soloists spice the melodic line with relaxed blue notes, instrumentally evoking the deep feeling for the blues articulated by the great women blues shouters. In the out chorus, trombonist Druie Bess joins trumpeters Albert Hinton and Slick Jackson for a rousing brass polyphony orchestrated with flair.[44] Stone fashioned "Boot To Boot" into an intricate masterpiece, using stop time and frequent breaks to divide the 198 bars into 29 structural divisions. Buoyed by the rhythm section, "Boot To Boot" races along, propelled by fleet exchanges between the soloists and ensemble. Stone's artful use of polyphony in the opening and out chorus, combined with his skillful voicing of the saxophone trio in the third section, easily matched the skill of Benny Carter, Don Redman, and other top eastern arrangers.[45] Stone's arrangements lifted the band to new heights, transcending the territorial tradition.

Just as the band ascended nationally, it abruptly plummeted, brought down by the death of Rock's father. Grief stricken and obligated to the family business, Rock turned the management of the band over to Stone. Bereft of Rock's steady management, the band languished. "I didn't know what to do with it," Stone admitted. "We just took a nosedive because I didn't know anything about . . . the business end."[46] Bookings became scarce and less lucrative. Without steady work, the Blues Serenaders faded. "I could never say the band broke up," Stone confessed. "It just kept evolving. Members would leave and we'd get somebody else. There was never a place where we said, 'Okay, this is it.'"[47] After merging, then parting with T Holder, Stone joined the George E. Lee band as music director and arranger. Stone returned to Kansas City with the Lee band in October 1929, bringing his career as a bandleader full circle. Freed from the burden of leadership, Stone concentrated on composing and arranging, his greatest gifts to the development of the Kansas City jazz tradition.

LIKE STONE, BANDLEADER WALTER PAGE came of age musically in Kansas City before venturing out into the territories. Musical scrappers, Walter Page and the Blue Devils ruled the territories, vanquishing all challengers in bare-knuckle battles of the bands. Jesse Stone recalled the fateful evening the Blue Devils routed the Blues Serenaders in an orchestra contest. "The biggest upset we [the Blues Serenaders] ever had in our life . . . happened to be in Sioux City, Iowa, . . . and it was a battle of the bands between Page and Jesse Stone. We got up on the stand first because we were considered like the house band there. We played there regularly. Well, we started out with some of our light things, little ballads. And these guys [the Blue Devils] hit right off the reel, *wham*, and they didn't let up all night long. They had a tough band."[48] Buster Smith attributed the band's prowess to the strength of the soloist. "We'd get off," Smith revealed. "We built the band around them solo things. We had Lips [Page] on trumpet over there and we had Dee Stewart . . . second trumpet. In other words we tried to be a band that could just get off instead of just read the music."[49] Although closely associated with Oklahoma and the Southwest territories, Page's career with the Blue Devils began and ended in Kansas City.

A large, barrel-chested youth with a mischievous grin, Walter Page started his musical career doubling on tuba and bass drum with neighborhood brass bands in his hometown, Gallatin, Missouri.[50] Moving to Kansas City with his widowed mother, Page attended Lincoln High School, where he studied under Major N. Clark Smith. Encouraged by Smith to pick up the double bass, Page modeled his powerful style after Wellman Braud, who came to Kansas City with John Wyckliffe's Ginger Orchestra in 1917. According to Page, "[Braud] came to Kansas City with John Wycliffe's band from Chicago for the five-day circuses put on by the Elks and Shriners. . . . I was sitting right in the front row of the high school auditorium and all I could hear was the oomp, oomp, oomp of the bass, and I said that's for me. I was just getting started with Bennie Moten then, perfecting my beat. Braud is my daddy. That's why I have the big beat. . . . [W]hen Braud got ahold of that bass, he hit those tones like hammers and made them jump right out of that box."[51] Summing up Page's forceful Braud-inspired technique, Eddie Durham observed, "[W]ithout amplification, a lot of guys weren't strong enough on bass fiddle. But Walter Page you could hear! He was like a house with a note."[52]

After graduating from Lincoln High in 1918, Page completed a three-year gas engine maintenance course. Changing career paths in 1921, he enrolled in the University of Kansas (KU) in Lawrence, Kansas, to major in public education. Taking advantage of the music program at KU, Page studied piano, voice, violin, sax, composition, and arranging. In contrast to Major N. Clark Smith's tacit approval of jazz, the white faculty at KU openly disdained jazz and discouraged students from playing it. In an article published on the front page of the student newspaper in 1921, Professor Harold Butler, Dean of the School of Fine Arts, derided jazz as "merely the animal side of music. It originated in the dancing dives of the South, and came into popularity by being copied in the dancing halls of New York and other large cities. Jazz is nothing but syncopated rhythm and has been the biggest cause of the undesirable dances which have been so prevalent of late."[53] Disregarding administrative admonitions against jazz, Page spent school breaks in Kansas City playing with Bennie Moten. He developed a taste for travel while working in the dining service for the Union Pacific railway during summer vacations. Page realized his musical ambition and desire to travel by joining the Blue Devils.

In late November 1922, the "Internationally Famous Blue Devils" arrived in Kansas City with Billy King's musical comedy revue, "Moonshine," for a week-long engagement at the Grand Theater. Accompanying Bessie Brown, Marguerite Scott, and Marshall "Garbage" Rodgers, along with a chorus of "creole beauties," the Blue Devils merited special mention in the local press.[54] The *Kansas City Sun* praised the Blue Devils as "the classiest aggregation of jazz artists now before the public. To say you have not heard jazz until you hear it rendered by this orchestra is nothing but the single truth."[55] Ethel Waters, then billed as "the world's greatest blues singer," joined the company as a headliner for a two-week encore performance.

Page hopped aboard as the Blue Devils pulled out of Kansas City for California, New Year's Day 1923.[56] The Billy King road show closed at the end of the season, stranding the band in the territories. The Blue Devils carried on playing hotels and theaters across Texas and Oklahoma. While on the road the band members developed a book of standards and originals. "We played the 'tab' shows for TOBA," Page recalled. "We got so we wouldn't play anything without music. I used to write from ear at one in the afternoon and by seven that night we'd have a complete arrangement. We had three arrangers, which meant thirty dollars extra, which we all drank up."[57] Moving across the Southwest, the Blue Devils grew in number, picking up leading local players.

HENRY "BUSTER" SMITH, slim and self-effacing with a gentle country manner, joined the Blue Devils in Dallas. Born on a farm near Altdorf, Texas, to a sharecropper family, Smith cut his musical teeth noodling on his family's organ.[58] While working the fields with his family near Dallas, Smith spied his future in a pawn shop window. "I saw a clarinet in a window in town one day and ran all the way back home to ask my mother if I could have it," Smith related. "It didn't cost but $3.50 so she told me I could buy it if I picked four hundred pounds of cotton a day. Well, I picked over four hundred pounds for five days, and then went back and bought that clarinet."[59] Mastering his new instrument, Smith joined the Voddie White Trio, playing casuals and Saturday-night fish fries in the Dallas area. A quick study, he conquered the alto saxophone in three days. Smith promptly established a reputation locally as an imaginative, facile soloist. In 1925, he joined the Blue Devils at the urging of band members impressed by his inventive technique.

Shortly after Smith came aboard, Walter Page assumed leadership of the Blue Devils. "Down in Texas we ran into the road company of *Shuffle Along*, and it turned out that our overture was the 'Shuffle Along Overture,' which we played by heart and it killed them," Page recalled. "That was our last appearance before disbanding. Emir Coleman wanted to go into politics, so I was asked to take over the band when he left. The touring company folded up, so I formed a small group and played around the same part of the country for a while."[60] While scuffling around Texas and Oklahoma, Page decided to expand the band to full size. Corralling a group of local movers and shakers in an Oklahoma City hotel room, Page persuaded them to bankroll the move. Over the next few years, Page augmented and upgraded the personnel of the band: adding Eddie Durham, trombone and guitar; Oran "Lips" Page, trumpet; Jimmy Rushing, vocals; and Bill Basie, piano. The footloose Durham did not stay with the Blue Devils long before joining Jesse Stone. The others, along with Buster Smith, became mainstays, supplying the solo firepower that propelled the Blue Devils to the top ranking regionally.

ORAN PAGE, LIKE HIS IDOL LOUIS ARMSTRONG, loved the limelight. Clowning on stage, Page sang in a gravelly voice, and his trumpet solos favored the upper register. Raised in Dallas, Page learned the rudiments of music from his widowed mother, a music educator.[61] As a youth, Page played with a juvenile brass band led by bass drummer Lux Alexander. During high school, he spent summers touring the South with minstrel shows and carnivals. On a jaunt to Atlanta, Page accompanied Bessie Smith. Page's mother sent him to college to be a doctor, but he left school for the life of a traveling musician. Slim with broad features and hair as glossy as his shoes, Page toured the country accompanying Ma Rainey on the TOBA circuit. Stopping in Chicago, Page made a pilgrimage to see his hero Louis Armstrong with the King Oliver band. Back in Texas, Page freelanced with Troy Floyd's band in San Antonio and Sugar Lou and Eddie's Orchestra at the Hotel Tyler in Tyler, Texas, before joining the Blue Devils. An accomplished player able to improvise effortlessly on chord changes, Page swiftly became a star soloist with the Blue Devils.

IT WASN'T LONG BEFORE vocalist Jimmy Rushing joined Page in the solo spotlight. Rushing, pudgy with bulging eyes and an engaging grin, became a Blue Devil in Oklahoma City. A versatile song stylist, Rushing moved comfortably between interpreting popular standards and shouting the blues. A consummate entertainer, the rotund Rushing seemed to defy gravity as he danced lightly across the stage.

Rushing grew up in Oklahoma City, surrounded by music.[62] His father played trumpet in the Knights of Pythias Band, and his mother played piano and sang in church. Doting parents, they shepherded the wayward Rushing to church choirs, glee clubs, and operatic productions. His father bought Rushing a violin and vigilantly monitored his practice schedule, to no avail. Rushing preferred vaudeville over the violin, particularly the blues shouters riding on the TOBA circuit. Ignoring his parents' disapproval, Rushing learned to play blues piano from his cousin Wesley Manning, one of the leading pianists in the area. "He was the No. 1 pianist for that part of the country for a long time," Rushing recalled. "My father objected to him teaching me because he thought I'd start playing the sporting houses like Wesley."[63] Realizing his father's worst fear, Rushing followed Manning's lead, sneaking out to play the piano and sing for his friends into the early hours of the morning.

In the early 1920s, Rushing left home to roam around the Midwest. In Chicago he checked out the bands and vocalists working on the South Side. His travels led to California, where he first sang professionally with the Sunnyland Jazz Orchestra, which featured Papa Mutt Carey and other New Orleans expatriates working in Los Angeles. Rushing occasionally worked with Jelly Roll Morton in Los Angeles, and much to his surprise, Morton encouraged his fledgling efforts at the piano. Homesickness reined in Rushing's wanderlust, and he returned to Oklahoma City. Back home he worked as a short-order cook in his father's café while singing on the side. After hearing Rushing in a cabaret one night in Oklahoma City, Walter Page invited him to join the Blue Devils. The Blue Devils lacked a strong vocalist, and Jimmy Rushing filled the bill. Ernie Williams, the Blue Devils' conductor and vocalist, specialized in ballads and blues, but struggled to be heard above the band. Rushing's bell-like voice soared above the band's volume without the help of a megaphone.

RUSHING AND WALTER PAGE brought pianist Bill Basie into the fold on July 4, 1928. Raised in Red Bank, a resort town on the New Jersey shore, Basie yearned to leave with the carnivals and circuses passing through each summer.[64] An indifferent student, young Basie worked in a local theater, cleaning up, operating the spotlight, and rewinding the films. A self-taught pianist, he worked his way up to the front of the theater, playing as an accompanist to the silent movies. Unable to read music, Basie learned to improvise with the flickering images on the screen. Honing his technique, Basie graduated to playing casuals with drummer Sonny Greer, who later made his mark with Duke Ellington's band. Following a short stint working in Asbury Park, New Jersey, Basie, in the mid 1920s, moved up to Harlem, arriving at the dawn of the "renaissance." Absorbing the rich musical environment, Basie made the rounds of the theaters and clubs dotting Harlem. The stride style pioneered by Fats Waller, James P. Johnson, Willie "the Lion" Smith, and other piano professors became his greatest influence. Waller befriended young Basie, introducing him to the organ. Although not very sophisticated musically, Basie managed to find a niche in Harlem, playing at small after-hours joints where he made the contacts that led to his first big break.

On the advice of Lou Henry, a friendly, more experienced musician, Basie auditioned for Katie Crippen's six-piece band, slated to join the "Hippity Hop" revue. Basie won the audition, and joined Katie Crippen and Her Kiddies to travel across the country on the Columbia vaudeville wheel, which toured downtown theaters for white audiences. "Our act, which was the only part of the show with sepia performers, was a special feature that used to be called the olio," Basie elaborated. "We didn't have any connection with any of the skits and production numbers or anything like that. We came on and did our thing, and that was it. We would open up and bring Katie Crippen on, and she sang and danced. . . . Katie Crippen was a very good entertainer. You had to be a real pro with strong audience appeal to get your act in a big show like 'Hippity Hop.'"[65] In late November 1922, "Hippity Hop," featuring Sugar Foot Snowball, the "Colored Harmonica Playing Fool," opened at the Gayety Theatre in Kansas City. Ironically, the same week "Moonshine" featuring the original Blue Devil Orchestra opened just a few blocks away at the Grand Theater. Although so close by, Basie did not explore the 18th and Vine area until the next years when the revue swung back through Kansas City.

Basie described stumbling upon the famed music district:

> We came to the corner of Eighteenth Street and wham! Everything along that street was lit up like klieg lights. It was one of the most fantastic sights I've ever seen in my life. We turned right there. We didn't figure that we needed to go any further on Troost. There were joints all lit up and going full blast on both sides of the street for several blocks. One of the first places I remember seeing was the Yellow Front Saloon. Another was the Sawdust Trail. And everywhere you went, there was at least a piano player and somebody singing, if not a combo or maybe a jam session. There was so much going on that I couldn't believe my eyes or ears . . . all of those joints along that strip were wide open, and there were ambulances and police cars with sirens just sitting out there ready to roll. . . . the action was greater than anything I ever heard of.[66]

Delighted by the area's atmosphere of abandon, Basie returned to 18th and Vine every night after work and made himself right at home through the early morning hours of revelry.

When "Hippity Hop" folded in 1925, Basie returned to working speakeasies and basement clubs in Harlem. With a heavy concentration of talent vying for a limited number of venues, competition for jobs in Harlem became fierce. On one occasion Claude Hopkins stole outright Basie's regular engagement. While working in one of his regular haunts, Leroy's, Basie happened to meet Harry Smith, a slender trumpet player with the Gonzelle White show who favored bowler hats. The two hit it off, and Smith encouraged Basie to audition for the piano slot in the White band. Underscoring his invitation, Smith escorted Basie to the band's rehearsal the next day. Pleased by Basie's easygoing temperament and versatility on the piano, White brought him into the band. Petite, with red hair and a fair complexion, White first established her career during the early 1920s, touring on the Columbia and Keith Junior circuits. An accomplished vocalist and nimble dancer, White concluded her show by taking a solo turn on alto saxophone. Her husband and manager, Ed Langford, played C-melody saxophone with the band and joined White on stage for short skits and comedy routines. Following Langford's lead, other band members doubled as entertainers

Somewhat shy and reserved, Basie marveled at band members' entertaining escapades on stage. "Harry Smith was a hell of a trumpet player, and he was also featured in the act as a dancer," Basie explained. "He could tap and do the buck and wing, kicks, splits, soft shoe, all those steps."[67] A veteran hoofer, Smith traveled the country in 1919 with a street carnival defending his title, "Champion Buck and Wing Dancer of the World," "against all comers."[68] Drummer Freddie Crump's on-stage feats amazed Basie. "He [Freddie Crump] did all of the fancy things that show-band drummers used to, like throwing his sticks in the air and catching them like a juggler without losing a beat," Basie elaborated. "He was a whole little act by himself, especially when it came to taking bows. He used to come dancing back in from the wings and hit the drums as he slid into a split. He used to grab the curtain and ride up with it, bowing and waving at the audience applauding."[69] The twenty-five-member White company featured a singing chorus line as well as top comedians, including: "Dusty" Fletcher, who later went on to fame with the national hit "Open the Door Richard"; "Jazz Lips" Richardson; and "Pigmeat" Markham. Known then as Rock Markham, his nickname "Pigmeat" came from a routine he performed with the show, where he danced and sang "I'm Sweet Papa Pigmeat. I got the Jordan River in my hips, and all the women is raving to be baptized."[70]

The White show played a string of dates around New York City before boarding the TOBA circuit. On the road, natural disasters and personal tragedy plagued the group. Members barely escaped New Orleans, besieged by the great flood of 1927. Ed Langford fell ill after playing a ballyhoo during a rainstorm in Indianapolis, then developed pneumonia, and died in Chicago. A true trouper, White accompanied his body back to Kansas City for burial, and then rejoined the show. Basie and other band members took Langford's place in the skits, and the show went on. Returning with her whole troupe to Kansas City, Gonzelle White and Her Big Jamboree opened a week-long engagement at the Lincoln Theater on July 4, 1927. The reviewer for the *Kansas City Call* applauded the show's pacing and the troupe's showmanship.

> The curtain rises on "The Big Jamboree" after the jazz orchestra renders an overture that wins applause. The comedians Rock Markum [Markham] and Willie Jackson appear with the chorus in the song and dance opening. They follow with Miss White and Harry Smith in a little comedy that concerns an unknown man "Jenkins." Then Markum and Miss Coly Edwards sing and dance "Round About Way to Heaven" and Mr Smith plays a cornet solo with the girls in a dance. Comedy features and musical dance numbers follow in quick

succession. Miss White and Willie Jackson score with a song and dance. The comedians and White form a jazz-harmony trio, and Jackson leads the girls in a Spanish dance, singing "Senorita Mine." A domestic drama has Miss White, Mr. Smith, Wm. Basie, Ruth Harris; full of action with the moral "The Wages of Sin is Death." There's more fun in the "Hot Dog" skit by the comedians. The band takes its position on the stage and accompanies several specialities [sic] including sensational dancing by Willie McKelvey, and Alfred Steeley; Mouth-harp selections by Leonard harmonica; saxaphone [sic] and cornet duet, Miss White and Mr. Smith; and songs with dances, Miss White and girls. After Mr. Markum does an eccentric wild dance the company closes with a "Gig Walk" song and dance. A good to look at bunch of singing and dancing girls, backed by a number of fancy draped scenes add class to the production.[71]

With this rather modest mention Basie arrived back in Kansas City, where he first established his career.

After closing at the Lincoln, the White revue paused in Kansas City, staying at the Eastside Hotel across the street from the Lincoln Theater. Basie indulged in the night life, becoming well acquainted with the sporting men who lorded over gambling, vice, and bootlegging. "It was during the time that the Gonzelle White show was playing at the Lincoln that I first met Piney Brown," Basie disclosed. "There were all these girls in the show, and Piney was the man-about-town in Kansas City in those days, and by the way, he was the nicest guy you'd ever want to meet in the world. When you were with him, you never had to worry about anything, because he always took care of the bill. I had already heard about him, and when he came by the theater and said he wanted to meet the show girls, I already knew who he was. So right away I said to myself, 'I got to figure a way to get in on this action.' . . . It was also during this time that I just met Ellis Burton. He was the one who ran the Yellow Front Café. . . . I used to go down there all the time. That was one of the first places in Kansas City where I got a chance to sit in on piano a few times."[72] Moving in and out of Kansas City during the next year, Basie often relied on the benevolence of his shady benefactors.

The White show next embarked on a tour of theaters in Oklahoma. During a layover in Tulsa, Basie first encountered the Blue Devils. As Basie slept late one morning in the hotel where the White show stayed, the Blue Devils passed by playing a ballyhoo in the street, drumming up a little business for an engagement that evening. Groggy from lack of sleep and the local homebrew Chocktaw beer he consumed the night before, Basie at first thought the music he heard came from a Victrola in the next room. Throwing on his clothes, he stumbled downstairs and joined the throng following the wagon. The group's verve and dynamics dazzled Basie. "Everybody seemed to be having so much fun just being up there playing together, and they looked good and sounded good to boot," Basie remarked. "There was such a team spirit among those guys, and it came out in the music, and you were part of it. Everything about them really got to me, and as things worked out, hearing them that day was probably the most important turning point in my musical career so far as my notions about what kind of music I really wanted to try to play was concerned."[73]

While playing a ballyhoo for the White show later that day, Basie noticed a number of Blue Devils checking him out from the crowd. Basie's command of the keyboard impressed band members, particularly Jimmy Rushing. "We'd stand through the ballyhoo until Basie would play, 'That guy's crazy,' we'd say, because he played so good," Rushing exclaimed.[74] Elbowing through the crowd, Rushing and Walter Page invited Basie to stop by the Blue Devils' dance that evening, an invitation Basie readily accepted. Hitting it off later that night, Rushing and Basie made arrangements to meet in Oklahoma City a few weeks later, when both bands would be in town. Kindred spirits, the two became fast friends. At Rushing's request, Basie sat in for the band's pianist one evening. Basie meshed well with band members, so Walter Page extended an open invitation to join the Blue Devils.

Flattered by Page's offer, Basie dutifully returned to Kansas City with the Gonzelle White show. However, unable to find steady gigs once back in Kansas City, the show languished. Basie freelanced around Kansas City, playing at the Yellow Front and other joints on 18th Street, garnering a measure of local acclaim. In early April 1928, Basie accompanied cornetist Harry S. Dorsey for the annual Wheatly-Provident Hospital fashion show extravaganza at Paseo Hall. "He just seemed to come from nowhere," Jap Allen remarked. "Overnight there he was playing part time in some of the night spots. Then he played for a while in one of the theaters before going on the road with the Blue Devils. He was a hit right away with the musicians as well as the public."[75]

Gonzelle White, seeking to revive the revue, booked a week-long engagement at the Pantages Theater in mid-April. Shortly before opening night, Basie entered the Old City Hospital in grave condition, afflicted with spinal meningitis. While Basie recuperated, the White show disbanded. Following his discharge, Basie returned to working in clubs and playing piano in local theaters, accompanying silent movies. Unable to get the Blue Devils off his mind, Basie contacted Walter Page. Dissatisfied with piano player Turk Thomas, who "played a galloping piano" with "no equilibrium," Page welcomed Basie to the band.[76] Basie traveled to Oklahoma, joining the Blue Devils on Independence Day 1928, exactly one year after arriving in Kansas City with the Gonzelle White show. Four months later, Basie returned to Kansas City as a star attraction with the Blue Devils.

The Blue Devils enjoyed a regular circuit of top engagements across the territories, but Walter Page, itching to take on the Moten band, wanted to move the band's headquarters from Oklahoma to Kansas City. Testing the waters, the Blue Devils premiered at 18th and Vine, with the help of George E. Lee. In exchange for the opportunity to work the Blue Devils' territory in Oklahoma, Lee publicly endorsed the Blue Devils' Kansas City date in an advertisement in the *Kansas City Call*. Lee hailed the Blue Devils as the "Syncopation Kings of the Southwest" and urged local fans to "give these visiting artists the reception of their lifetime." The advertisement for the dances billed Basie as "pianist and director;" Walter Page, manager; Oran Page, trumpeter; James Rushing, "golden voiced tenor;" and Henry Smith, "King of sax."[77] The Blue Devil Orchestra opened at Paseo Hall on October 28, 1928, with a follow-up Halloween dance. One thousand seven hundred gaily attired dance fans streamed in between heavy rains to celebrate Halloween with the Blue Devils. The *Kansas City Call* reported the "Blue Devils were as hot as though they had just been blasted from the lower regions. And how the crowd liked the music! They encored each number vociferously and couldn't seem to get enough."[78] The Blue Devils played regularly at Paseo Hall during November 1928, battling George E. Lee in late November. Working in and around Kansas City, Page wanted to battle Moten in the "worst way," but Moten wisely kept his distance and, during the next few years, waged a war of attrition picking off Page's best men one by one.

5

Blue Devil Blues

"That's all right baby, baby, that's all right for you. . . .
after all I been to you, baby that's the way you do."

—Walter Page's Blue Devils, "Blue Devil Blues," 1929

MORE BY COINCIDENCE THAN DESIGN, Andy Kirk tended to be in the right place at the right time. His good fortune and the band's stellar musicianship quickly vaulted the Twelve Clouds of Joy into the national limelight. The move to Kansas City marked the first of several giant leaps that carried the band from Oklahoma City to the grand Roseland Ballroom in New York. In early July 1929, the Twelve Clouds of Joy opened at Kansas City's Pla-Mor Ballroom. Bennett Stydham's gracious introduction made nervous band members feel right at home. "Stydham came up on the stand and introduced us to the dancers: 'Ladies and gentlemen, this is Andy Kirk and his Twelve Clouds of Joy,'" Kirk recalled. "'We brought them in from Oklahoma where everybody loves them. We know you'll love them too. Let's welcome Andy Kirk and the band!' They did. And every Cloud's face that I could see from behind my sousaphone had a big grin."[1]

The Twelve Clouds of Joy's style and music well suited the dancers gliding across the immense spring-loaded dance floor at the Pla-Mor. The band, decked out in white tuxedos, specialized in popular tunes, waltzes, ballads, novelties, with a little hot jazz to spice the mix. "Casey Jones," a holdover from the Holder band, brought down the house. "We put on a ten-minute show every night with loud, fast stuff and it used to break everybody up," Kirk explained.

One of our big entertainment numbers was the novelty "Casey Jones." We dressed up in engineers' black caps and tied red bandanas around our necks.

Just before going into our routine I would borrow a cigarette from one of the smokers . . . take the mouth piece off the sousaphone and blow a lot of smoke into the tubing. Massey sang the verse, then the whole band would come in on "'Casey Jones, mounted to the cabin, Casey Jones, with the throttle in his hand' . . ." By the time I got out front, smoke was pouring out of the bell of my horn. Allen Durham was imitating the drive shaft of a train engine with his trombone, and Big Jim Lawson was dancing a jig as he "oiled" the "drive shaft" with his trumpet. The crowds loved it, especially white audiences. They'd gather around the bandstand and clap and yell, "Let's get hot. Come on, get hot."[2]

Like Moten and Lee, Kirk moved easily between both sides of town, playing the Pla-Mor Ballroom and Paseo Hall. Dance fans at 18th and Vine warmly embraced the band as their own. Band members reciprocated, adopting Kansas City as their new hometown. Kirk and his wife Mary joined the social whirl of the professional class. Band members became familiar figures in the community, playing baseball against the Moten and Lee bands on the Parade Way Sunday afternoons. Mary Lou Williams found Kansas City to be a "heavenly" place. "Yes, Kaycee was a place to be enjoyed, even if you were without funds," Williams fondly reminisced. "People would make you a loan without you asking for it, would look at you and tell if you were hungry and put things right. There was the best food to be had: the finest barbecue, crawdads, and other seafood. There were the races, and swimming, and the beautiful Swope Park."[3]

Unfortunately, a dark cloud trailed the band from Tulsa. Shortly after the Clouds of Joy settled in Kansas City, the American Federation of Musicians slapped band members with a heavy fine. While setting up shop in Kansas City, band members maintained their affiliation with the white musicians' local union in Tulsa. "At the time the State of Oklahoma had segregation laws that prevented us [the Clouds of Joy] from belonging to the all-white musicians' local 94 in Tulsa," Kirk confided. "Although we had lived and worked in that jurisdiction for over three years, we remained under the traveling band status. That meant any contract we filed must show 10 percent above existing local scale, according to the laws of the AFM [American Federation of Musicians]. This we always did, and that local always accepted our contract without question. But naturally the members of the Tulsa local wanted to play the best spot—which we had—but each time we deposited our contract with the white local there it was accepted."[4] The secretary of Local 94, Daddy Fox, resented the Kirk band's success and raised the scale for the band's final engagement in Tulsa without notifying Kirk or the management of the Crystal City Park. The contrived infraction triggered a $1,800 fine by the national union and prevented the band from playing union engagements in Kansas City until Kirk settled the fine. Fortunately for Kirk, Bennett Stydham stepped in and helped pay the fine. In the end, the dispute worked to the Kirk band's advantage. Band members switched their affiliation to Kansas City's Local 627, freeing them to play anywhere in the country, unmolested by the

whims of local unions—white or African American. The Clouds of Joy immediately benefited from the change in headquarters and union affiliation. Located in the "heart of America," Kansas City provided easy access to regional
and national entertainment circuits.

Between extended engagements at the Pla-Mor, the Clouds of Joy toured
theaters and ballrooms across Iowa, Kansas, and Oklahoma, traveling on the
same circuit as the George E. Lee band. The two bandleaders became close
friends, agreeing on a uniform rate well above scale for their bands. "We
worked out a business agreement so that we wouldn't be cutting each other's
throats," Kirk explained. "We both agreed to forget about scale and ask for
some real money. Our bands were getting very popular locally then and there
was plenty of work around for both of us, so we set up a scale which neither of
us would go under. We weren't concerned with what the other bands got
because we were more commercial and did a lot of novelties which the other
jazz bands like Bennie Moten's weren't doing."[5]

A fortuitous encounter with Fletcher Henderson and a recording session
for Brunswick propelled the Clouds of Joy to the brink of national prominence. While playing nightly at the Pla-Mor, the Clouds of Joy often shared
the stage with visiting bands, taking on all comers in battle of the bands. Squar-
ing off against Fletcher Henderson, the "King of Jazz," in early September
1929, Kirk first realized the standard the band needed to achieve to compete
in the national arena. "Fletcher Henderson was the band that really opened
our ears," Kirk related. "When they came in to guest for a night, the Clouds
of Joy stood around the bandstand, soaking up the sound. Their 16 pieces, of
course, delivered a bigger sound than our 12, but it wasn't just the numbers
that made the impact. Their beat was different from ours. They had a two-
beat drive, powerhouse all the time. We played four-beat, a little bounce-beat
style. They had what we called the Eastern sound, and they did a lot of show
tunes."[6] Similar in personality and style, Kirk and Henderson hit it off famously. Henderson helped Kirk out by contributing several fresh arrangements to the Clouds of Joy band book.

A few weeks later, Henderson and Kirk competed at Paseo Hall. The Clouds
of Joy rose to the occasion, approaching parity with the more experienced
and famed Henderson band. Covering the battle for the *Kansas City Call*,
"Dance Gossip" columnist Earl Wilkins relished the David and Goliath
matchup. "And a mighty battle it was with palms going to both orchestras.
The huge crowd seemed in its applause to give an edge to the novelty numbers, melody, and blues of Kirk although an appreciable group obviously preferred the masterly arrangements of Henderson and his New Yorkers.
Hundreds of people did not dance at all but moved from one end of the hall to
the other to hear each orchestra close up. . . . Both bands were pleased with
their reception and the crowd was tickled to death with the music."[7] A few

weeks later, Henderson wired Kirk, inviting the Clouds of Joy to fill in for his band at the Roseland Ballroom in New York, starting in January 1930.

Readying the band for the long haul east, Kirk embarked on a jaunt of one-night stands across Kansas and Oklahoma. Back in Kansas City in late October, the Kirk band opened at the Cuban Gardens, mobster Johnny Lazia's casino, located north of the river next to the Riverside Park Jockey Club, the unofficial municipal race track. The band's engagement ended abruptly after an angry exchange of words between Billy Massey and the club's manager. Mary Lou Williams recalled the band's first brush with the sinister side of Kansas City nightlife. "Andy was playing tuba, and the band was conducted by our singer, Billy Massey. Billy was a man not easily scared, and one day at the new job he ran off his mouth to the boss," Williams related. "The hood concluded he was crazy (which was not far wrong), and told all the band to pack and leave—but fast. The rest of the guys were too nice, he said, for him to think about killing Billy."[8] Acting immediately on the recommendation, the band made a beeline back to the Pla-Mor.

Shortly after retreating to the safety of the Pla-Mor, the Kirk Band recorded for the Brunswick label with the inadvertent help of local entrepreneur Winston Holmes. After reluctantly folding his Meritt label in 1927, Holmes returned to freelancing, producing sessions, and recording as a featured artist for the Gennett and Paramount labels. In early October 1929, he struck a deal with the Brunswick label in Chicago to record Lottie Beaman, Sylvester Kimbrough, Paul Banks, and the George E. Lee Novelty Singing Orchestra. Eager to end Victor Records' dominance over Kansas City talent, Brunswick jumped at Holmes's entrée to the scene.[9] Executives Jack Kapp and Dick Voynow along with J. Mayo Williams, supervisor of race recordings, arrived in Kansas City in early November to make arrangements for the sessions and scout other local talent.

Kapp and company auditioned a number of local groups before settling on the Blue Devils and the Clouds of Joy. When the Clouds of Joy's regular pianist, Marion Jackson, failed to show for the audition at the Pla-Mor, Kirk recruited John Williams's wife, Mary Lou, who occasionally filled in with the band. "I got all the boys together and told them to be on time, and the next day they were all there, all except Marion Jackson, who was playing piano with me then," Kirk recounted. "He was somewhat of a ladies' man and must have had something on that day. We waited around for him a little while until Kapp started to get impatient. I asked John Williams [he replaced Fats Wall] to call his wife Mary Lou, who he had been telling me about and to get her over to the Pla-Mor in a hurry so we could get on with the audition." Easing into the piano chair, Mary Lou performed like a regular member of the band, leaving the executives from Brunswick none the wiser. Particularly taken with Mary Lou, Kapp added the Clouds of Joy to the sessions scheduled to start the next week in the studio of radio station WDAF, located in the Kansas City Star building.

Having performed mainly stock arrangements of popular standards for white dancers, Kirk and the Clouds of Joy had yet to develop an original book. Kirk, desperate for fresh material to record, enlisted Mary Lou Williams to score new compositions for the sessions. The two stayed up for several nights furiously writing charts. Williams hurriedly learned the art of arranging. "Kirk liked my ideas, though I could not set them down on paper," she confessed. "He would sit up as long as 12 hours at a stretch, taking down my ideas for arrangements, and I got so sick of the method that I began putting them down myself. I hadn't studied theory, but asked Kirk about chords and the voicing register. In about 15 minutes I had memorized what I wanted. That's how I started writing. My first attempt, 'Messa Stomp' [Mess-A-Stomp] was beyond the range of half of the instruments."[10]

Since Marion Jackson failed to make the audition and Kapp expected Mary Lou Williams to be at the piano, Kirk brought her in for the sessions. The band recorded eight selections: six as Andy Kirk and His Twelve Clouds of Joy and two as John Williams and His Memphis Stompers. Catering to Kapp and Mayo Williams's desire to target the race market, the Kirk band emphasized stomps, blues, and novelties. The band led off with its most advanced arrangement, "Mess-A-Stomp." A blues taken at medium bounce tempo, "Mess-A-Stomp" begins with a short introduction by the band, heralding John Harrington's burnished clarinet solo supported by riffs laid down by the brass section. Bill Dirvin's pointed banjo solo blends with an eight-bar interlude featuring the reeds contributing a chorus before backing off and setting a riff behind Gene Prince's floating eight-bar trumpet solo. Mary Lou Williams's piano solo reveals a muscular, two-fisted pianist, moving effortlessly across the full range of the keyboard. After 12 bars of chromatic riffing, by the sections, punctuated by a brief banjo solo, the band takes it home with a shout chorus.[11] "Mess-A-Stomp" marked a strong composing and performance debut for Williams and won the band a contract with Brunswick.

The ensuing two small group recordings "Blue Clarinet Stomp" and "Cloudy" highlight the band's soloists. "Blue Clarinet Stomp," showcases well-executed solos by John Harrington, clarinet, John Williams, baritone saxophone, and Claude Williams doubling on guitar and violin. Drummer Ed "Crackshot" McNeil's shaded, swinging cymbal work adds texture to the rhythm section, featuring Kirk on tuba and Bill Dirvin on guitar. Harry "Big Jim" Lawson wraps things up nicely with a scat vocal. The lazy tempo of Andy Kirk's "Cloudy" allows the soloists ample opportunity to stretch out, especially on a bright trombone solo by Allen Durham. Mary Lou Williams harmonically shades her brilliantly executed solo with clustered blue notes a half-step apart, similar to bent blue notes played on a wind instrument.[12]

Mimicking the sound of a locomotive, "Casey Jones Special" careens along at a break-neck tempo, before arriving at its tongue-in-cheek destination of "Hicksville." "Sumpin' Slow and Low" and "Lotta Sax Appeal," recorded by John Williams and His Memphis Stompers, are a study in contrasts. As the title implies, "Sumpin' Slow and Low" is taken at a lazy tempo and features a round of solos in the low register. "Lotta Sax Appeal" moves along at a lively tempo, propelled by soloists playfully challenging each other with the reed and brass sections echoing the soloists' musical dialogue with riffs. The final two selections recorded for Brunswick, "Corky Stomp" and "Froggy Bottom," feature Williams's harmonically imaginative piano style, foreshadowing her later solo piano recordings. Ironically, while relegated to the role as band wife, Mary Lou Williams made the greatest contribution to the success of the band's first recording session.[13]

Like Mary Lou Williams with the Kirk band, Jesse Stone's direction and compositions vastly improved the Lee band's performance in the studio. After joining Lee, Stone enriched the band's book with sharp arrangements of popular standards and his own compositions. A natural educator, Stone tutored band members individually on the basics of music and drilled the sections. Following two months of preparation, the Lee band entered the studio on November 6 to record two vocals by Lee, "If I Could Be With You One Hour Tonight" and "St. James Infirmary," along with two Jesse Stone original instrumentals, "Paseo Street" and "Ruff Scufflin'." The band returned to the studio on November 8 to record two more selections featuring Julia on vocals, "He's Tall Dark and Handsome" and "Won't You Come Over to My House."

Stone modeled the arrangements of "Paseo Street" and "Ruff Scufflin'" after the style of the eastern bands, particularly Fletcher Henderson and McKinney's Cotton Pickers. His ambition as an arranger overreaches the ability of some band members. The reed and brass sections lack the crispness demanded by the intricate interplay of Stone's arrangements, which featured tricky trios, duos, and short solos with breaks. While trumpeter Harold Knox, trombonist Jimmy Jones, and saxophonist Budd Johnson contribute clean solos, squeaky alto breaks by Clarence Taylor and Herman Walder mar the sessions.

The band is more at ease accompanying Lee's vocals on the less demanding arrangements of "If I Could Be with You One Hour Tonight," and "St. James Infirmary." The 1926 hit "If I Could Be with You One Hour Tonight" became a jazz standard after the immensely popular McKinney's Cotton Pickers adopted it as a theme song. Lee dispenses with the tender longing of the verse and lustily charges right into the chorus, "If I could be with you I'd love you strong, if I could be with you the whole night long." The powerful emotion of Lee's vocal style overwhelmed the subtlety and nuance of the lyric and transformed the tender song of yearning into a passionate promise of satisfaction.

In 1926, Phil Baxter privately published the original version of "St. James Infirmary" as "Gambler's Blues." Although not copyrighted or widely published, "St. James Infirmary" became a jazz standard after Louis Armstrong recorded an up-tempo version for the OKeh label in December 1928. The Lee band takes "St. James Infirmary" at a slower tempo, better fitting the somber mood of the lyric: "I went to St. James Infirmary and saw my baby there, stretched out on a long white table so sweet, so cold, so fair." The rhythm section precisely marks time, echoing the pace of a funeral procession. The next year, Cab Calloway's recording of "St. James Infirmary," inspired by Lee's version, quashed Lee's hope for greater exposure.

The two selections, "He's Tall Dark and Handsome" and "Won't You Come Over to My House," typify risqué songs, which Julia referred to as those her "mother taught her not to sing." Julia's vocal range rises from contralto to mezzo soprano, embellished by a rapid vibrato gained during her early classical vocal training with Major N. Clark Smith. Her assured, syncopated barrelhouse piano work contrasts her lilting vocals. The George E. Lee Brunswick recordings captured the band as a work in progress. They had vastly improved over the Meritt sessions two years earlier, but were not quite up to the task of Stone's advanced arrangements.

The Blue Devils maintained close ties to Kansas City during their travels far and wide across the Midwest in two seven-passenger Cadillacs with a trailer full of instruments bringing up the rear. Catching wind of the pending Brunswick sessions, the Blue Devils hastily returned to Kansas City and won the audition. Pressed for time, Kapp worked the Blue Devils in for two selections at the tail end of the sessions. The band composed and rehearsed "Blue Devil Blues" and "There's a Squabblin'" specifically for the session, then never played them again. The occasion briefly reunited the Blue Devils with Basie, who had left the band the previous spring. "They [the Blue Devils] all knew him [Basie], and they were all close, like brothers," trombonist Druie Bess explained. "He just went in and took Charlie Washington's place on the session. Charlie didn't care, he was a young, sporty guy, and he just went out and drank a little whiskey."[14]

Basie's staid piano introduces "Blue Devil Blues," leading to a riff set by the ensemble, buttressed by an understated blues-tinged trumpet solo by Lips Page. Buster Smith follows with an imaginative three-octave clarinet solo, peppered with 16th and 32nd notes and supported by the rhythm section, which was led by Walter Page on bass horn. Jimmy Rushing's plaintive, behind-the-beat vocal delivery fits the lazy simplicity of the lyric, "that's all right baby, baby, that's all right for you. . . . [A]fter all I been to you, baby, that's the way you do." Page's muted trumpet flourishes in the two-bar rests accentuate Rushing's vocal delivery. The theme and mood of "Blue Devil Blues" establishes a stylistic motif often employed by Rushing and Basie during their long association.[15]

"There's a Squabblin'" represents the culmination of the distinguishing characteristics of the territorial bands and anticipates the golden age of Kansas City jazz style during the 1930s. Taken in 2/4 time, "There's a Squabblin'" employs a simple riff-driven head arrangement to facilitate the exuberant interplay between the sections and soloists. Lips Page's staccato muted trumpet solo is skillfully structured and brilliantly executed. Buster Smith, taking a turn on clarinet and alto saxophone, shows a robustness of ideas and execution, foreshadowing his direct influence on the advanced technique of Charlie Parker. Walter Page steps out of the rhythm section for a well-executed low-register baritone saxophone dialogue with the reed section. The hard-swinging rhythm section, led by Page's pizzicato bass, is a hallmark in the development of a pure Kansas City style. Page's two-beat line, contrasted by the four-beat rhythm of the guitar and combined with Alvin Burrough's smooth cymbal work, first establishes the signature rhythm that provided the foundation of Kansas City's supple swinging style.[16] A Basie original, "There's a Squabblin'" foreshadows the hard-swinging style he later developed as a member of the Moten band and then perfected with his own band at the Reno Club in Kansas City.

Kirk fared better professionally from the Brunswick sessions than Lee, Page, or Winston Holmes. Impressing Kapp right off the bat, the Clouds of Joy landed a two-year contract with Brunswick. Bearing the Brunswick banner, the Kirk band played leading ballrooms and theaters on its way east to replace Fletcher Henderson at the Roseland Ballroom in January 1930. Lee's recordings sold well in Kansas City, thanks to Winston Holmes's local promotion. "If I Could Be With You" and "Paseo Street" sold more than 2,000 copies to Kansas City fans during the first week of their advance release.[17] Despite the strong local sales, Brunswick passed on signing Lee to a contract. Nevertheless, Lee continued to play up his brief association, touting his band as Brunswick recording artists for years to come. Brunswick assigned the Blue Devils' recording to its subsidiary label, Vocalion, targeting ethnic, jazz, and blues record buyers. Unfortunately for the Blue Devils, the onset of the Great Depression, triggered by the stock market crash in late October 1929, devastated the market for race recordings.

The economic panic that followed forced Brunswick and other labels to concentrate on recording and promoting the well-established bands in their rosters. As the Depression deepened, record sales plummeted from a record high of 104 million in 1927 to 6 million in 1932. During the same period, the production of phonographs plunged from 987,000 to 40,000.[18] The nose dive in record and phonograph sales financially devastated independent African American music stores that were spawned by the race-record industry. The Brunswick sessions marked Winston Holmes's swan song as a record producer. Within a few years, hard times forced Holmes to close his spacious music company on 18th Street and open a small crowded shop around the

corner on Vine that specialized in repairing radios and piano tuning. Strapped
for cash, Holmes, the proud impresario of the race music industry, sold off his
back stock of race records for nickels and dimes on the dollar.

As the Depression ravaged the entertainment industry nationally, Kansas
City managed to hold its own as the entertainment Mecca of the Midwest.
The Depression actually enriched Kansas City's musical stock. Musicians from
the hard-hit Southwest, particularly Texas and Oklahoma, migrated to Kansas City in droves, fortifying existing bands and breeding a new generation of
bands, notably Bill Little and His Little Billies and Jap Allen and the Southern Troubadours.[19] By late 1929, the musicians union's ranks outgrew its
modest headquarters in the Rialto Building at 18th and Vine. The increased
membership and the strong leadership of newly elected president William
Shaw enabled the union to buy a building for its new headquarters, fulfilling
a long-time dream of members.[20]

Tall, gangly, and taciturn, Shaw began his professional career playing pic-
colo and flute with the Richards and Pringle Minstrel show. During World
War I, Shaw served with a U.S. Army band. Returning to civilian life, Shaw
performed with various minstrel shows before settling down to work as a bar-
ber. Shaw moved to Kansas City in 1925 and opened the Goldenwest Barbershop on 18th Street across from the Moten & Hayes Music Shop. Elected
President in 1928, Shaw transformed the union, instilling pride, discipline,
and professionalism in the ranks. He even went as far as to require members
to march in the Kansas City Labor Day parade. Shaw dramatically increased
membership by recruiting bands and musicians arriving from the Southwest,
bringing errant members back into the fold, and persuading local clubs and
theaters to become union houses. Under Shaw's stewardship, the union bought
a plain brick two-story apartment building and small house at 1823-25 Highland for its headquarters. The musicians drafted their dream plans for studios, a conservatory of music, and a dance hall on the second floor of their
new building.

Taking the lead, Shaw organized a mammoth benefit dance at Paseo Hall
in early December 1929. Accompanied by much ballyhoo, the union fielded
six bands for the first annual Musicians' Ball. The *Kansas City Call* reported
that dance fans jam-packed Paseo Hall throughout the evening festivities,
inspiring the bands to new musical heights.

> The crowd did everything but hang on the ceiling. The lobby was jammed; the
> dance floor was jammed; the seats along the wall were jammed; and the balcony
> was groaning with too much population. And maybe you think those six or-
> chestras didn't play with that sort of crowd for inspiration! There were more
> varieties of melody, rhythm, blues and stomp music than the old dance palace
> has heard in a long time. George E. Lee and his novelty singing Brunswick
> orchestra got the crowd in a good humor with a flawless performance. Paul

Bank's nattily attired Rhythm Aces followed in a way that made everybody happy. Andy Kirk's Twelve Clouds of Joy came next with a burst of joy that made the hall rock. Bennie Moten's Victor recording orchestra made its large following happy with the type of music which has made it widely famous and Bennie himself got out of bed to fill this engagement. And George Wilkerson and his Musical Magnets bore up the tradition and got hot in the approved manner.[21]

The resounding success of the ball financed the remodeling of the new headquarters.

The union dedicated its new home on Sunday, May 4, during National Music Week, an annual event sponsored by the American Federation of Musicians. A panoramic group photo of members proudly lined up in front of their new union hall commemorated the event. The celebration began promptly at 4 P.M. with a parade of the union members, led by a fifty-piece marching band. The festivities continued the next evening with a battle of the bands at Paseo Hall, pitting eight bands in a battle royal: Paul Banks's Ten Rhythm Aces versus Bill Little and His Little Bills; Elmer Payne's Music Masters against Julius Banks's Red Devils; Andy Kirk's Twelve Clouds of Joy opposing Jasper Allen's Southern Troubadours; and Bennie Moten and His Fourteen Victor Artists battling George E. Lee and His Brunswick Recorders. The contest commenced at 9 P.M. and continued until daybreak, with the combatants exchanging musical volleys from the bandstands on either side of the hall.

The battles at the musician balls were usually waged in the spirit of a Texas death match in professional wrestling, more for show than blood, but the contest between Moten and Lee assumed deeper meaning. It capped a year-long struggle between the two bandleaders for regional superiority. According to the *Kansas City Call*, in late April 1929 the George E. Lee band bested the Moten band in a battle at the Frog Hop Ballroom in St. Joseph, Missouri, before a crowd of 4,000 dancers.[22] The defeat called into question Moten's regional superiority. Over the years, the original core group of the Moten band had remained relatively stable. Moten paid well, so Hayes, Leonard, Walder, and other members of the old guard stayed with the band. But adding new members failed to remedy the band's lack of a strong vocalist to front the band, deft soloists to lead the sections, and an arranger to bring the band up to the level of the eastern bands. Frustrated by losing ground to Lee, Moten contemplated changing the band's personnel and musical direction.

Moten long coveted the outstanding soloists in the Blue Devils. Initially, he tried to take over the band wholesale, making his intentions known with a news release published in mid-June 1929 by the *Kansas City Call*. "Bennie Moten of the Bennie Moten's Victor Recording orchestra fame has taken over the Walter Page orchestra, the Blue Devils and will operate it as a unit of the Moten Orchestras. The new unit opens at the new Cinderella Gardens, Little Rock, Arkansas. According to Mr. Moten, the new unit will be about as hot as anything on the road and is expected to keep busy."[23] Although, in the end, the announcement turned out to be premature, Moten did persuade some of the Blue Devils to join him. Buster Smith mused, "Bennie tried to get me first to leave the Blue Devils but I wouldn't do it. I didn't want to go off and leave Page, Rushing, and Lips and all of them, but the first thing I knew they went off and left me."[24]

Initially rebuffed by the Blue Devils, Moten expanded the band, adding his nephew Ira Alexander "Bus" Smith and Eddie Durham. Bearing a striking resemblance to Moten, Smith came aboard as director and pianist. A stronger entertainer than musician, Smith had developed a forceful stage presence while touring with the Gonzelle White show, where he preceded Basie as pianist. Joining the Moten band in Oklahoma City, Smith at first found little to do on the bandstand. "I had no job," he groused. "My job was sitting there on the bandstand looking at my watch. I said to myself, 'man, I can't do this, I'm used to trucking.'" Choosing an instrument he could play while conducting the band, Smith bought a sixty-bass accordion and mastered it in his spare time. "I drove everyone out of the rooming house trying to learn it," Smith chuckled. "I got five tunes down and played choruses only on those. Bennie kept referring to me as his kid brother, so I legalized the name Moten. Guys would say to him, who is this kid, better keep him in, he's forty-percent of the band."[25]

While Bus hogged the spotlight, conducting the band onstage, Eddie Durham quietly set a new musical course for the group. Trombonist, guitarist, and gifted arranger, Durham enriched the band book with fresh compositions. Originally from San Marcos, Texas, Durham began his musical career co-leading his family's band with his brother Allen.[26] Striking out on his own, Durham passed through the ranks of Mitchell's Joys, Gene Coy's Black Aces, and a number of other Texas territorial bands. Lanky and handsome, Durham honed his writing and arranging skills as a member of the 101 Ranch Circus band. "That's where I really taught myself to write, to express my own voicing, because we had a lot of horns to play around with," Durham pronounced. "The circus band was a big brass band, a parade band. We had four trombones, two or three French horns, and peck horns."[27] Durham worked with trumpeter Edgar Battle's Dixie Ramblers, a twelve-piece band, featuring tenor saxophonist Herschel Evans, before joining the Blue Devils. A freelancer at heart, Durham shortly left the Blue Devils for the Blues Serenaders. After the demise of the Blues Serenaders, Durham joined the Moten band. An outsider brought in by Moten to modernize the band's style, Durham clashed with the old guard. Looking back, Durham summed up the band's primary weakness: "The style was set by Thamon Hayes' trombone; Woodie Walder's clarinet, which he would take apart and play in sections; Harlan Leonard's alto sax; Vernon Page's tuba; and Bennie's brother [nephew] doubling on piano and accordion."[28] During the next several years, Durham, along with Basie, amended the lineup while revolutionizing the style of the Moten band.

The Moten band returned to Kansas City in mid-July 1929 for a six-month engagement at the El Torreon Ballroom. Basie, standing in the throng assembled in the early morning hours on 18th Street waiting to greet band members, resolved to "connive" his way into the band. "I waited along with the crowd, and it was kind of like standing around waiting for the hometown team to get back. . . . [P]retty soon the first car, carrying Bennie Moten himself, pulled in. I never will forget that," Basie remembered. "It was a Chrysler, and Bus Moten was driving. Then the other car, carrying the rest of the band, pulled in right behind him, and everybody crowded around."[29] Before Basie could ingratiate himself into the Moten organization, the band left for a Victor recording session in Chicago. Durham, only a member for a short time, had yet to influence the band's musical direction. The session produced the usual fare of blues, stomps, breakdowns, and rags, rendered in the old style.

Wrapping up the recordings session in short order, the band promptly returned to Kansas City for a big homecoming dance at Paseo Hall. Watching the band from the crowd at Paseo Hall, Basie became even more intent on becoming a band member. "I really dug them. I came away more sold on them than ever. I wouldn't say that I thought that they could chop the Blue Devils or anything like that, because I still don't think they could do that," Basie observed. "But they had a special kind of class, and they also looked like they had it made in some ways, while the Blue Devils were still out there struggling from gig to gig."[30] Tired of scuffling around the Yellow Front Tavern and other clubs playing for tips, Basie yearned to join the Moten organization, but the band already had two pianists.

Basie found entrée to the band through Eddie Durham. In late summer 1929, the two became chummy while sitting in during late-night jam sessions at the Yellow Front and Subway. Basie, unable to read music, let alone write out arrangements for a full band, asked Durham to orchestrate a couple of standards he thought would work for the Moten band. Basie played the part for each section on the piano, while Durham wrote out the arrangements. They presented the new arrangements at the band's next rehearsal. Pleased, Moten invited Basie to accompany the band to Wichita, Kansas, to work up more arrangements with Durham.

Little by little, Moten steadily brought Basie along. In Wichita, Moten called Basie onstage for a few numbers. Back in Kansas City, Moten let his protege sit in during the band's regular engagement at the El Torreon. Moten and Basie shared piano duties, delighting audiences with their four-handed piano duets, executed with more flair than virtuosity. Basie viewed the opportunity to get close to Moten as a marvelous learning experience. "It put me so close to Bennie himself and the way he handled the band from the piano. That's not what I had in mind when I came up with the idea of two pianos.

That was just a little something extra that turned out to be one of the most important experiences a future bandleader could ever have."[31] An earnest apprentice, Basie carefully watched Moten on and off the stage.

Moten, busy tending to band business, gladly relinquished piano duties to Basie. While working six nights a week at the El Torreon, the band added a Monday-night dance at the Labor Temple. In late September, Moten inaugurated the first in a series of break-o'-day dances at the Labor Temple, beginning Saturday nights at 1 A.M. after the band's regular engagement at the El Torreon and continuing until daybreak. With Bus Moten concentrating on accordion and Bennie Moten distracted by his business interests, the band truly needed a full-time pianist, and Basie fit the bill. Each band member contributed a dollar a week toward Basie's pay and Moten furnished the rest, bringing his salary up to $15 per week.

Taking charge of the band musically, Basie and Durham prepared for the next recording session in Chicago, crafting arrangements of original compositions and rehearsing the band. The band left Kansas City on October 22, 1929, and spent the following two days in the studio working with Ralph Peer. The influence of Basie and Durham is apparent. Basie coauthored with Moten six of the nine selections recorded. Durham's arrangements sharpened the execution of the sections, affording a crispness and fluidity previously lacking, particularly on "Jones Law Blues" and "Boot It." The solos throughout the sessions are more relaxed and fully realized, yet still lacking in virtuosity, with the exception of Ed Lewis's fine trumpet solos on "Bandbox Shuffle" and "Rit-Dit-Ray" and Durham's trombone on "Every Day Blues" and "Mary Lee." Durham's brilliant pioneering guitar solos brightened the sound of the band. To be heard above the band, Durham attached a resonator the size of a pie tin on his guitar. Basie largely replaced Moten on piano, contributing a liberal number of stride-inspired solos. Bus Moten's accordion solos were executed with verve, but increasingly out of place with the timbre of the band. Overall, the band moved to a more eastern sound, a direction fostered by Moten. Basie observed, "[W]hat Moten had in mind was not just to be the best band in the territory, but one that would be in the same big-league class with Fletcher Henderson, Duke Ellington, Chick Webb, Claude Hopkins and McKinney's Cotton Pickers."[32]

Once back in Kansas City, Moten, Basie, and Durham recruited Jimmy Rushing from the Blue Devils. Rushing made his debut with the band on Friday, December 13, 1929, for a dance at the Labor Temple. At first, he had trouble adjusting to the Moten band's unusual accent on the beat. "When I first went to Kansas City, Bennie Moten's band had a little different beat than we [Blue Devils] used to carry," Rushing explained. "Their accent was on the first and third, although they played four. It sounded almost like a train coming. . . . I couldn't get with that beat at first. I liked that rhythm, but I didn't dig it too good. It took me a month before I got used to it. . . . In Oklahoma, where I had come from, the beat was more even. And New Orleans was more of less even when they used a four."[33] With the help of the former Blue Devils, Moten managed to regain parity with Lee locally and compete with the eastern bands on their own turf.

Armed with his new lineup, Moten challenged Lee to a battle for the "supremacy of Kansas City" at Paseo Hall in late December 1929. The *Kansas City Call* announced the showdown:

> All the grudges are up on the table and in sight where whoever will may see. George Lee and Bennie Moten have finally agreed to fight it out musically in a knock-down, drag-out band battle at Paseo Hall. . . . Bennie issued the challenge. The decision will be given by the audience and both George Lee's Brunswick recording orchestra and Bennie Moten's Victor recording orchestra are primed for the battle win, lose or draw. Followers of George seem to have no fear of the outcome of the contest. "With George's singing and recent additions to his band, there isn't any orchestra out in this part of the country which can touch him," one frequenter of dances said Thursday. "There'll be a lot of good music at this dance for I admit that Bennie is good, but I still believe that he can't touch George." Bennie's friends are equally confident of victory. One man well known in Kansas City orchestra circles for years said, "Bennie had a good orchestra before George and he is constantly making improvements in it. In my opinion he has the best band Kansas City ever had. When he added James Rushing to do his singing he made a master stroke. He will have no difficulty in proving his supremacy at the meeting Monday night."[34]

After all the hype building up to the event, Earl Wilkins declared no winner in his "Dance Gossip" column the next week, indicating the two bands fought to a draw. After matching Lee, Moten continued to refine the band's personnel and style, moving ever closer to the sound of the eastern bands.

During 1930, the Moten band played a series of long-term engagements at the El Torreon and Fairyland Park, spending little time on the road. Staying close to home gave Basie and Durham the opportunity to work up arrangements of new compositions and hone the sections' execution. By April, the band showed noticeable improvement and distinctly different style. Earl Wilkins recognized Durham's contribution to the band's new style. "This ['Travelin'] is one of the arrangements which is making young Durham, Bennie's arranger an enviable reputation among musicians in the city. Durham is good and the arrangements for the orchestra show it more all the time."[35]

In early May, the Moten band opened for the summer season at Fairyland Park. Celebrating the auspicious occasion, Moten ordered new band uniforms with maroon coats and vests, white striped trousers, and two-toned tan shoes. Basie, having worn a makeshift uniform for nearly a year, eagerly donned the new uniform and felt like a regular band member for the first time. Secure in his position with the Moten organization, Basie put down roots in the community and married Vivian Winn, a slender, attractive, well-respected member of the social set. Winn, formerly a cashier at the Lincoln Theater, worked as a clerk in the school district before marrying Basie. Earl Wilkins wished the young couple well in his regular column. "William Basie, well known and talented pianist for Bennie Moten, has secured for himself a charming bride in the person of the equally well known Miss Vivian Winn. Both young people are popular and I wish for them everything in reason for happiness."[36] An independent modern woman, Winn became Vivian Winn Basie. The toast of the town, the couple made the rounds of social functions and dances at Paseo Hall.

The arrival of the great bands from the East intensified the social whirl at Paseo Hall. Kansas City, offering lucrative engagements at the El Torreon, Pla-Mor, and Paseo Hall, became a regular stop for top eastern bands headed west. Like the big local three, Moten, Kirk, and Lee, out-of-town bands played engagements for white audiences at the El Torreon or Pla-Mor ballrooms, followed by Monday-night dates for African Americans at Paseo Hall. Dance fans at 18th and Vine were familiar with the eastern bands from newspaper coverage and recordings, but had seen few outside of Fletcher Henderson's band and the Alabamians. Arriving in 1930, McKinney's Cotton Pickers and the Duke Ellington band dazzled the aficionados crowding the bandstand at Paseo Hall.

Based at the Graystone Ballroom in Detroit, McKinney's Cotton Pickers embarked on a tour of the Midwest in late 1929, on the way to open in New York after the first of the year. In Kansas City, the band played a week-long engagement at the Pla-Mor followed by a dance at Paseo Hall. The Cotton Pickers immediately captured the fancy of fans at Paseo Hall, who reportedly "howled clapped stomped and surged around the platform for more and more."[37] In mid-January, the band returned by popular demand to battle George E. Lee's band at Paseo Hall. The Cotton Pickers' sharp arrangements, ensemble excellence, showmanship, and strong vocals influenced Kansas City bands considerably—particularly Bennie Moten. Local bands adapted the Cotton Pickers' theme song "I Want a Little Girl" and performed it as a blues. To some extent, Eddie Durham modeled the arrangements for the Moten band after the style of the Cotton Pickers. Moten later bought arrangements of "Roses of Picardy," "Love Brings a Little Gift of Love," "Just a Kiss," and "Mighty Lak a Rose" from Don Redman, the arranger for the Cotton Pickers.

In late July 1930, Duke Ellington and crew, on their way to Hollywood to appear with Amos and Andy in the film *Check and Double Check*, stopped in Kansas City. The hastily arranged tour west marked Ellington's first excursion outside of New York in five years. For his debut in Kansas City, Ellington played a battle of the bands at Paseo Hall against Lee. Kansas City music fans, already familiar with Ellington's music through his reputation and recordings, flocked to Paseo Hall for a peek at the already legendary pianist and bandleader. The *Kansas City Call* noted Ellington's highly anticipated debut in Kansas City. "Everybody was there—all the people that usually go to dances and hundreds of others who never go. White faces were there in abundance, among them the manager and radio man from the Pla-Mor and officials from the El Torreon. The boxes and balcony were full of listeners, and a solid phalanx of spectators twenty deep turned perspiring but marveling faces up at the boys from New York who could do such amazing tricks with their instruments. People were jammed into every available and unavailable cranny at the east end of the hall where the band played: they even stood precariously balanced in the windows." Ellington's "weird, wild jungle music enchanted the audience."[38] Thamon Hayes and other Moten band members stopped by Paseo Hall after their regular engagement at Fairyland Park. Beholding the Ellington band in action, Moten band members became aware of the virtuosity and style required to achieve Moten's goal of competing against national bands and succeeding in the East.

That September Moten brought Paul Webster, a strong soloist, back into the band to lead the trumpet section for a late October recording session.[39] Unable to break away to Chicago, the band recorded in Kansas City. Ralph Peer, accompanied by two assistants, brought a portable recording unit to Kansas City and set up a temporary studio in Lincoln Hall. The recording engineers draped the walls with curtains and covered the floor with thick rugs to dampen the sound. Usually, the band's recording sessions were hurried affairs, staged on the fly in Chicago between engagements, but Peer and Moten took their time for this session. With the Great Depression casting a pall over the record industry, the top brass at Victor wanted to record only "surefire hits." The *Kansas City Call* reported the Moten band spent "five hours on one number alone and four hours on several others." As a precaution, four takes of each tune were recorded on wax masters, and Peer made onsite selections of the best take for Victor's consideration. Not knowing if and when they would enter the studio again, Moten and Peer further hedged their bets by recording eighteen selections in just four days.[40]

The recordings capture Basie and Durham's transformation of the band. During the previous year, Basie and Durham had steadily shifted the band from the simple stomp-down Kansas City style to a more polished sound modeled after, yet distinct from, the eastern bands. The brass and reed sections rose to the occasion, skillfully maneuvering Durham's increasingly complex arrangements with heightened precision and sophistication. The sections were given a stronger sense of swing through Durham's unique application of riffs, an orchestral technique of repeating short melodic phrases, rooted in the call-and-response tradition. Eastern bands commonly used riffs underneath soloists. Durham employed riffs in a different manner for renditions of "Oh Eddie!" and "Professor Hot Stuff," bringing them to the forefront with the brass riffing against the reeds for counterpoint. Durham's unique arrangements established a distinguishing characteristic of Kansas City jazz style. Throughout the sessions, the rhythm section was more subdued and unified, providing greater support for the sections and soloists. While the saxophone section still lacked imaginative, strong soloists, the brass section had gained an impressive get-off soloist in Paul Webster, who contributed inventive muted trumpet solos on "Oh Eddie!," "New Moten Stomp," "That Too, Do," and "As Long As I Have You." Basie steps out of the rhythm section for confident piano solos on "Oh Eddie!," "Mack's Rhythm," "That Too, Do," and "You Made Me Happy," and pays tribute to one of his principal influences, Fats Waller, by scatting brightly through "Somebody Stole My Gal." The title of Basie's composition "The Count," recorded during the session, foreshadows his later self-appointed ascent to jazz royalty.

A versatile song stylist, Jimmy Rushing moved effortlessly between the popular standard "Liza Lee" and the blues "That Too, Do." Following a six-bar modulation by the full band and an interlude, featuring a round of solos, Rushing nimbly glides through the lighthearted lyrics of "Liza Lee." His impassioned delivery of "That Too, Do" captures the blue mood of the chorus: "sent for you yesterday, here you come today, baby you can't love me and treat me that a way." The sympathetic instrumental accompaniment by Webster, Basie, and other band members underscores Rushing's deep feeling for the blues. The Moten band fared well from the session, with Victor rejecting only one selection, "Break O' Day Shuffle," rendered in the old Kansas City stomp-'em-down style favored by the dancers at the break-o'-day dances.

Preparing for a major eastern tour to support the new recordings, Moten engaged Broadway producer Aaron Gates to liven up and polish the band's stage show. Gates added veteran tap dancers Roy Ellis and Billy Grayson to keep the show rolling between sets. Dressing up the band's presentation, he fashioned costumes and designed choreography for the band and Jimmy Rushing. Moten premiered the new stage show during a week-long run at the Mainstreet Theatre in early January 1931. Earl Wilkins, sneaking in with the band opening night, gave readers of his "Dance Gossip" column a glimpse of the band's new stage show:

> The act ahead finishes, the rear curtain goes up, the lights blare on the boys in the orchestra, and they cut loose with a hot number which is guaranteed to take the roof off. And it darn near does! The audience claps and roars as the band swings into its second number. Bus Moten is out front, dapper as always, cutting with that baton, pressing the band to better and better efforts. They swing into "Travelin," and Rushing steps out from the wings to do the vocalization. He is dressed in blue overalls, an old gray hat, and wears a red bandanna about his neck: over his shoulder he sports a stick with a bundle tied in an old handker-

chief. Slowly he sidles across the stage as he sings the number. As he finishes, he skips off the stage, and the house comes down with applause. Then Grayson and Ellis strut out for their fast tap-dancing number. They get a big hand from the audience in their two appearances. And so the ever-hotter music goes on for the thirty minutes that the band plays.[41]

The heartfelt response from the hometown audience at the Mainstreet bode well for the band's upcoming eastern tour.

In late February, the Moten band took off eastward. Vivian Winn Basie and other band wives joined nearly a hundred well-wishers jamming the sidewalk in front of the Moten-Hayes music shop. With driver Lyman Darden at the wheel of the new bus, the band worked its way east, playing theaters and ballrooms. Oran "Lips" Page joined the band in Dayton, Ohio, more than ably filling the first trumpet chair vacated by Paul Webster earlier in the year. Page joined Rushing in the spotlight, doubling as an entertainer and principal get-off soloist. At the Graystone Ballroom in Cincinnati, the band battled Edwards' Collegians before an audience of 4,000, a skirmish broadcast nationally. Thamon Hayes reported to the *Kansas City Call* the perils of the band's adventures on the road east, ranging from a date at one juke joint in Louisville with "many a fight with plenty of whisky bottles in evidence and the who struck John, which follows too free imbibing" to a journey "over mountainous road with a flock of sharp curves and yawning valleys waiting beneath to make everybody nervous."[42]

Arriving in Baltimore, the Moten band bumped into the Clouds of Joy. After closing at the Roseland, the Kirk band had stayed mainly in the East, touring New York and New England. While on the road, the band went through a near complete turnover of the rhythm section. Impressed by Eddie Durham's pioneering guitar technique, Kirk asked violinist Claude Williams to step back in the rhythm section and concentrate on guitar. Williams resisted, preferring to solo on the violin. When Williams fell ill, the band left him and his violin behind. Bill Dirvin, equally adept on banjo and guitar, agreed to set down his banjo in favor of the guitar. The band suffered a setback with the loss of drummer Edward "Crackshot" McNeil to health problems. A master percussionist, McNeil's flashy bell and chimes work charmed the audiences, while his easy roll moved the Clouds smoothly along.[43] Ben Thigpen, a dependable timekeeper, replaced McNeil. Mary Lou Williams joined as a full-time member after Kirk finally put aside his reservations about having a woman in the band. At first, she played piano duets with Marion Jackson, similar to Moten and Basie in the Moten band. Finally, during an engagement at the Pearl Theater, Kirk let Jackson go and Williams assumed leadership of the rhythm section, becoming the Clouds of Joy's shining star.

At the Pearl Theater, the band joined forces with Cab Calloway's older sister, Blanche. An experienced entertainer, brimming with personality,

Calloway stepped into leadership of the group on-stage, easily eclipsing vo-calist and director Billy Massey. Sam Steiffel, the owner of the Pearl and Blanche's manager, aspired to use her association with Cab, then the hottest ticket in the business, to build a power base similar to Moe Gale, the owner of the Savoy in New York. Gale required acts booked into the Savoy to sign contracts with his management agency, steadily building an impressive stable of artists. Seeking to follow suit, Steiffel attempted to maneuver Blanche into leadership of the Clouds of Joy.

Steiffel's scheme came to light when upcoming engagements for Blanche at the Pearl Theater listed the band as Blanche Calloway and her own Twelve Clouds of Joy. "Steiffel . . . decided she looked good with the band behind her," Kirk recalled. "I was playing tuba then and we didn't have a front man except Billy Massey, our vocalist. . . . Steiffel placed two extra men in my band who were supposed to try and talk them into going with Blanche and leaving me."[44]

Just as Calloway's takeover of the Clouds of Joy seemed inevitable, Moten unwittingly came to Kirk's rescue. While comparing notes in Baltimore, Moten informed Kirk that Local 627 wanted the Clouds of Joy to fill a seasonal en-gagement at Winnwood Beach, a summer resort north of Kansas City. Wary of Steiffel's attempt to take over the Clouds of Joy, Kirk and loyal band mem-bers split with Calloway and worked their way back to Kansas City. On the way out, Kirk recommended Jap Allen as a replacement band to Calloway. Acting on the tip, she immediately sent for tenor saxophonist Ben Webster, pianist Clyde Hart, and other Allen band members to form the nucleus of her new band.

As the Clouds of Joy pulled back to Kansas City, the Moten band forged on playing a string of increasingly prestigious one-nighters down and back up the East Coast. Premiering in Washington, D.C., the Moten band played the Masonic Temple. Band members lingered in Washington for a little sight-seeing, touring Howard University and visiting the top of the Washington Monument. Moving on to Wilmington, Delaware, they learned the steps to a new dance sensation, the Lindy Hop, named in honor of Charles Lindbergh. In Philadelphia, the band opened at the Pearl Theater against heavy compe-tition from Dave Peyton, Horace Henderson, Fletcher Henderson, and Noble Sissle, all playing in the area at the same time. The Pearl hailed the Moten band as "The Hottest Band this side of Hades." The motif extended to the band's music stands adorned with little devils. True to its billing, the Moten band packed the Pearl for two shows daily. Writing to Earl Wilkins, Thamon Hayes marveled how "the aisles of the theater were packed and that people stood in line for a block for tickets."[45]

The Moten band opened at the Savoy Ballroom in New York during the first week of April, sharing a triple bill with the San Domingo Band and Cato's Orchestra. The high-stepping dancers at the Savoy loved the band's western stomp style, because it differed from the eastern bands. Gates's choreography brought the band's stage presentation closer to par with the elaborate stage shows featured by the eastern bands. Rushing's version of "Rocking Chair" and the dancing of Ellis and Grayson delighted the audience. Band members knew they had truly arrived when the manager of the Savoy threw a party in their honor, inviting Cab Calloway, Fletcher Henderson, and Chick Webb. Savoring the sights and sounds of Harlem, Moten, Basie, and other band members proudly strutted up and down Seventh Avenue, rubbing elbows with the uptown crowd on Striver's Row.

The band opened a week-long run at the Lafayette Theater on Saturday, April 11. Advance publicity in the *New York Age* proclaimed the band "one of the greatest colored orchestras in the country. The most extravagant claims are being made for this band. Irvin and Flournoy Miller went to see the band perform in Philadelphia last week and expressed the opinion that they are greater than Duke Ellington's Orchestra. . . . The twenty member band have been hard at work rehearsing the music for the show so they will render as well as their famous 'specialties.'"[46] Featured with the revue "Rhythm Bound," the Moten band lived up to its press. Two weeks later, the *New York Age* reported the bands recently featured at the Lafayette including Duke Ellington, Cab Calloway, Fletcher Henderson, Blanche Calloway, Charlie Johnson, Noble Sissle, Bennie Moten, Marion Hardy, and Luis Russell, "have all been well received."[47] The ranking of the Moten band in the *New York Age* amounted to more than hype. Connie's Inn and the Savoy Ballroom offered the band steady employment, but Moten declined, choosing instead to return to Kansas City for a summer engagement at Fairyland Park. Harry Duncan, the park's manager, needed a surefire attraction to fill Fairyland's ballroom, which had seen better days. Out of loyalty to Duncan, Moten took the engagement at Fairyland rather than staying in New York. Unfortunately, the decision to return to Kansas City proved to be a poor choice for the band.

The Clouds of Joy drifted into Kansas City ahead of the Moten band. Band members gratefully returned home after what Mary Lou Williams described as "what seemed like a year of one-nighters."[48] In mid-May, the Clouds of Joy opened at Winnwood Beach, a summer resort located eight miles northeast of Kansas City. A medium-sized resort, known as "the Atlantic City of the West," Winnwood featured thirty-five acres of waterways, amusement rides, a sideshow, a boardwalk complete with a spacious ballroom stretching out over the swimming lake, modeled after the one in Atlantic City. Small rental cabins dotted the grounds, and families flocked to them seeking relief from the heat and humidity of Kansas City. Road weary, the Clouds of Joy gladly settled down for the summer engagement at Winnwood Beach, savoring the opportunity for a little rest and relaxation.

The Moten band returned to Kansas City a few weeks later. Fortified by the successful eastern tour, the band sported a new musical poise and confidence. Reviewing the homecoming dance at Paseo Hall, the *Kansas City Call* noted the band's newfound savoir faire, singling out Lips Page's crowd-pleasing mugging. "The band is undeniably better than ever. It seems to have a new confidence and assurance which give it the true snap of the big time bands. The new trumpet player, Orrin [Oran] 'Lips' Page, was an instant hit with the dancers."[49] More than an entertainer, Page's broad range and musical sophistication enabled Durham to extend the band's harmonic reach.

Initially, adding Page's voice to the band posed a challenge for Durham. "I was playing valve trombone in order to help the trumpets," Durham explained.

> I worked very hard, playing awful high with the trumpets to give a three-trumpet effect, then switching back to make a two-trombone sound. There was a lot of pressure on the brass, but those guys wouldn't play a sixth or ninth chord. They were playing the fifth, tonic, and third, and they couldn't hear the sixth. So then Moten brought Lips Page into the band. "What's he gonna play?" the guys wanted to know. "He's all right, but we don't need another horn." Then I stepped the band up to ninth chords, and they could hear a ninth better than they could a sixth. Lips was pretty true on his horn and he could hear the sixth, so I gave him that and played the ninth myself. That's how we started getting five-part harmony in the brass, and they came to see why we had needed another horn. There was nobody playing *their* note, where before they'd been saying "you playin' my note? Get off my note!"[50]

Moten readily reestablished his domination of Kansas City's top venues, playing nightly at Fairyland and staging regular Saturday-night break-o'-day dances at Paseo Hall. Feeling his oats, Moten challenged McKinney's Cotton Pickers to a battle of the bands at Paseo Hall. Moten publicly expressed confidence in the band's readiness to compete with top national bands in an interview with Earl Wilkins. "Before I took the band east in the spring, the fellows felt that they were pretty good, but they didn't have complete confidence in themselves," Moten confided.

> They had heard so much about the good bands around New York that they weren't at all certain that they could measure up to the pace set by the big fellows. They then went east and all. Kansas City knows what happened. The folks out there were kind enough to give the band a great big hand wherever it went. For some reason they liked us a lot. That treatment gave the fellows confidence. They feel that now they are in a class with the best of them. They have been working hard and are prepared to meet anyone. I am not forgetting that McKinney has a very, very good band. We just don't feel afraid of them, that's all. We are going to prove once and for all for the home folks that our band, which they have patronized so generously can hold its own with anyone. We will all feel cheap if we don't win and you can just bet that we'll all be fighting and playing the best kind of jazz we know how.[51]

Publicly throwing down the gauntlet, Moten put his reputation on the line.

The Moten band locked horns with McKinney's Cotton Pickers in late June. Despite intense heat that was blamed for four deaths earlier in the day, 1,300 people attended the event. The Cotton Pickers carried a majority of the evening, playing from 9 P.M. until 12:45 A.M. Arriving late from Fairyland Park, the Moten band played seven or eight numbers to the apathetic crowd sapped by the heat. Earl Wilkins declared no victor in his "Dance Gossip" column, but cryptically quoted an anonymous correspondent who signed herself "public sentiment," who felt "McKinney played much better than Bennie and that Bennie got 'well oiled.'"[52]

Stung by the public humiliation, Moten began seriously considering changes in the band's lineup. However, faced with a forty-five-week tour of the East, Moten, for the time being, maintained the status quo.

The Moten band left Kansas City in mid-September, traveling caravan style with some band members driving their own cars behind the band bus. A few band wives joined their husbands on the trip. Basie, accompanied by Vivian, drove his new Pontiac roadster. Although, Vivian, put off by Basie's drinking and carousing, left the tour midway and abruptly returned to Kansas City. The tour, booked by Sam Steiffel, covered much of the same territory as the band's spring trip. Working its way to New York, the band played ballrooms and theaters in major cities en route. On the East Coast, the band joined a five-band tour. Basie felt the band more than held its own with other bands. "The special tour that Associated Colored Orchestra concern had set up was advertised as a 'Battle of Music.' It featured five big dance orchestras playing against each other on the same bill," Basie recalled.

> The other four were Chick Webb, representing New York; Blanche Calloway, representing Washington; Zack Whyte from Cincinnati; and Johnson's Happy Pals from down in Richmond, Virginia. . . . [T]hose five bands created a lot of excitement and got us some good newspaper publicity, especially when we played Pittsburgh. . . . They really liked the Moten band in Pittsburgh. The *Courier* gave us big headlines on the entertainment page and ran a big picture of the whole band on stage to announce that the Battle of Music was a coming event at the Knights of Pythias Temple in October. Then a few weeks later, the same picture was printed again to announce that we were coming back for a one-night stand, and that was also when the *Courier* said that Bennie Moten's band had won the Battle of Music at the Pythias temple the week before by popular demand.[53]

The band did not fare as well with audiences in New York. Arriving in New York, the Moten band played a white R.K.O. theater downtown and the Savoy Ballroom before opening a week-long engagement at the Lafayette in mid-December. Ed Lewis disclosed how New York dance fans expecting to hear the western stomp-down style gave the band a cool reception. "The real mistake he [Moten] made was when he went East and played the same stuff the eastern bands were playing for years! He was a flop, because the people expected the same western music he was famous for, and in fact we almost got stranded. It was the saddest thing he ever did." Lewis added that the decision to emulate the eastern bands sparked a dispute between the old guard and the former Blue Devils, ending with four long-time members receiving their walking papers. "That was one of the factors that caused the band to split up," Lewis divulged. "Bennie gave notice to four guys: Vernon Page on tuba, Woodie Walder, Harlan Leonard, and Booker Washington. There was a clique of guys in the band that wanted to bring their friends in, and Bennie went along with them."[54] By mid-January 1932, rumors of the changes filtered back to Kansas City, prompting a denial by Earl Wilkins, in the *Kansas City Call*. "There are a number of stories circulating about Bennie Moten's outfit. I have looked into them too, and I can report that: (1) Bennie's band is now in New York; (2) that the band is intact and has not even considered breaking up; and (3) that no members of the band have come home as has been reported."[55]

Already embroiled in turmoil, the band suffered a devastating financial blow when Steiffel failed to pay members three weeks of back wages for the New York engagements. Acting quickly, Moten barely averted financial disaster by filing a grievance with the local union in New York. Breaking with Steiffel, Moten engaged Maceo Birch, an experienced showman, to book and manage the band. On the return trip to Kansas City, the band stopped in Chicago for dates at the Paradise Theater and the Grand Terrace, filling in for Earl Hines. While in Chicago, Moten hired Ben Webster and alto saxophonist Eddie Barefield to replace Walder and Leonard. Webster, hoboing back to Kansas City from a brief stint with Blanche Calloway, and Barefield, stranded in Chicago after a dispute with the Chicago musicians union, eagerly joined the band. For Woody Walder and Harlan Leonard, being replaced while traveling with the band added insult to injury.

On the heels of the band's return to Kansas City in early February 1932, Thamon Hayes and Ed Lewis registered their displeasure by resigning in solidarity with Walder, Leonard, Booker Washington, and Vernon Page, bringing to a close the first great Bennie Moten band. The changes came at a great cost. The disaffected musicians regrouped and haunted Moten with a vengeance, undermining his dominance of Kansas City and the Midwest region and causing his band to spend an inordinate amount of time on the road when jobs were scarce. Ironically, in the end, Moten's dream of success in the East, which had originally prompted the changes in the band's style and personnel, proved to be only that—a dream dissipated in the harsh realities of the growing Depression.

6

Moten's Swing

AFTER RELUCTANTLY ACCEPTING Ed Lewis's and Thamon Hayes's resignations, Bennie Moten patched the band back together with top-notch players. Elmer Crumbley, a yeoman trombonist, replaced Hayes. Joe Keyes and Joe Smith joined Lips Page, rounding out the trumpet section. Keyes, a skilled section player and strong soloist when sober, joined the band following a brief stint with Blanche Calloway. Smith, noted for his stage antics and outstanding muted trumpet style, came aboard from McKinney's Cotton Pickers. Moten scored a real coup when Walter Page joined the band.[1] Over the years, Basie, Durham, Rushing, and Moten had tried their best to recruit Page, to no avail.

In early February 1932, Page finally relented and became a member of the Moten band, on the heels of a turn of fortune by the Blue Devils. In early December 1930, the Blue Devils closed out a long-term engagement at the Ritz Ballroom in Oklahoma City and launched a tour of the northern territories, sponsored by the National Orchestra Service, a small firm based in Omaha. The band returned to Kansas City in the fall of 1931 for an extended engagement at the White House Tavern, a rambling white-washed roadhouse out in the county at 82nd and Troost. While playing at the White House, the band suffered a major loss with the death of trumpeter Harry Smith, Bill Basie's old comrade from the Gonzelle White days. Following the breakup of the White show, Smith, a spirited soloist and experienced entertainer but hard drinker, bounced around, working briefly with Chauncey Downs and Jap Allen before hitting the road with Victoria Spivey's road show. Back in Kansas City for a big 1930 New Year's Eve celebration at Paseo Hall, Smith left Spivey's revue for the Blue Devils, succeeding Lips Page. An apt replacement, Smith, earlier on, had greatly influenced Page's style and stage manner.[2] With the band for less than a year, the trumpeter reportedly died on his knees in the Booker T Hotel on December 29, 1931, of acute alcoholism. Walter Page, Smith's third cousin, lost a relative, close friend, and the band's main get-off soloist.

Page replaced Smith with a brash, young hotshot trumpeter, setting in motion a chain of events that eventually led to his resignation as leader of the Blue Devils. "We got better and better and by 1931 I felt it was time to make the big time. We made up our minds we were going to make it to New York and we started out that way but something happened," Page disclosed.

> I had big ideas then, and wasn't asleep, because we put aside money in the treasury, had two new touring cars, two dress uniforms, good instruments and a great band. We played a fifteen-week engagement for National Orchestra Service and then I worked a gig at the White Horse [House] Tavern in Kansas City. I was having some trouble with one of my trumpet players. He was a half-breed and used to get juiced a lot. I used to teach him his music everyday, until he became like my son. I drilled him on trumpet and he had a beautiful tone . . . taught him his accents and I never played trumpet in my life. I put him in first chair and he made it. We all used to date white girls up in Sioux City because there wasn't much discrimination and he got in some trouble with one of them. I wanted to take him out of the band and get a replacement and was trying to get Jim Youngblood, a great piano player away from T Holder's Clouds of Joy, who were playing in Des Moines at the time. This trumpet player caused me to lose Youngblood because he couldn't get along with him and when I sent a wire telling Youngblood to forget about the job, he turns around and goes to the white local in Des Moines and files a complaint through the national head-quarters. After I finished up my stay at the White Horse [House] I report to local 627 in Kansas City, and what was staring me in the face, international blackball . . . $250.00 fine. With the money I was sending home to my wife and three kids back in Oklahoma City plus paying off the fine, I didn't have any money left so I turned the band over to [James] Simpson and told him to fill our engagements. . . . I struggled around with some four- and five-piece com-bos in hotels there and finally got a big offer to join Bennie Moten. . . . Bennie wasn't doing so good himself when I joined, although his new band was better than his other one. . . . Even though Moten raided my own band before, he had one of the biggest hearts I know of.[3]

The rhythm section, led by Page, playing four beats to the bar on the string bass, in favor of the bass horn, which was limited to a two-beat rhythm, gave the new Moten band a looser, freer swinging style.

Eddie Durham underscored Page's vital contribution to the band's new style. "I remember when the band started swinging. . . . Walter Page had played sousaphone, but he played good baritone saxophone, too, and he started doubling on baritone and bass with the Blue Devils. . . . [T]hen I got an idea about the rhythm. 'Who wants a bass fiddle in a band?' everybody wanted to know. They preferred sousaphone in a dancehall because you could hear it better. Without amplification, a lot of guys weren't strong enough on bass fiddle. But Walter Page you could hear! He was like a house with a note," Durham exclaimed. "He didn't have the best ear, but he worked hard, and the string bass was in demand. How was his sound produced? I think it's in the coordination of the stroke in the head. The bass is one of the greatest things in the world for rhythm, but instead, of writing a two-beat bass on the fifth tonic, I kept it moving on chromatics to the chord. It sounded good, but when they saw it on paper, musicians said, 'This has gotta be out of tune!' Walter Page is the guy that created that walkin', walkin' [bass]."[4] Page's powerful, fluid string bass playing combined with the walking bass line revolutionized the Moten band's rhythm and allowed them to truly swing for the first time.

Moten, delighted with the new lineup but concerned about Kansas City fans' reaction to the departure of long-time band members, justified the personnel changes in an interview with Earl Wilkins published in the *Kansas City Call*. "As people in Kansas City know, I have always tried to keep my orchestra upon a high level," Moten asserted. "I have done my best to make improvements wherever I could do so with benefit. This new change, although it removes some faces which are familiar to dance fans here, is, I believe a move for the better. It is my intention to keep ever striving for greater and greater perfection. Only by following that course can I keep faith with the hundreds of friends this band has—friends who expect us to keep going up the ladder of national recognition." Moten concluded on a note of goodwill toward Hayes and other former band members. "Thamon and, for that matter the rest of the boys too, are still on good terms with me and I wish them well."[5]

In the same issue of the *Kansas City Call*, Hayes confirmed the end of his eleven-year association with Moten and announced the formation of his new band. Hayes publicly echoed Moten's statement of continued friendship, tempered by the fact he intended to compete with Moten. "Bennie and I are still good friends. I am sure that even though we are now competitors, we will continue to be on most cordial terms."[6] The public display of goodwill masked Hayes's antipathy for Moten. Wasting little time, Hayes assembled a new band to exact his revenge.

Building on the core of musicians cast-off from the Moten band, Hayes added Richard Smith to the trumpet section. Lanky with high cheeks and an infectious smile, Smith joined the band from Harold Jones's Brownskin Syncopators in Lincoln, Nebraska. Originally from Kansas City, Smith graduated with a degree in pharmacology from the University of Iowa before launching his music career. In mid-February, Hayes raided the George E. Lee band in New Orleans, sending bus fares to drummer Samuel "Baby" Lovett, saxophonist Herman Walder, and, most importantly, the gifted arranger, composer, and pianist Jesse Stone. Sick of traveling great distances between engagements for little pay, the three readily abandoned the Lee band.

"He [George Lee] heard about us getting these tickets and we had to hide out from him," Herman Walder reported. "We saw George Lee pulling up beside us, like he's gonna make us get off the bus, or something like that. But man, we got dug down in the seat . . . and slipped out."[7] Lastly, Vic Dickenson, a gangly veteran trombonist, formerly with the Zack Whyte band in Cincinnati, joined, bringing the band up to the standard twelve members.

Stone rehearsed the new band in secret at Thamon Hayes's house. Band members kept a low profile, waiting to ambush Moten at the mammoth musicians ball staged by Local 627 at Paseo Hall on March 7, 1932.[8] The union lined up nine bands for the event: Bennie Moten, Simpson's Blue Devils, Andy Kirk, Jap Allen and His Famous St. Louis Band, Paul Banks, A. C. Hayden and His Night Owls, George E. Lee and His New Recorders, Bill Little, and the Thamon Hayes band. Hyping the upcoming battle, the *Kansas City Call* touted the Hayes band as the "new wonder band of accomplished musicians. First appearance!"[9]

Musical director Jesse Stone drilled the Hayes band rigorously, preparing for the upcoming battle with the Moten band. "We were rehearsing from the beginning I think three days a week, finally added another day, and then as we neared our first time playing we rehearsed five days a week," Stone divulged. "Every rehearsal was from a half hour to an hour of class. [We covered] progressions, chord instruction, and all types of things. They would ask me questions and I would try to answer. They would even ask me musical history, how things evolved, and I taught them scale formation, and how the scale is based on steps, how chords are derived from the tones on the scale. . . . I drilled them more than George Lee's group because we had such a short time to get ready." Grinning, Stone added, "[W]e had something to look forward to."[10]

Band members wanted their unveiling to be a "Cinderella thing." Harlan Leonard's mother-in-law provided the finery for the ball, buying the band brown Eaton uniforms with yellow lapels and stripes down the side of the pants.[11] Kansas City's musical community eagerly anticipated the band's debut. The *Kansas City Call* reported: "One of the acknowledged features of the evening will be the first appearance of Thamon Hayes and his band. This organization is composed of men well known for their work in other orchestras here in Kansas City. They were assembled only recently but hard rehearsal work has smoothed them down already to the status of an obviously good band. Their debut is being watched with unconcealed interest by dancers and musicians alike."[12]

Premiering at the musician's ball, surrounded by friends and admirers, the Hayes band took the stage by storm, blowing away the Moten band. Earl Wilkins fairly gushed over the Hayes band's performance:

> Judged solely by popular acclaim the feature of the evening was the first appearance of Thamon Hayes and his band. Going on late at something after

midnight, the Hayes band received from the crowd such an ovation as has rarely been tendered any orchestra ever to play the hall. When Maceo Birch, master of ceremonies, announced that the next band to play would be Thamon Hayes and his band, the crowd went wild. There were hoarse cries, shrill whistles, staccato hand clapping, and thuddings of feet on the floor. Nattily attired in new uniforms of rich tan with shirts and ties to match, this new band made a pleasing appearance. Before they started their stunt, the crowd insisted that Thamon Hayes, the organizer, take a bow. And then the Hayes group swung into its numbers. The dancers were interested. They stopped dancing and milled about the platform to watch. They crowded the balcony rail, straining to see the men in action. The first number rocked them, and they went into frenzies before the Hayes band had finished. There were cries of "Play it boy!" "Listen to those fellows go!" "They've really got a band, haven't they?" The Hayes organization has a pleasing combination of the kind of rhythm which has made Bennie Moten's orchestra famous, and the trick style which has stood George Lee in such good stead. Their one novelty number, an imitation of an old-fashioned Holy Roller meeting, with the lead trumpet "preaching" and the lead trombone "praying" turned the dancers into admiring watchers.[13]

Members of the Moten band, overconfident and drunk, found the Hayes band a hard act to follow. Eddie Barefield clearly recalled the circumstances leading to Hayes's rout of the Moten band. "They had all these bands over there and all the fine girls were out and everything, and Bennie Moten's band was going to play last because he was considered to be the king around Kansas City," Barefield related.

So we go over to the hall, and everybody's playing. But of course, most of the crowd is waiting for Bennie's band. They're the big shots. So we are there, but we are not really paying any attention to anybody else. We're too busy socializing, but then just before the time for us to go on, Thamon Hayes went on, and Big Ed Lewis and those guys took off, and they were knocking the back out of that place, and they really were going over big with the crowd. Meanwhile, with all that socializing, when the time came for us to go up there and wipe everybody out, just about everybody in Bennie's band was drunk. We couldn't get ourselves together to save our lives that night. Eddie Durham was drunk. Jack Washington was sick. Ben Webster was drunk. Basie was drunk. Lips was drunk. The whole brass section was drunk and of course, Joe Keys [Keyes] was completely cut. We went up there on that stage and stumbled through something, but Thamon and those cats tore us up that night.[14]

Hayes's band member Booker Washington recalled chaos erupting on the bandstand during the Moten band's set. "Bennie Moten got up on the bandstand after we finished playing, and his band got into a fight. The trumpet player, Joe Smith, and another person in the band got into a fight up on the bandstand."[15]

Hayes graciously credited band members for the evening's victory in the *Kansas City Call.* "The fellows have all worked hard in the past and will continue to do so to give the public the very best we've got. Much of the credit for the band's achievement so far must go to Jesse Stone, the director, who is handling our arrangements."[16] The Hayes band found favor with Kansas City audiences, playing regularly at Paseo Hall and major social events in the community, including the annual fashion show at Convention Hall and the Easter Dance at the Labor Temple. In mid-May the Hayes band opened for the season at Fairyland Park, an engagement held by the Moten band the two previous summers.

The Moten band, still reeling from the fiasco at the Musicians' Ball, embarked on a six-week tour of the South. Stopping at the Casino Ballroom in Memphis, the band presented a new composition, "Love," to W. C. Handy, the Father of the Blues. Swinging across the South, the band played Oklahoma City and Shreveport, Louisiana, and then barnstormed across Texas, where they performed at major hotels and ballrooms. Writing to Earl Wilkins from Beaumont, Basie praised the band's new hot trombonist Dan Minor, formerly with Alphonso Trent, and assured the readers of the *Kansas City Call* "that the organization was working hard and improving all the time."[17]

Earl Wilkins, reviewing the band's homecoming dance in late April at Paseo Hall, noted the band's increased unity and showmanship. "On his tour, he [Moten] rehearsed steadily to make his new members a smoothly working unit in their cooperation with the older members of the band. Joe Smith on the trumpet is a real find for anyone's band. His antics with his muted instrument left the dancers asking for more. Dan Minor, the new trombone player, is another man who worked well. The way Walter Page handles his bass viol is a feature which was well received. Bus Moten, director, has unlimbered even more since I last saw him. His sinuous jiggling and writhing is one of the things you will have to see to appreciate."[18] While on the road, Basie and Durham totally revamped the band's book, creating orchestral arrangements of "Honeysuckle Rose," "I Can't Give You Anything but Love," "I Want a Little Girl," and other popular standards. The last vestiges of the stomps, blues, and breakdowns previously featured by the band fell by the wayside. Satisfied with the overhaul of the band, Moten lined up a late-spring tour to the East, securing engagements in Indianapolis, Louisville, and Cincinnati, capped by two weeks at Coney Island and four weeks in New England.

The East Coast dates fell through, delaying the tour, as the Great Depression swept across the country, shuttering clubs and ballrooms in small and medium-sized towns. Theaters barely held their own by giving away dishes with paid admission to attract crowds. Trimming expenses, theater owners cut back on stage productions and bands. Moten, misjudging the impact of the country's economic downturn, persisted, striking a deal with the National Music Service Corporation of Cincinnati for a six-month tour of the East.

Leaving town in late June 1932, accompanied by little fanfare, the Moten band embarked on what turned out to be a long, hard trip.

While the Moten band trudged east, Hayes and Kirk prudently stayed close to home. The Hayes band spent the summer of 1932 at Fairyland Park, filling out its schedule with choice dates in the 18th and Vine area. The band broadcast nightly over KMBC from Fairyland Park, gaining broader recognition. The fledgling Columbia Broadcasting System distributed the band's Wednesday-night broadcasts to affiliates in seventeen states, stretching from the Midwest to the West Coast. In June, CBS picked up the band's broadcasts three nights a week. These pioneering network broadcasts established the Hayes band's reputation throughout the western region, creating a ready market at the conclusion of the season at Fairyland.

The Kirk band played an extended engagement at Wild Wood Lakes, a modest resort similar to Winnwood Beach. Having experienced firsthand the effects of the Depression, Kirk settled into the summer engagement, content to be a big fish in a little pond. Kirk recalled how the Clouds of Joy "just got back to Kansas City before everything dropped dead in the East. The work was still good in and around Kansas City, even though the Depression was going full blast. After that summer [1931] we went on tour through Arkansas and Oklahoma for the Malco Theatre Chain. They had a great many houses around the Southwest, but nobody had any money to go into these theaters with. . . . We gave a final concert in Memphis, which was John Williams' home, and just did get back to Kansas City. When we got back home, there was no Depression! The town was jumping!"[19]

The bright nightlife swirled around the hundreds of saloons and nightclubs liberally sprinkled from downtown south to "out in the county," just beyond the city limits. During Prohibition, liquor flowed freely throughout the city, unchecked by local authorities. Clubs flouted state and federal laws against gambling, offering games of chance for gamblers of all stripes. When pressed, local police mounted raids, rounding up the usual suspects, more for show than law enforcement. Once downtown, the courts unceremoniously cut the suspects loose. When federal agents raided clubs, municipal judges, resenting interference by the federal government, simply dismissed the charges. Authorities, acting on numerous complaints by the *Kansas City Call*, raided the notorious East Side Musicians Club at 12th and Highland over one hundred times without securing a single conviction, before federal agents finally locked the door because of a liquor violation. "The East Side Musicians suffered a series of raids at the hands of Kansas City police, but the raiders were never able to get evidence enough to convict the club of gambling. The records of the North Side court show 106 dismissals and not a single conviction. Naturally the musicians were very sure of themselves. On the 100th raid, they set out to celebrate and made it a good one by serenading Chief of Police John L. Miles, with a band playing 'I Can't Give You Anything but Love.'"[20]

In the summer of 1932, with the Democrats running on a platform promising the repeal of Prohibition and the probable election of Franklin Delano Roosevelt, club owners hedged their bets, remodeling old haunts and opening new clubs weekly. The Hawaiian Gardens opened in mid-July at the former site of the Black and Tan Cotton Club, located on the southeast corner of Charlotte Street and Independence Avenue. Like the Black and Tan Cotton Club, the Hawaiian Gardens catered to both races but seated them in separate balconies. The Gardens advertised in the *Kansas City Call*, which in turn praised the club's decor, modeled after a Honolulu nightclub. "The tropical effects are heightened by a profusion of gorgeous palms. Soft lights wafted from Japanese lanterns enhance the oriental beauty of the place." Vocalist and entertainer Sadie McKinney, formerly with McKinney's Cotton Pickers, headlined the show, accompanied by the Hawaiian Gardens Serenaders, a seven-piece band featuring drummer Abie Price, entertainer Jimmy Ruffin, and pianist Pete Johnson. Singing bartender Joe Turner put on a show of his own behind the well-stocked bar, entertaining the crowd with his rendition of "It Don't Mean a Thing If it Haven't [sic] Got That Swing," while busily pouring drinks. Out of the chute, the club created a sensation, attracting nearly 5,000 patrons opening weekend.[21]

Pete Johnson and Joe Turner first met at the Backbiters' Club, a private club on Independence Avenue, haunted by the underworld figures. Turner, a tall strapping youth with bulging eyes and a broad toothy grin, managed to slip past the doorman and sit in with the band led by Johnson. "The windows were painted over on the inside, and during the day I sneaked in and scraped off enough paint so me and my buddies could watch the people dancing all night," Turner confided. "My brother-in-law was the doorman, and his job was to shake down the customers, search them to see if they were carryin' guns—anything like that. I couldn't get in at night with him around, but when he took another job I drew a mustache on my face with my mother's eyebrow pencil and dressed up in my daddy's hat and one of his shirts. I was already tall, and I'd slip the hat down over my eyes and go in with a crowd. The musicians would tell me, 'Go home, little boy,' but I'd bug them and say I could sing, and finally one night they let me. There was no mike in those days, but I got up there and sang the blues songs, and they were surprised I could keep time so good and that I had such a strong voice."[22] Turner's rough-and-tumble style of blues shouting perfectly complemented Johnson's two-fisted, percussive technique of boogie-woogie piano. The two formed a musical partnership, which in later years carried them to Carnegie Hall.

Native Kansas Citians, Johnson and Turner came of age, musically and otherwise, in the speakeasies lining 12th Street.[23] Growing up without fathers, they became the men of their homes at an early age. Johnson's mother, incapable of making ends meet after her husband abandoned the family, placed young Pete in an orphanage, a common practice of the day. Johnson, malnourished and neglected, escaped and made his way back home. A brawny, quiet child with big eyes and a shy smile, Johnson left school in the fifth grade to work as a manual laborer with his Uncle Charles "Smash" Johnson. A day laborer and talented pianist, Uncle Charles inspired young Pete to become a musician. "Uncle Smash was quite a pianist at that time and played the best jobs in the territory," Johnson recounted. "He was often called to play on the river boats that traveled the Missouri River, and the movie houses in and around Kansas City, where he was accompanying silent films."[24] Picking up the drums, young Johnson studied with Charles Watts before beginning his professional career accompanying pianists Ernest Nichols and Louis "Bootie" Johnson. Switching to piano, Johnson frequently sat in for "Bootie," who often drank too much and missed jobs. Johnson soon established a reputation as an up-and-coming pianist, freelancing around town, playing rent parties and saloons for drinks and tips. A childhood friend, drummer Murl Johnson often accompanied Johnson on his nightly rounds. "Pete would play the piano all night and the people would buy him drinks just to hear him play the blues," Johnson explained. "Sometimes we would go into a joint and he would play the piano to rest the man that worked there. He would always want me to play drums. We would be out all night and would not have the carfare home, which was only a nickel, and would have to walk home. As the years went by Pete began to get better and the club revues would have him play for them. Pete had a great ear as he could catch a song right away. All you had to do was hum the tune and he had it."[25]

Like Johnson, Joe Turner grew up streetwise. After losing her husband in a train accident in 1915, Turner's mother raised four-year-old Joe and his older sister Katie with the help of a large extended family. Surrounded by music at home, Turner began singing as a child. "Ever since I was a kid I had singing on my mind. I started singing around the house," Turner remembered. "We had records—Bessie Smith and Mamie Smith and Ethel Waters. . . . I used to listen to an uncle by marriage named Charlie Fisher. He played piano in a night club, and he also played on a piano in the hall downstairs in our house, which was like an apartment building. He taught me the new tunes, and I listened to two other uncles, who played guitar and banjo and violin."[26] Turner, at the age of twelve, broke both legs jumping out of a second-story window to escape a fire. Initially, doctors doubted he would ever get back up on his feet, but after a year of crawling around on the floor, Turner, a tall, powerful youth, pulled himself up on chair backs and by sheer will learned to walk again.

Leaving school in the sixth grade, Turner enrolled in an education of a different sort, apprenticing with blind street singers and jug bands on 12th Street. After finally getting his foot in the door of the Backbiters' Club, Turner stepped up professionally by joining Pete Johnson and Murl Johnson on the bandstand. Once established, the band relocated to the Black and Tan Cotton

Club. Serving double duty, Turner began his career as a singing bartender. "We moved to the Black and Tan club, which had been a furniture store and had a balcony and all," Turner detailed. "An Italian named Frankie owned the place, and he wanted to make me the manager. I said I didn't want that but I would get the entertainers and the waiters if he'd let me learn to tend bar. The bartender was Kingfish, and he was older. Part of my job was to get the bootleg whiskey and part was to take off my apron and sing with the band when things were quiet. Kansas City was wide open, and sometimes the last show would begin at five in the morning."[27] Joe and Pete got along well with the gangsters who owned the Black and Tan. When the club closed and re-opened as the Hawaiian Gardens, they remained at their posts behind the bar and at the piano.

The mobsters who lorded over the clubs on 12th and 18th Streets regarded musicians as little more than fixtures, on par with bar stools and pianos. Musicians served at the club owners' pleasure, subject to abrupt mood swings, ranging from generous to lethal. Intimidated by the owners of the Hawaiian Gardens, bandleader Abie Price bought a handgun for protection. When Price accidentally shot off several of his toes, the leadership of the band fell to Pete Johnson. Joe Turner, billed in advertisements in the *Kansas City Call* as the "singing bartender," shared the spotlight with Johnson. The blatant disregard of the Volstead Act prompted action by federal agents. Temporarily putting a damper on Kansas City's nightlife, the feds shut down eleven clubs, including the Hawaiian Gardens, Kit Kat Club, Scotland Yard, and the Subway Cabaret. Johnson and other band members were arrested in the Hawaiian Gardens raid. When federal agents subpoenaed Johnson, on the advice of the owners of the Hawaiian Gardens, he refused to testify. The not-so-fortunate Turner landed in jail. Musicians playing in big bands at the resorts and amusement parks across town escaped the legal indignities suffered by Johnson, Turner, and the other freelancers who worked the joints on 12th and 18th Streets.

With the Moten band on the road in the East, Hayes and Kirk enjoyed free rein over top jobs in Kansas City and the Midwest. Well aware of the effects of the Depression, they chose out-of-town dates judiciously. Closing out the Fairyland Park engagement in late August, the Hayes band toured the western territory, concentrating on states covered by the KMBC broadcasts. The Clouds of Joy, after concluding the summer season at Wild Wood Lakes, played an engagement at the Arena in Denver to a packed house. The band's new vocalist, Pha Terrell, enchanted Denver audiences. Reed thin with an incredibly high range, Terrell became a band member in Kansas City right before the Denver trip. Specializing in torch songs and popular standards, Terrell's vocal approach suited the polished style of the Clouds of Joy. Kirk credited Terrell with the band's ensuing acclaim. "Pha Terrell's vocals helped make our band successful right from the start when we were getting big nationally. He was a Kansas City boy, working as a hoofer and muscle man fronting for some joint on 18th Street owned by one of the syndicates in town in the early thirties," Kirk related. "Leo Davis, who was with me in Morrison's band back in Denver . . . told me about him and to go down and listen to him. I heard him do one number and thought he would go well with the band, and asked him if he would like to join. He was very happy that I asked him because he was just around twenty-one then. I made him the front man and he could sing a good jazz tune when he wanted, but all he had to do was to hear those girls swoon when he sang ballads like 'Dedicated to You,' and that was it; he didn't sing anything else then. The boys in the band used to kid him about his high voice, and they thought he was soft because of that, but they soon found out. He wouldn't say much, just went into action, and that was it. He was a real ladies man and a great singer."[28] Between short tours of the Midwest, the Kirk and Hayes bands returned to the security of Kansas City.

In contrast, the Moten band's long trip east led to near disaster. After leaving Kansas City, the band spent two months in Ohio, playing Akron, Dayton, Irontown, and Cincinnati. While in Ohio, Moten fleshed out the band's stage show, adding the Sterling Russell vocal trio and Josephine Garrison, a multi-talented entertainer. The National Music Service Corporation booked mostly one-night stands, forcing the band to travel great distances between dates for little pay. Worse yet, National failed to secure sufficient dates to carry the band to the East Coast. Moten contemplated canceling the eastern leg of the trip after an engagement at the Graystone Ballroom in Dayton, but instead decided to forge ahead to the Pearl Theater in Philadelphia. Moten traveled ahead of the band, hustling up jobs along the way. Basie recalled the band's hard journey east. "I don't know how many towns we hit during the next five or six weeks of that trip as we barnstormed our way east again. But we got stranded in quite a few of them," Basie remarked. "That don't mean that we were not having a ball or anything like that. It just means that we'd come into a town and play a great gig and then we wouldn't know where the hell we were going next. So we'd have to stay there until Bennie and the advance man came up with another arrangement somewhere. Then we would pack up and roll again. Of course, we were not eating a lot of steak and chicken dinners during those times. It was more like hot dogs, sardines and crackers, or cheese and crackers, and soda pop and bootleg whiskey, things like that."[29]

Arriving in Philadelphia in early December, the band opened at the Pearl Theater. After the first week, the owner Sam Steiffel pulled Moten aside and complained about the band's limited repertoire. Frantic for new material, Moten asked Basie and Durham to work up a couple of new compositions. Repairing to the basement, Basie and Durham fashioned a head arrangement, "Moten's Swing," based on the changes to the popular standard, "You're Driving Me Crazy." The catchy new number hit with audiences, stopping the show nightly. Band members, anticipating their first full pay in some time, spent lavishly, putting everything from lodging to drinks on their tabs. Instead they came up empty handed on payday. During a previous engagement at the Pearl, Moten borrowed money from Stieffel for new band uniforms. Stieffel collected the debt by attaching the band's wages and impounding the bus. Luckily, Moten met a local booking agent, Archie Robinson, who generously squired the band around in an ancient bus.

From Philadelphia, the band traveled to Camden, New Jersey, to record for Victor. Eddie Barefield vividly recalled the band's increasingly desperate circumstances. "Now we were all very hungry, but somewhere or other Archie found a rabbit. We pulled off the highway to a pool hall, where they made a big tub of stew with this one rabbit. I always figured it was a cat, because I couldn't understand where he'd find a rabbit in Philadelphia or Camden," Barefield confided. "Take the head off and you wouldn't be able to tell the difference. I always made a joke of it and kidded Basie about having had some cat stew. Anyway, it tasted very good. We stood around the pool table sopping up the gravy and stuff with bread until the tub was empty, and then we went over to the church they used as a studio."[30]

Entering the studio in Camden on December 13, 1932, the Moten band recorded ten selections in one marathon session. Eddie Barefield's "Toby" and Basie and Durham's "Moten's Swing" displayed a rare brilliance and originality. Although the band consciously emulated the style of the eastern bands on stage, these two selections transcend that influence to create a vigorous hard-swinging style. Eddie Barefield attributed the stylistic difference to the use of riffs and head arrangements. "We cooked up a lot of 'head' arrangements," Barefield reported. "If someone knew the melody, we'd play that first. Then Ben [Webster] would take a solo, and I might take one. Lips Page would come down next and play ten, fifteen or twenty choruses, while we set up riffs behind, a different riff for each chorus. . . . [T]he reason the Moten band was so much looser was because it had so little written material. The playing was freer, but we didn't just grab a bunch of notes and play 'em without any division. No matter how many notes you play, you divide them into some kind of form. The music has to be divided and accented. . . . [T]he way we played on those records, with those fast tempos, was the way we played every night. We didn't have any music, but we sure used to swing!"[31]

The accented brass and reed sections gave the band a more aggressive and expansive sound, particularly on "Moten's Swing" and the popular standard "Blue Room," in which the sections totally absorb and elaborate on Richard Rodger's original theme, building to a climax of riffs that totally transcend the melody in a joyous out-chorus.[32] Taken at breakneck speed, "Toby" showcases the band's impressive soloists who were urged by shouting riffs from the brass and reed sections. Basie artfully paraphrases "Rhapsody in Blue" in the introduction followed by a round of masterful solos by Eddie Durham, doubling on guitar and trombone; Lips Page; Eddie Barefield, switching easily from alto to clarinet; Count Basie; and Dan Minor. The brass and reed sections alternately punctuate the solos with inventive, concise riffs. The loose structure collectively improvised by the band imparts a strong sense of swing, a hallmark of the Kansas City jazz style.

More tightly structured and crisply executed than "Toby," "Moten's Swing" heralds the golden age of the Kansas City jazz style. Basie introduces the first chorus with a confident, eight-bar stride piano solo, segueing into a forceful contrasting riff exchange between the brass and reed sections. In the follow-up eight-bar interlude, Basie, supported by Walter Page's pulsating bass, punctuates short melodic riff statements with rests. The sax section launches the second chorus with a riffed melody phrase intensified by short rests, echoing Basie's use of space in the interlude. In the bridge Durham contributes four rollicking two-bar phrases on guitar, followed by a second eight-bar melodic riff interlude by the reeds. Barefield introduces the third chorus with a broad melodically phrased alto solo, alternately contrasted by the riffing brass section, Basie's sparse accompaniment, and Durham's ringing guitar. The brass section closes out the chorus by restating the melody from the initial sixteen-bar section of the chorus. Lips Page introduces the fourth chorus changing keys to A-flat major with six-bar phrases followed by short two-bar phrases. Page climaxes his solo with a high concert C. The brass and reed sections then come together for a joyous, melodic out chorus, concluding with Basie's chime-like ending. Distinctively, "Moten's Swing" builds to a climax in the out chorus, which, ironically, states the melody for the first time.[33] The collective improvisation from head arrangements, fueled by the driving rhythm section and the supporting soloists and riffing sections, established a new style of freer orchestral jazz that foreshadowed the Swing Era.

Leaving Camden right after the session, the band traveled south, hitting Richmond and Newport News, Virginia, before swinging west for dates in Columbus and Cincinnati, Ohio. Basie recalled how homesick band members were:

> A lot of the fellows began to get restless, because they wanted to be back in Kansas City with their families for the holidays. They were getting letters and telegrams and long-distance calls, and things were getting to be a little strained, and some of them started to cut out for home. . . . Ben Webster was probably the first to go because, although he was not married, he was very close to his relatives. He was always ready to head back home. . . . I think just about everybody who had left had gone by railroad. Of course, some of them had to wire home for money. I don't remember what route we took out of Cincinnati, but Bennie got us out of there somehow and we tried to pick up a little change on the way. But things were really rough in all of those little towns across Indiana and Missouri, and when we finally did make it back into Kansas City, we were pretty raggedy.[34]

Arriving in time for a late December homecoming dance, Moten expressed the band's gratitude to be back. He told the *Kansas City American* "there is no place like Kansas City for that warm home-like atmosphere. You can say for the boys and myself that 'we are glad to be home again.'"[35]

Moten's happiness in Kansas City was short lived. While on the road, he neglected to arrange bookings for the band's return home. Once back, Moten faced stiff competition from Kirk, Hayes, and Clarence Love. The Clouds of Joy had already locked up many social events and big seasonal engagements, including New Year's Eve and Valentine's Day at Paseo Hall. The Hayes band held a long-term engagement at the Castle Supper Club, an upscale cabaret located at the former Dreamland Hall. The Clarence Love band, a young band that mostly played white venues, occupied the bandstand at the El Torreon Ballroom, usually a reliable engagement for Moten.

The lack of local work forced the Moten band to resume regional touring. Departing for Oklahoma in mid-January 1933, the band played dates in Muskogee, Tulsa, and Forest Park in Oklahoma City. Moten hoped to return to New York and replace Cab Calloway at the Cotton Club in February, but the opportunity fell through, so the band continued barnstorming through Louisiana, Georgia, Alabama, Tennessee, Mississippi, Arkansas, Oklahoma, and Iowa. The constant traveling took a toll on the band's personnel. While on the road, four band members resigned, including the entire saxophone section. Moten gathered replacements on the fly, adding tenor saxophonist Herschel Evans in San Antonio. A brilliant soloist, Evans modeled his big-tone style after Coleman Hawkins. Bespectacled and reserved, Evans provided a counterpoint to Lips Page's onstage antics. In Mississippi, Moten filled out the reed section with Jesse Washington and E. Perry Crump. Jesse Washington's brother Harry replaced long-time band member Leroy Berry on banjo.

In early May 1933, the Moten band returned to Kansas City for the third annual musicians ball at Paseo Hall. Despite having lost 74 members in the previous year, Local 627 managed to field seven bands for the ball: Bennie Moten and his Victor Recorders, George E. Lee and his Brunswick Novelty Orchestra, Andy Kirk and his Twelve Clouds of Joy, Thamon Hayes and his Wonder Band, Paul Banks and his Rhythm Aces, Clarence Love and his Orchestra, and Ernest Williams and his Thirteen Original Blue Devils. Like the Moten band, the Blue Devils had recently retreated to Kansas City after a catastrophic tour to the East Coast.

After Walter Page's departure in early 1932, the Blue Devils persevered in fits and starts under a rapid succession of leaders. Trumpeter James Simpson initially inherited the band from Page. Simpson, ill equipped to lead the band, turned the leadership over to former Moten vocalist Bill Little in the summer of 1932. Little left the group in the early fall of 1932 after being seriously injured in an automobile wreck. Assuming the reins, trumpeter Leroy "Snake" White, a long-time member, led the band on a road trip east, sponsored by a

St. Louis booking agent. Stranded with no money in Beckly, West Virginia, the band members struggled to make it back to St. Louis. Moten, in the process of rebuilding his band once again, sent a car to rescue Buster Smith, Lester Young, and other top players.

Smith explained how, in the end, the commonwealth philosophy undermined the Blue Devils. "A commonwealth band was what the trouble was. . . . [T]he thing is there's thirteen of us, whenever we wanted to do something, accept a job, we have to sit down and have a discussion, and we'd always have voting on it and seven would vote for it and six would vote against it. Or vice versa," Smith explained. "It looked like everywhere we'd get a chance to get a good job somewhere, that seven would vote against; they'd want a little more money. Like when we got to Cincinnati, Fats Waller was playing at [radio station] WLW, and he had a little four- or five-piece band. He liked us and wanted us to sit in with him out there and work regularly. He offered us, I think it was eight hundred dollars a week. We wasn't doing anything there. . . . [S]o we got to talking on it, and seven of 'em said we ought to get a thousand dollars, . . . 'That's Fats Waller, he's making plenty of money.' We couldn't never get together on it so we ended up going on back down to Virginia. Went all the way to Newport News and that's where we got stranded there."[36] Without a strong leader like Kirk or Moten to chart the band's course, the Blue Devils faltered from lack of unity in the ranks. Filtering back to Kansas City, band members came together under the leadership of vocalist Ernie Williams for the May 1933 musicians ball, but soon after they went their separate ways. Talented soloists, they found plenty of work in the elegant clubs opening with the lifting of Prohibition.

The swearing in of President Franklin D. Roosevelt in March 1933, along with the passage of the Cullen Act by Congress, permitting the sale of 3.2 percent alcoholic beer and light wine, created opportunities for new nightclubs. Grander clubs opened, like 18th and Vine's new Cherry Blossom, which threw its doors open on April 8, 1933, within hours of the Cullen Act becoming law. The spacious and well-appointed Cherry Blossom occupied the site of the former Eblon Theater at 1822 Vine, right across from the Booker T Hotel. The *Kansas City Call* made special note of its elaborate oriental décor: "The [dance] floor is surrounded by chromium posts placed at equal distance with gold laced ropes connecting the posts." The orchestra platform featured "a large Japanese God placed at the rear . . . overlooking the dancers. The musicians racks are concealed behind pictures depicting the famous rolling hills of Japan. The exterior of the platform is done in vivid colors with emblems of dragons and other characteristic Japanese monsters as decorations. On the walls are painted pictures of Oriental landscapes. The roof is a canopy of pink and blue which forms a sweeping drape. Two or three rows of tables are placed around the dancing floor. Soft carpets are laid down the sides of the floor, forming aisles."[37]

On opening night, the Cherry Blossom overflowed with patrons; a line of people waiting to get in stretched half a block down Vine Street. Fresh from their brush with the law at the Hawaiian Gardens, Joe Turner and Kingfish manned the bar, serving thirsty patrons, while twelve waitresses, clad in bright Japanese costumes, briskly circulated among the petite tables neatly lined up in rows. George E. Lee's Orchestra headlined the revue, which featured a host of entertainers. The *Kansas City Call* captured the excitement of the action-packed stage show opening night:

> The first floor show came on around 12:15 o'clock. Jesse [Patsy] Scott danced and sang in a manner which proved a big hit with the spectators; Corinne Russell did several specialities; L. C. [Speedy] Huggins, well known tap dancer of Greater Kansas City, gave an excellent demonstration; the Three Chocolate Drops [Leroy Reed, Willie Williams, and James McFadden] proved a sensation with an exhibition of the latest in intricate and fancy dance steps. Probably the biggest hit of the evening was little Baby Mason, a six-year-old girl who could tap dance like a veteran. She stopped the show after the first few steps she took. Another who instantly became popular with the patrons was Pearl Madison, entertainer from Milwaukee, who has performed in several well known clubs throughout the Middlewest. She sang and danced several times. Jimmy Ruffins made himself liked by the crowd as master of ceremonies with his novel manner of entertaining and singing. His voice was especially pleasing. George E. Lee's orchestra scored the "Porter's Love Song" and "Rosetta." Julia Lee's rendition of the ever popular "Exactly Like You" was well received.[38]

Open all day and night, the Cherry Blossom quickly became a popular gathering place where drowsy late-night revelers staggered out in broad daylight just in time for the porters to set up lunch for the social set. With a well-deserved reputation as a place where things were just "beginning to begin" at 3 o'clock in the morning, the Cherry Blossom became a haven for early morning jam sessions.

The Lee band played for dancers and anchored the floor show, which changed weekly. The steady stream of entertainers passing through the Cherry Blossom spotlighted well-known veterans of vaudeville like Strange Man, "World's Greatest Song and Dance Man." Vaudeville circuits, in decline since the introduction of talking films, collapsed under the weight of the Great Depression. The breakup of TOBA and other vaudeville circuits left entertainers and musicians in limbo. They found new opportunities in the numerous clubs springing up across the nation. Long in the vanguard of violating the Volstead Act, Kansas City club owners promptly converted existing speakeasies to legitimate taverns, and new nightclubs opened weekly.

The new clubs gave the Cherry Blossom stiff competition. In early May, Bennie Moten opened at the Crystal Palace in the former Blue Room at the Street Hotel. The Castle Supper Club became Club Ritz, featuring a band led by pianist Sam Price. Ellis Burton remodeled the Yellow Front, creating his own Oriental Garden featuring LaForest Dent and His Rhythmic Gents. Paseo Hall closed briefly for a quick make-over, before reopening as the Harlem Night Club on July 1. The Harlem Night Club's all-star review headlined by Erskine Tate and His Grand Terrace Orchestra from Chicago brought together veteran entertainers from across the country, including blues singer Hattie Noels; Muriel Zolenger from "Dixie on Parade;" Lawrence and Wallace from the Club Leisure in Chicago; Kid Charleston, former featured dancer with Duke Ellington; Daisy Boone from the Grand Terrace; and May Richards, formerly with the Cotton Club. Much to the dismay of African American dance fans, within a few weeks of its opening, the Harlem Night Club became a whites-only establishment—imposing Jim Crow policy to one of the most revered institutions in the 18th and Vine area. Finding the doors to the Harlem Night Club slammed shut in their faces, African American patrons switched to the Cherry Blossom.

In early July, the Moten band moved from the Crystal Palace to the Cherry Blossom. Basie wrote the fast-paced stage show, modeled after revues in Harlem and Chicago. For the next several months the band remained at the Cherry Blossom, accompanying the floor show and playing for dancers. Basie and the other band members liked the easy atmosphere of the Cherry Blossom, but Moten had other ideas. Always ambitious, Moten wanted to join forces with Lee at the larger Harlem Night Club. Rumors about the possible merger stirred up discontent among band members. In mid-September, Moten approached the band about changing venues. Band members, already restive about alleged irregularities in the band's bar tab, revolted, calling a meeting to vote on Moten's leadership. Led by Basie, band members who wanted to stay at the Cherry Blossom voted Moten out of his own band. Basie then jockeyed ahead of Walter Page into leadership of the group.

Later, Basie coyly recalled his role in the little palace coup:

Bennie still had a lot of big plans for the band, and something was not going right at the Cherry Blossom, and there was some dissatisfaction among some of the musicians. I won't go into all of that. . . . But what it all came down to was that he (Moten) wanted to pull the band out and try to get into something else. I think he had something cooking with George E. Lee that he wanted to bring the band in on. But it seemed like a lot of the guys wanted to stay put. So Bennie called a meeting to find out how things stood, and that led to one of the hardest and saddest decisions I ever had to make in my life. Because then it all got to the point where the main question was Bennie himself, and they wanted to take a vote to see whether or not they were going to keep him as the leader. So Bennie said something like, "Well if that's the way you feel and you're positive that's what you want to do, okay." And he just walked on out so they could vote their honest opinion.

Basie claimed to have gone "along with whatever the band decided," but an announcement of the event in the *Kansas City Call* disclosed his zeal in seizing the opportunity to take over the band.[39] The day after the vote, the *Call* proclaimed Basie the new owner and manager of the Moten band. "Bennie Moten's band according to an announcement made Thursday, is now under the new management that of 'Count' William Basie, who is now owner and manager. Walter Page, former owner of the Blue Devil's band, is assistant manager, and Jack Washington is secretary and treasurer. . . . The 'Count' says the aggregation will play sweet and swinging music. The band will be known as 'Count' Basie and his Cherry Blossom Victor Recording orchestra and will continue to be the feature attraction at the popular Vine Street night club."[40] Basie made minor changes in the personnel. He gave Jesse and Harry Washington, the brothers who ran up the band's bar tab, their walking papers, and then brought in Buster Smith to lead the saxophone section.[41] In one fell swoop, Basie deposed Moten and elevated himself to royalty, assuming the title, Count Basie.

Moten hurriedly pieced together a new band that combined veterans of the territorial bands and eager younger musicians.[42] Three weeks after being ejected by his former band, Moten opened with a new band at the Breakers club on the outskirts of St. Joseph, Missouri. Returning to Kansas City in early October, the new Moten band opened for a short run at the El Torreon. No longer one of Kansas City's top venues, the El Torreon struggled to compete with the number of spacious, smart, new nightclubs recently opened in downtown Kansas City and "out in the county." While the cavernous El Torreon presented bands for dancing, the clubs showcased bands along with elaborate stage shows that featured comedians, dancers, and entertainers in an intimate setting. Unlike ballrooms, forced to maintain public decorum and eschew serving liquor, the clubs dispensed highballs, a strong draw for patrons parched by years of Prohibition.

Unable to rely on the El Torreon for steady employment, Moten joined forces with George E. Lee at the Harlem Night Club in late October 1933. Putting aside their long-running rivalry, the two merged the best players from both bands to create the Moten-Lee band. They complemented each other with Moten taking care of business behind the scenes and Lee entertaining on stage. Competing for crowds with more fashionable venues downtown, impresario Maceo Birch created a flashy floor show featuring dancers and comedians. The Harlem Night Club courted white patrons in earnest by advertising in theater bills and in the *Kansas City Journal-Post*. The "Night Club Notes" column in the *Kansas City Journal-Post* noted the improvement in the quality of entertainment and ambience of the club.

The Harlem club has made a real scoop in the night club field. It has consolidated the bands of Bennie Moten, Victor recording artist, and George E. Lee,

Brunswick recording artist, and formed a new band under joint leadership. . . . With the best musicians from the two orchestras and several new artists in the group . . . the new 15-piece band will be directed by Buster Moten and his accordion, play the arrangements of Eddie Durham and feature George and Julia Lee as soloists. . . . And in addition to presenting its superlative new band, the Harlem club, now newly decorated and properly ventilated and heated, of-fers the fastest 45-minute floor show three times nightly that has been seen in a Kansas City cabaret. The entertainers include Maseo [Maceo] Birch, master-of-ceremonies; the Four Dancing Covans; Daisy and Edith, rope jumping dancers of exceptional merit; "Jelly Bean" Johnson, Ethel Willis, Bobby Davis, Shorty and Ruby and the Six Sepia Steppers. When you're hitting the high spots, don't miss the Harlem.[43]

With the help of the *Kansas City Journal-Post* and the combined drawing power of Moten and Lee, the Harlem Club attracted throngs of white patrons, eager to sample the flavor of New York's legendary Harlem without straying far from downtown Kansas City.

The metamorphosis of Paseo Hall into the Harlem Club robbed the 18th and Vine community of a cherished institution, and it was the only dance hall capable of accommodating visiting bands.[44] Filling the void, the Roseland Ballroom, located at 1413-15 Troost, opened its doors to African American patrons in late October. Billed as the "largest and most exclusive ball room in the middle west," the Roseland easily accommodated 3,000 patrons.[45] At the grand opening Halloween night, Count Basie and his orchestra shared a double bill with Jimmy Bell and His Chocolate Dandies. Christening the community's new ballroom, Basie opened the show with a set from 9 to 10:30 P.M. before returning to his regular stand at the Cherry Blossom. Picking up the beat from Basie, the Jimmy Bell band continued the celebration until 2:30 A.M.

Once established, the Roseland became the leading African American venue for national bands. The Fletcher Henderson Orchestra, taking a thirty-day break from an eight-year run at the Roseland Ballroom in New York, played the new Roseland in Kansas City on December 18, 1933. The *Kansas City Call* reported that the Henderson band "failed to draw as the Fletcher Henderson of old," with only 500 patrons attending. The band still boasted plenty of star power, including saxophonist Coleman Hawkins, trumpeter Henry "Red" Allen, bass player John Kirby, and trombonist Dickie Wells, but a new generation of bandleaders had eclipsed Henderson's popularity. The *Kansas City Call* attributed the lackluster turnout to the wealth of bands enjoyed by Kansas City audiences during the previous year. "It wasn't be-cause Henderson's music wasn't good, but more because dance band follow-ers have been treated to so much good music in the past year. They have danced to Cab Calloway's brand of music, Noble Sissle, Earl Hines, Blanche Calloway, Harriet Calloway, Claude Hopkins and a number of other bands."[46] Closing out the evening at the Roseland early, Coleman Hawkins and other members of the Henderson band stopped by the Cherry Blossom where Count Basie held court, right across the street from where they were staying at the Booker T Hotel.

Coleman "Bean" Hawkins, the reigning king of the tenor saxophone, did not engage in musical jousting at jam sessions. He had everything to lose and nothing to gain from cutting contests. The late-night session at the Cherry Blossom proved to be the exception to the rule. Egged on by fellow band members and challenged by Lester Young and the other saxophonists prowling on stage, Hawkins strolled across the street to the Booker T and returned with his horn. Count Basie detailed the circumstances leading to the night of the legendary cutting contest, ending with Lester Young dethroning Hawkins as king of the tenor saxophone during an all-night freewheeling jam session. "Herschel and Ben Webster and Lester and a few others were up there jamming, and Hawkins came by and decided to get his horn," Basie recounted.

> Somebody kept asking him to play, so he finally went across the street to the hotel, and when he came back in with his horn, I was sitting at a table with John Kirby and some friends, and John thought that something was unusual. "I ain't never seen that happen before," he said. "I ain't either," I said. Because that was something that Hawk didn't do in those days. Nobody had ever seen Hawk bring his horn in somewhere to get into a jam session. That's the main thing I remember about that night. Because it was so strange. All of those other saxophone players were up there calling for their favorite tunes, and then Hawk went up there, and he knew all of the tunes, and he started calling for all of those hard keys, like E-flat and B-natural. That took care of quite a few local characters right away. Not many piano players were too eager to mess with that stuff. I know I wasn't going up there.[47]

As the tenor battle raged on, exhausting all pianists brave enough to venture into the fray, Mary Lou Williams came to the rescue. "The word went around that Hawkins was in the Cherry Blossom, and within about half an hour there were Lester Young, Ben Webster, Herschel Evans, Herman Walder and one or two unknown tenors piling in the club to blow. Ben [Bean] didn't know the Kaycee tenormen were so terrific, and he couldn't get himself together though he played all morning," Williams related.

> I happened to be nodding that night, and around 4 a.m. I awoke to hear someone pecking on my screen. I opened the window on Ben Webster. He was saying: "Get up, pussycat, we're jammin' and all the pianists are tired out now. Hawkins has got his shirt off and is still blowing. You got to come down." Sure enough, when we got there Hawkins was in his singlet taking turns with the Kaycee men. It seems he had run into something he didn't expect. Lester's style was light and, as I said, it took him maybe five choruses to warm up. But then he would really blow; then you couldn't handle him on a cutting session. That was how Hawkins got hung up. The Henderson band was playing in St.

Louis that evening, and Bean knew he ought to be on the way. But he kept trying to blow something to beat Ben and Herschel and Lester. When at last he gave up, he got straight in his car and drove to St. Louis. I heard he'd just bought a new Cadillac and that he burnt it out trying to make the job on time. Yes, Hawkins was king until he met those crazy Kansas City tenormen.[48]

Bassist Gene Ramey credited Young's victory to his creativity, flowing from the philosophy of Kansas City soloists: "Lester had a very spacey sound at the end of '33. . . . He would play a phrase and maybe lay out three beats before he'd come in with another phrase. You know, instead of more continuous staying on style. . . . Prez had kind of loosened up. . . . Hawk was cutting everybody out. Until Prez got him. He tore Hawk apart. He tore Hawk up so bad he missed a date in St. Louis. Hawk was still trying to get him at twelve o'clock the next day. Seemed like the longer Prez played, the longer the headcutting session went on, the better Prez got. He played more creative things. The adage in Kansas City was . . . *say something on your horn*, not just show off your versatility and ability to execute. *Tell us a story, and don't let it be a lie.* Let it *mean* something, if it's only one note."[49] Embellished with each retelling, the legend of Young's victory over Hawkins grew to mythic proportions, and in the process became a metaphor for the ascendance of the Kansas City jazz style.

While the Kirk, Moten-Lee, and Hayes bands followed the money, playing for white audiences, the Basie band preferred performing for the gamblers, hustlers, and prostitutes flocking to the late-night sessions at the Cherry Blossom. Gene Ramey attributed the Basie band's popularity to band members' fraternizing with the sporting community. "Basie's band built up their popularity on socializing. I mean the big following they had in and around Kansas City," Ramey revealed. "But that band didn't believe in going out with steady black people. They'd head straight for the pimps and prostitutes and hang out with them. Those people were like great advertisement for Basie. They didn't dig Andy Kirk. They said he was too uppity. But Basie was down there, lying in the gutter, getting drunk with them. He'd have patches on his pants and everything. All of his band was like that."[50] Basie's behavior did not sit well with his wife Vivian, accustomed to traveling in more refined social circles. Agreeing to disagree, the two had not lived together since the previous July. Weary of Basie's drinking and public philandering, Vivian filed for divorce on January 24, 1934. A front-page article in the *Kansas City Call* reported Vivian's charges against Basie of "non-support, mental cruelty, desertion and drunkenness."[51] That same week, the Cherry Blossom unexpectedly closed when a van showed up and hauled off all the fixtures. Worse yet, the club managers disappeared without paying the band and twenty other employees.

The owners of the Booker T Hotel bought the building and reopened the Cherry Blossom, putting Basie back to work, but Vivian's allegations seriously damaged his reputation with the social elite in the 18th and Vine community. As a result, Basie became a persona non grata to the many social clubs that held functions and celebrations at the Cherry Blossom. Basie quietly granted Vivian's divorce petition in late March, and left town with the band to open at a hotel in Little Rock, Arkansas. Shortly after arriving in Little Rock, Lester Young left the band to replace Coleman Hawkins in the Fletcher Henderson band. When Hawkins quit the Henderson band, band members who had been at the Cherry Blossom the night of the cutting contest urged Henderson to hire Young as a replacement. Quickly finding the Henderson band a bad fit, Young returned to Kansas City and joined the Kirk band. Basie, possessing more zeal than business acumen, failed to line up further bookings after the band closed the hotel engagement in Little Rock. One by one members deserted the band. Lips Page and Jimmy Rushing returned to Kansas City in June, and rejoined the Moten band. Finally only Basie and drummer Jo Jones, then known as Joe, remained. They played odd jobs for tips in joints to make ends meet and slept in a car. Swallowing his pride, Basie returned to Kansas City in late summer, seeking to reestablish his reputation and make amends with Moten.

While Basie initially faltered as a bandleader, Harlan Leonard successfully made the transition from sideman to leader under considerably different circumstances. Unlike Basie's overthrow of Moten, Leonard assumed leadership of the Hayes band with Hayes's blessing. The fall of 1933 arrived with great promise for the Hayes band. Coming off a summer engagement on the riverboat *Idlewild*, the band left Kansas City for an eight-week engagement in Peoria, Illinois. Moving on to Chicago in mid-November, the band opened at the new Club Morocco, an upscale nightclub, rivaling the Grand Terrace. Opening night, Earl Hines and his entire band from the Grand Terrace stopped by to check out the competition and wish the Hayes band well. During the second week at the Morocco, the Hayes band, now billed as the Rockets, began broadcasting over the CBS network from WBBN. Just as the Hayes band started to gain entry to Chicago, the local musicians union headed by James Petrillo locked the door. "We stayed there [Club Morocco] about four or five weeks and the union said we couldn't stay there any longer because we were a traveling band," Booker Washington recalled. "They refused [to let us in the local union]. . . . [W]e did give a farewell dance, but they finally said, 'That's the end of it.' So we had to come back home again."[52]

Jesse Stone stayed on in Chicago to organize a new band for the Club Morocco. Stone's departure left the band without an arranger, composer, or front man. Fortunately, Stone let Hayes keep the band book, which enabled the band to carry on without an arranger on staff. Before leaving Chicago, Hayes hired George Ramsey, a tall slender dancer, to replace Stone as conductor and entertainer. Charles Goodwin explained that Ramsey came aboard more for show than as a musical leader. "Then they had guys that wasn't conductors, they were more or less dancers and things like that. . . . They would have personalities with the band by being in front of them and pretending to direct. . . . It didn't hamper the band any because they didn't pay any attention to him. It was a good thing to show. . . . He could run across the stage and make a big split, you know, added things to the band, introduce the numbers."[53]

Returning to Kansas City in early December, Hayes hired pianist Rozelle Claxton to fill the creative void left by Stone's exit. A budding composer and arranger, Claxton briefly worked with the Moten band before the merger of the Moten-Lee bands. The Hayes band alternated between the new Roseland Ballroom and the Labor Temple before they were hired for an extended engagement at the Royal Gardens at 5th and Virginia in Kansas City, Kansas. In late March 1934, the Hayes band replaced Clarence Love at the El Torreon Ballroom. Skirting union payscale, the band chipped in $3 each to pay Ramsey. Feeling shortchanged, Ramsey turned the band in to Local 627. The union fined Thamon Hayes $500 and each band member $100. Outraged by the betrayal, the hotheaded Herman Walder attacked Ramsey in front of the union hall. "That cat was standing out in front of the place down there [the musicians union]. And he says to me, this dancer, 'Man, I'm sorry about that, man,'" Walder fumed. "'I'm sorry I turned you cats in.' I said, 'What do you mean, sorry man? That's my living, man! My kids go hungry by this.' BAM! I knocked that cat down and he started running, and Harlan [Leonard] trying to catch him, and we run him out of town."[54] Frustrated by the fine, Thamon Hayes resigned as leader in June 1934. Slated to start a summer engagement at Winnwood Beach, band members chose Harlan Leonard as their new leader and renamed the band Harlan Leonard's Kansas City Rockets.

As Leonard launched his career as a bandleader, Basie worked his way back into Moten's good graces. While scuffling around Kansas City playing for tips in the joints on 18th Street, Basie found love and redemption. Two years earlier, during the Moten band's farewell appearance at the Lafayette Theater, Basie became smitten with a young dancer named Catherine Morgan, performing with the Whitman Sisters. Although, at the time too young for him to approach, Catherine lingered on Basie's mind. During a big Labor Day stomp at the Labor Temple sponsored by Local 627, Basie spied Catherine working as a fan dancer under the name Katherine Scott. Stepping backstage after the show, Basie attempted to introduce himself. Katherine rebuffed Basie's advances and accused him of trying to peek behind her fans. Basie quickly exited, but the brief encounter held the promise of romance with Catherine, and indeed she later became his wife. Reconnecting with the community, Basie played organ for services at the Centennial A. M. E. Church. In late September, Basie arranged the music for a program held at the church on the "Negro and the New Deal," featuring the Moten band. During the program, Basie performed a new composition, "I Lost," co-written by Roy Dorsey,

Harry Smith's half brother. With Moten in attendance, the title of Basie's new composition assumed deeper meaning. The joint appearance led to Basie's reconciliation with Moten.

Basie kept busy that fall playing the organ for church services and on his own radio program over WHB. Moving up in mid-October, Basie joined the house band, accompanying vaudeville revues produced by Maceo Birch at the New Centre Theater at 15th and Troost Avenue. In November, the revue from the New Centre moved to the Harlem Night Club, which brought Basie closer to the Moten band. For the club, Basie and Birch developed a snappy revue that featured vaudeville veteran S. H. Dudley, Jr. Basie gradually worked his way back into the Moten band and became a full-time member again in January 1935. Ironically, the band included Lips Page, Jimmy Rushing, Herschel Evans, and other musicians Basie had wrested from Moten at the Cherry Blossom. Once again flush, footloose, and fancy free, Basie resumed his late-night carousing in the clubs lining 12th and 18th Streets.

With the blush off the Cherry Blossom, the Sunset Club at 12th and Highland became the new hot ticket in town. Owned by Felix Payne and managed by Walter "Piney" Brown, a popular sportsman, the often-raided Eastside Musicians Club at 12th and Woodland reopened as the Eastside Musicians Sunset Club in November 1933. The opening-night gala sported an all-star lineup spotlighting: "Little Skippy," a shake dancer from St. Louis; Miss Josephine Byrd, an entertainer formerly with the stage production "Green Pastures"; and Joe Turner, "moaning the blues throughout the night." Eddie Durham and Lips Page sat in with the house band, Pete and His Little Peters, featuring Pete Johnson, drummer Murl Johnson, and alto saxophonist Walter Knight. The advertisement of the grand opening in the *Kansas City Call* trumpeted a number of visiting luminaries, including George and Julia Lee, the Moten band, Maceo Birch, and the floor show from the Harlem Club. In the announcement, Count Basie invited everyone to "meet us there every morning."[55]

The Sunset quickly developed a reputation for its late-night sessions, where even "whites swing out." Dave E. Dexter, Jr., a journalist covering the local music scene for the *Kansas City Journal-Post*, *Metronome*, and *Down Beat*, judged the Sunset as the top music club in Kansas City:

> There Pete and a 3-piece band (around 3 a.m. others sat in until sometimes Pete would look around from his chair and see six saxes and four trumpets taking turns in the jams) played dance music—all blues—with Joe shouting and yelling "Well Good Mawin' Glory," or, more often, "Roll 'Em Pete, and let 'em jump for Joy." Beer was served in tall tin cans, by the quart, and it was 15 cents a serving, pay when it's put on the table in front of you please. Pete kept a jigger of gin filled near his keyboard, sipping it quietly, never becoming noisy. When they "felt it," Pete and Joe would start a boogie which might run any-where from 10 to 75 consecutive choruses, Joe singing a few, Pete takin' a few,

the tenor comin' in and so on. Occasionally the colored patrons got excited and threw themselves on the floor, completely hysterical by the rhythm and atmosphere. A brown arm reaching over from the bar shoved these persons out of the way, under a table. It wasn't considered good etiquette to interfere when Pete and Joe were "on the jump."[56]

Musicians flocked to the after-hours sessions at the Sunset, to bask in Piney Brown's legendary generosity. Eddie Barefield fondly remembered Brown's benevolence. "Piney was like a patron saint to all musicians. He used to take care of them," Barefield recalled. "In fact, he was like a father to me. . . . Most all the playing and jamming happened at Piney's Place. Piney was a man, he didn't care how much it cost; . . . If you needed money to pay your rent, he would give it to you and take you out and buy you booze. He was a man you could always depend on for something if you needed it."[57] A charming ladies man and lucky gambler, Piney Brown first established his reputation for generosity to musicians as the manager of the Subway Club located below street level at 1516 18th Street.[58] A small casual joint with a low ceiling, the Subway served as a popular gathering spot for musicians needing a loan, a meal or just a place to hang out and jam. Eddie Barefield marveled that Piney made any money at the Subway, considering his magnanimity with musicians. "I don't think he made any money off the Subway, because he gave away too much. . . . When you went down there to play, you could go down there any night and get juiced and eat and do whatever you wanted to do. If you came there as a musician it never cost you anything."[59] Musicians reciprocated Piney's largess by flocking to the newly opened Sunset Club to sit in with Pete and Joe, making it an instant success. A modestly appointed, deep and narrow saloon with gambling in the back room, the Sunset enjoyed a certain cachet, attracting such visiting dignitaries as Duke Ellington, Cab Calloway, and the entire Harlem Renaissance basketball team. Not everyone appreciated the early morning revelry at the Sunset. Andy Kirk, living right around the corner at 1212 Woodland, complained about the nightly musical ruckus. "Turner and boogie-woogie pianist Pete Johnson kept rolling out blues till four and five in the morning. I didn't have to go to the club. It came to me through the windows, " Kirk groused. "Sometimes I'd get so disgusted: all that blues shouting and boogie-woogie kept me awake."[60] Understandably, the Sunset never enjoyed the same enthusiastic endorsement from Kirk it received from Lee, Moten, and Basie.

Lee and Moten dissolved their partnership when the Harlem Night Club closed at the end of 1934. Lee worked briefly with Harlan Leonard's Rockets before returning to his roots, singing with small ensembles in the joints on 12th and 18th Streets. His sister Julia struck out on her own and opened at Milton Morris' new club, Milton's at 3507 Troost Avenue. The son of Jewish Russian immigrants, Morris worked his way up from newspaper boy to owner of a drugstore called the Rendevous. Circumventing the law of the land, he sold liquor for medicinal purposes. More bottled-in-bond crossed the counter than aspirin. A raconteur and bon vivant, Morris forged strong ties to the Pendergast machine and the wise guys in the north end. During the late 1920s, Morris operated the Hey Hay Club, a speakeasy at 4th and Cherry. Morris later opened his namesake Milton's after selling his interest in the Hey Hay Club, effectively severing his ties to the north end.

With Prohibition drawing to a close, the genial Morris no longer needed the surly gangsters, who were increasingly drawing the scrutiny of the federal authorities. An air-conditioned refuge from Kansas City's sweltering summers, Milton's became a popular destination for both locals and tourists hungry for a taste of Kansas City nightlife. Julia Lee specialized in crowd-pleasing risqué songs, such as "Two Old Maids in a Folding Bed" and "I've Got a Crush on the Fuller Brush Man." After surviving a horrendous car accident while touring with her brother's band, Lee lost her taste for travel. So, she willingly settled in for a long-term engagement at Milton's, where she made good money from the generous tips patrons stuffed in the winking kitty perched on top of the piano.[61]

Splitting amicably with Lee, Moten set his sights once again on success in the East. Reunited with key members of his former band, Moten organized a spring tour to New York. Preparing the band for the long haul, Moten resumed touring regionally. He spent most of January 1935 in Tulsa, Oklahoma, where the band played to packed houses at the Dixie Theater. The band returned to Kansas City for a farewell engagement as part of the annual spring musicians ball held on March 11 at Paseo Hall, which had recently reverted to an African American club with the closing of the Harlem Night Club. The annual battle of the bands featured: Paul Banks' Rhythm Aces; Andy Kirk and His Twelve Clouds of Joy; Clarence Love Orchestra; Harlan Leonard's Rockets; and Bennie Moten's Big fifteen-piece band. Special guest attractions included: S. H. Dudley, Jr., and Maceo Birch's Coco-Nut Grove Revue, "When Harlem Comes to Kay See"; Deacon Moore's Singing Band from the Muehlebach Hotel; and the Jeter & Pillars Plantation Grill Band from St. Louis. The Kansas City Call reported that it was one of the largest crowds ever to attend a musicians ball with 1,800 "dance lovers . . . celebrating their homecoming at Paseo Hall. . . . It wasn't a dance crowd. It was a throng that absorbed swing and rhythm from Harlan Leonard's Kansas City Rockets and later on from Kansas City's premiere maestro, Bennie Moten himself and band." Deacon Moore declined an invitation to play after Moten, explaining he "preferred listening to the Moten swing instead."[62]

Following the musicians ball, the band left for an engagement at the Rainbow Room in Denver. Moten stayed behind in Kansas City to tend to last-minute details before launching the New York tour. Plagued by throat infections, Moten decided to have his tonsils removed before hitting the road to the East Coast. Moten checked into Wheatly-Provident Hospital on April 1, trusting his close friend and head surgeon, Dr. Hubert W. Bruce, to perform the tonsillectomy. The routine procedure ended in tragedy for both men. During the operation, Bruce accidentally severed an artery in Moten's throat. As Bruce frantically attempted to stem the blood gushing from the artery, Moten bled to death on the operating table. Rumors circulated in the community that the two spent the evening before the operation drinking and carousing, and this caused the hung-over Bruce's hand to slip during the surgery. Ed Lewis clarified the events leading to Moten's death. "He [Moten] had a wonderful surgeon, Dr. Bruce, who was one of the finest in the Midwest. A lot of people blamed Bruce for Bennie's death, but it wasn't his fault," Lewis revealed. "Bennie was a nervous type of person, and they had to use novocaine because he wouldn't let them put him to sleep. He got frightened when he felt the knife, and jumped, severed an artery and bled to death. It really wasn't Dr. Bruce's fault, but people in Kansas City were so hurt over it that the poor fellow had to leave town. He had one of the largest practices in the Midwest and he had to give that up."[63] According to the autopsy report, Moten died of coronary sclerosis on April 2, 1935.

Word of Moten's death reached band members as they prepared to take the stage at the Rainbow Room. Bus Moten immediately returned to Kansas City to make arrangements for his uncle's funeral. The rest of the band remained in Denver to fulfill the engagement, so they missed Moten's funeral, held on Saturday, April 6 in the auditorium of the Centennial A. M. E. Church at 19th and Woodland. The community, which so often celebrated to the music of Bennie Moten, came together for the solemn occasion. Covering the funeral in the *Kansas City Call*, L. Herbert Henegan observed that "it was the largest funeral Kansas City had witnessed in 20 years. . . . Thousands of both races from all walks of life, filled every available space . . . and overflowed far out into the street during the last rites for Bennie Moten, beloved and widely known orchestra leader." A steady stream of men, women, and children of all races filed by Moten's body, lying in state on the rostrum, surrounded by a mountain of flowers. Members of Harlan Leonard's Rockets stood sentinel at either end of the casket in full band uniform. Outside the church a brass band from Local 627 played hymns as mourners filled the church to the rafters. Delivering the eulogy, the Reverend Mr. Reynolds expounded on the value of a good name. "'There's wealth in a good name,' he said. 'Bennie Moten, a Kansas City boy, born in a humble home, began his musical career at four years of age. He touched men in every walk of life in his work. He touched them at the bottom and at the top, but kept his manhood and his good name. He was both brave and courageous. Bennie Moten was a master builder of men in a symphonic whole. Men served Bennie Moten because he had that something that drew them to him and because they loved to serve him.'" After the benediction, the funeral procession made its way through the 18th and Vine area, flanked by two motorcycle patrolmen clearing traffic.

The brass band followed playing a mournful dirge. Throngs of admirers lining the streets wept openly as the hearse bearing Moten's body passed. Turning onto 15th Street, the procession quickened its pace, moving into the traffic lane headed for Highland Cemetery.[64]

Moten's death ended a musical legacy stretching from the dawn of the Jazz Age to the genesis of a pure Kansas City jazz style. Although not an outstanding musician or composer, Moten cultivated the growth of Kansas City Jazz from its roots in ragtime and blues to the flowering of a fresh vigorous swinging style. He did so as a good businessman and adept manager of talented musicians. He afforded them the support and financial security needed to advance musically. Eddie Durham rated Moten as "one of the greatest leaders that ever was. . . . He just knew what to do and how to treat the men, everything like that. And he was the same with the men, exactly 100 percent."[65]

The undisciplined, but creative team of Count Basie and Eddie Durham thrived in the easy atmosphere of the Moten band, in which they were given free rein to revamp the personnel and sound of the band, and in the process created a new style of Kansas City Jazz. Moten promoted the tradition he fostered by touring and recording as Bennie Moten's Kansas City Orchestra. While the Clouds of Joy also helped establish Kansas City's reputation, bandleader Andy Kirk's association with Kansas City was not as direct as Moten's. The Clouds of Joy could have floated in from anywhere. The Moten band clearly originated from Kansas City, stylistically and geographically. Moten's national tours and recordings blazed the trail for bands and musicians ensuing from Kansas City. Ironically, while Moten traveled to New York to further the cause of his band and Kansas City Jazz, John Hammond and other New York music moguls journeyed to Kansas City. In search of new talent, they were lured by late night radio broadcasts from the Reno Club on 12th Street led by Count Basie, the most direct heir to Moten's legacy.

7

Until the Real Thing Comes Along

If that ain't love, it will have to do,
until the real thing comes along.

—Andy Kirk and His 12 Clouds of Joy,
"Until the Real Thing Comes Along," 1936

FOLLOWING BENNIE MOTEN'S DEATH, his nephew Bus attempted, in vain, to keep the band going under Bennie's name. In mid-April 1935, the Bennie Moten Orchestra, directed by Bus Moten, opened at the Cocoanut Grove, a spacious nightclub sporting a Hawaiian theme complete with palm trees and dancers decked out as hula girls. Located at the busy intersection of 27th and Troost Avenue, the Cocoanut Grove had only recently opened its doors to African American patronage. Basie left the band during the second week of the engagement, as he felt "with Bennie Moten himself gone, it just wasn't the same anymore."[1] Count Basie got along well with Bus and left on good terms, but other band members found Bus to be overbearing, an unwelcome change from Bennie's laid-back leadership. "He'd [Bus] holler at the boys 'cause somebody'd make a note wrong or somebody'd be late," Buster Smith declared. "He'd fuss and raise sin. Bennie was a fine skillful [leader]; he was very cooperative. Know how to talk to you, never would get mad whatever you did. He was a good fella."[2] Bus managed to keep a semblance of the original band going under Bennie's name for the next year, but one by one, key members deserted until it became the Bennie Moten band in name only. Finally Bus could no longer financially sustain the big band, so he disbanded it and formed a small combo with George E. Lee.

In early summer 1935, Basie worked his way into a regular slot at the Reno Club, which occupied the ground floor of a nondescript two-story red brick building, located near the northeast corner of 12th and Cherry, just east of the newly constructed towering art deco Jackson County Courthouse on the eastern edge of downtown. The Reno, a small boisterous L-shaped saloon, featured a long bar in the front that buttressed a modest oyster-shell bandstand tucked beneath the balcony in the back. Prostitutes from next door, arrayed in shades of scarlet, perched in the balcony like exotic birds, dispensing knockout drops to unsuspecting cattle men. While sitting in for Bill Chowning, the pianist with the house band at the Reno for a couple of weeks, Basie struck up a friendship with the owner, Sol Stibel. It wasn't long before Basie appropriated Chowning's job and moved up to assume leadership of the small ensemble that featured Slim Freeman, a veteran saxophonist formerly with T Holder, Andy Kirk, Bennie Moten, and George E. Lee. Bankrolled by Stibel, Basie revamped the band by bringing in Buster Smith, Jimmy Rushing, Lips Page, and other old friends from the Blue Devils and Moten band. In mid-July, Count Basie and His Barons of Rhythm premiered at the Reno Club, the "biggest little club in the world," playing for dancers and accompanying the floor show featuring Mr. Shorty & Mr. Bumpsky's Revue, along with tap dancer Dorothy Lee. A small cardboard hand-lettered sign inserted in the window advertised the band's debut to the crowds flowing down 12th Street. Regular radio broadcasts from the Reno introduced the band to the broader audience across the Midwest and eventually brought it to the national forefront.

Radio station W9XBY, located "at the top" end of the AM dial at 1580 kilohertz, broadcast the opening night festivities from the Reno Club. Licensed to First National Television, Inc., an experimental television and radio engineering school, W9XBY went live on December 31, 1934. One of four hi-fidelity stations in the United States licensed to broadcast at twice the normal bandwidth of other AM stations, W9XBY served as a hands-on classroom for radio engineering students. A nonaffiliated station, W9XBY relied on remote broadcasts for evening programming and on-the-job training for students. These young white students, hailing mostly from rural areas, received an education of a different sort as they broadcast from African American churches and nightclubs across the city. By popular demand, W9XBY broadcast the Basie band from the Reno weeknights from 11:30 to 12 P.M. and Saturdays from 12:30 to 1 A.M. W9XBY's 1,000-watt signal usually only covered the Kansas City metropolitan area, but late at night under favorable atmospheric conditions, its broadcasts carried east to Chicago, as far north as Canada, west to Denver, and across the South.

In late October 1935, Walter Page came aboard, thus rounding out the reunion of key former members of the Blue Devils. An advertisement in the *Kansas City Journal-Post* announced Page's arrival, heralding him as "Baron Walter 'Biggon' Page." In the advertisement Basie invited "all musicians and all entertainers to the 'Spook' breakfast party Monday morning."[3] Basie printed formal invitations proclaiming:

Leader!   Orchestra!   Entertainers!
You are hereby summoned to appear
at the
Club Reno
602 East 12th Street
for the First of a series of
Spook Breakfast Parties
to begin
Monday Morning
from Four on
Kindly Make Reservations Early, giving name of Club
HArrison 9591   Count Basie

The popular breakfast dances that Basie had frequented in Harlem years earlier inspired the spook breakfasts. "That was something I remembered from years ago, back in New York. . . . Spook was an *in* jive word among entertainers in those days," Basie explained. "It really didn't have anything to do with color or ghost directly. It was something that entertainers used to call themselves. I don't really know where that came from. Maybe it had something to do with being mostly nighttime people. So we kept late hours, spooky hours. The hours when spooks came out."[4] Beginning at 4 A.M. on Mondays and continuing all day, the spook breakfasts became a popular haunt for musicians and entertainers.

Trumpeter Richard Smith distinctly recalled the excitement surrounding the early morning sessions:

Picture Kansas City's 12th and Cherry in 1935 with the Club Reno almost at its Northeast corner, and parked there, almost seeming to lean against it, a John Agnos lunch wagon, horse-drawn and stacked high with liver, pig snoots and ears, hog maws, fish, chicken and pork tenderloins. Pick up a sandwich on your way into this musty, smoke-hazed room, squeezing past the hustlers, grifters, solicitors and off-duty musicians, to find a seat as close as you can to the bandstand. . . . The Reno Club's early Monday morning "Spook" Breakfasts would often be sparked by the heralded appearance of Big Joe Turner who, always surrounded by a cheering section from his Sunset Crystal Palace gig, would come in to "work out" with Sol's "Girl Friday," vivacious Chrystianna [Christianna] Buckner. Chrystianna had a song and dance for everyone, and people especially liked "Two Old Maids" and "I Ain't Giving Nothin' Away." Out on the floor, with patent leather hair gleaming, would be Reno Club's highly polished "Hot Lips" Paige [Page] with white handkerchief in hand doing his "Louis Armstrong" on "When It's Sleepy Time Down South." Backing him up was . . . the Reno Club band. Nine brilliant instrumental satellites of sound responding to the sonic radiance of their personable mentor, Bill Basie. . . . At the club on such early Monday mornings would be found Jo Jones, "Big Un" Page and trumpeter Joe Keyes, jammed up against the north wall, almost popping out of that back door next to the unfenced dirt yard.

Standing room at the back alley was a bleacher of sorts, for the overflow of patrons on heavy nights, and for musicians, black and white, who wanted to listen "closer" to the band. The repartee between those on both sides of that back door was often more entertaining than the floor show on the inside. Drinks purchased by the bandmen could be shuttled through the door at half price. Some outside purchases would sometimes meet with disaster on the return trip by falling into the hands of "Big Un," who would down it with one gulp, throw the glass out the door and tell the luckless buyer to "Go to Hell." With John Agnos's lunch wagon parked at the alley's Cherry Street entrance, there sometimes was more business transacted through the back end of the Reno Club than through the front door.[5]

The late-night broadcasts over W9XBY and the wildly popular spook breakfasts established Basie's career as a bandleader.

While Basie launched his band locally, Andy Kirk and the Clouds of Joy finally succeeded nationally after enduring several years of professional dips and curves. Wrapping up a short but successful run at the Vanity Fair, an upscale downtown club, in late October 1933, Kirk discovered that few of the nightclubs that opened across the city in the wake of Prohibition's repeal could sustain a band the size of the Clouds of Joy. The El Torreon Ballroom, with its attendance in decline, offered only sporadic employment. Facing slim prospects, Kirk took a break in the spring of 1934 to rehearse and refresh the band's repertoire.

The lull in the band's busy performing schedule triggered a turnover in personnel. The band's two star soloists, tenor saxophonist Ben Webster and trumpeter Irving "Mouse" Randolph, left to join the Fletcher Henderson band. In turn, Lester Young returned to Kansas City from a short stint with the Henderson band to take Ben Webster's place. Randolph, prohibited by Kirk from leaving the band until he found a suitable replacement, recruited Vertna Saunders. Before long, Young and Saunders moved on too. "We'd rehearse nearly every day, and played all of Mary Lou Williams's arrangements. Then they'd say we got a job next Saturday, but we're going to rehearse in the meantime," Saunders complained. "The same thing happened the next week. . . . [W]e went along with it maybe a month or six weeks, but things kept getting worse financially, so one day Lester says, 'I'm going to Minneapolis,' so I said, 'well, I'm going to St. Louis.'"[6] Texan Buddy Tate, a competent get-off soloist with a straight-ahead style and big tone, replaced Young, and Bob Hall, a trumpeter with a full beautiful tone, succeeded Saunders.

With work scarce in Kansas City, the Clouds of Joy spent the summer and fall of 1934 traveling across the South and western territories, with frequent stops in Memphis, John Williams's hometown. Kirk, desperate to get back into the national limelight, struck a deal to accompany blues singer Mamie Smith on a string of one-nighters to the East Coast. His strategy paid off, and in the spring of 1935 the Clouds of Joy landed in the East for a stint at the

Vendome, the leading club in Buffalo, New York. The band went over well, and the management promised Kirk an extended return engagement, but at the last minute reneged. Instead, they held over the popular Willie Bryant band, which had followed the Clouds of Joy into the club. Broke and stranded, Kirk struck a deal with Bill McKinney for the Clouds of Joy to tour the Midwest as a unit of the McKinney's Cotton Pickers. Laying over in Cincinnati, Kirk seriously considered giving up the band and returning to the comfort of his post office job in Denver. Luckily, the ever faithful Ben Thigpen and Earl Thompson convinced Kirk to stay the course. Less vested members deserted the band. Buddy Tate, unable to bear the financial hardship, headed home. "We paid some dues with Andy, man, things really were bad, you have no idea," Tate sighed. "I quit and went back to Dallas."[7] Kirk replaced Tate with Dick Wilson, a strikingly handsome showman with advanced ideas and technique, and took the band back home to Kansas City.

Once home, the band's fortunes turned. In late May 1935, the Clouds of Joy opened for the season at Fairyland Park, which gave band members a measure of financial security and stabilized the personnel. With the opportunity to regroup, Kirk updated the Clouds' sound by developing a band book of hot and sweet tunes rendered in the rhythmic swinging style recently popularized by Benny Goodman. He then contacted Jack Kapp, his former liaison at Brunswick Records who had founded the American branch of Decca Records in 1934. Kapp swiftly built an impressive stable of vocalists and bands by raiding the rosters of Brunswick, Columbia, and Victor. Cashing in on leading vocalists and bands at cut-rate prices, Decca sold recordings by Bing Crosby, Louis Armstrong, Guy Lombardo, the Mills Brothers, Isham Jones, and Jimmy Lunceford for 35 cents each or three for a dollar. Hoping to duplicate Decca's success with the Lunceford band, Kapp invited the Clouds of Joy to come to New York to record. The band seized on the opportunity, eager to return to New York and get back in the studio. Another fortuitous encounter provided the band with an avenue to New York. While playing at Fairyland Park, Kirk happened to meet George Crowe, a young talent scout affiliated with band manager Joe Glaser. Impressed by the Clouds of Joy, Crowe recommended the band to Glaser, who lined up an eastern tour for the band.

Arriving on the East Coast in mid-February 1936, the Clouds of Joy played an extended engagement at the Club Astoria, a black-and-tan club in Baltimore, before moving on to New York City to record for Decca. Kirk pressed Mary Lou Williams to craft fresh arrangements of older material and to create new compositions for the sessions. Williams worked nonstop in one creative burst, just as she had for the band's first recording session in 1929. Looking back, Williams marveled at the sheer volume of her output. "Never have I written so many things so quickly in my entire career," she mused. "I must have done twenty in one week, including 'Cloudy,' 'Corky,' and 'Froggy

Bottom' [all new arrangements], 'Steppin' Pretty' and 'Walkin' and Swingin''
For nights I could not leave my room, having my meals brought in to me.
And at 7 a.m. I was up again for another session."[8] Williams earned $3 for
each new arrangement above her salary of $75 per week.

Kirk and Kapp clashed in the studio: Kapp wanted to record novelty and
swing tunes, while Kirk hoped for a ballad to appeal to white audiences. In
the end, the two reached a compromise that provided Kapp with ample recordings for the swing market and Kirk a crossover ballad. Moving in and out
of New York, the Kirk band recorded sixteen selections between March 2 and
April 7. Kirk and Kapp took their time, recording only one to three selections
per session. At Kapp's urging the band recorded a number of novelty tunes
including "Git," "I'se a Muggin'," "Give Her a Pint (And She'll Tell All),"
and "All the Jive is Gone," rendered in the popular hep harmony style of the
day. Kapp also insisted the band re-record "Lotta Sax Appeal," "Froggy Bottom," "Corky," and "Cloudy" from the earlier Brunswick sessions. Williams's
arrangements totally refashioned these standards from their earlier stomp-
down style to a gracefully swinging modern mode. The band's new musical
direction is best represented by Williams's original, "Walkin' and Swingin',"
written specifically for the session. Taken at a bright tempo, "Walkin' and
Swingin'" bounces along buoyed with the reed and brass sections alternating
between playing the melody straight and riffing off it. Expanding her musical
palette, Williams explored new orchestral possibilities with "Walkin' and
Swingin'." Williams explained, "'Walkin' and Swingin'' was one of those numbers musicians liked to play. I had tried out trumpet combining saxes to make
the sound of five reeds, and this was different and effective."[9]

Throughout the session, Kirk urged Kapp to audition a popular ballad favored by Kansas City audiences. Kapp ignored Kirk's request, insisting the
band record "Christopher Columbus," a wildly popular new song written by
Andy Razaf and Leon "Chu" Berry. Fletcher Henderson had recently adopted
"Christopher Columbus" as his band's theme song and planned to record it
later that month for the Vocalion label. Acting on insider information, Kapp
endeavored to beat Henderson and Vocalion to the punch by having the Clouds
of Joy record it first. Kirk agreed to record "Christopher Columbus" if Kapp
would listen to the band's special ballad. "I told him okay we'd make it, but
that I wanted him to listen to something special we had," Kirk asserted. "He
said to make his tune first and then we'd talk about it. We made 'Christopher
Columbus' and it became a big hit for us. While he was bragging to everybody about what a fine job we did with that tune, I told him I had a couple of
ballads I wanted him to listen to. He looked at me like I was crazy, and asked
me what was I trying to do, go high hat on him? He said he had plenty of
bands for that and not to waste the talent we had, but to keep on making the
type of numbers we had made our reputation with. I finally got him to listen
to one chorus of 'Until the Real Thing Comes Along.'"[10] Kapp let the band

record "Until the Real Thing Comes Along," but after listening to the playback he had second thoughts about the lyrics' indelicate grammar and coarse imagery. Kapp hired Sammy Cahn and Saul Chaplin to polish the lyrics. Working in concert, the two smoothed out the grammar and spiffed up the imagery, changing the refrain from "I would work for you / I'd slave for you / work my body to a grave for you / If that ain't love / It's got to do / Until the real thing comes along" to "I would work for you / I'd slave for you / I'd be a beggar or a knave for you / If that ain't love / It will have to do /Until the real thing comes along."[11] Returning to the studio on April 2, 1936, the band recorded "Until the Real Thing Comes Along" with the new lyrics.

A Kansas City standard, the song came to Kirk through a circuitous route. "(It Will Have To Do) Until the Real Thing Comes Along" evolved from "'Till the Real Thing Comes Along" written by lyricist Mann Holiner and composer Alberta Nichols for Lew Leslie's 1931 stage production *Rhapsody in Black*, which featured Ethel Waters. Members of the Three Chocolate Drops picked up on the song during a January 1933 performance of the production at the Shubert Theater in Kansas City. Unable to remember the exact lyrics, the Three Chocolate Drops improvised a variation of "'Til the Real Thing Comes Along," performing it at the Cherry Blossom and other cabarets in the 18th and Vine area. Basie, Kirk, and other local bands picked up on the Chocolate Drops' version, known as the "Slave Song." Saxophonist Slim Freeman astutely copyrighted the "Slave Song," much to the later dismay of Kirk, who claimed Freeman had no more to do with the creation of the song than a "bucket." Initially unimpressed, Kapp put "Until the Real Thing Comes Along" on the back burner and rushed the master for "Christopher Columbus" into production.

Decca released "Christopher Columbus" before the Clouds of Joy wrapped up the final recording session. It hit instantly, lifting the Clouds of Joy to top billing in theaters and ballrooms along the East Coast. On Easter Sunday 1936, the Clouds of Joy headlined a show at the Savoy Ballroom in Harlem with Chick Webb and the Fess Williams Sextette featuring pianist James P. Johnson. In Philadelphia, the band played the Elks annual dance on Easter Monday. Louis Armstrong, in town for another engagement, joined the band as a featured guest for the evening. Moving on to Washington, D.C., the Clouds of Joy played the prestigious Howard Theater. Kirk received a glut of offers from clubs, ballrooms, and theaters across the country, but instead returned to Kansas City to honor a previous commitment to Harry Duncan for a summer-long engagement at Fairyland Park.

The Clouds of Joy opened at Fairyland Park in mid-May 1936. Riding high on the crest of "Christopher Columbus" and Mary Lou Williams's new arrangements, the band rose to new popularity. The *Kansas City Call* described the band's transformation in a review of a battle of the bands against Jimmy Lunceford at Paseo Hall. "Andy and his boys held down the bandstand from

9 until 10:30 and the Clouds 'went to town' in a big way. Led by the dynamic and crooning Pha Terrell, the Clouds literally brought gasps from hundreds of early arrivals with their swing rhythm. This is a new Kirk, the Kirk that the East raved over some weeks ago. When they broke down and played 'Christopher Columbus' the crowd went wild."[12]

Released in early summer, "Until the Real Thing Comes Along" created a heavy demand for the Clouds of Joy. Making the song his own, singer Pha Terrell emphasized the final "comes along" with a heartfelt, soaring false coda. Unmoved by the flood of offers from across the country, Kirk honored his agreement with Harry Duncan and spent the summer in Kansas City. Delighted local fans flocked to Fairyland Park in record numbers to dance to the Clouds of Joy and cool off in the immense crystal pool. During the summer of 1936, the hottest on record in Kansas City, temperatures exceeded one hundred degrees during forty-one days.[13] At night, whole families sought refuge from the oppressive heat by dragging their bedding to the nearest park to sleep in the open under the canopy of stars.

As the Kirk band achieved national acclaim, booking agents and record company executives rushed to Kansas City. Journalist Dave E. Dexter, Jr., gave the industry insiders entrée to leading local bands and musicians. A native Kansas Citian, Dexter covered the local scene for the *Kansas City Journal-Post*. Dexter grew up in the northeast area, a close-knit predominately Italian and Irish working-class neighborhood. While attending Northeast High School, he faithfully followed the bands at the Pla-Mor, El Torreon, and Winnwood Beach. Dexter shunned dates with girls, going stag to absorb the music undistracted. He became acquainted with the more earthy musical delights in the clubs on 12th and 18th Streets, digging small combos, blues shouters, and barrelhouse pianists while sipping bootleg needle beer with his high school buddies. As an undergraduate at Missouri Valley College in Marshall, Missouri, Dexter covered sports news for the *Kansas City Star*. While studying journalism at the University of Missouri in Columbia, he covered the Kansas City music scene for *Down Beat* and *Metronome*, earning $5 for each article published. Dexter left school in the spring of 1936 and signed on with the *Kansas City Journal-Post* to write obituaries. Dexter directly took over the "Night Club Notes" column, which covered his first love: music in local clubs, hotels, and ballrooms. With his three-piece suits and matinee-idol looks, Dexter cut a dashing figure on his nightly circuit of clubs and ballrooms. Not content with covering the usual fare of white bands and clubs, Dexter introduced his readers to African American bands and clubs, taking special care to mention events sponsored by Local 627.

Dexter loved the Basie band but detested the Reno Club, considering it an unworthy venue for the band. Endeavoring to break the band nationally, Dexter tipped fellow *Down Beat* contributor and impresario John Hammond to Basie's broadcasts over W9XBY. Born into the upper class, Hammond early on developed a taste for blues and jazz. After dropping out of Yale, he pursued his vocation with great success, recording Bessie Smith for the Columbia label, producing Billie Holiday's sessions with Teddy Wilson, and helping Benny Goodman form his big band. While in Chicago with the Goodman band at the Congress Hotel, Hammond tuned into the Basie band's late-night broadcast. Hammond praised the band's broadcasts in *Down Beat*, but dawdled at checking out the band personally. Impatient with Hammond's inaction, Dexter, a natural born devil's advocate, goaded Hammond and other music magnates in an unaccredited article about the Basie band in the July 1936 issue of *Down Beat*.

While musicians and swing connoisseurs come away from a session with Basie talking to themselves with amazement, the bright business men who spend thousands of dollars to import name bands for Kansas City dancers, continue to pass up an opportunity to put the town on the musical map a la Coon Sanders in 1921.

With a couple of years seasoning Count Basie's Orchestra will probably rank with any band in the country for top honors in the swing division. Hammond, Mills or some other music mogul will give them the push that should come from Kaysee's hotel and restaurant big shots. Meanwhile Basie's squad huddles together in the darkest corner of a dive known as the Reno Club, one of the town's most unsavory holes. There they swing some of the country's finest arrangements under the noses of pimps, bags and shipping clerks who may or may not appreciate them fully, but who, it is certain cannot pay them a living wage.

One can imagine lots more life in Basie's music than is evident at one of the Club Reno sittings. Perhaps the clean pure air of W9XBY'S studio brings the boys out of it when they broadcast. But even in the smoke-filled darkness of the rough n' ready Reno one gets a tremendous boot listening to Basie's riders. His front rank men are Lester Young, who lackadaisically plays tenor sax 'til "who laid the chunk;" Clifford McTier [McTyer], guitar; George Hunt, trombone; Walter Page, bass and Mack Washington [Willie McWashington], drums. The rhythms furnished by Basie, McTier, Washington and Page are as solid as a booker's head, and, give a rich, stimulating background to the solos.

Buster Smith, first alto sax, does the arranging, carrying out Basie's ideas with taste and finesse. It is a real pleasure to watch Basie's men play such arrangements as Savoy Stomp without looking at the scores. They get in the groove together and work from memory without missing a note.

Basie's own rating spots Young, Page, Mack Washington and Hunt as his outstanding men. The others especially Buster Smith, rank far above the average colored musician in tone and execution. Full personnel of the band is as follows:

    Count Bill Basie, piano and leader
    Buster Smith, 1st sax and arranger
    Jack Washington, 3rd sax
    Lester Young, 1st tenor

Slim Freeman, 2nd tenor
Joe Keys [Keyes], 1st trumpet
Dee Stewart, 2nd trumpet
Carl Smith, 3rd trumpet
George Hunt, trombone
Walter Page, bass
Mack Washington, drums
Clifford McTier, guitar
Alice Dickson, singer
Jimmy Rushing, singer

Basie was scheduled to leave the Reno early in June in order to rehearse his band for recording. His plans after that are uncertain at this writing, but he will doubtless be signed up by some astute booker for a good Eastern spot, while Kansas City goes smugly on its way, unconscious of the laxity of these who are supposed to bring its public real entertainment and music.[14]

Following the publication of Dexter's tirade, John Hammond and Joe Glaser heeded the challenge and raced to Kansas City in late July. By coincidence, they arrived the same evening: Glaser accompanied Louis Armstrong for a concert at the Municipal Auditorium and Hammond arrived alone. Aristocratic with a wiry brush cut and a toothy grin, Hammond registered at the elegant Muehlebach Hotel and rendezvoused with Dexter. Together they made the rounds, trailed by Glaser. Despite the swelling popularity of "Until the Real Thing Comes Along," the smooth style of the Clouds of Joy at Fairyland Park did not suit Hammond's musical taste.

Glaser, on the other hand, seized the opportunity to capitalize on his earlier association with Kirk and locked the Clouds of Joy into a long-term contract. While Glaser lingered at Fairyland Park wooing Kirk, Hammond and Dexter made a beeline to 12th Street. Hammond hit it off with Pete Johnson and Joe Turner at the Sunset, but passed on the other band members, who were drunk and musically off that evening.

Amused by the unsavory characters and illicit activities surrounding the Reno Club, Hammond fell absolutely in love with the Basie band. "I walked down to 12th Street to a dingy building with a second floor which must have been a whorehouse, because there were girls lounging on the stairway," Hammond revealed.

On the street level was the Reno Club with signs advertising domestic Scotch for 10 cents, imported Scotch for 15 cents, and beer 5 cents. Hot dogs were 10 cents, hamburgers were 15 cents, and drinks served at tables were 25 cents. There was no cover, no minimum, and there was a show which included chorus girls and the Basie band with Jimmy Rushing and Hattie Noel as vocalists. It was quite a bargain. The first thing I saw was the high bandstand, at the top of which sat Jo Jones surrounded by his drums, Basie sat at the left of Walter Page and his bass crowded as close to the front line as he could get. . . . The band

played long sets, working almost constantly. . . . I noticed an open window behind the bandstand at which occasional transactions took place; I assumed that
"tea" was being passed. . . . But the band! . . . for me there has never been anything like the early Basie band. It had its shortcomings. Its sound was occasionally raw and raucous, but you expected it to erupt and sooner or later it did.[15]

Back in New York, Hammond praised Kansas City's music scene in general and above all the Basie band in a September 1936 article in *Down Beat*,
confirming Dexter's earlier assessment of the band's potential.

Hearing Count Basie's band is an experience I will never forget. The stage was
all set for a complete disillusionment, for I had been plugging the band only from
its radio work, sight unseen. I was almost scared to go near it, lest I might have to
retract some of the raves I have been scattering about. But after spending only
one night in the place I came away convinced that the band has the makings of
the finest the country has ever known (it isn't far from that state right now).

The first thing that flabbergasted me was the realization that all the music I
had been hearing over W9XBY every night was from a mere ten piece group:
three rhythm, three saxes, four brass. The voicing of the arrangements is so
deft that the band had sounded at least like a five brass four reed combination.
Then there was the work of the rhythm section, with Walter Page on bass, Joe
[Jo] Jones, drums and the Count on piano. The only section I have ever heard
even remotely comparable to it is the four piece one of Albert Ammons in
Chicago when Israel Crosby was still on bass, but even Ammons' doesn't begin
to have the versatility that belongs to the Count's.

Page is one of the great bass players of the world, with a wonderful tone,
flawless technique, and infinite experience. Jones, who is a recent replacement,
is about as near perfection as the best drummers can come, and Count Basie on
piano—well, there just aren't any words for him. He has all the solidity and
endurance of Fats Waller, most of Teddy Wilson's technique and some of his
taste, plus a style that is definitely his own. He actually swings a band that is
already rocking more than any I have known.

As a section, the brass is fine, although I would feel safer about my superla-
tives if I could hear it some place other than the excellent shell at the Reno,
which could flatter any section. The trombone is not quite so assured as he had
seemed over the air, and the trumpeter Lips Page was definitely at a disadvan-
tage due to a temporarily wrenched leg. Outstanding in the reeds, of course, is
Lester Young, who would be an asset to any band in the country on tenor. He
is the kind of guy who just likes to make music, with the result that he is always
to be found jamming in some unlikely joint. Buster Smith, the first alto and an
important arranger, is no slouch either, for his technique is unlimited and his
tone quite free from the cloying quality which colored alto men took over from
the Lombardo tribe.

Hammond concluded by revealing his intent to shape the band's development. "The leader himself is a consummate natural showman, and his men

have that infectious enthusiasm that inspires an audience. What ever rough edges there still are can either be removed or made more jagged, preferably the latter."[16] Immediately taking a personal interest in the band's future, Hammond persuaded Willard Alexander, one of the top agents at MCA, to add Basie to the agency's roster led by Benny Goodman. Acting quickly on Hammond's recommendation, Alexander booked a fall tour to the East Coast for the band, starting with an engagement at the Grand Terrace in Chicago.

Poised on the brink of national success, Basie suffered a major setback when arranger Buster Smith and soloist Lips Page left the band. Smith, unimpressed with John Hammond's overtures, departed in late August to join Claude Hopkins in Chicago. Joe Glaser wooed Page into a management contract at the Reno. Glaser hoped the band would follow suit, but Basie declined the opportunity, preferring to cast his lot with Hammond and Alexander. Page signed on with Glaser as a single, delighted to be represented by the same agency as his hero Armstrong.

Much to the chagrin of the departed members, Basie did finally claim the band's overdo recognition. "We'd heard so much about how somebody was going to come and get the band and make it big," Smith related. "I just didn't think anything about it—figured it was just more talk—so I left. Lips left too, before I did. We hadn't been gone long before I heard Basie broadcasting from the Grand Terrace in Chicago, and I was a little surprised—and a little sorry I hadn't stayed with them."[17]

The loss of Smith and Page, along with Willard Alexander's desire to expand the band, forced Basie to regroup right before the band's national debut. Initially, Basie wanted to simply replace Smith and Page, and then take the nine-piece band on the road. Willard Alexander however insisted on expanding the band before embarking on the tour. Given the opportunity to assemble a big band, Basie knew exactly the sound he wanted. "I already had some pretty clear ideas about how I wanted the band to sound like," Basie recounted. "I knew how I wanted each section to sound. So I also knew what each guy should sound like. I knew what I wanted them there for. Even back when I was dictating those arrangements to Eddie Durham for Bennie Moten's band, I could actually hear the band playing those passages while we were working on them."[18]

While still in residence at the Reno Club, Basie carefully began building the band, working section by section, recruiting new players and sending for old friends.

> So I think the first thing we started on was the trombone section, when we got [George] Hunt, also called Rabbit. . . . Then later we added Dan Minor. These two trombones were all we had in that section for the rest of the time we were in Kansas City.

Boss Tom Pendergast and wife, 1936. Tom Pendergast was the man who made Kansas City the draw for entertainment and nightlife until tax evasion brought him down in 1939. Kansas City was the never the same after. *Driggs Collection.*

T. J. Pendergast Wholesale Liquor Co., Inc., Kansas City, 1930s. This liquor distribution company provided Pendergast with a large source of income, as it supplied all the taverns and night clubs in Kansas City. *Driggs Collection.*

Tom Pendergast Home, Ward Parkway, Kansas City, c. 1938. Payoffs from a variety of sources helped account for Boss Tom Pendergast's sumptuous home on Ward Parkway. He installed a wire to Riverside Race Track, where his losses on the ponies caused him to dip into the state insurance fund. *Driggs Collection.*

Mary Lou Williams, pianist/arranger for Andy Kirk's Orchestra, Denver, 1940.
Surrounded by admiring fans, Mary Lou Williams, Andy Kirk's great soloist and
principal arranger, takes time out at Denver's Rainbow Ballroom in 1940. *Photo by
Roland Shreves; Driggs Collection.*

Facing page, bottom: Andy Kirk's Clouds of Joy, Mary Lou Williams, piano;
Rainbow Ballroom, Denver, 1935. *Left to right:* Earl Thompson, Ted Donnelly,
Bob Hall, Harry Lawson, Andy Kirk, Ted Brinson, Ed Thigpen, Booker Collins,
Mary Lou Williams, Dick Wilson, John Williams, John Harrington, Pha Terrell.
Kirk's Clouds of Joy were on their way up in 1935 when the band was appearing at
Denver's Rainbow Ballroom. One man, middle trumpeter Bob Hall, dropped and
was replaced by Paul King when they finally broke into the big time in 1936 and
started recording for Decca Records. *Driggs Collection.*

Reno Club, 12th and Cherry, Kansas City, 1938. From 1935 to 1939 this club flourished, starting Count Basie on his way to fame, through Bus Moten, Bill Martin, and finally Oliver Todd, before the place was closed in the cleanup of 1939. *Driggs Collection.*

Facing page, top: Hot Lips Page and Bus Moten Band, Reno Club, 12th and Cherry, Kansas City, c. November 1936. *Left to right:* Bus Moten, piano; Jesse Price, drums; Billy Hadnott, bass; Orville DeMoss, alto sax; Hot Lips Page, trumpet; Robert Hibbler, trumpet; unkown, alto sax; Dee Stewart, trumpet; Odell West, tenor sax. Hot Lips Page was signed by Joe Glaser and went to New York after this engagement. Bus Moten was a hothead, despite having good men, and lost the job almost immediately. *Driggs Collection.*

Facing page, bottom: Interior of the Reno Club, 12th and Cherry, Kansas City, 1937. *Left to right:* Prince Albert, trumpet; Bill Searcy, piano; Paul Gunther, drums; Lowell Pointer, bass; Curtyse Foster, tenor sax; Roy "Buck" Douglas, tenor sax; Bill Martin, trumpet; Ray "Bill" Douglas, first alto sax; Christianna Buckner, dancer. It was on this bandstand that Count Basie's career was launched in 1935. *Courtesy Curtyse Foster; Driggs Collection.*

The Rockets at the Spinning Wheel, 12th and Troost, Kansas City, 1937. *Left to right*: Pete Johnson, piano; Booker Washington, trumpet; Herman Walder, alto sax; Leonard "Jack" Johnson, bass; Woody Walder, tenor sax; Baby Lovett, drums. This break-off unit from the Harlan Leonard band kept this job for three years. Pete Johnson, an inveterate ladies' man, left and was replaced by Elbert "Coots" Dye. *Driggs Collection.*

Buster Smith and Odell West, Lucille's Paradise, Kansas City, 1938. *Photo by William Vandivert, courtesy Rita Vandivert.*

Murl Johnson, drums; "Coots" Dye, piano; Lucille Webb, owner, at mike. Lucille's Paradise, Kansas City, 1938. *Photo by William Vandivert, courtesy Rita Vandivert; Driggs Collection.*

Margaret "Countess" Johnson, piano, Kansas City, 1938. Countess Johnson substituted for Mary Lou Williams in Andy Kirk's band and hardly anyone knew the difference. She also had her own combos. She died of tuberculosis in 1939. *Driggs Collection.*

Famous Kansas City location, 18th and Vine, 1940s. This area was central to Kansas City's nightlife. *Driggs Collection.*

Joe Keyes, trumpet, c. 1939. A gifted first trumpet player with Bennie Moten and Count Basie, he was undependable and often became drunk. He drowned in 1950. *Photo by Danny Barker; Driggs Collection.*

Count Basie's Kansas City Seven, New York City, 1940. *Left to right*: Jo Jones, drums; Walter Page, bass; Buddy Tate, tenor sax; Count Basie, piano; Freddie Green, guitar; Buck Clayton, trumpet; Dicky Wells, trombone. *Driggs Collection.*

Herschel Evans soloing on "Blue & Sentimental" with the Count Basie Band, Famous Door, 52nd Street, New York City, July 1938. Released on Decca Records, this number made Evans better known. *Photo by Otto Hagel; Driggs Collection.*

Lester Young with the Count Basie Band, Famous Door, New York City, 1938.
A rare moment of laughter. *Photo by Otto Hagel; Driggs Collection.*

Harlan Leonard's Rockets, College Inn, Kansas City, 1940. Winston Williams, bass; Henry Bridges, tenor sax; Darwin Jones, alto sax; Myra Taylor, vocals. Williams and Bridges were two of the reasons Harlan Leonard's band was the hottest in town in 1940. *Photo by George Costello; Driggs Collection.*

Harlan Leonard's Rockets, RCA Studios, Chicago, 1940. *Left to right*: Richmond Henderson, trombone; Jimmie Keith, tenor sax/arranger; Edward "Peeny" Johnson, first trumpet; James Ross, trumpet/arranger; Harlan Leonard, first alto sax; William Smith, trumpet; Darwin Jones, third alto sax/vocals; Winston Williams, bass; Henry Bridges, tenor sax; Jesse Price, drums; William S. Smith, piano. Harlan Leonard's band was recording for Bluebird records. *Driggs Collection.*

Jesse "Country" Price, College Inn, Kansas City. Price came to Kansas City from Memphis in 1932 and worked his way up to top drummer after Jo Jones left with Count Basie in 1936. He was the driving force in Harlan Leonard's Rockets at the College Inn in 1940. *Photo by John Randazzo; Driggs Collection.*

Charlie Parker, Kansas City, 1940. On his way up, Parker poses at a dime-store photomat. *Driggs Collection.*

Charlie Parker, alto sax, and Gene Ramey, bass, Kansas City, 1940. Parker was the last and perhaps greatest star to come out of Kansas City. *Photo by Robert Armstrong; Driggs Collection.*

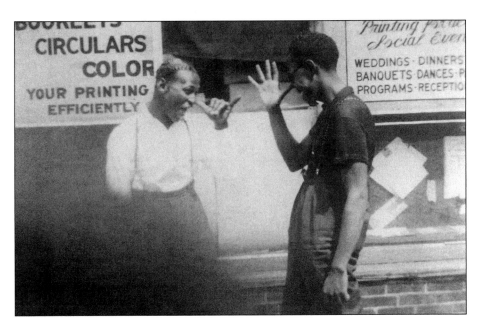

Jesse Price and Charlie Parker, Kansas City, summer 1938. Price dug Parker and induced Buster Smith to hire him for the job they held down at Lucille's Band Box. *Courtesy Lord Bud Calver; Driggs Collection.*

Jay McShann, 1940. *Left to right*: Gene Ramey, bass; Jay McShann, piano; Gus
Johnson, drums; Walter Brown, vocalist; Joe Baird, trombone; Bill Nolan, vocalist;
Orville Minor, trumpet. On a one-nighter in Wichita, McShann had three vocalists
on his way to New York in 1942. Bill Nolan, to the left of Walter Brown, dropped
out. *Photo by Robert Armstrong; Driggs Collection.*

Then Herschel Evans came back from California, and that was the beginning of the two tenors. Herschel and Lester had been pretty close friends ever since the days when I was at the Cherry Blossom, and they used to swap gigs between the band I had in there and the one Bennie Moten and George E. Lee had over at Club Harlem. Now, with two bad soloists like that in the same reed section, we really had something special. But I actually didn't begin to realize how special that was until a little later on.

Herschel also brought Buck Clayton into the band. He and Buck had come in from Los Angeles around the same time. So when Herschel found out that we needed somebody in the trumpet section because Lips Page was leaving to go out under the management of Joe Glaser, he said he had a cat named Buck Clayton who played a lot of trumpet, and he brought him in. Buck had been in China with a band, and he had also had his own band in Los Angeles for awhile. When Herschel brought him in, he was in town because he was from Parsons, Kansas, and he was stopping off on his way east to join Willie Bryant's band in New York. But when he came into the Reno and sat in with us, he changed his mind about going on to New York at that time. . . . Herschel and Buck also found us a new alto player when Buster Smith decided to cut out on us. . . . So Herschel and Buck got in touch with Couchy [Chaughey] Roberts back in Los Angeles, and he came and joined us. Couchy had been in Buck's band in China, so all Buck and Herschel had to do was say the word and he came.

Rounding out the group, Basie sent for violinist and guitarist Claude Williams, then working in Chicago.[19]

Still lacking an arranger for the fourteen-piece band, Basie fell back on Buster Smith's head arrangements for the original nine-piece band. Basie figured the band could wing it and improvise collectively off the head arrangements until he could hire an arranger to develop a book of new, original compositions. Basie's decision resulted in a rough start for the band, despite John Hammond's best efforts to smooth the way.

Before pulling out of Kansas City, Basie and crew played a double bill with Duke Ellington at Paseo Hall on November 2. Dance fans packed Paseo Hall for royal entertainment by the Duke and the Count. According to the *Kansas City Call*, "Ellington went to town on 'It Don't Mean a Thing,' 'Stormy Weather,' 'Solitude,' 'Troubled Waters' and several other numbers that had the huge crowd applauding raucously."[20] The review ambiguously reported the Basie band "played with their usual gusto." Claude Williams remembered that the Basie band was caught ill prepared to share the bill with the more polished and experienced Ellington band. "Duke Ellington blew us out of the other side of the hall because we didn't have arrangements," Williams revealed. "All of Basie's arrangements were for nine pieces not a twelve-piece band, so we had to play head arrangements. The band wasn't ready."[21] Right after the engagement, as the band prepared to board its new bus and depart for Chicago, Ellington joined the crowd of well-wishers gathered outside the hall to see the band off. Pulling Basie aside, Ellington graciously assured him "you can make it."[22] Little did Ellington realize that Basie was destined to become one of his principal rivals in the years to come.

Following Fletcher Henderson into the Grand Terrace in early November, the freewheeling Basie band initially sounded pretty rough. Hammond marveled that Ed Fox, the manager of the Grand Terrace, did not fire the band right off the bat. Buck Clayton blamed the new musicians who were added at the last minute for the band's rocky start. "Our reputation, before we came out east, was built on nine pieces, and I don't think we ever had a bad night in Kansas City, but when we added five or six men it made a lot of difference," Clayton confided. "The band had to be enlarged to go out on the road, but it slowed everything down and made it sluggish, because those extra men were not exactly the best musicians."[23]

Jazz critic George Simon echoed Clayton's opinion. Reviewing the broadcasts from the Grand Terrace over the NBC Blue Network, Simon lambasted the band's intonation in his *Metronome* column. "True, the band does swing, and it's only been caught on the air where, 't'is said, copyright restrictions don't allow to play some of its best tunes. But that sax section is so invariably out of tune. And if you think that sax section sounds out of tune, catch the brass! And if you think the brass by itself is out of tune, catch the intonation of the band as a whole!! Swing Is Swing, but music is music, too. Here's hoping the outfit sounds better in person."[24] Simon's sharp criticism of the Basie band stemmed, in part, from his rivalry with Hammond, a regular contributor to *Down Beat*, *Metronome*'s principal competitor. Hammond's blatant self-interest in hyping the group further fueled the feud with Simon. Fletcher Henderson came to the band's rescue by loaning Basie arrangements from his band book. Once equipped with a few proper arrangements, the band showed a marked improvement. The *Kansas City Call* quoted a *Chicago News* review that declared "Basie has one of the most exciting bands in creation, possessing a rhythmic abandon that is non-existent north of their homes, Kansas City."[25]

While in Chicago, Hammond hustled Basie, Jimmy Rushing, Walter Page, Jo Jones, and Lester Young into the studio to record for the Vocalion label. A split lip prevented Buck Clayton from participating, so Carl Smith sat in on trumpet. Hammond recorded the ensemble under the pseudonym Jones-Smith Incorporated, because Basie had already signed a contract with Decca. Before Hammond could get Basie under contract to Brunswick, Jack Kapp's brother Dave, masquerading as a friend of Hammond, had convinced Basie to sign with Decca. Unfair at best, the three-year Decca contract paid the full band a flat rate of $750 with no royalties. Skirting the band's contract with Decca, Hammond ushered the small group into the studio under a pseudonym and trumped the Kapp brothers.

Hammond's offer of a recording session caught Basie and other band members by surprise. "John asked me if I wanted to record. I didn't have my library and didn't know what the heck we were going to do," Basie declared. "So we just sat down and came up with four tunes and had a nice ball on the session."[26] The band wrapped up the session in only three hours. Jimmy Rushing kept his overcoat on during the entire session. Lacking original material, the band collectively improvised on the standards "Shoe Shine Boy," "Oh, Lady Be Good," "Boogie Woogie," and "Evenin'." Without the baggage of the larger band, the core members easily came together, as they had so many nights before at the Reno Club. Making his debut on record, Lester Young dominates "Shoe Shine Boy" and "Oh, Lady Be Good." Supported by Page's sturdy walking-bass line, Basie introduces the melody of "Oh, Lady Be Good" in the first chorus with riffs and licks. Following Basie's loose statement, Young confidently takes charge, gliding through two, thirty-two-bar choruses building idea on idea, crafting a splendidly improvised structure. The forceful rhythm section gracefully anticipates Young's inventive phrases. Jones, playing a thrown-together drum set with no bass drum, uses rim shots to accentuate Young's flowing solos. Smith's muted trumpet takes the lead for the next chorus, only to be eclipsed by Young's supporting riffs. In the out chorus, Basie jumps in at the bridge, truncating the first sixteen bars before Young and Smith wrap things up neatly in the last eight bars with a shout chorus of riffs in true Kansas City fashion.[27] Forced to obscurely attribute the sessions to Jones-Smith, Inc., Vocalion failed to cash in on Basie's growing stature. Nevertheless, Hammond triumphed artistically over the Kapp brothers in capturing the raw essence of the Basie band in all its glory right out of the Reno Club.

After closing out a five-week stand at the Grand Terrace, the Basie band played a string of one-nighters to the East Coast. Arriving in New York City at the height of the Christmas season, the band opened opposite the Woody Herman band at the Roseland Ballroom. The band still lacked original material and suitable arrangements, but it showed a vast improvement over its inauspicious debut at the Grand Terrace. Based on the band's broadcasts from the Roseland, George Simon tempered his previous criticism by noting the band's increased polish and potential for greatness:

> The result of the Count's tactics is vast improvement in the band. That's especially obvious in the outfit's weakest department, intonation. Though the men still suffer from an inability to sustain notes on the same even pitch—a fault that crops up mostly in slow tunes—they do sound in tune when it comes to biting off notes or even playing some smartly written figures.
>
> Right now it's those written figures that make the band stand out and show promise of really amounting to something in the future. There's some brilliantly conceived stuff there: figures that not only swing in their own right, but which also fit into some cleverly worked out swing patterns. The men are beginning to feel them more than they did at first: they're relaxing more, and consequently deriving greater benefits from them.

Simon praised the rhythm section but criticized the brass and reed sections as well as the band's repertoire.

> The two melody sections, as mentioned before, are responsible for holding back the band. Intonation and blend are not yet good. In colored sax sections that's sometimes overlooked, but it can't be in brass units. There are as compensation a few outstanding soloists. In the brass the only new man, Buck Clayton, sends you with interesting stuff played with much feeling. Lester Young and Herschel Evans both carry off their share of hot tenor passages adequately enough. . . . Unfortunately, not as much can be said for the selection of tunes; here the library is woefully weak. The band plays very few current pops, and those it does play it plays very badly. There's no getting away from the fact that it's dependent almost entirely upon its limited selection of specials.[28]

Hammond and Basie, well aware of the band's shortcomings, had little time to make changes before heading into the first Decca recording session. Entering the studio on January 21, 1937, the band recorded two standards, "Honeysuckle Rose" and "Pennies from Heaven," along with two originals "Swingin' at the Daisy Chain" and "Roseland Shuffle." While Rushing's spirited vocals save the day on the popular standard "Pennies from Heaven," the instrumentals lack the coherent structure requisite to fully realize and sustain the melodic ideas expressed by the ensemble as a whole. This is particularly evident on "Roseland Shuffle," a blatant adaptation of "Shoe Shine Boy," recorded earlier for Vocalion as Jones-Smith, Inc. Following a forceful contrasting riff statement by the full ensemble, Basie and Lester Young carry the melody with alternating choruses before yielding to the saxophone and brass sections' riff interplay, which ambles to an abrupt conclusion. Listening to the results of the session, it became clear to Basie and Hammond that, despite the strength of the rhythm section and overall solo excellence, without sharp arrangements of strong original compositions, the band could not successfully compete with Duke Ellington, Jimmy Lunceford, and other more polished bands. Increasingly concerned with the outfit's slow progress, Hammond and Basie adjusted the personnel and expanded the repertoire.

Leaving New York in early February, the band opened at the Chatterbox Room in the Hotel William Penn in Pittsburgh. The stuffy white crowd at the Chatterbox soon gave way to college kids attracted by the band's nightly broadcasts over WCAE. The band happily complied with the younger set's demands for swing music of the wildest sort. Shortly after opening at the Chatterbox, Hammond and Basie gave Claude Williams, Joe Keyes, and Carl Smith their walking papers. Hammond, irritated by Williams's assertive violin solos, wanted a guitarist dedicated to playing rhythm. Ironically, George Simon, the band's strongest critic, had praised Williams's violin and guitar work in his review of the band's Roseland performance. Basie deferred to Hammond, and Freddie Green, a quiet, steady rhythm player, replaced Williams. Tuning up the trumpet section, Basie replaced Joe Keyes with Ed Lewis, an old friend from Kansas City, and Carl Smith with Bobby Moore from New York.

When the band returned to New York in late March, Hammond introduced Basie to Billie Holiday. Basie fell under the spell of her elegance and talent. "And she was something. I was really turned on by her," Basie confessed. "She knocked me out. I thought she was so pretty. A very, very attractive lady. And when she sang, it was an altogether different style. I hadn't heard anything like it, and I was all for it, and I told John I sure would like to have her come and work with the band if it could be arranged. And naturally John agreed, because he already had the same idea before he took me to hear her. . . . [A]nd she did very well that everybody immediately fell in love with her. When she rehearsed with the band, it was really just a matter of getting her tunes like she wanted them. Because she knew how she wanted to sound, and you couldn't tell her what to do. You wouldn't know what to tell her. She had her own style, and it was to remain that way. Sometimes she would bring in new things and she would dictate the way she'd like them done. That's how she got her book with us. She never left her own style. Nobody sounded like her."[29] Holiday's contract with Brunswick prevented her from recording with the Basie band for the Decca label. However, Holiday and Hammond freely used Basie band members as sidemen for her recording sessions.

Following dates at the Apollo Theater and Savoy Ballroom, the band opened at the Nixon Grand Theater in Philadelphia during mid-April. While at the Grand Theater, Basie and Hammond further refined the personnel of the band by replacing alto saxophonist Chaughey Roberts with handsome Earl Warren, a strong section player and entertaining crooner. A few months later, Eddie Durham, Basie's musical alter ego from the Moten band, joined as staff arranger and composer, charged with tightening the sections and developing the band book. Except for a few originals written for the Decca recording sessions, the band relied on special arrangements of popular standards purchased by Basie in New York. Still somewhat unsophisticated musically, Basie needed a collaborator to extend and orchestrate his ideas. Fortunately, over the years, Hammond had stayed in touch with Durham. Hammond, putting his considerable charm to work, persuaded Durham, then working as an arranger for Jimmy Lunceford, to join the Basie band. Willard Alexander sweetened the deal, paying Durham the princely sum of $150 per week—$75 for arranging and $75 for playing in the band—more than twice his salary with Lunceford. A freelancer at heart, Durham signed on for one year. In early June 1937, right after a battle of the bands between Basie and Lunceford in Hartford, Connecticut, the valet simply moved Durham's bags from Lunceford's to Basie's band bus.

Basie and Durham quickly renewed their creative partnership. As before, Durham fleshed out Basie's rough ideas and shaped them into supple arrangements. Taking advantage of a long break in the band's touring schedule, the two rehearsed the band and worked up fresh head arrangements in the basement of the Woodside Hotel in Harlem, the band's headquarters.

"We got together down there at least three times a week, and we made some great head arrangements down there during those sessions, and those guys in each section remembered everything," Basie remarked. "I don't know how they did it, but they really did. So by the time we got through with a tune, it was an arrangement. People thought it was written out."

> It was like the Blue Devils. We always had somebody in those sections who was a leader, who could start something and get those ensembles going. I mean while somebody would be soloing in the reed section, the brasses would have something going in the background, and the reed section would have something to go with that. And while the brass section had something going, somebody in the reed section might be playing a solo. When a trumpet player would have something going, the band would have something. While he's playing the first chorus, they'd be getting something going down there in the reeds. That's all they needed, and the next chorus just followed.
>
> That's where we were at. That's the way it went down. Those guys knew just where to come in and they came in. And the thing about it that was so fantastic was this: *Once those guys played something, they could damn near play it exactly the same the next night.* That's what really happened. Of course, I'm sitting there at the piano catching notes and all, and I knew just how I wanted to use the different things they used to come up with. So I'd say something like "Okay, take that one a half tone down; go ahead down with it and then go for something." We'd do that, and they would remember their notes, and a lot of times the heads that we made down there in that basement were a lot better than things that were written out.[30]

The next Decca session captured the band's immense improvement, brought about by Durham's arrangements of Basie's ideas. On July 7, the band recorded four selections: "Smarty," "One O'Clock Jump," "Listen My Children," and "John's Idea." The session's finest moment, "One O'Clock Jump," fully realizes the relaxed hard-swinging style Basie and Durham cooked up in the basement of the Woodside Hotel. Based on a twelve-bar blues head arrangement called "Blue Balls," originally composed by Basie, Durham, and Buster Smith as members of the Moten band, "One O'Clock Jump" ushers in the Basie band's golden age. The driving rhythm section led by Basie's confident rolling piano introduces the theme in F major and sets the rollicking mood, leading to spirited twelve-bar solos by Herschel Evans, George Hunt on trombone, Lester Young, and Buck Clayton, all in Db major. Restrained riffs by the counter sections underscore and accentuate the round of stellar solos. Basie and the rhythm section return for twelve bars before the trumpet, trombone, and saxophone sections take things home with three choruses of exuberant riffs, establishing the band's familiar signature.[31] Distinguished by its catchy melody and infectious riffs, "One O'Clock Jump" became an overnight hit with dance fans and record buyers. Basie straightaway capitalized on the growing popularity of swing with considerable help from Hammond and the "King of Swing," Benny Goodman.

The previous spring, Benny Goodman boldly breached the color barrier by forming a quartet with pianist Teddy Wilson and vibraphonist Lionel Hampton, bringing the first integrated band to the public. Goodman's brave stand against musical segregation loosened public attitudes toward integrated groups and opened the doors to white hotels and dance palaces for African American bands. The Basie band, one of Goodman's favorites, benefited greatly from the relaxation of the color barrier. "In my opinion, there is nothing like the pure swing this outfit has, from the moment it starts playing until it stops—and the rhythm section of this band: Basie himself on piano, Walter Page on bass, Joe Jones on drums, and Freddie Green playing guitar, is in a class by itself," Goodman observed. "Basie and Page were plugging along in some cellar joint in Kansas City, working for starvation wages, with just about no hope of getting anyplace. I happened to catch them one night around that time [while we were at the Congress Hotel] on some little station call[ed] W9XBY, and the kick I got out of hearing them was terrific. It was only right that somebody should do something about seeing that they got a hearing."[32]

True to his word, Goodman helped John Hammond bring the band to the MCA roster. Goodman also prominently featured Basie, Freddie Green, Walter Page, Lester Young, and Buck Clayton and other core members during his historic Carnegie Hall concert on January 16, 1938, the wildly successful debut of swing in New York's preeminent concert venue. Boosted by Hammond and Goodman, the Basie band quickly ascended to the upper rank of bands nationally. Basie maintained his affiliation with Local 627 but never again based his band in Kansas City.

As Basie struggled to establish his band nationally, the Kirk band moved up in popularity on the phenomenal success of "Until the Real Thing Comes Along." Barraged by offers of management deals and out-of-town engagements, Kirk chose to spend the summer of 1936 in Kansas City, honoring his contract with Fairyland Park. "We had several offers to leave Kansas City just before we made the big-time. Both John Hammond and Willard Alexander who had come to Kansas City to hear Basie at the Reno Club, heard my band at Fairyland Park. The same night, Craig, the owner of the Blossom Heath in Oklahoma, asked me to open the winter season for him, and Charlie Buchanan of the Savoy called me long distance from New York. They all wanted 'Until the Real Thing Comes Along.' Joe Glaser was staying at the Muehlbach Hotel and told me not to sign with anyone until I'd thought his offer over. He wired me plane tickets from Chicago and that was it."[33] Kirk never looked back.

Wrapping up the season at Fairyland Park, the Clouds of Joy unceremoniously left Kansas City, zigzagging on a string of one-nighters leading to the East Coast. Arriving in New York, the band recorded again for the Decca label on December 9, 1936. Much to Kirk's dismay, Jack Kapp, hoping to duplicate the popularity of "Until the Real Thing Comes Along," wanted to record mostly ballads. "I had a hard time getting him to record any more jazz; he wanted everything schmaltz. We had a lot of good tunes in our book, but he wanted the opposite of what he said before . . . 'Dedicated to You,' 'Poor Butterfly,' and things like that," Kirk complained. "I was always hoping to get in some more jazz numbers, but the other things were commercial then and they made a lot of money for us."[34]

Kapp brought three tunes to the session: "Fifty-Second Street," "The Lady Who Swings the Band," and "Dedicated to You," written by Sammy Cahn and Saul Chaplin, the team that refined the original version of "Until the Real Thing Comes Along." Giving into Kapp's desire for another hit ballad, Kirk cast "Dedicated to You" and the other ballad "What Will I Tell My Heart" in the mold of "Until the Real Thing Comes Along," complete with a lilting falsetto ending by Pha Terrell. "Fifty-Second Street," a paean to New York City's famed swing street, showcased vocalist Harry Mills and the exuberant piano work of Mary Lou Williams. The lyrics of "The Lady Who Swings the Band" introduced Mary Lou Williams to the country as the creative force behind the band, and made her an instant celebrity.

> In Kansas City, there's a pretty girl named Mary Lou, and she plays her
>   piano in a manner, that is ultra new
> Here of late she's playing with the band. Let me tell you of this baby at the
>   Baby Grand
> When You hear a hot trombone, who's the power behind the moan? It's the
>   lady who swings the band!

Kapp's instincts paid off. "What Will I Tell My Heart," backed by "The Lady Who Swings the Band" hit big, selling over 45,000 copies within three months of release, giving the band the needed follow-up hit to "Until the Real Thing Comes Along."[35]

While in New York, the Clouds of Joy played the Savoy Ballroom and Apollo Theater to favorable reviews. In the same column in which George Simon so severely criticized the intonation of the Basie band, he fairly raved about the Clouds of Joy, praising Mary Lou Williams and Dick Wilson. "In person that Kirk bunch is all it's cracked up to be. Terrific swing, and intonation that's about as fine as you'd find in any colored band. And at least two soloists who are bound to send you: little Mary Lou Williams on piano, and big John [Dick] Wilson on tenor saxophone."[36] With talent to match his good looks, Wilson cut a striking figure on stage. Kirk felt that Wilson "could play tenor with anyone then. He was way ahead of his time."[37] Wilson, Mary Lou Williams, and Pha Terrell gave the band the star power needed to compete with Earl Hines, Jimmie Lunceford, Duke Ellington, and other leading bands.

Joe Glaser further leveled the playing field by steering the band to Rockwell-O'Keefe, a leading booking agency, insuring steady employment in top venues from coast to coast.

Leaving New York, the Clouds of Joy opened at the Howard Theater in Washington, D.C., for a midnight show on New Year's Eve featuring comedienne Jackie Mabley, later known as Moms. Glaser, taking a cue from Duke Ellington and Count Basie, billed Kirk as the Sultan of Syncopation. Worn out, Kirk fell seriously ill at the conclusion of the week-long engagement. Leaving Kirk behind to recuperate, the band left for an eight-week engagement at the Trianon Ballroom in Cleveland. With the limelight focused on Mary Lou, Dick Wilson, and Pha Terrell, the audience scarcely noticed Kirk's absence. Broadcasts from the Trianon over the NBC network furthered the band's national reputation. Kirk reunited with the band at the conclusion of the engagement at the Trianon Ballroom for a recording session in New York on February 15, 1937. Dissatisfied with the results of the session, Kapp held the masters back and scheduled a follow-up session for April 17. With "Until the Real Thing Comes Along" having sold over 100,000 copies and "What Will I Tell My Heart" still going strong, Kapp felt little pressure to rush additional recordings to the market. Unfortunately, by pressuring Kirk to record mainly commercial hits, Kapp stifled the band's creativity in the studio and on the bandstand. At engagements, the band had to faithfully recreate their recorded hits, playing them note for note, leaving little room for collective improvisation or get-off solos.

During the spring of 1937, the band toured widely, playing a series of one-night stands, often traveling great distances between engagements. One-night stands earned more money than long-term engagements, so Glaser and Rockwell-O'Keefe stretched the band's routing whenever possible. Kirk estimated that the band traveled 50,000 miles during their first year on the road. Kirk, ably navigating Jim Crow restrictions, loved traveling and the people he met while on the road. "You always hear about one-nighters, how awful they were: 'Man, those one-nighters are killing me. They're a drag, man.' I want to talk about how *good* one-nighters were," he proclaimed.

If it hadn't been for one-nighters, I wouldn't have met Mrs. Mary McLeod Bethune, and Dr. George Washington Carver and a lot of other wonderful people whose names aren't in anybody's "Who's Who." But because of them we could do those one-nighters, which were such a necessary part of our business.

We couldn't stay in the white hotels where the white bands stayed. I'm glad now we couldn't. We'd have missed out on a whole country full of folks who put us up in their homes, cooked dinners and breakfasts for us, told us how to get along in Alabama and Mississippi, helped us out in trouble and became our friends for life. All those "lovely folks we met"—to quote my own lyrics—weren't rich or famous, most of them, but they were heroes and heroines to Andy Kirk and His Twelve Clouds of Joy.[38]

In contrast, Mary Lou Williams loathed life on the road. She found the constant touring and long distances between engagements grueling. "I remember jumping from St. Louis to Canada: over 750 miles in one day. We played St. Louis until 3 a.m., slept and left for Canada around 11 a.m., and arrived at ten that night—one hour late for the job. . . . I often wonder what an agent would do if he had to travel with the band he was booking," Williams pondered. "After the release of our Decca records, in 1936, the Kirk band traveled five or six thousand miles a week on one-nighters all through the South, repeating most of the dates before coming West again. . . . We got little chance to hear local musicians, though, for we arrived in most places in time to play, and left right afterwards. I have gone to sleep with my fur coat on, near freezing, and woken up in the car hours later wet from perspiration in the sub-tropics of Florida." Making matters worse, Williams, Terrell, Wilson, and other band members reaped little profit from the band's national acclaim.

Having abandoned the old commonwealth philosophy back in the territories, Kirk kept a substantial cut of the money. While living cheaply in Kansas City, band members accepted the disparity in pay, but the added expense of living on the road bred dissatisfaction in the ranks, especially with Mary Lou Williams. "Our sidemen were only making eight and a half dollars a night, and paying two or three bucks for decent rooms," Williams declared. "Since they had gone through hardships to keep the band intact, I thought they deserved at least 15 dollars. I made 75 a week, with arranging, and I think Pha Terrell got less." Williams supplemented her income by writing arrangements for other bandleaders. Demand for her talent grew after Benny Goodman commissioned her to write fresh compositions and arrangements for his band. "I was writing for some half dozen bands each week. As we were making perhaps 500 miles per night, I used to write in the car by flashlight between engagements," Williams mused. "Benny Goodman requested a blues and I did 'Roll 'Em' and several others for him. One week I was called on for twelve arrangements, including a couple for Louis Armstrong and Earl Hines, and I was beginning to get telegrams from Gus Arnheim, Glen Gray, Tommy Dorsey and many more like them."[39] Ironically, when "Roll 'Em" became a hit for Benny Goodman, Jack Kapp encouraged the Kirk band to record a boogie in the same vein. Williams readily complied, composing "Little Joe from Chicago," dedicated to Joe Glaser and Joe Louis.

In early May 1937, the band returned to Kansas City in triumph for a homecoming weekend at the Pla-Mor Ballroom. Fans packed the dance floor, delighted to sway and dip once again to the sweet strains of the Clouds of Joy. Declining a follow-up Monday date for the fans at 18th and Vine, the band moved on to St. Louis, before swinging across the south for a long stand at the Cotton Club in Los Angeles. While crisscrossing the country playing one-night stands, the Clouds of Joy often laid over in Kansas City for engagements at the Pla-Mor. Band members, denied accommodations downtown, stayed in the 18th and Vine area, carousing in clubs and renewing old friendships. Oddly, while in town, the band seldom played dates for African American audiences. Having hit the big time, the band shared only memories with the 18th and Vine community. Like Basie, Kirk, once established nationally, dropped Kansas City as a headquarters.

Harlan Leonard attempted to follow suit and break out nationally, but with little luck. Shortly after Kirk and Basie left Kansas City for good, Harlan Leonard set his sights on establishing the Rockets nationally. Unlike Basie, who became a bandleader by default, resulting from the tragic death of Bennie Moten, Harlan Leonard smoothly made the transition from sideman to leader. Under Leonard's assured guidance, the Rockets remained on a steady course, with all members staying aboard except for Vic Dickenson. After concluding the summer 1934 engagement at Winnwood Beach, the Rockets played mainly in the 18th and Vine community with a regular Sunday night dance at Dreamland Hall, a medium-sized hall at 22nd and Cottage, adorned with elaborate wood carvings. The band specialized in social events and dances, playing more than fifty such affairs during the winter of 1934 and spring of 1935. In mid-summer, the Rockets ventured out in the territories, touring ballrooms and theaters across Oklahoma. Moving on to Louisville, Kentucky, the Rockets spent August and September playing on the riverboat *Idlewild*, formerly based in Kansas City. Back home in October, the band resumed its regular schedule of social affairs, holiday celebrations, and Sunday night dances at Dreamland Hall. In the spring of 1936, the Rockets settled into a long-term engagement at the new Harlem Club on Troost.

In early fall, Dave Kapp scouted the Leonard band while he was in Kansas City to sign the Basie band to a Decca contract. Fearful of losing promising local talent to another label, Kapp invited the band to record for the Decca label in Chicago. In mid-December 1936, the Rockets opened at the Cotton Club, an upscale white establishment on Chicago's west side, playing for dancers and accompanying the stage show. The Rockets' entertaining novelty style suited the old-fashioned taste of the club's upper-class patrons. With a steady engagement and the promise of a recording session, the future looked bright for the band, but a run-in with the Chicago union ended both opportunities. As before, the Chicago union refused to grant the Rockets resident status or permission to record for Decca, which forced the band to close at the Cotton Club in mid-January 1937. Following a farewell engagement to a packed house at the Savoy Ballroom, Leonard retreated to Kansas City, hoping to straighten things out with the Chicago union. Frustrated by being locked out by the Chicago union and teetering on the brink of financial disaster, the Rockets disbanded. Leonard explained to the *Kansas City Call* that the Rockets' breakup resulted not from hard feelings: "Out of fairness to the former members of the Kansas City Rockets . . . I might say the band did not split as the result of any arguments. Neither is there any malicious feeling among the former members. . . . An unavoidable economic condition has severed a great organization."[40]

Woody and Herman Walder formed a splinter group, the Rocket Swing Unit, and opened at the Spinning Wheel, a cavern-like dive on 12th Street. Happy to be back in Kansas City, Herman Walder disavowed out-of-town engagements. "I says, if I ever get back to Kansas City, man, this stuff is gone with me, this traveling," Walder declared. "I had enough with it. I called a cat, name of Moon Eye, he owned the Spinning Wheel, and he sent money for six cats. . . . Rozelle Claxton on piano, and little Jack Johnson on the bass, Baby Lovett on drums, Booker Washington on trumpet, my brother Woodie on tenor [saxophone and] clarinet, and myself [on alto saxophone]. . . . I held that job down for three years. I said, the road never get me nomore."[41] Pete Johnson, fresh from the Sunset Club, soon replaced Rozelle Claxton on piano. Playing long hours, band members made more money than they did with the Leonard band, sometimes as much as $16 a man per night thanks to the kitty. Like most clubs in Kansas City, the Spinning Wheel bandstand featured a large open-mouth caricature of a cat that blinked its eyes when fed tips for the band. Band members made only $4 per night, forcing them to rely heavily on the generosity of the steady stream of patrons who fed the kitty. For the time being, Herman Walder, Baby Lovett, and other local musicians made a good living playing the joints crowding either side of 12th Street.

After the breakup of the Rockets, Leonard quickly rebounded, acquiring a fresh batch of promising young musicians recently back in Kansas City from a tour of the Northern territories and Canada with Tommy Douglas. After a few engagements in Kansas City, the band split with Douglas, a brilliant musician but an overbearing bandleader. Tenor saxophonist Jimmy Keith tried to keep the group together, but failed to secure enough steady engagements, so he turned the leadership over to Leonard. Assuming the helm of an already organized band, Leonard did not miss a beat as a bandleader. The announcement of the Rockets' breakup in the *Kansas City Call* also noted Leonard's takeover of the former Tommy Douglas band. Cashing in on his strong ties to the community, Leonard lined up a regular Sunday night engagement at Dreamland Hall, then rounded out the schedule with a steady stream of social engagements. Leonard initially wanted to call his new band the Kansas Citians, but on second thought revived the Kansas City Rockets.

The new Rockets bore little resemblance to the former band. While the original Rockets featured veterans of the Moten, Lee, and territorial bands, who favored the earlier stomp-down style, the new edition of the Rockets included young players who preferred the modern technique championed by Tommy Douglas.[42] Short and wiry with a rich full tone, Jimmy Keith led the saxophone section. As the principal get-off soloist, Keith helped develop the band book and created special arrangements of standards. Tall and slender with dreamy eyes, alto saxophonist Darwin Jones doubled as featured vocalist and rendered ballads in the style of Pha Terrell. Edward "Peeny" Johnson, a solid section player with a sharp brilliant sound, led the trumpet section. Trumpeter James Ross, a modernist specializing in gliding upper-register solos, helped Keith develop the band's book. The new Kansas City Rockets held great promise, but since it needed seasoning to realize its full potential, Leonard stayed in Kansas City, biding his time to refine the band's sound and develop an original book. As Leonard struggled to whip his young protégés in shape, he received stiff competition from the rise of two new bands led by pianists Jay McShann, a recent arrival from Muskogee, Oklahoma, and former Blue Devil Buster Smith.

8

Roll 'Em, Pete

"Roll It, Boy,
Let 'Em Jump For Joy."

—Pete Johnson and Joe Turner,
"Roll 'Em, Pete," 1938

PIANIST JAY MCSHANN arrived in Kansas City by serendipity. During a lay-over on a bus trip to visit his uncle in Omaha, Nebraska, in late fall 1936, McShann stopped by the Reno Club to catch a set or two of the Count Basie band. Stepping into the dark, smoky confines of the club, he instead found Bus Moten's swing combo on the stage. "I stopped in Kansas City and I had a two or three hour layover on the bus. . . . So I went down to the Reno Club," McShann recounted. "Basie had already gone east with the big band. I knew these musicians who were working for Bus, two or three of them from Tulsa. So they said, 'What are you doing in town?' I said, 'I was on my way to Omaha, the gig closed in Kansas, so I thought I would go to Omaha, hang around with my uncle and see what's happening musically.' Bill Hadnott said, 'Man, you don't want to go to Omaha. Take my keys, stay at my apartment and I will stay at my girlfriend's apartment and I'll guarantee you'll get a gig first two or three days in town. You don't want to go there, Kansas City is where it's happen-ing.'"[1] Accepting Hadnott's offer on impulse, McShann stayed in Kansas City.

Slim and genial, with an angular face animated by light brown eyes, a dimpled chin, and a winning grin, McShann cut his musical teeth in the south-western territorial-band tradition. Born in Muskogee, Oklahoma, the young-est of four children, McShann grew up in a staunchly religious family.[2] His father worked as a delivery man for a furniture company that carried records as a sideline. Young McShann first discovered the blues while picking over the chipped records littering the bed of his father's truck. "That was the 'Back Water Blues' by Bessie Smith and James P. Johnson," McShann recalled. "After I heard that, I was hooked on the blues."[3] Inspired by Johnson and other early piano greats, McShann, started pecking out blues and simple tunes on the old upright piano in the parlor, much to his parents' disapproval. Undeterred, he practiced on the sly while his parents attended church. "As a kid I used to pick out things on the piano while I listened to records by the blues singers like Mamie Smith and Clara Smith," McShann said. "My parents didn't like that kind of music and wouldn't let me play them very long and would come in and turn them off. They'd go off the church and then I'd get an hour or so to practice. My parents always thought I was in church earlier until one day one of the nuns was passing by, heard me playing, and told my parents, and I really caught it."[4]

Listening to Earl "Fatha" Hines's late-night broadcasts from the Grand Terrace in Chicago sparked McShann's interest in jazz. Seeing Bennie Moten, Clarence Love, and other great territorial bands passing through Muskogee inspired him to become a professional musician. While still in high school, McShann joined a small jazz combo led by saxophonist Don Byas. Facing little competition locally, the band frequently played multiple engagements in a single night. At first, Byas and McShann's parents fretted over finding their sons straggling home in the early morning light, but grew supportive after realizing the two usually returned with their pockets full of money. With the country still in the grip of the Great Depression, every dollar coming into the household counted.

After graduating from high school, McShann went to Nashville, intent on earning enough money over the course of the summer to attend Fisk University. Finding work scarce, McShann left Nashville, riding the rails back to Muskogee, arriving home exhausted and covered with soot. A restless youth, McShann soon left home again, this time for good, following his wanderlust to join the Grey Brothers band in Tulsa. When the opportunity with the Grey brothers fell through, McShann became stranded in Tulsa. While searching the city for work, McShann stumbled across saxophonist Al Denny's big band rehearsing without a pianist. McShann, unable to read music, quickly memorized the band's repertoire before auditioning for the piano slot. "When they started talking about what they were going to do for a piano player, I went up to see one of them and said, 'Look man, I think I can play those tunes.' He said, 'You can? well come on up then!' They put the music in front of me and they thought I was reading it. 'Man,' they said, 'we've got a cat here who can read, fake and everything!' I had a good ear, but they soon found out I couldn't read. Then they helped me, and I learned fast."[5] A quick study, McShann promptly eclipsed the musical sophistication of other band members.

Leaving the Denny band after a few months, McShann joined a small ensemble headed for Arkansas City, Kansas, a bustling border town perched on a rocky bluff at the confluence of the Walnut and Arkansas Rivers. Kansas, a dry state since 1880, prohibited the manufacture and sale of alcohol. As a result, Arkansas City offered little in the way of nightlife. The band barely scraped by, playing weekends in tin-roofed roadhouses that served 3.2 beer on the outskirts of town. With time on his hands, McShann enrolled in Arkansas City Junior College. Running out of money after a year of slim pickings, McShann left Arkansas City to join Eddie Hill and His Bostonians at the Bluebird Ballroom in Shawnee, Oklahoma, located thirty miles east of Oklahoma City.[6] At the end of a six-month engagement at the Bluebird, the band headed for the deep southwestern territories, playing small towns across Arizona and New Mexico, before settling into an extended engagement at a resort in the mountains twenty miles outside Albuquerque. When a love triangle involving Hill ended in multiple suicides, band members loaded him on a train headed for California. With the end of the Bostonians, McShann briefly returned to Arkansas City where he played duets with a drummer until a statewide crackdown on unregulated beer sales shuttered the roadhouses.[7] Broke and discouraged, he grabbed a bus to visit his uncle Odie in Omaha.

Staying in Kansas City on a lark, McShann freelanced in the Lone Star and other clubs lining 12th and 18th Street. McShann received his nickname "Hootie" one night after becoming literally intoxicated by Kansas City's nightlife. "I remember the first time I went to the Greenleaf Club and the guys said we got a new cat in town," McShann chuckled. "They told the bartender to 'fix us that special drink you fixed for us a couple of nights ago. We got a new cat gonna sit in here and blow tonight.' They had pale beer, and they put alcohol in the bottom. It was hot in the summer, and it was so cold you could see the frost on the outside of the container. . . . [I]t tasted so good and cold, I said wow. They said, 'man, you ready for another,' and I replied, 'yeah.' After about the third one they said when you going to blow. I said I was ready, but when I tried to get up I couldn't get out of the seat. They said, 'man, this cat come up here and got hootied.' So from then on the cats started calling me Hootie."[8] A hale-and-well-met fellow, McShann easily found a niche in Kansas City's musical community.

While sitting in around town, McShann swiftly established a reputation as an up-and-coming pianist, equally adept at boogie-woogie, blues, and jazz. Elmer Hopkins, a veteran drummer, hired McShann for a steady engagement at the Monroe Inn, a cozy, working-class neighborhood bar on Independence Avenue, in the northeast section of town. Journalist Dave Dexter, living at his parents' home just a few blocks north of the Monroe Inn, happened to hear McShann while passing by one evening. Dexter became a regular fixture at the club, sitting alone at the bar chasing cups of steaming black coffee with ice-cold beer, intently listening to McShann. Convinced he found a raw talent equal to Basie, Dexter championed McShann in the *Kansas City Journal-Post* and *Metronome*. In his regular column covering the Kansas City scene for

Metronome in March 1937, Dexter declared McShann the top local pianist: "Jay McShann, negro pianist, a sensation here, heard nightly at the Monroe Inn out Northeast. . . . Also playing with McShann is Lawrence Hopkins, drummer one of the best in the city now since Andy Kirk and Count Basie and their units have gone East. Both McShann and Hopkins deserve a better spot."[9]

McShann, laid back and unassuming, shrugged off Dexter's recommendation that he and Hopkins move up to a more worthy venue. For the time being, McShann preferred sticking with his job at the Monroe Inn, which ended early enough for him to check out the action in other clubs. McShann first met Charlie Parker during a late-night sojourn down 12th Street. "We'd always get through about 1:00 or 1:30, so that would give us a chance to go in and catch what was happening in town," McShann recalled. "That's how I happened to hear Bird one night. He was in the Bar Lu Duc nightclub at 12th and Charlotte. Music was piped out in the street. So we stopped to see who was blowing. Bird was sitting up there blowing. I said, 'man, where you been.' He said 'I'm from Kansas City.' I said, 'I thought I'd met all the musicians in town.' He said he had 'been working with George Lee [Wilkerson] down in the Ozarks. It's hard to get musicians to go to the Ozarks, and I wanted to do a little woodsheddin'. So I went to the Ozarks with George Lee [Wilkerson].'. . . I said, 'man, you sure sound different.' He said, 'maybe we will get a chance to work together.' I said, 'always hopin'.'"[10] McShann's chance meeting with Parker on 12th Street set the stage for their future musical partnership.

Already a journeyman soloist, Parker learned his craft prowling the alleys behind the clubs where Kansas City Jazz flourished. Originally from Kansas City, Kansas, Parker and his parents, Addie and Charles, moved to the Missouri side in the mid-1920s. Charles, an alcoholic, abandoned the family in the early 1930s.[11] Addie, a kind-hearted pillar of strength, took in and raised as her own Charlie's half brother, John, her husband's child with another woman. Forced to fend for herself and her family, Addie promptly found work cleaning the Western Telegraph office in the Union Station and bought a roomy two-story building at 1516 Olive in the heart of the 18th and Vine district.[12] Parker, a bright but indifferent student, except in music, attended Lincoln High School. In his freshman year Parker joined the Lincoln High band, which was directed by Alonzo Lewis. Lacking an instrument of his own, Parker picked up the school's tuba. Pleased by her son's interest in music, but appalled by his choice of instrument, Addie bought Parker a beat-up alto saxophone for $45, then invested an even larger sum to get it in working order.[13] "School did one great thing for him; he was given a tuba to play," Addie related. "I didn't go for that; it was so heavy and funny coiled around him with just his head sticking out, so I got him another instrument [alto saxophone]. He started playing at thirteen. He was never interested in sports. All he cared about was music and reading."[14] A playful youth with large expressive eyes, a charming smile, and a deep booming voice, Parker continued his musical apprenticeship, hanging around the clubs on 12th and 18th Streets, just a short stroll from his home.

After Addie left for work, Parker embarked on his nightly rounds of clubs with his treasured alto in a rumpled brown shopping bag, tucked tightly under his arm. Drummer Ernest Daniels, a childhood friend, often accompanied Parker on his late-night journeys. Daniels fondly recalled Parker as having "a very nice disposition, kind of happy-go-lucky. During that time they had the [cartoon] comic strip Popeye, Charlie used to imitate Popeye's deep-toned voice, and make that deep-toned tone on his horn."[15] According to Dave Dexter, Parker "could charm the leaves from the trees."[16] Practicing diligently, Parker progressed rapidly and was soon invited to play occasional dates with a band led by Andy Kirk's wife, Mary. John Williams squired the two to their engagements. Mary Lou Williams recalled Parker being in "knee-pants" at the time, sounding "good," but not getting the "rhythm and stuff" quite right.[17]

In July 1935, Parker joined the Ten Chords of Rhythm, a dance band led by pianist Lawrence Keyes. A large burly youth with talent to match his cockiness, Keyes took Parker under his wing at Lincoln High. "Bird played baritone horn in the [Lincoln] band, but off the stand he was fascinated with the piano, and he used to bother me to show him chords," Keyes disclosed. "I was three years older than him. I was a sophomore, and he was a freshman. We became good friends. It was a triumvirate because there was another guy whom Charlie admired tremendously, and the three of us would hang out in each other's houses, practicing and talking music day and night. . . . The name of the third fellow was Robert Simpson and he played trombone remarkably. To say Charlie admired him is perhaps too mild, Charlie worshiped him and was in his company a great deal."[18] Later, Simpson's untimely death during an operation at the age of nineteen devastated Parker.

Hailed in the *Kansas City Call* as "Kansas City's Newest Dance Orchestra," the Ten Chords of Rhythm, featuring "Elmer Brown, K. C.'s own Little Cab and those four boys of syncopated harmony, the Solid Senders," premiered at Lincoln Hall on August 4, 1935. By September, the Chords of Rhythm grew to twelve members.[19] Primarily a dance band, the Chords of Rhythm specialized in popular standards like "Accent on Youth," "Isn't This a Lovely Day," "Lulu's Back in Town," "Sweet and Slow," "St. Louis Blues," "Twelfth Street Rag," "Avalon," and its theme, "Sentimental Mood." Although nonunion, members made good money, earning ten to twelve dollars each per night from their cut of the 25 cent admission fee at Lincoln Hall.

The band's amateur status suited Lincoln Hall, but, in order to play Paseo Hall and other larger ballrooms, members were required to join Local 627. George E. Lee brought Parker and other band members into the union. Lee, still popular in the community but without a regular band, hired the Chords of Rhythm for a Halloween dance at Paseo Hall. For the occasion, Lee helped pay band members' initiation fee.[20] Hyping the event, Lee shamelessly touted the band as George E. Lee and His Original Brunswick Recording Orchestra. Ironically, band members made more money as nonunion freelancers than regular union members. Given short shrift on engagements doled out by the union, the band spent November and December playing halls and ballrooms in small towns just outside of Kansas City. The Chords of Rhythm played its swan song at a Paseo Hall Christmas dance, accompanying singer and dancer Christianna Buckner from the Reno Club. Failing to find steady work in the wake of the Christmas date with Buckner, the Chords of Rhythm faded from the scene.

Stepping out on his own as a soloist, Parker freelanced on 12th Street. He regularly sat in with the band at Greenleaf Gardens, a few blocks east of the Reno Club, where the Basie band held court. After hours, Parker haunted the spook breakfasts at the Reno, shadowing his idols Lester Young and Buster Smith. Too young to enter the front door, Parker loitered in the alley behind the Reno, and mingled with veteran musicians waiting their turn on the band stand. Bassist Gene Ramey frequented the early morning spook breakfasts with Parker. Ramey recounted, "Basie had a nine-piece band, and they worked a tough schedule—from 8:30 to 5:00 in the morning. After that, the jam sessions would begin. People stopped by on their way to work, and there was the 'sportin' life' set who never worked, and musicians of any big band that was in town—like Dorsey or Garber. Sometimes there would be as many as a hundred musicians waiting to get on the stand." The gravel alleyway behind the Reno served as an informal music school for Ramey, Parker, and other young up-and-coming musicians. "In K.C. there is a wonderful tradition where a more experienced musician tries to help a new one," Ramey stated. "An alto player called Prof. (Buster) Smith used to help Bird get his horn better. Effergee Ware, a guitarist, coached a whole group of us, teaching us cycles, chords, and progressions. We would sit in the park, practicing all night long."[21]

Just 15 years old and already playing professionally, Parker became an astute student of the tradition. More confident than capable, Parker eagerly elbowed his way into jam sessions, much to the frustration of more experienced musicians, who considered him a pest. Gene Ramey explained how jam sessions in Kansas City assumed deeper meaning, akin to rites of passage. "Jam sessions in a sense were constant trials of manhood. Different sections of the band would set difficult riffs behind soloists and, sometimes, they would see if they could lose each other," Ramey reported. "Usually it was one man who became the goat. He might then come in for some kidding. Charlie would shoot back to his teasers' and censors' remarks like, 'Play your own horn' or 'Stick to your script.'" During the early summer of 1936, Parker attempted to prove his manhood during a spook breakfast at the Reno Club. Ramey, accompanying Parker to the session, witnessed drummer Jo Jones's legendary rebuke of Parker. "We were to jam with Basie, and Charlie made no answer," Ramey confided. "Jo Jones waited until Bird started to play and, suddenly, in order to show how he felt about Bird, he threw a cymbal across the dance floor. It fell with a deafening sound, and Bird, in humiliation, packed up his instrument and left." Ramey felt Parker's public embarrassment stiffened his resolve to master his instrument. "However, this gave Bird a big determination to play. 'I'll fix these cats,' he used to say. 'Everybody's laughing at me now, but just wait and see.'"[22]

Stung by Jo Jones's rebuff, Parker joined a union-sponsored band led by veteran bassist George Wilkerson, playing a summer engagement at a Musser's Ozark Tavern near Eldon, Missouri, located in the flinty, hickory and oak tree–carpeted Ozark mountains, 150 miles south of Kansas City. After the creation of the huge dragon-shaped Lake of the Ozarks in 1931, Eldon became a popular summer resort area, attracting scores of vacationers from Oklahoma, Arkansas, and Kansas. The rustic clubs and roadhouses, constructed from russet-colored Ozark rocks framed by sturdy oak timbers, afforded steady employment for bands, ranging from hillbilly string ensembles to jazz combos. Traversing the narrow winding roads hugging the steep Ozark hills presented a perilous proposition at best, so band members usually stayed on location. Retreating to the Ozarks, Parker found refuge in the hills, woodshedding on his alto saxophone, preparing for his return to 12th Street.

The engagement stretched into the fall. Taking a break, Parker and other band members returned home for Thanksgiving dinner with their families. Heading back to Eldon Thanksgiving evening, band members traveled caravan style in two sedans. Three miles north of Eldon, the car carrying Parker, Wilkerson, and Ernest Daniels hit a patch of ice, careened off the road, and rolled over several times, throwing the three musicians out of the car. The force of the crash broke several of Parker's ribs, hurled Daniels sixty feet, puncturing one of his lungs, and critically injured Wilkerson. Other band members and Mr. Musser, the club owner, traveling a block ahead, hurried back to the scene of the accident and rushed the three to the hospital in Eldon, where Wilkerson died in the early morning hours.[23]

Mr. Musser generously paid all the medical bills and replaced Daniels's drums and Parker's silver Conn alto, which was destroyed in the accident. Daniels considered the accident a watershed incident in Bird's career. Daniels accounted, "I consider it a turning point in Bird's life, because he got a little money out of a lawsuit we had against Mr. Musser, who made no objection to this suit, feeling his liability coverage would help us (he was a big man, reputed to practically own the town of Eldon, Missouri). With this money Charlie bought a new Selmer, whose action I hear is a little faster than the other kinds of altos—It gave him a lift."[24] Parker's newfound virtuosity astounded Gene Ramey and other musicians familiar with his previous style. "Basie's 'Jones-Smith' record had come out, and Bird startled everybody by playing Lester Young's solo on 'Lady Be Good' note for note," Ramey related. "'Here comes this guy,' the cats used to say. 'He's a drag!' They couldn't believe it, because six months before he had been like a crying saxophone player."[25] Barely sixteen years old, Parker came of age musically during that summer spent in the Ozarks. While Parker established his reputation as a deft soloist, McShann emerged as a top local band leader.

McShann left the Monroe Inn in early May 1937 to fill in for the pianist in trumpeter Dee "Prince" Stewart's band at Club Continental, a smart night-club located downtown near 12th and Wyandotte. Catering to the younger set, Club Continental featured fine dining, a spacious dance floor, and three stage shows nightly. Advertisements for the club billed the Stewart band as arriving direct from New York's famed Ubangi Club, but in reality the band moved over from the Reno Club.[26] Stewart, a regular member of the Bus Moten band at the Reno, took over the band and cut Moten out of the action after securing the engagement at the Continental in early 1937. Ill-tempered and quick with his fists, Stewart led the band in name only, so Buster Smith stepped in as the de-facto leader, dealing with band members and writing arrangements. Smith's arrangements impressed McShann. "Buster had his own stuff that he had written including 'The Old Southland.' He had a lot of good tunes he heard from other bands," observed McShann. "Buster could write, and he had a good book he kept himself like 'Rockin' in Rhythm.'"[27]

When Stewart's regular pianist returned in August 1937, McShann joined forces with drummer Harold Gadson and opened at Wolf's Buffet, a bustling tavern located on the north-west corner of 18th and Vine. Patrons attracted by the reasonably priced buffet piled high with chicken, spaghetti, and rows of side dishes lingered for the floor show. Petite, athletic shake dancers and jaded female impersonators rounded out the evening's fare. McShann en-joyed being in the center of festivities on 18th street. "At 18th and Vine, there was a club on each side of the street. Wolf's was on one side of the street; Hymie's was on the other side right across from Wolf's," McShann remem-bered. "Pete [Johnson] would come out of Hymie's and go right over to Wolf's. Leave Wolf's and go right over to Hymie's. Right down the street they had another club upstairs there, and Lucille's too. That was four clubs right in there together. You'd find one club all full and packed. The next hour the next club would be full and packed. It'd just go around like that. People'd make the rounds and catch everything."[28] Feeling right at home in the bright nightlife, McShann settled into a steady engagement at Wolf's.

In mid-February 1938, Buster Smith and Charlie Parker arrived on 18th Street, opening at Lucille's Paradise, just a few blocks east of Wolf's. Origi-nally established in 1935 as a small barbeque stand, nestled upstairs above the bustling crowds, Lucille's steadily expanded, growing into a sophisticated roost for professionals and social clubs. Gregarious and comely, Lucille Webb, the owner, personally greeted patrons flocking to her namesake. A long bar domi-nated the busy entryway, facing booths trimmed in green and red. Small tables crowded the main room where the band entertained patrons nightly until 7 o'clock the next morning. Initially, Lucille's featured the Three Swing Men of Swing, a string trio showcasing Claude Williams on violin. After expanding the club to accommodate two hundred patrons, Lucille brought in the former Club Continental orchestra led by Buster Smith.

When the Stewart band closed at the Club Continental in early 1938, Buster Smith seized the opportunity to form his own band. Enlisting key players from the Stewart band, Smith rounded out the roster with Charlie Parker and other promising young musicians. Smith became a father figure, musically and otherwise, to young Parker. "He used to call me his dad, and I called him my boy," Smith mused. "I couldn't get rid of him. He was always up under me. In my band we'd split the solos. If I took two, he'd take two, if I took three, he'd take three, and so forth. He always wanted me to take the first solo. I guess he thought he'd learn something that way. He did play like me quite a bit I guess. But after a while, anything I could make on my horn he could make too—and make something better out of it. We used to do that double time stuff all the time. Only we called it double tongue sometimes in those days. I used to do a lot of that on clarinet. Then I started doing it on alto and Charlie heard me doing it and he started playing it."[29] Working side by side at Lucille's, Smith passed his musical legacy to Parker.

In early April, Smith crossed paths once again with Basie. Since leaving the Reno Club, a year and a half earlier, the Basie band steadily rose in ranking, recording for Decca and playing top venues across the country. While establishing the band nationally, Basie wanted to bring Smith back into the fold as an arranger, but some long-time band members vetoed the idea. Their collective rejection stung Smith. "Basie wanted me to come back but some of the boys in the band said, 'Aw, don't take Buster back, he went off and left us.' So Basie said, 'Bus, some of the boys are a little hot, so just stick around a while till they cool off and then come on back.' But I never did go back as a member of the band."[30] Adding insult to injury, Basie neglected to credit Smith as co-composer of the band's biggest hit, "One O'Clock Jump."

Returning to Kansas City in triumph, Basie played an April 9 engagement for white dance fans at the Pla-Mor, followed two days later by a dance for a racially mixed crowd of 3,000 at the cavernous Municipal Auditorium located just a short stroll west from the Reno Club. Since Local 627 sponsored the dance at the Municipal Auditorium, union rules requiring a local band to open came into play. Anticipating a packed house, William Shaw chose two bands for the occasion: the Tommy Douglas band and Buster Smith and His Paradise Orchestra. For Parker, sharing the stage with the Basie band, particularly Jo Jones, who had publicly humiliated him at the Reno Club years earlier, amounted to sweet vindication. In contrast, Smith's reunion with Basie and their former band mates from the Reno Club became a bittersweet reminder of what might have been.

Leaving Kansas City, Basie continued a short tour of the Midwest before returning to New York for a date at the Apollo Theater. In a farewell interview in the *Kansas City Call*, Basie acknowledged his debt of gratitude to friends in the 18th and Vine area and to Bennie Moten. "Throughout my engagements in the east, I have always said that I would be glad to get back on Eighteenth and Vine and mingle with the boys who are responsible for my successes. . . . Each new success the band has, I always think of Bennie and feel that he would be proud of the boys in the band, many of whom played with him during his career."[31] Basie made no mention of his long association with Smith.

With few other options, Smith returned to his regular engagement at Lucille's Paradise. Smith, Parker, and scores of other musicians, relying on the clubs peppering 12th and 18th for their livelihood, soon became casualties in a cultural war between Boss Tom Pendergast, the head of the local democratic political machine, and Missouri Governor Lloyd Stark over Kansas City's blatant disregard of state liquor, prostitution, and gambling laws.

GOVERNOR STARK, elected in 1936 with the help of Kansas City's democratic machine, turned on Pendergast once he was in office. Journalist Willam Reddig, in his book *Tom's Town*, a history of Kansas City and the Pendergast machine, chronicled the political feud between Stark and Pendergast that led to the crackdown in Kansas City.

> This third phenomenon was the entry into the 1936 [Missouri Governor] campaign of the apple man from Louisiana, Missouri, Lloyd Stark, developer of Stark's Delicious, who came forward with Big Tom's blessing and shortly thereafter turned into the Jack the Giant Killer of the reform. Stark won the Democratic nomination for governor with Pendergast delivering another record vote from Jackson County and went on to win the final election with the Democratic ballots in Pendergast's county establishing an all-time high. This Mr. Stark was strictly an apple knocker despite the fact that he gave a deceptive opening number as an apple polisher. . . . A severe, humorless man with the eyes of a zealot and the mouth of a Puritan, he gave all the Kansas City boys a chill and they quickly abandoned hope of warming up to him. A man with a jaw as ugly as Big Tom's, and something of an eccentric on physical culture, Stark didn't seem to know when he was being intimidated. A former Navy officer and a former Army officer as well, he knew a thing or two himself about the strategy of infiltration and surprise, insinuating himself into the good graces of the St. Louis Democrats at the same time he was working the old hocus-pocus on the Kansas City machine. And he was an ingrate. He showed no appreciation at all when the Goats [Pendergast's democratic faction] produced the damnedest biggest primary vote ever counted in Jackson County to win the nomination for Stark.[32]

Gearing up for a future run for a United States Senate seat from Missouri, Stark could ill afford to ignore the national bad press about the vice and corruption in Kansas City, that continued unabated under his watch.

Kansas City had long enjoyed a national reputation as a mecca for vice. In 1933, a United Press article published by newspapers across the country designated Kansas City as the "crime capital" of the nation, reporting "Kansas City, 'the Heart of America,' has become a national crime capital, refuge of gun men who find other communities inhospitable. The rackets levy a toll of $25,000,000 to $30,000,000 a year—an amazing total in a community of half a million."[33] Since Pendergast controlled Missouri's Democratic party, which dominated all branches of government, state authorities ignored the flagrant violation of state liquor, gambling, and prostitution laws in Kansas City. Governor Stark proved to be another matter. Once sworn into office, Stark, seeking to diminish Pendergast's influence and snag the Democratic Senate nomination in 1940, enforced Missouri's liquor laws with a vengeance. As the owner of T. J. Pendergast Liquor Wholesale Company, the principal supplier of liquor in Kansas City, Pendergast stood to lose considerably from the enforcement of state liquor laws. Pendergast initially stymied Stark's crusade by convincing him to appoint Thomas F. Fitzgerald, a loyalist to the Democratic machine in Kansas City, to state liquor control supervisor. When Stark directed Fitzgerald to immediately crack down on Kansas City, he instead focused on St. Joseph and St. Louis. Frustrated, Stark fired Fitzgerald and took aim at Kansas City himself.[34]

A series of articles by syndicated columnist Westbrook Pegler chronicling the widespread corruption and vice in Kansas City published nationally in mid-February 1938 spurred on Stark's cleanup effort. In the four-part series, Pegler painted a lurid portrait of an utterly corrupt city where the promotion of vice amounted to a major civic industry. In an interview with Pegler, Henry F. McElroy, city manager and Pendergast crony, characterized Kansas City as "a machine or gang town, run by the organization of Tom Pendergast." McElroy attributed the proliferation of tawdry nightlife to "public demand."[35] Immediately following the publication of Pegler's litany of vices fostered by the Pendergast machine, Stark's agents descended on Kansas City, enforcing state liquor restrictions to the letter of the law and forcing clubs on 12th and 18th Streets to shut down at 2 A.M. and remain closed on Sunday. The curtailed operating hours immediately eroded the quantity and quality of nightlife in Kansas City. Facing decreased revenues from the loss of late night and early morning customers, club owners scaled back on entertainment by replacing musicians with jukeboxes. Musicians relying exclusively on club work soon found themselves looking for day jobs.

JAY MCSHANN MANAGED to get out of Wolf's ahead of the crackdown, abetted by a little luck and the help of a wealthy patron. A few months before the cleanup began in earnest, Local 627 President William Shaw introduced McShann to Walter Bales, Jr., a local bon vivant and executive with Traveler's Insurance. An amateur pianist with a taste for blues and boogie-woogie, Bales enjoyed playing duets with African American pianists plying their trade on 12th and 18th Streets. Basie, while in residence at the Reno Club, regularly joined Bales in the studios of Jenkins Music Company for an afternoon of four-handed piano. The two became close, and Bales helped finance Basie's departure from Kansas City. Needing a new partner, Bales contacted William Shaw at Local 627 about getting together with McShann. Meeting the unaffected McShann for the first time, Bales thought Shaw had sent over the wrong pianist. Sitting down at the piano, McShann immediately put Bales's doubts to rest and the two became fast friends, frequently getting together at Jenkins to play duets.

Well-connected, Bales nudged McShann's career along, recommending him for casual engagements at Kansas City's exclusive country clubs, where he entertained local movers and shakers. The white Local 34 had long held a monopoly on country club and society engagements, but, with Bales's help and his own natural charm, McShann managed to breach the color line. McShann marveled at the generosity of his new clientele. "I went out there and did that date [Kansas City Country Club] and boy, oh, boy I got a lot of tips," McShann gleefully recalled. "I had my pockets full of money. When I got through playing the guy said, 'I got this bushel basket full of booze,' and I said 'I'll take it.' So he said, 'How much I owe you for tonight,' and I said, 'I don't know.' He said, 'Well, make up you mind and I'll be back in a minute and make out a check for you.' So he went on up front and came back and said, 'You remember how much you want for the night.' I said, 'No, I haven't quite got it together yet.' And he said, 'Will $25.00 be all right?' I said 'Oh, yes, yes.' I wanted to holler. I wanted to jump up and down and holler. I made so much in tips I didn't think I would be paid. I came in that night through 18th Street and started giving away bottles."[36]

In early April 1938, McShann moved uptown, opening at Clair Martin's Plaza Tavern, located in the heart of the Country Club Plaza, a fashionable shopping district west of 47th and Main Street. The Plaza, modeled after Kansas City's sister city Seville, Spain, featured then, as it does now, blocks of specialty shops and professional offices with red-tiled roofs, imported ornate wrought iron grillwork, and bright terra-cotta trim. Martin's, a wide shallow club, richly appointed with a row of leather booths neatly lined up opposite the chic art-deco bar, catered to the country club district's wealthy social elite and young professionals. McShann assembled a crack band for the engagement, including: Bob Mabane, tenor; Edward "Popeye" Hale, alto; and his cousin Pete McShann on drums. Initially, McShann wanted to hire Billy Hadnott for the bass slot. Finding Hadnott unavailable for a few weeks, McShann hired Gene Ramey on a temporary basis. After playing a few nights with Ramey, McShann decided he preferred Ramey over Hadnott.

Like McShann, Ramey came out of the southwest territorial band tradition.[37] Originally from Austin, Texas, Ramey launched his musical career playing sousaphone with George Corley's Royal Aces. In 1932, Ramey moved to Kansas City, Kansas, on a musical scholarship to Western University. Inspired by his mentor Walter Page, Ramey switched to string bass. With a slight build and thin, double-jointed fingers, Ramey at first struggled just to push the bass strings down to the neck of the bass to create notes. Compensating for his pliant fingers, Ramey developed a double-fingering technique, giving him strength enough to coax notes out of the bass. After graduating from Western, Ramey played a short stint with Bus Moten before joining trumpeter Oliver Todd's Hottentots, a young ten-piece dance band based in Kansas City, Kansas. In early April 1936, Oliver Todd resigned, and pianist Margaret Johnson took over leadership of the group, changing its name to Royal Rhythm. In keeping with the royal theme, Johnson billed herself as "Countess" Margaret Johnson. Tall, willowy, and zestful with slender agile fingers, Johnson idolized Mary Lou Williams, whose solos she memorized from records.

A CHILD PRODIGY like Mary Lou, Margaret Johnson made her performing debut at the age of three playing "Shine for Jesus" at a Baptist convention in Chanute, Kansas, where she was born September 28, 1919. Her family moved to Kansas City, Kansas, where she attended Sumner High School. Independent and ambitious, Johnson formed a small ensemble that played for school events and local dances. During her junior year in 1934, Johnson merged bands with Oliver Todd to form the ten-piece Hottentots. When Todd left the band in April 1936, the leadership fell to Johnson, who was well respected by the band members. Her execution and style impressed Gene Ramey. "Countess Johnson didn't show any effort when she played," Ramey declared. "Her style was different, between Earl Hines and Basie's but nearer to Earl's. She was fast and powerful, and she said something."[38] In his "These Make News" column in the Kansas City Call, E. Leroy Brown, Jr., confirmed Ramey's assessment of Johnson's brilliance in a review of Johnson's band at a dance in Topeka, Kansas. "She (Johnson) was . . . truly going to town. No jive. All of the jitterbugs were on hand to listen to her do her number and she did it. When the dance had come to its scheduled time of closing, the crowd persuaded her to stay over for another hour and give them more of that torrid music that she was pouring out."[39]

In late spring 1938, Andy Kirk recruited Johnson to fill in for Mary Lou Williams, who had taken ill while the Clouds of Joy played a Pan-Hellenic dance at the University of Missouri in Columbia. According to an article in Down Beat by Dave Dexter, quoted in the Kansas City Call, Kirk contacted William Shaw who recommended Johnson. "Desperate—Kirk wired William Shaw, head of the AFM Musicians 627 in Kansas City. 'Must have good pianist to succeed Mary Lou,' said Kirk in the telegram, 'Send one soonest.' Shaw didn't hesitate. He had heard of Miss Johnson. He knew she had practiced Miss Williams' style for many months, and copied her choruses as soon as they were released on records. So Miss Johnson was sent to Columbia, where she amazed Kirk and his gang with her remarkable technique. The payoff, however, as *Down Beat* tells it, was the fact that for the next four months everywhere Kirk's famous band played, including Kansas City the home town dancers thought the Countess was Mary Lou!"[40] Touring across the country with the Clouds of Joy, Johnson played Williams's solos note for note, leaving audiences none the wiser.

Many musicians in Kansas City including Ramey judged Johnson a superior pianist to Williams. "She [Johnson] was very good," Ramey stated. "And everybody said she was better than Mary Lou."[41] After Williams returned to the Kirk band, Johnson stayed in New York. In September, on the recommendation of her old flame Lester Young, she recorded four numbers accompanying Billie Holiday for the Vocalion label. Shortly after the session, Johnson fell ill from tuberculosis. Thinking she had contracted a bad cold, Johnson returned to Kansas City in November to recuperate before returning to New York. While in town she formed a band and accompanied Pha Terrell on the Vine Street Varieties. Continuing to suffer from declining health, Johnson convalesced at her mother's home in Kansas City, Kansas, where she died on July 13, 1939. Ironically, a few months after Countess Margaret Johnson's untimely death, an article on the International Sweethearts of Rhythm in the *Kansas City Call* announced the need for an "embryonic Mary Lou Williams" to join the band.[42]

THE ROYAL RHYTHM disbanded shortly after Johnson hit the road with Andy Kirk, which freed Ramey to join McShann as a regular member. Once established at Martin's, McShann refined and expanded the band. Gus Johnson replaced Pete McShann on drums and Billy Smith joined on trumpet, bringing the group up to seven members. A doorway connected the tavern to an adjacent cafeteria also owned by Martin. The band played soft music from 8 to 10 P.M. at the tavern, then moved over to the cafeteria to serve up swing renditions of popular standards for the young country club set. "They loved him [McShann] at Martin's," Ramey exclaimed. "They were promoting their chicken-in-a-basket then, and I made up a song about it to the melody of 'Pennies From Heaven.' We'd sing it there and on the radio, and it turned out to be a great thing. Society people would come from all over to order this chicken that would 'knock you out.'"[43] Dave Dexter lauded the new band in his "Notes From the Night Clubs" column in the *Kansas City Journal-Post*: "Jay McShann and his barrelhouse tempos are attracting patronage to Clair Martin's tavern on the Country Club plaza. McShann, only 21 years old, plays the finest swing piano in the Middle West. Bob Mabane and Edward Hale sing and the spot is becoming known as a meeting place for musicians and those who follow the latest trends in modern rhythm treatments of popular tunes."[44] With help from Dexter and Bales, McShann achieved local acclaim and a comfortable niche at Martin's, and made good money playing for Kansas City's social elite.

As McShann eased into a long-term engagement at Martin's, Pete Johnson and Joe Turner left Kansas City for New York. John Hammond, while in Kansas City scouting Basie in the summer of 1936, pledged to help Johnson and Turner get established in New York. In the spring of 1938, Hammond made good on his promise and negotiated a contract on their behalf with the Music Corporation of America, as well as a short run at the Famous Door, a cozy club on 52nd Street. Unbeknownst to Hammond, Johnson and Turner had parted ways several years earlier over money at the Sunset Club. Like most musicians in Kansas City, they relied on the kitty for their livelihood. Turner worked behind the bar pouring drinks and singing requests for customers, who in turn fed the kitty on top of the piano. During his breaks, Johnson, a ladies man, floated from table to table buying drinks for the women in the club. To Turner's dismay, Johnson dipped deeply into the kitty for his dalliances, leaving little money to split at the end of the evening. Rather than confronting Johnson, Turner let it slide and moved across the street to the Lone Star.[45]

Prompted by Hammond's offer, encouraged the two reunited in a musical marriage of convenience. Tired of working long hours with the Rocket Swing Unit at the Spinning Wheel, Johnson jumped at Hammond's offer. In contrast, Turner agreed to Hammond's proposal with reluctance. Hammond had attempted to bring Turner to New York on several prior occasions, offering to pair him with the Basie and Goodman bands, to no avail. Turner had declined Hammond's overtures, feeling more comfortable working the clubs on 12th and 18th Streets. With Governor Stark's cleanup sweeping away club work, Turner finally relented. In late May, Johnson and Turner opened at the Famous Door, where the Basie band got its start in New York. Like Basie, they initially got off to a rough start.

Having arrived in New York during the off-season, Tuner and Johnson had little luck finding work after closing at the Famous Door. Worse yet, a guest appearance at the famed Apollo Theater arranged by Hammond turned out to be an unmitigated disaster. Johnson's wife Marge related, "Instead of letting Joe and Pete do a blues number, they were told to do a ballad. 'I'm Glad for Your Sake, I'm Sorry for Mine.' The audience began stamping their feet and beating their hands together. Joe and Pete couldn't imagine what was happening—until curtains were closed. To quote Pete: 'It's a good thing they closed them or they'd been throwing rocks at us.' Louis Armstrong was on the same program, and, as they passed him, he said, 'That's Show Business.' Later, Pete realized what was meant by that remark: If you're going to appear before the public, do your best number first and you can stay on; if you don't do that, you might not get on."[46] Discouraged by the lack of jobs and hostile reception at the Apollo, Johnson and Turner returned to Kansas City in early July, to wait for another shot at New York. While attempting to establish Turner and Johnson in New York, Hammond also helped advance Harlan Leonard's Rockets nationally.

After taking over the former Tommy Douglas band in February 1937, Leonard set about molding the undisciplined young members into a professional unit.[47] The band possessed plenty of raw talent, but lacked a strong composer and arranger, which forced Leonard to rely on stock and head arrangements of standards. The Rockets spent the spring and summer of 1937 playing at the Harlem Club on Troost Avenue, before launching a fall tour of the South with dates in Arkansas, Texas, Oklahoma, Louisiana, Mississippi, and Louisville, Kentucky. The band developed a strong following in Louisville while playing a ten-day engagement on the steamer *Idlewild*, formerly based in Kansas City. While on the road, the Rockets started coming together as a unit. Reviewing an October dance in St. Joseph, Missouri, *Kansas City Call* columnist Leroy Brown noted the band's increased polish and "originality."[48] While encouraged by the band's gradual improvement, Leonard realized he needed an experienced arranger and composer comparable to Eddie Durham or Mary Lou Williams to meet the standard set by Basie and Kirk. Later that month, when pianist Robert Wilson fell ill and left the band, Leonard enlisted Rozelle Claxton, a promising young composer and arranger, originally from Memphis. Taking charge as director and principal arranger, Claxton refashioned the band book by reworking the specials of popular swing standards and creating sharp arrangements of his own compositions.

Leonard spent the winter and spring of 1938 in Kansas City rehearsing and readying the band for a summer tour of the South and Midwest. Before embarking on the tour in the early hours of June 18, the band gathered in front of Local 627, surrounded by well-wishers. Covering the band's departure for the *Kansas City Call*, Leroy Brown captured the significance of the moment to the community and the band members: "It was well that these friends turned out to witness the cats leaving for it let them know just how many people they would be disappointing if they let them down. Of course this is not going to take place for Harlan and the rest of the cats are 'ready,' prepared, as one might say, to enter the big time circles and make good."[49] Brown's prediction proved premature. Returning home in August from the successful southern tour, the Rockets finished out the season at Fairyland Park, replacing Red Blackburn's University of Kansas college swing band. At the beginning of the summer, Harry Duncan, unable to find a local African American band on a par with Moten's or Kirk's, took a chance on the Blackburn band. Dancers, more accustomed to the hot and sweet style of the African American bands usually featured at Fairyland, gave the Blackburn band a lukewarm reception. When ballroom attendance sagged in mid-summer, dragging down the park's numbers, lanky young John Tumino replaced Duncan as manager of the ballroom. Tumino discharged the Blackburn band and engaged the Rockets, thus salvaging the rest of the season. The Rockets rose to the occasion, packing the ballroom nightly. Leroy Brown trumpeted the band's vast improvement in the *Kansas City Call*:

> For the past year Leonard has been building his aggregation until now he is almost over the edge. Several sore spots in the band have been eliminated and the band to date is one of the best swing bands in the country, barring none. Following in the footsteps of Andy Kirk and Count Basie, Leonard would have to be good and he is good. With Rozell [Rozelle] Claxton doing the arranging and playing those torrid numbers on the piano, Leonard can boast one of the most valuable men in the theatrical world today. Claxton has revised several old numbers for the band and has written new tunes which are soon to be released. Aiding Claxton in the arranging end of the orchestra are James Keith, tenor sax man, and James Ross, first trumpet. These two versatile artists are key men in the orchestra. Both are well schooled in music and capable of doing justice for themselves wherever they perform. Vocal honors of the orchestra fall upon Darwin Jones. A youth from Red Oak, Iowa, this "cat" plays sax in the orchestra and does the vocalizing on the "sweet" numbers. So great has been this lad's popularity that night after night rounds of applause have greeted him on his Fairyland park engagement.[50]

Taking a personal interest in the band, Tumino offered Leonard a contract for the next season.

Riding high into the fall, the Rockets played a busy schedule of club dates and social engagements rounded out by Sunday night dances at Dreamland Hall. A late September visit by Benny Goodman brought Leonard his first big break. In town for a week engagement at the Tower Theater, Goodman, accompanied by Martha Tilton and other band members, stopped by Dreamland Hall to check out the Rockets for Willard Alexander at MCA. Favorably impressed, Goodman recommended the band to Alexander. Dave Dexter and John Hammond had been lobbying Alexander on Leonard's behalf for months, but with little success. The nod from Benny Goodman finally did the trick and Alexander made the trek to Kansas City. Arriving in mid-October, he spent two hours auditioning the band before catching the 9 P.M. flight back to New York. Leonard, delighted by the audition, expressed confidence in the band's ability and future with MCA in a statement to the *Kansas City Call*, "Through the splendid cooperation of two well-known critics of today, Dave Dexter of our own Kansas City *Journal* and John Hammond, wealthy New York critic, I have for some time been negotiating with Music Corporation of America regarding my band which is fast reaching that stage of perfection and polish which will assure its future." Leonard declared the audition a success and predicted the band would be leaving town shortly. "I have every reason to believe that we will be with our many Kansas City friends only a few short months more."[51]

Alexander unexpectedly passed on signing the band, which caught Leonard off guard. Frustrated by the Basie band's rocky start, followed by Joe Turner's and Pete Johnson's cool reception in New York, Alexander balked at taking on another rough unknown group from Kansas City. Covering the audition for the *Kansas City Call*, LeRoy Brown reported that Alexander "was not satisfied with certain instruments in the band" and felt "there were changes that would have to be made before the boys would be able to step into the big time rackets." Brown optimistically concluded, "Although some replacements will be made it is almost a certainty that Leonard's stay in Kansas City is going to be short."⁵² Stymied by the missed opportunity, Leonard adjusted the band's lineup. Tuning up the rhythm section, he replaced Ben Curtis on bass with Winston Williams, a young disciple of Walter Page, and ordered drummer Edward Philips to take drum lessons. Leonard then enlisted Charlie Parker to lead the saxophone section. Parker came to the band a fully realized soloist, seasoned by his tenure with Buster Smith and a short stint with the McShann band at Martin's.

Buster Smith moved to New York City in July 1938, and left Parker in charge of the band. Smith, promising to send for the band once he became established, left Kansas City with high hopes, which were quickly dashed by the harsh realities of New York's music scene. Arriving in New York, Smith discovered the local musicians union required a three-month waiting period for new members. While waiting to join the union, Smith eked out a living selling a few arrangements to Artie Shaw and Count Basie. Once in the union, Smith freelanced with Don Redman, Lips Page, and other bandleaders, and gave up hope of bringing Parker and the band to New York. Without Smith's steady leadership, the band fell apart. Parker, ill equipped to manage his own affairs, much less that of a band, missed jobs and alienated club owners. Parker's capricious nature was compounded by his growing dependence on narcotics.

PARKER HAD DABBLED in drugs for a number of years, mainly Benzedrine and marijuana, easily available in the deep North End and the clubs on 12th Street. Having developed a taste for the pain-killers prescribed for his broken ribs, Parker graduated to shooting morphine and heroin. Addie scolded her errant son to no avail, and narcotics became as much a part of Parker's routine as a cup of coffee in the morning. A doting mother, she looked the other way when her household appliances disappeared only to turn up at the corner pawnshop.⁵³ Initially, Parker's prodigious appetite for narcotics had little effect on his musical development. Apprenticing with Buster Smith, he evolved into a facile improviser with endless ideas. Following the demise of the Smith band, Parker bounced around from group to group for several months before landing in the Jay McShann band at Martin's.

McShann wanted to work with Parker since their first meeting at the Bar Lu Duc, but the opportunity did not come to pass until the fall of 1938. Closing out a fifteen-week run at Martin's in late July, McShann expanded the band to ten pieces and opened at the Club Continental, playing for dancers and accompanying the stage show. Covering McShann's move in the *Kansas City Journal-Post*, Dave Dexter proclaimed "swing critics" judged the ten-piece McShann band the "best in the city," in effect, ranking the new band above the Rockets.[54] When Dee Stewart, fronting a new band, replaced the McShann band at the Club Continental in late October, drummer Gus Johnson and alto saxophonist Edward Hale stayed on with the Stewart band. Returning to Martin's in early November, McShann replaced Johnson with Jesse Price and Hale with Charlie Parker. Price and Parker stepped into the spotlight as featured soloists with the band. An advertisement for a joint appearance of the McShann and Leonard bands at the Gold Crown Tap Room in mid-November touted Price as the "mad drummer" and Parker as "Little Charlie Parker, saxophonist."[55]

A few weeks later, Parker left McShann to join Leonard, drawing his first paycheck for 75 cents on November 29.[56] LeRoy Brown noted an immediate improvement in the Rockets. "Harlan Leonard and his Kansas City Rockets now include three new faces. They are Winston Williams, bass; William Smith, third trumpet; and Charley Barry [Parker], alto sax. These changes have greatly improved the band and with a few minor changes in arrangements there is certain to be more heard from this fine Kansas City aggregation."[57] As a featured soloist with the Leonard band, Parker's star rose locally. In mid-December, he appeared on the *Vine Street Varieties*, a weekly radio revue, with an all-star group drawn from the Leonard band, led by Jesse Price.[58] Broadcast over WHB Saturday afternoons from 3 to 4 P.M. from the Lincoln Theatre, the *Varieties* showcased Julia Lee, Jay McShann, Harlan Leonard, the Rocket Swing Unit, Pete Johnson, Joe Turner, and other top local musicians.[59] Lionel Hampton, Teddy Wilson, and other visiting musicians often stopped by to sit in with the house band. Sharing the bill with Prince Zulong, "a torture-defying, fire-eating, and glass-walking" mystic, the Price band performed "Old Man Mose," "Lady Be Good," and "Honeysuckle Rose."[60] Not wanting to lose his new star performers or be outdone by Price, Leonard brought the full band featuring Parker to the *Vine Street Varieties* the following week.

Pleased with his young protégé , Leonard groomed Parker for stardom with the band. An advertisement in the *Kansas City Call* announcing a Christmas night dance at Dreamland Hall billed Parker as "saxophonist supreme," a strong statement in a town where saxophones reigned.[61] The Rockets received a boost when *Down Beat* ranked Rozelle Claxton among leading national pianists and arrangers in the January 1939 reader's poll. Although he ranked near the bottom rung in both categories, it gave the relatively unknown Claxton and the Leonard band a step-up. Dave Dexter, a fan of Claxton, who left Kansas City the previous fall for a staff position with *Down Beat* in Chicago, squeezed him into the poll to rate, by association, the Rockets with other national bands. In the same issue, Dexter covered the recent changes in the Rocket's personnel, generously reporting the addition of Parker to the lineup, despite his antipathy for the cocky young saxophonist.

Since falling victim to one of Parker's pranks years earlier, Dexter had grown to detest Parker.[62] In his history of jazz, *The Jazz Story*, Dexter strongly expressed his contempt for Parker, describing him as a "spoiled brat" who "horsed around in Kansas City, in his late teens, goosing musicians on the stand, stealing packs of cigarets [sic] from their cases."[63] Just as Parker gained his first national press in *Down Beat*, Leonard fired him. Beset by drug problems, Parker missed engagements with little explanation, which caused Leonard to let him go in mid-January 1939. Deeply disappointed in his young charge, Leonard simply explained, "We could never count on him showing up."[64] Buoyed by Claxton's recognition and the coverage of the Rockets in *Down Beat*, Leonard set his sights on national success and had little time to deal with the unreliable Parker. Stung by Leonard's dismissal, Parker hopped a freight bound for New York City to seek his musical father, Buster Smith.

Just as Parker hoboed east, Joe Turner and Pete Johnson returned to New York in grand style to premiere at Carnegie Hall. John Hammond, taking a cue from Benny Goodman's wildly successful Carnegie Hall debut in December 1937, staged an ambitious concert, tracing the growth of African American music from its roots in spirituals to the flowering of swing. Lacking the money to produce the gala concert on his own, Hammond turned to an unlikely partner, Eric Bernay, the publisher of *The New Masses*, a Marxist publication. With "From Spirituals to Swing," Hammond sought to introduce New York's social elite to the rich tapestry of African American music and cultivate an audience for a new club in which he owned a stake, Café Society, located on Sheridan Square in the Village. During the fall of 1938, while planning "Spirituals to Swing," Hammond and Benny Goodman bailed out Barney Josephson, when the club went broke after the second week of operation. Buying into Café Society, Hammond realized his dream of presenting his favorite musicians and recent discoveries to an appreciative racially mixed audience in a sophisticated setting. He strongly felt Café Society should be "a place where known and unknown performers could be heard, where jazz, blues and gospel were blended, where all my favorite performers could appear, where Negro patrons were as welcome as whites."[65] While symbolically embracing African American patrons, Hammond ardently courted New York's wealthy social elite that inspired the club's name.

Assembling the program for the "Spirituals to Swing" concert, Hammond gathered artists representing different regions and stages in the development of African American music. Along the way, he generously gave a number of relatively unknown musicians their first break. Traveling to Durham, North Carolina, Hammond sought out Blind Boy Fuller for the concert. Finding

Fuller in jail for shooting at his wife, Hammond engaged Fuller's cohort Sonny Terry, a blind harmonica player. While in North Carolina, he auditioned Mitchell's Christian Singers, an a cappella quartet of laborers and convinced them to come to New York. Originally, Hammond wanted legendary delta bluesman Robert Johnson on the bill. After learning of Johnson's untimely death, Hammond brought in Big Bill Broonzy from Arkansas. Rising gospel star Sister Rosetta Tharpe, direct from the Cotton Club, happily brought her fervent style of Holy Roller gospel music to the stage of Carnegie Hall. Trumpeter Tommy Ladnier and soprano saxophonist Sidney Bechet represented the New Orleans tradition. Pianists Albert Ammons and Meade Lux Lewis performed Chicago-style boogie-woogie. Hammond paired a relatively unknown blues singer, Ruby Smith, who was rumored to be related to Bessie Smith, with pianist James P. Johnson. Pete Johnson and Joe Turner arrived fresh from the Lone Star Club in Kansas City. The Basie band headlined the event and supplied the house rhythm section.

Staged on December 23, 1938, the concert, dedicated to the memory of Bessie Smith, caught the fancy of New York's cultural elite. Selling the hall out to the rafters, Hammond seated the overflow on stage in folding chairs. "Spirituals to Swing" hit with the concertgoers more accustomed to opera and classical music. H. Howard Taubman, the reviewer for the *New York Times*, marveled at the power and breadth of the program. "An evening of American Negro music shook the stage, the rafters and the audience. . . . There were spirituals, Holy Roller hymns, harmonica playing, blues, boogie woogie piano playing, early New Orleans jazz, soft swing and finally—without adjectives—swing. . . . A good time was had by all—except, perhaps, by the manager of the hall, who might have been wondering whether the walls would come tumbling down."[66] Concertgoers loved Mitchell's Christian Singers, Sonny Terry and Meade Lux Lewis, Albert Ammons with Pete Johnson, performing as the Boogie Woogie Trio. Although afforded only scant rehearsal time, Johnson, Lewis, and Ammons came together as a unit for a three-piano boogie-woogie session. Lewis and Ammons left the stage, and Johnson brought out Joe Turner. Mindful of Louis Armstrong's advice following their fiasco at the Apollo Theater, Johnson and Turner launched into their strongest numbers, "Roll 'Em, Pete" and "It's Alright, Baby." Much to Hammond's delight, "Joe shoved the mike out of his way, as though flicking lint from a lapel, picked up the beat, and started shouting the blues in an open-throated tone that carried to the far reaches of the hall."[67] The audience went wild over their raw energetic performance.

The second half of the three-and-a-half hour program showcased the Basie Band featuring Jimmy Rushing and Helen Humes. During the set, Lips Page joined the Basie band on stage for their first reunion since the Reno Club. Introducing Page, Hammond reminisced about first hearing the nine-piece Basie band at the Reno Club. Lips and the band improvised "Blues with Lips," rekindling the spirit of the legendary late-night sessions at the Reno Club and giving the audience a taste of pure Kansas City style. While "Spirituals to Swing" aspired to present the full spectrum of the African American tradition, Hammond weighted the program in favor of Kansas City by featuring prominently Johnson, Turner, and the members of the Basie band. They immediately benefited from the exposure. The Basie Band moved up in the national ranking of bands, placing fourth in the January 1939 *Down Beat* poll for best swing band. Pete Johnson and Joe Turner joined Billie Holiday, Albert Ammons, and Meade Lux Lewis for an extended run at Café Society. Turner and Johnson's regular appearances on Benny Goodman's radio program and the release of their first recording, "Roll 'Em, Pete," established their careers nationally. With "Spirituals to Swing," Hammond validated Kansas City's national reputation as a cradle of jazz alongside New Orleans, Chicago, and New York.

ON THE SAME DAY Hammond celebrated Kansas City Jazz at Carnegie Hall, Missouri Governor Lloyd Stark declared all-out war on the gambling, vice, corruption, and flagrant violation of liquor laws that had fostered the tradition of jazz in the city. Fed up with local reluctance to comply with state laws, Stark directed Missouri's Attorney General to marshal his forces and use whatever means necessary to clean up Kansas City. In his order, published on the front page of the *Kansas City Star* on December 23, 1938, Stark charged "that the gambling racket is carried on openly in defiance of the law and without protest from any official heads of the city's government; that houses of prostitution flourish within the very shadows of the courthouse and city hall, and the inmates solicit openly, unashamed and unafraid of official authority. . . . It is apparent to all that there is an open and notorious violation of the liquor laws of Missouri and an utter disregard and disrespect for the provisions of that act."[68] The ensuing raids on the clubs, houses of prostitution, and gambling dens by an army of state agents had a chilling effect on nightlife in Kansas City.

Columnist Leroy Brown protested the crackdown in the *Kansas City Call*:

The lid is back on the night clubs in this burg these days and consequently the "drag" with its subsequent outlets for fast living is again draped in its cloth of black and bears every resemblance of a mourning widow. Yes a widow who has lost her husband, two children and best dog all in one week. One would think that just because the present probe is centered on the gambling racket that the night clubs and beer parlors would more or less be exempt from strictly adhering to the closing hour law but that is not so. You see my dear friends, most of the beer parlors and so-called night clubs are just fronts for the horrible and distasteful "crap shooting" that takes place within its rear portals. This is not true in all cases but in those cases where only the selling of drinks and dancing takes place the investigating group must see to it that they close at midnight.[69]

The crackdown padlocked the venerable Reno and Chesterfield Clubs, along with eight other popular nightclubs. Authorities hauled musicians off to jail along with patrons. William Shaw spent many sleepless nights bailing union members out of jail in the early hours of the morning. Work in clubs became so scarce many local musicians took day jobs to support their families.

By April, even Boss Tom Pendergast required the services of a bail bondsman after being indicted on several counts of federal income tax evasion. For years Pendergast profited from the suckers flocking to Riverside Park and the gambling dens liberally sprinkled throughout the city. Ironically, in the end, Pendergast proved to be the biggest sucker of all, falling victim to his own gambling empire. Beginning in 1933, Pendergast, a compulsive gambler, lost up to a million dollars a year at the racetrack. To support his obsession, he put the touch on associates for increasingly large sums of money and engineered an insurance graft scheme. The large drafts of cash Pendergast used to cover his bets caught the attention of Maurice Milligan, a crusading federal district attorney investigating the machine since 1934. On Good Friday, April 7, 1939, a federal grand jury fielded by J. Edgar Hoover indicted Pendergast for income tax evasion. On May 22, Pendergast pleaded guilty to two counts of tax evasion. The judge sentenced Pendergast to a year and a day in federal prison and fined him $5,000.[70]

With Pendergast safely tucked away in the federal penitentiary at Leavenworth, Kansas, reformers, sporting small brooms primly pinned to their lapels, cleaned up the town, sweeping 12th Street clean of all vestiges of vice. Federal agents broke up a narcotics ring reportedly raking in an estimated $12 million a year.[71] Raids on gambling houses by federal and state authorities sent sporting men scurrying out of town. The ladies on 14th Street soon found that "tricks ain't walkin'," and left for more tolerant climes. By early January 1941, the fevered cleanup reached such a self-righteous pitch that local authorities banned Julia Lee for performing risqué songs. After shutting down Milton's for a month on a liquor violation, Kansas City's liquor control department banished Julia Lee from returning to Milton's "because of the type of song she sang and the way she sang it." Lee had learned the songs in question—"The Fuller Brush Man," "Handy Man," and "Two Old Maids"— from the music book *Songs My Father Taught Me Not to Sing*, which she had picked up at Jenkins Music Company. Milton Morris publicly protested, buying recordings of the songs from Jenkins and offering to play them for liquor control. Lee defended herself, simply stating "these same songs have been sung in some of the finest homes in Kansas City."[72] Influential friends came to Lee's rescue, and she soon returned to her regular post at Milton's. Years later, Morris claimed to have "paid a kid five bucks" to push the liquor control agent responsible for Lee's public humiliation down a flight of stairs during a baseball game.[73] Morris's gesture struck a blow for the intemperate spirit of old Kaycee, but the reformers in control of city hall ultimately won the war on vice and corruption. The crackdown on nightlife in Kansas City hastened the exodus of musicians and bands. Facing diminished opportunities, Leonard and McShann abandoned Kansas City for the bright lights of New York, following in the wake of the Kirk and Basie bands, only to be swept under by the swelling tide of war.

9

Hootie's Blues

"Hello little girl, don't you remember me. . . . time ain't been so long, but I had break you see, well I'm doing all right found me a kewpie doll. . . . she lives two flights up and she sends me with a smile."

—Jay McShann, "Hootie Blues," 1941

JAY MCSHANN AND HARLAN LEONARD managed to escape the full force of the local cleanup and break out nationally, with a little luck and help from Dave Dexter. In the fall of 1938, Dexter joined *Down Beat* in Chicago. Confidently moving into his new position as associate editor, Dexter brought a new professionalism to the musician's monthly. "Within days I was writing, or rewriting from a dozen unpaid volunteer correspondents in the major cities, at least 80 percent of the news and features in each issue," Dexter proudly recalled. "I selected the photos and composed their captions. I pasted up the dummy of each page, corrected typographical errors, and arranged the physical layout of each story, writing every headline myself."[1] Dexter wrote under numerous pseudonyms to give the illusion of a large staff. The barely twenty-three-year-old Dexter, still sporting his funny Kansas City haircut, trimmed high and tight on the sides, emerged as a powerhouse in the music industry, in deciding which records merited review and what bands deserved ink. Once established at *Down Beat*, Dexter wielded his considerable influence to advance the McShann and Leonard bands nationally, while continuing to champion the Kansas City tradition.

In early February 1939, Dexter brought Jay McShann to Chicago for an engagement at the newly opened Off-Beat Club, an offshoot of *Down Beat*, located below the popular Three Deuces Club on State Street. The Off-Beat attracted scores of musicians and industry insiders who hoped to appear in

Down Beat. Dexter originally wanted to bring in Joe Turner and Pete Johnson, at the time riding high on the popularity of their hit recording "Roll 'Em, Pete." Finding Turner and Johnson otherwise engaged at Café Society, Dexter wired Jay McShann at Martin's. Jumping at the opportunity, McShann and Gene Ramey drove all night through sleet and snow, arriving at the Off-Beat just in time for a brief rehearsal with an all-star bill headlined by Anita O'Day, Wingy Manone, and Jimmy McPartland's jam band.

Dexter, covering McShann's debut in Chicago for the *Kansas City Call*, predicted the young bandleader would soon follow Kirk and Basie to national prominence. "Another Kansas City boy has made good in big-time music circles. Following in the steps of Count Basie, Andy Kirk, Pete Johnson, Joe Turner, Eddie Durham and two dozen other artists who got their first real 'push' in the Heart of America city, Jay McShann this week opened spectacularly at the new Off-Beat club with his own trio."[2] An impressive parade of bandleaders led by Paul Whiteman, Red Nichols, Bob Crosby, and Ina Ray Hutton stopped by bearing best wishes. Following a five-week run, McShann and Ramey returned to Martin's in Kansas City. Encouraged by his brush with fame in Chicago, McShann wanted to enlarge the band, but Dexter, who loved the small band, discouraged the thought.

While introducing McShann to Chicago audiences, Dexter helped Harlan Leonard win a recording contract with the Bluebird label and a management agreement with MCA. In the same article in which Dexter touted McShann's success at the Off-Beat, he also predicted big things for the Rockets. "Next in line for the move upward is Harlan Leonard's band, which may soon get the call from one of several large agencies here [Chicago] and in New York. Several recordings of the Leonard band were received here last week, and they are being used as samples for the ear of MCA, CRA [Consolidated Radio Artists] and Rockwell-O'Keefe scouts in Chicago, all of whom are interested in the band."[3] Dexter shopped the demos to Bluebird, securing a contract for the Rockets, more on the strength of his recommendation than the quality of the band's performance.[4] The contract with Bluebird bode well for the Rockets' future. Launched in 1932 by Victor records as a budget label for the race, hillbilly, and ethnic markets, Bluebird's roster of bands grew steadily over the years to include Glenn Miller, Artie Shaw, Charlie Barnet, and other leading white bands. Bluebird sold records by top bands for 35 cents each, capturing a lion's share of the lucrative swing market. The affiliation with Bluebird positioned the Rockets to surge to top national ranking propelled by a hit record along the lines of "One O'Clock Jump" or "Until the Real Thing Comes Along."

At Dexter's urging, John Hammond returned to Kansas City in early May 1939 and auditioned the Rockets for MCA. Leroy Brown delightedly pronounced the audition a qualified success. "Harlan and the boys played several hit tunes for Hammonds [Hammond], who could be seen sitting passively 'digging' all the strong and weak points of the aggregation. Following the audition he went into a huddle with Harlan and the orchestra leader emerged smiling as if he had run into a million dollars."[5]

Set to sign with MCA in the fall, Leonard adjusted the band's lineup and enhanced the band book during a summer engagement at Fairyland Park. In the rhythm section, drummer Jesse Price, a precise timekeeper and tireless soloist influenced by Jo Jones, replaced Edward Phillips. Pianist William Smith, a strong rhythmic player with a deft left hand inspired by Count Basie and Mary Lou Williams, succeeded Rozelle Claxton, who left the Rockets for the Ernie Fields band. Guitarist Efferagee Ware, like Freddie Green, concentrated on playing rhythm, rarely soloing. Bassist Winston Williams carried a steady beat. Shoring up the trombone section, Leonard added Fred Beckett, a fluid imaginative improviser who loved the solo spotlight. Beckett's wife, Helen Rothwell, a blues singer in the popular style of the day, joined as featured vocalist. In September, Henry Bridges, a powerful soulful soloist originally from Paris, Texas, replaced Freddie Culliver. Kindred souls, Bridges and Jimmy Keith challenged each other like Lester Young and Herschel Evans in the Basie Band. In the trumpet section, William "Smitty" Smith, a traditionalist favoring Louis Armstrong, provided a counterpoint to James Ross's fiery, upper-register modern solos. Ross, a budding composer and arranger, helped build the band book by contributing a snappy original composition, "Hairless Joe Jump," inspired by Hairless Joe, a character in Al Capp's popular comic strip, *Lil' Abner*. In early October, Leonard signed a seven-year contract with MCA, joining Basie in the Negro band department, headed by Maceo Birch.

Later that month, the Rockets embarked on a short midwestern tour under MCA's sponsorship, kicking off with a weekend dance for the annual Kentuckiana Institute Jamboree at the Armory in Louisville, Kentucky. The Rockets played swing standards for jitterbugs and accompanied a lively floor show headlined by Maxine Sullivan's New York Revue. The racially segregated audience, with whites perched in the balcony and African Americans milling around the dance floor, warmly greeted the Rockets, wildly applauding the antics of "the mad drummer" Jesse Price and calling balladeer Darwin Jones back for several encores. Maxine Sullivan, bounding on stage for the finale, brought down the house with her novelty swing hit "Loch Lomond." The ongoing popularity of "Loch Lomond," originally recorded in 1937, established and sustained Sullivan's career. Leonard, watching Sullivan delight the crowd, realized a charismatic female vocalist with a hit popular song could be the band's ticket to success. Leaving Louisville, the Rockets ranged across the territories from Kentucky to South Dakota.

The Rockets returned to Kansas City in late fall for a short engagement at the Century Room, a spacious club located upstairs on Broadway at 36th Street. Operated by John Tumino, the manager of the dance pavilion at Fairyland Park, the Century Room sported a round bar in the center of the room, circled by neatly arranged tables separated by a spacious recessed dance floor. Tumino, capitalizing on his contacts from Fairyland, booked national and top local bands. Young swing devotees and jitterbugs, attracted by the modest cover charge at the door, crowded the dance floor. While playing nightly at the Century Room, Leonard prepared the band for its upcoming Bluebird recording session and national debut. Dexter gave the Rockets another boost for Christmas, by ranking the band and individual members in the December 1939 annual *Down Beat* reader's poll. The Rockets, yet to record or play outside the Midwest, came in twenty-ninth, above Cab Calloway, Earl Hines, Ella Fitzgerald, and other more established bands. James Ross rated sixteenth in the trumpet poll over Charley Teagarden, Henry "Red" Allen, and a host of more well-known players.

In early January 1940, the Rockets opened at the elegant Trianon Ballroom in Chicago and recorded six selections for the Bluebird label. Caught short of enough new material to carry the all-day session, Leonard fell back on two old war-horse arrangements from earlier editions of the Rockets, Jesse Stone's "Snaky Feelings" and Richard Smith's "My Gal Sal," along with a stock arrangement of Mario Dorcey's "Contact." James Ross worked up arrangements for "Rockin' with the Rockets," "Skee," and "Hairless Joe Jump," released as "Hairy Joe Jump." The three new originals employ the distinguishing elements of the Kansas City jazz style: sections riffing in counterpoint, punctuated by solos and anchored by the steady pulse of the rhythm section, but in keeping with the decorum of the white bands in the Bluebird roster. The Rockets played with restraint and precision of execution. Of the originals, "Hairy Joe Jump" held the greatest promise of hitting nationally and establishing the band. Taken at medium-swing tempo, the brass and reed sections lightly introduce the theme in the first chorus with contrasting riffs capped by a four-bar interlude. William "Smitty" Smith takes charge in the middle chorus with a jauntily executed muted trumpet solo challenged by an inventive Lester Young–inspired solo turn on tenor saxophone by Jimmy Keith. Pianist William Smith follows with a harmonically advanced sixteen-bar solo influenced by Mary Lou Williams, leading to a full-throttle solo by James Ross, accented by drummer Jesse Price's rim shots and a muscular turn by tenor saxophonist Henry Bridges. In the final chorus, the band forcefully restates the theme, taking things home in fine fashion.

Once released, a reviewer for *Down Beat* favorably compared "Hairy Joe Jump" to "One O'Clock Jump." Unfortunately, it sold only modestly.[6] Charlie Barnet and a number of other bands covered "Hairy Joe Jump," but recorded it as "Southern Fried." In the end, the Rockets benefited little from the song's national popularity.

Before leaving Chicago, Leonard stumbled across the charismatic female vocalist he had been seeking since Louisville. Petite and spirited with a broad grin and hearty laugh, Myra Taylor joined the Rockets after a chance encounter with band members. While visiting her pianist at the hotel where

Leonard and the Rockets were staying, Taylor met Jimmy Keith and several other band members. At her pianist's prodding, Taylor sang her signature song, "This is My Night to Dream," for their new friends. Keith dashed down the hall, returning with Leonard in tow. Following an impromptu audition, Leonard offered her a spot with the band. In between jobs, Taylor readily accepted Leonard's offer. "I was flat broke," Taylor mused, "I had been playing the Three Deuces with Lil Armstrong, Baby Dodds, and Lonnie Johnson. After our New Years Eve show, the owners torched the club, and I lost my gowns and arrangements. All I had left was the dress I had on, so Harlan's offer was a godsend."[7] Taylor brought bountiful experience as a vocalist and entertainer to the Rockets.

Originally from Bonner Springs, Kansas, just a few miles west of Kansas City, Taylor began her career as a dancer at the Sunset and Reno Clubs. " I had to sneak through the back window of the Sunset, because I was underage, but I could walk right in the front door of the Reno," Taylor declared. "I always got the job with my dancing and kept it with my singing."[8] Taylor hit the road in 1937, traveling widely across the Midwest, working with the Red Perkins band at the Harlem Nightclub in Omaha and Clarence Love at the 25 Club in Dallas. Moving on to Chicago, she performed around town with Roy Eldridge and Stuff Smith at the Three Deuces, Horace Henderson at Swingland, Red Saunders at Club Delisa, and Earl Hines at the Grand Terrace. A quick wit with flawless comedic timing and a crowd-pleasing natural vocal style, Taylor returned to Kansas City with the Rockets. Former Blue Devil Ernie Williams soon joined Myra in the vocal lineup. Williams, a relaxed blues stylist in the classic Kansas City tradition, also fronted the band, freeing Leonard to concentrate on taking care of business. Getting ready for the Rockets' debut in New York City, Leonard rehearsed the band daily for two weeks at Local 627. Before launching the tour, the Rockets opened for the Jimmy Lunceford band at the Municipal Auditorium. Leonard, cultivating his new protégé, gave Taylor star billing for the date. At the end of January 1940, Leonard and the Rockets pulled out of Kansas City bound for the grand Golden Gate Ballroom in Harlem, intent on duplicating the triumph of the Kirk and Basie bands.

THE McSHANN BAND followed the Rockets into the Century Room in early January 1940. During the previous year, McShann teetered on the brink of national fame while maintaining his base in Kansas City, alternating between Martin's and the Club Continental with frequent appearances in the *Vine Street Varieties*. In June 1939, Sharon A. Pease profiled McShann in his "Swing Piano Styles" column in *Down Beat*, an honor usually reserved for nationally established pianists. Pease introduced the relatively unknown McShann to the broad national audience, chronicling the young bandleader's career in detail. Analyzing McShann's original composition "Hootie Blues," Pease favorably compared the young pianist's style to Mary Lou Williams, Count Basie, and Pete Johnson. Pease concluded by confidently predicting, "You'll be hearing more of Jay McShann one of these days."[9] Dexter followed up with a letter recommending the McShann band to Jack Kapp. Always on the lookout for fresh talent from Kansas City, Kapp dispatched J. Mayo Williams, head of Decca's race department, to check out the McShann Band at Martin's. Williams, instantly impressed with the band's hard-swinging style reminiscent of the Basie band at the Reno Club, signed McShann to a contract on the spot and set a date for a recording session later that fall in Chicago.

Buoyed by best wishes from a parade of admirers, the McShann band headed for Chicago on November 11, 1939, to record for Decca.[10] McShann, planning on a marathon session, supplemented three William Scott originals—"Blame It on Me," "Why Did it Have to be You," and the band's theme "Jiggin' With Jay"—with special arrangements of the standards—"Losing My Heart," "Diane," "Margie," and "Annie Laurie." Just as the band entered the recording studio, the Chicago union stepped in and thwarted the session. "We went up to Chicago, but I didn't know I was supposed to turn in a contract to the local union," McShann revealed. "Well the Chicago union found out about the session when we were getting ready to record and they stopped the session. So we didn't get a chance to record. We had to come on back to Kansas City."[11] McShann returned home with a promise from Williams and Kapp of another recording session in the near future.

Opening at the Century Room, McShann cut a management deal with John Tumino and expanded the band to twelve pieces for the upcoming Decca recording session. In mid-February 1940, McShann added trumpeter Bernard "Buddy" Anderson and trombonist Joe Baird, who brought the band up to nine members. Anderson, whose ideas outreached his execution, came to the band from Tulsa, where he had worked with Henry Bridges and guitarist Charlie Christian. A month later, McShann, bankrolled by Walter Bales, traveled to Omaha and raided the Nat Towles band, one of the leading territorial bands of the day. Arriving during a Monday-night jam session hosted by Towles, McShann picked off band members. "All the musicians were coming in, so every time I heard a cat I liked I'd send him a drink and have him come over," McShann confided. "They all could leave town, but they owed Towles money, so I said, 'Okay, I'll see you at 7 o'clock in the morning to get you the money you need to pay your debts before you leave town.' One band member told Nat, 'There's a guy in town trying to get your musicians.' Nat said, 'I'm not worried because they all owe me money.' He didn't know I had plenty of money from Walter Bales, who told me to call or go down to the Traveler's Insurance office if I needed more. I told all the musicians I'd meet them at 7 o'clock in the morning. I went down to Traveler's, and I knew the clerk was caught off guard, because here's a black musician coming in asking for a couple of hundred dollars, and this must be a heist."[12] Fortunately for McShann,

Bales called just in time to assure the nervous employee that everything was on the up and up.

McShann returned to Kansas City with the musicians needed to fully realize the band. Guitarist Leonard "Lucky" Enois, a strong rhythm player and lyrical soloist influenced by Charlie Christian, filled out the rhythm section. Harold "Al" Bruce, an undisciplined lead player fond of the upper register, joined Anderson and Minor in the trumpet section. Trombonist Leo Williams, a reliable section player and competent soloist, added a needed second voice to the trombone section. William Scott adapted the band's book to accommodate the increased size, voicing out the sections by setting little riffs so the band did not miss a beat. On Easter Sunday, March 24, McShann and his brand-new twelve-piece Decca Recording Orchestra battled Lawrence Keyes and His Fifteen Deans of Swing in front of 2,500 dance fans at the Roseland Ballroom.

During the course of the evening, McShann reconciled with Charlie Parker, who had returned to Kansas City from New York the previous fall for his father's funeral. Parker's physically grueling journey east led to a musical epiphany, similar to his realization in the Ozarks years earlier. Cut loose by Harlan Leonard in early 1940, Parker headed east, turning up on Buster Smith's doorstep in New York, considerably worse for the wear. Dismayed by Parker's condition, the kindhearted Smith took his young protégé in over his wife's objections. "Charlie got downhearted when it looked like I wasn't gonna send for them, so he just caught a train and hoboed up there [New York], came up there where I was." Smith recollected. "He sure did look awful when he got in. He'd worn his shoes so long that his legs were all swollen up. He stayed up there with me for a good while at my apartment. During the day my wife worked and I was always out looking around, and I let him stay at my place and sleep in my bed. He'd go out and blow all night somewhere and then come in and go to sleep in my bed. I'd make him leave in the afternoon before my wife came home. She didn't like him sleeping in our bed because he wouldn't pull his clothes off before he went to bed. He was always like that. He would go down to Monroe's and play all night long. The boys were beginning to listen to him then."[13]

Unable to find regular work beyond jamming at Monroe's for tips, Parker took a job washing dishes at Jimmy's Chicken Shack, a popular Harlem eatery. While working in the kitchen, Parker listened closely to Art Tatum, who often stopped by to sit in. He absorbed the piano master's technique of harmonic substitution and interpolating melodies. Since his days of "going out of key" with Buster Smith at Lucille's Paradise, Parker had been searching for a fresh harmonic approach. During a jam session at Dan Wall's Chili House with guitarist Biddy Fleet, Parker finally articulated what he had been hearing. "I remember one night before Monroe's I was jamming in a chili house on Seventh Avenue between 139th and 140th," Parker described. "Now I'd been getting bored with the stereotyped changes that were being used all the time at the time, and I kept thinking there's bound to be something else. I could hear it sometimes but I couldn't play it."

"Well, that night, I was working over *Cherokee*, and, as I did, I found that by using the higher intervals of a chord as a melody line and backing them with appropriately related changes, I could play the thing I'd been hearing. I came alive."[14] Parker later downplayed the significance of his discovery, which sparked the bop revolution, simply stating, "I'm accused of having been one of the pioneers." Despite his disclaimer, Parker first took flight on the wings of his musical breakthrough at Wall's.[15]

In late summer, Parker, weary of washing dishes and eager to launch his career, joined entertainer Banjo Burney Robinson's band, bound for a hotel engagement in Annapolis, Maryland. Parker received word of his father's death while playing with Robinson.[16] The senior Parker, a footloose alcoholic, died in Memphis from a stab wound, inflicted by a woman in the heat of an argument. Although the two had separated years earlier, Addie made arrangements for her husband's funeral. Parker, returning to Kansas City in September to be by his mother's side, fretted over his father's condition. "Charles could hardly recognize the body, it was in horrible shape from loss of blood," Addie Parker remembered. "'Mama, what made him do it?' Charles asked." His mother simply replied, "He liked the lady, I guess."[17] Like his father, Parker had a predilection for alcohol and substance abuse, but, out of necessity, had cleaned up his act. Living meagerly in New York forced him to nip his budding habit. Working on the road with Robinson, far from his sources, further separated him from temptation.

After the funeral, Parker stayed in Kansas City, moving into his mother's house on Olive Street. Finding club work on 12th and 18th Streets scarce in the wake of the cleanup, Parker joined Lawrence Keyes's Deans of Swing, a young band originally formed by students at R. T. Coles Vocational School. Like Keyes's earlier band, the Chords of Rhythm, the Deans of Swing played primarily at Lincoln Hall, with odd dates at the Blue Room in the Street's Hotel and the Century Room. After the Easter battle between the Keyes and McShann bands, Parker moved over to the McShann band.[18] Although Parker had abruptly abandoned the McShann band at Martin's for the Leonard band the previous year, McShann welcomed home his musical prodigal son to the newly expanded band. Parker's dedication and leadership pleasantly surprised McShann. "He [Parker] was pretty straight then and an inspiration to our band. He was serious about his music then, and I put him in charge of the band when I wasn't there," McShann disclosed. "He'd keep a notebook and took down the time when the guys used to make rehearsals and when they were late, etc. He'd really get tight if they didn't take their music seriously. I used to work on him by telling him the brass section and the rhythm were in terrific shape, and they'd blow his reed section right out of the hall. This made him work to keep them in top form, and it would also make the rest of the band work."[19]

McShann, Parker, and William Scott tightened the band's sections and developed an original book during a spring engagement at a walk-a-thon, held in the cavernous ice-hockey arena attached to the back of the Pla-Mor. As the contestants staggered around the arena watching the clock, McShann rehearsed the sections, sending the reeds upstairs, while leaving the brass on the bandstand and then switching the two. "After opening at the walk-a-thon in the arena at the Pla-Mor we got the band together by using the loft as a rehearsal space," McShann recalled. "I sent Scotty [William Scott] and the reed section up there to rehearse. I kept the brass and the rhythm section on the stage. When the brass went upstairs to rehearse, the reeds would come down with the band. At the walk-a-thon, they had these games they would pull to eliminate so many people a night. After four or five months about everybody would be eliminated except for two or three people. By the time everybody was eliminated we had a book of 250 or 300 tunes and about 150 head tunes. I often wondered how in the world those guys could remember those head tunes, but they would remember 'em." Parker, drawing from his remarkable ability to play from memory, guided other members of the saxophone section to the right notes. "What really helped was having Bird in that big band," McShann observed. "When Bird was in the section, you would see him turn, especially on those head tunes he would be giving this cat his note. He'd give him the note he wanted him to make. He might tell 'em, and if he didn't tell 'em, he'd play it for 'em. And if you see him turning this way he'd be giving this cat his note. Sometimes they'd get off on the wrong notes. Then after a while they would all come together."[20]

After the walk-a-thon wound down in early summer, the McShann band opened for the season at Fairyland Park. Covering the band's debut at Fairyland in *Down Beat*, Bob Locke noted the band's vast improvement, brought about by the rigorous rehearsals at the Pla-Mor. "Jay McShann busted the season record when he opened at the Fairyland Park ballroom the last week in June as house ork, dragging in 400 terps [dancers] for the opening Tuesday which is generally an off night. . . . The 14-piece outfit has improved beyond the imagination of any one who hasn't heard it, and should be 1941's sepia sensation. . . . Every man has his heart in his job."[21]

While the McShann band rose locally, the Rockets fizzled nationally. The year 1940 began on an upbeat for the Rockets. They left Kansas City in late January and played dates in Pittsburgh, Philadelphia, and Trenton, New Jersey, followed by a four-week engagement at the newly opened Golden Gate Ballroom in Harlem at 142nd and Lenox Avenue. The palatial Golden Gate quickly rivaled the famed Savoy, located a block south, as the top ballroom in Harlem and claimed the favor of the dapper gangsters who lorded over the numbers and narcotics rackets. Opening on February 12, the Rockets joined a rodeo of bands that featured Les Hite, Claude Hopkins, Coleman Hawkins, and organist Milt Herth's trio. Dancers and onlookers circulated between four bandstands, while the bands bandied sets in a continuous musical marathon from 4 P.M. to 4 A.M. The Rockets were a hit with New York audiences, especially charming Myra Taylor, who mixed easily with the crowd, stepping off the stage to cavort with the jitterbugs on the dance floor. Impressed by her verve, a representative from MCA offered Taylor an exclusive contract as a single, but she declined out of loyalty to Leonard. After the first week, the Rockets settled in for an additional three-week engagement opposite the Coleman Hawkins band. Nightly broadcasts from the Golden Gate over the Columbia network gave the band its first national exposure and the opportunity to promote its Bluebird recordings.

While in New York, the band recorded four more selections for Bluebird. Once again caught short of enough strong new compositions to cover the session, Leonard relied on two standbys from the early band book: Rozelle Claxton's "Parade of the Stompers" and Richard Smith's arrangement of "I'm in a Weary Mood." Desperate for fresh material, Leonard contacted his old friends Buster Smith and Eddie Durham, then freelancing around New York. Smith crafted a simple, straightforward arrangement for "Ride My Blues Away," which featured Ernie Williams's half-shouted blues style inspired by Jimmy Rushing and Joe Turner. Durham supplied Leonard with an arrangement of a new popular tune, "I Don't Want to Set the World on Fire," originally scored for publication as a ballad, the tempo intended by the composers. The producer for the session, however, insisted that the band give it an uptempo treatment to appeal to jitterbugs. Durham's loose hard-swinging arrangement lifted the band to new heights, and the song's catchy melody and novel lyrics perfectly suited Myra Taylor's personality and playful style, but the brisk tempo overwhelmed the tender sentiment of the lyrics. Satisfied with the take, Leonard left the studio convinced he had recorded the hit destined to take the Rockets to the top.

Before leaving New York, Leonard hired pianist Tadley "Tad" Dameron, a progressive composer and arranger in the eastern style. Originally from Cleveland, Dameron attended the Oberlin Conservatory of Music. He began playing professionally with modernist trumpeter Freddie Webster in Chicago before serving a short stint as music director for Blanche Calloway. Dameron, an aspiring freelance composer and arranger, supplied arrangements to Andy Kirk, Benny Carter, Teddy Hill, and Horace Henderson. Down on his luck, after being fired by Vido Musso, Dameron readily cast his lot with the Rockets. Continuing the MCA tour, the Rockets played in Bridgeport, Connecticut, and Rochester, New York, sharing the bill with the Andrews Sisters. In Pittsburgh, the Rockets battled the Charlie Barnet band, featuring Lena Horne, at the Syria Mosque, drawing a crowd of 4,500. These engagements marked the beginning of the end of the Rockets.

During the Rockets' return trip to Kansas City, MCA dissolved its Negro band department, letting go Maceo Birch and merging its rosters of African American and white bands. Ideally, this put the African American bands on equal footing with the white bands, but in reality they received short shrift from the realignment. While white bands ranged freely across the country, playing week-long engagements at theaters, hotels, and ballrooms—African American bands, restricted by Jim Crow practice, relied heavily on one-nighters, which required circuitous routing. Birch's departure left the Rockets and other African American bands without an advocate at MCA. Dismissing the banner headline in the *Kansas City Call* proclaiming "MCA Jilted Negro Bands," Leonard downplayed the significance of the move, stating, "everything will be okay."[22] Leonard's optimism proved to be unfounded. MCA abruptly dropped the Rockets. Maceo Birch, taking his career full circle, returned to Kansas City to manage the Blue Room in Street's Hotel. Leonard resumed his former routine, playing at the Blue Room and Lincoln and Paseo Halls while filling out the band's schedule with social engagements. Leonard, striving to re-establish the band regionally, renewed his association with John Tumino, who had recently started his own booking agency.

Building on his contacts at the Century Room and Fairyland Park, Tumino established Consolidated Orchestras of America, a booking and management firm with contacts across the Midwest. Guided by Tumino, Leonard traveled a regional circuit, playing ballrooms, country clubs, and college dances across Missouri, Kansas, and Nebraska. The *Kansas City Call* noted Myra Taylor's popularity with "college students, swing fans, jitterbugs and music critics." She reportedly "wowed 'em" during her performance at the opening ceremonies launching the 1940 Monarchs season at Ruppert Field, the home of the Kansas City Blues.[23] Earlier in the year while anticipating big things from MCA, Leonard had balked at committing the Rockets to the upcoming season at Fairyland Park, and in turn Tumino awarded McShann the lucrative summer engagement. Leonard's miscalculation forced the band to spend the summer playing a considerably less prestigious engagement at Eddie Spitz's White House Garden, located out in the county on Troost Avenue near 84th. Surveying the Kansas City scene in *Down Beat*, Bob Locke judged the Rockets "deserve better pickings than they're getting."[24] Frustrated by the recent setbacks with MCA and Fairyland Park, Leonard pinned his hopes on Dameron's new compositions, slated for recording in mid-July, to put the Rockets back on track nationally.

Ironically, while writing new material for the Rockets, Dameron quietly slipped the McShann band arrangements on the side. "Tad was supposed to get them [the Rockets] ready to go back to the big time. He was writing and coming up with stuff," McShann revealed.

One day Tad came over to my rehearsal with some music and said, "Play this." We put the number down, and the cats played it. He said, "Man, this sounds like a complete different number the way you phrase so much different than Harlan. I like the way you all phrase." Harlan's band would cut their notes off, but we held them as long as we could. Dameron said, "Look, I will give you this number. I got another number, just let me hear so many bars." We played a few measures of that, and he said, "I'll give that number to you." I said, "the first chance I get some money, I'm going to lay some money on you and you write along just as you are doing for Harlan, but right now my money's short." And he said, "Okay." I got a chance to get a lot of stuff from him during that time. Every chance he got he'd lay some arrangement on me.[25]

Despite his dalliance with the McShann band, Dameron managed to pen enough originals to carry the Rockets' next recording session. Unlike the previous session for Bluebird, held amid a whirlwind tour, the Rockets quietly slipped in and out of Chicago for the July 15 session without playing an accompanying engagement. Dameron's new arrangements moved the band away from the distinctive Kansas City style to a more generic sound. His swing originals, "Rock and Ride" and "400 Swing," employ tight stylized riffs in the manner of the eastern bands, rather than the loose call-and-response Kansas City–inspired style, perfected by the Basie band. The band's overall delivery is clipped and sharply delineated, accented by carefully structured solos executed with precise intonation. Dameron's lush arrangement of the ballad "A-La-Bridges" wonderfully underscores Henry Bridges's big warm tone and supple modern trombone style of Fred Beckett. The ballad, "My Dream," featuring vocalist Darwin Jones, emulates the sweet style of Pha Terrell with the Kirk band, complete with Jones rendering a falsetto coda. Leonard filled out the session with an obligatory blues and novelty number. A holdover from the band's earlier style, "Please Don't Squabble," arranged by James Ross, served as a suitable vehicle for Ernie Williams's half-shouted blues vocal style. Inspired by Ella Fitzgerald's hit "A-Tisket A-Tasket," Eddie Durham's arrangement of the novelty "My Pop Gave Me a Nickel" featured Myra Taylor's playful vocal style and bubbling personality. Dameron's arrangements, consciously modeled after those of Glenn Miller, Artie Shaw, and the other white bands in Bluebird's roster, gave the Rockets a reasonable shot at commercial success, but a poor publishing decision by Leonard ultimately undermined any chance of a hit record bringing the band back to national prominence.

Like most bandleaders, Leonard took co-writing credit for compositions contributed by band members. Disregarding a growing dispute between the American Society of Composers, Authors and Publishers (ASCAP) and the radio networks, Leonard registered Dameron's new creations with ASCAP, as he had with the band's previous compositions. Established in 1914, ASCAP controlled most copyrighted music. ASCAP charged the radio networks a blanket performance fee based on the station's advertising revenue for use of its catalog. At the beginning of 1939, ASCAP sharply hiked its fees for radio stations. The National Association of Broadcasters (NAB) revolted and established a rival publishing firm, Broadcast Music Incorporated (BMI), on April 1. Young composers, already feeling unfairly treated by ASCAP, flocked to BMI where their compositions were assured airplay. BMI filled out its catalog by buying publishing houses wholesale and creating new arrangements of music in the public domain. Leonard and other bandleaders found themselves caught in the middle of the high-stakes stalemate.[26]

Unconcerned by the dispute, Leonard returned to Chicago on November 13 and recorded eight more selections for Bluebird. Dameron, long gone for greener pastures, left behind enough new compositions for the session. Sticking to his tried and true mix of styles, Leonard recorded five swing numbers— "Dameron Stomp," "Society Steps Out," "Too Much," "Keep Rockin'," and "Take 'Em"—along with "Mistreated," a blues number that featured Ernie Williams, and a ballad called "It Couldn't Be You," which showcased the smooth vocal style of Darwin Jones. A novelty number, "Dig It," that featured Myra Taylor rounded out the session. While most bandleaders switched their affiliation from ASCAP to BMI, going so far as changing their well-established theme songs to insure jukebox and radio play, Leonard doggedly stuck with ASCAP. Unfortunately for Leonard, Bluebird rejected half of the recordings out of hand because of the looming ASCAP ban and jukebox boycott.

The dispute between ASCAP and the NAB culminated with NAB calling for a ban on all ASCAP music on radio airwaves to become effective January 1, 1941. Anticipating the ban, stations curtailed band remotes and boycotted ASCAP-registered songs. Leonard, like other bandleaders affiliated with ASCAP, found himself out in the cold, unable to broadcast, even locally, songs the Rockets recorded for Bluebird. The *Kansas City Call* noted the ban's impact on the Rockets. "Now that the BMI ban has forced ASCAP tunes off the air Harlan's air time has been cut down owing to the fact orchestras are having difficulty in finding enough good tunes for nightly radio appearances."[27] Compounding matters, jukebox operators joined the ASCAP ban, closing the only other avenue for promoting new recordings.

Bluebird released Leonard's lone hope for a hit, "I Don't Want to Set the World on Fire," in late November, just in time for the Christmas season. Registered with BMI, assuring airplay, "I Don't Want to Set the World on Fire" failed to click with the record-buying public. In the end, the up-tempo swing treatment of the ballad, at the producer's insistence, robbed Leonard of the hit that could have catapulted the Rockets to the top, much like what "Until the Real Thing Comes Along" did for the Kirk band.

After the Williams Quartet recorded "I Don't Want to Set the World on Fire" as a ballad, Tommy Tucker and other bandleaders picked up on the slower-tempo version. The ballad version became immensely popular, selling 100,000 copies of sheet music. Released in September 1941, the Ink Spots recording became a sensation; it sold over 135,000 records in five days and then racked up an additional 80,000 unfilled orders. Covering the phenomenal popularity of the tune, the Associated Negro Press syndicate recognized the Rockets as the first band to record it, but noted that it initially "failed to catch on."[28] Stymied by his bad luck with MCA and Bluebird, Leonard temporarily put his dream of national success on the shelf.

As LEONARD RETRENCHED in Kansas City, a host of his contemporaries gathered in New York to record the first 78-rpm album set celebrating the Kansas City jazz tradition. Dave Dexter, no longer content to just write about music for *Down Beat*, started freelancing for Decca, producing and writing liner notes for 78-rpm album sets drawn from previously released material. After assembling a number of successful reissues, including an anthology of the Basie band, Dexter pitched Jack Kapp an album of Kansas City Jazz featuring the bands and musicians who defined the style. Having already cashed in on Basie and Kirk, Kapp heartily agreed to Dexter's proposal. Dexter enthusiastically took control of the project. After six months of planning, a veritable Who's Who of Kansas City musicians passed through Decca's studio perched fourteen floors above West 57th Street, overlooking the bare trees of Central Park.[29] Dexter personally supervised the sessions that celebrated the Kansas City style.

Andy Kirk and the Clouds of Joy drove from Portland, Maine, to New York for the first session on November 7, staying up for thirty-six hours straight. With an eye on authentic repertoire, Dexter and Kirk kicked off the set with "12th Street Rag," Euday Bowman's ragtime classic, and "The Count," penned by Basie as a member of the Moten band. Mary Lou Williams fashioned fresh arrangements for the session, updating and reinvigorating the two evergreens. Williams transforms the quaint syncopated melody of "12th Street Rag" into a hard-swinging anthem to Kansas City style. Following a fanfare introduction by the brass, the reed section introduces the theme, underscored by the riffing brass section. An eight-bar piano romp by Williams leads to a succession of solos punctuated by the riffing sections totally absorbing the melody. Taking things home, the full band exuberantly restates the original theme by ingeniously elongating the note values, simulating the three-against-four note pattern. Williams revamps "The Count," crafting a loose-swinging tribute to the Basie band in her own distinct style. The full band introduces the theme in a medium swing tempo, giving way to a round of spirited solos, propelled by the relaxed drive of the rhythm section. In the manner of the Basie band, Williams accentuates the solos with pronounced riffs, climaxing with the full band riffing in the out chorus. Freed of Jack Kapp's heavy hand in the studio, the Clouds of Joy ascended to new heights of swing and originality.

Dexter held a second session on November 11, recording six selections: "627 Stomp," by Pete Johnson's Band; "Piney Brown Blues," featuring Joe Turner and His Fly Cats; "South" and "Lafayette," with Hot Lips Page's

Orchestra; and "Moten's Swing" and "I Want a Little Girl" by Eddie Durham's Orchestra. For economy sake, the bands fronted by Johnson, Turner, and Page shared the same rhythm and reed section, with minor variations. The rhythm section featured former Blue Devil Abe Bolar, bass; George E. Lee alumnus A. G. Godley, drums; and King Cole guitarist John Collins. Three veterans of the territorial band tradition—Eddie Barefield doubling on alto saxophone and clarinet, Don Stovall on alto saxophone, and Don Byas on tenor saxophone—came together for the reed section. Coming to the studio prepared, Durham brought an ensemble from his recently formed big band, featuring Buster Smith on alto saxophone and Joe Keyes on trumpet.

Sharing composing credits, Johnson and Dexter dedicated "627 Stomp" to William Shaw and Local 627. In his liner notes for the set, Dexter captured the excitement generated by the interaction between band members. "'627 Stomp' is taken at bright tempo and is Johnson's side from the intro to the out chorus. The first half of the side is all piano. . . . [T]he saxes start riffing at Pete's half-way point. Don Stovall's alto cuts through for two 12-bar 'go' choruses and then Eddie Barefield lets loose with two more, on clarinet. Eddie plays similarly to the way the clarinetist did on the old Moten records. But he should, for it was Eddie Barefield who played those choruses! Pete takes it away from him just as the saxes, augmented by Page's horn, start a different, more exciting riff in the background. Gradually Pete builds up to a tremendous climax, driving his keys hard, his feet beating a stiff rhythm on the carpet below. It's a barrel-house finish with every man out for himself."[30] As further homage to Local 627, Dexter featured a photo of its modest headquarters on the front cover of the album set.

Barefield then suggested a tribute to their old friend Little Piney Brown. Joe Turner sketched out the lyrics in five minutes, and, after a brief consultation with Johnson, the band, minus the reed section, cut "Piney Brown Blues." Dexter recounted how the mood of the "Piney Brown Blues" remained so true to the feel of the late-night sessions on 12th Street; band members were temporarily transported back to the Sunset Club. "Pete's sparkling introduction gives Joe an entrance. And the next four choruses are all his. 'I shook hands with Piney Brown and I could hardly keep from crying,' Turner shouts. And over in the far corner, Pete smiled from the piano. Lips Page, blowing a muted obligato, looked around and winked. The stuff was on wax and they knew it. 'I swear we've got it right this time,' said Johnson. 'Sounds like the old Sunset Club back home.'"[31] In a broader sense, "Piney Brown Blues" eulogized the passing of the bright nightlife on 12th Street personified by the legendary Piney Brown. The most popular recording from the sessions, "Piney Brown Blues" backed by "627 Stomp," went on to sell over 400,000 copies after Jack Kapp released it as a single targeted for jukebox play.[32]

Lips Page closely emulated the style of the Moten Band for his two selections. Working with Eddie Durham, Page sketched a simple head arrangement based on the Moten band's original recording of "South," but modernized it, making it more palatable to contemporary tastes. Oddly, in referencing Page's version of the Moten recording, Dexter placed Eddie Barefield and Count Basie on the original session, remarking how Barefield recreated his original solo and Johnson emulated Basie's solo, when neither musician were with the Moten band at the time of the recording. Since issued in 1928, "South" remained popular on jukeboxes, causing Dexter to misjudge its provenance. On the companion side, Page and company recorded "Lafayette," in which they recreated the true sound of the Moten band. Dexter enthusiastically detailed the similarities between the original and Page's cover. "The idea on this number was to copy the 1931 [1932] arrangement faithfully and re-create the Moten music. Particularly reminiscent of the Moten aggregation is the three-way sax chorus immediately following Johnson's first piano solo, in which he tries to play solo exactly as Basie did on the Moten waxing. . . . Byas' tenor, Page's open-horn, with the saxes setting up a liquid riff behind him, and Pete's 'does-this-sound-like Basie?' piano lead up to Stovall's brilliant alto contribution. The full band then takes command with Page's trumpet playing lead. Godley's four-drum breaks are strictly 1932, but fit in nicely anyway."[33] Page, failing to make it big in New York after leaving the Basie band at the Reno Club, waxed nostalgic for the pure Kansas City style he helped pioneer.

Unlike Page, Durham had no interest in faithfully reproducing the style of the Moten band. Eight years after composing the original arrangement of "Moten's Swing," Durham crafted an updated version specifically for the Kansas City Jazz session. Although Dexter described the new arrangement as a "faithful interpretation," Durham departed from the style of his original, choosing a more laid-back tempo and de-emphasizing the compound riffs that distinguished the earlier Moten version in favor of his floating electric guitar solos and Buster Smith's fluid alto-saxophone work. In a nod to the original, the reed section brightly riffs through the last two choruses, which are accented by Durham's guitar fills. In his liner notes, Dexter explored in great detail the significance of "Moten's Swing," while barely mentioning Durham's rendition, indicating his disappointment with the new treatment.

Durham's lazy arrangement of McKinney's Cotton Pickers' flag-waver, "I Want a Little Girl," better suited Dexter. "This new version is taken at an easy drag tempo and features the leader's guitar plucking almost exclusively, although there are brief individual contributions by Lem C. Johnson, tenor; Conrad Frederick, piano; and Joe Keys [Keyes], muted trumpet in that order. Durham's orchestration of this pop tune shows his solid knowledge of scoring, for it comes off the turntable as a soft subtle bit of jazz. The rhythm section can be felt from the down beat, and particularly worthy of attention is the ensemble passage in which the saxes and the guitar cleverly 'spread' apart harmonically, achieve an uncommon tonal quality."[34] Durham, having moved beyond the Kansas City tradition, foreshadowed future trends in his contribution to the set.

Dexter, seeking to capture the elusive spirit of a late-night Kansas Çity jam session, enlisted Mary Lou Williams to lead a small group drawn from the Kirk band for the final session on November 18. Williams, frazzled by the rigors of traveling and frustrated by her meager pay, gladly grabbed the opportunity to lead, if in name only, her own band, the Kansas City Seven. Getting down to business in the studio, Williams refashioned two war-horses from the early Moten band, "Baby Dear" and "Harmony Blues." The results delighted Dexter. In his liner notes, Dexter lavishly praised her arrangements and piano work on "Baby Dear." "Mary Lou uses a small band, culled from the larger Andy Kirk group, and effectively creates, via her ingenious scoring talents to create a pseudo-jam session in which each soloist takes turns and gets two shots at the mike before the last bar. The tempo is bright. And particularly interesting are the leader's solo efforts. Her light, but deft and rhythmic figures, notably in the treble, are convincingly unique." Dexter, a follower of Williams's career since her early days in Kansas City, praised her originality as a pianist. "Although Mary Lou insists that Art Tatum and Earl Hines influenced her style in formative years, today there remains little of either Tatum or Hines in her manner of expressing herself on a keyboard."[35] While on the road with the Clouds of Joy, Williams, by popular demand, had to faithfully recreate her piano solos from the band's recordings. In the studio at the helm of her own ensemble she freely expressed her highly individual style.

Dexter noted that Williams chose "Harmony Blues" because she felt it was the "best blues the Moten gang ever played." Williams's arrangement transformed the original blues form into a lush ballad showcasing Dick Wilson's luxurious tenor work. Dexter, feeling Wilson had not received the recognition he deserved, took the opportunity to laud his talent. "Harold Baker's sharp, bell-toned horn leads the way from the opening beat here. But even more important than Baker's brilliant conceptions, and the contributions of the leader, are Dick Wilson's deep, gorgeously-phrased tenor saxophone improvisations. Rarely is Wilson heard in a slow blues groove. 'Harmony Blues' shows his skill to excellent advantage, and for no other reason, is thus a great record."[36] Given the opportunity to lead her own group, Williams began considering her options.

Basie's contract with Columbia prevented his participation in the session, forcing Dexter to round out the set with two previously released selections by the Basie band, "Good Morning Blues" and "Doggin' Around." Dexter annotated the album with extensive liner notes featuring an overview of the development of Kansas City Jazz and brief biographical sketches of all participants. Dressing up the set, he graced the inside of the front and back covers with photos of the musicians who came together to create the album. Dexter proudly included his own portrait, which stands in sharp relief to the black faces surrounding it. With his maiden voyage as record producer, Dexter cemented Kansas City's reputation as a cradle of jazz equal to New Orleans and Chicago. In the liner notes, he drew a distinction between the three jazz centers, advancing Kansas City ahead of New Orleans and Chicago. "For Kansas City style jazz actually is *Southwestern* jazz. All the bands from the west of the Mississippi River, it seems, play somewhat alike, stressing a beat, piano solos, riffing by the saxes, *and always coordinated together!* The early New Orleans bands never used a piano. Nor a saxophone. And instead of organized jamming, the idea seemed to be all 'bash' together, and have the solos clash. Chicago style (don't miss Decca Album No. 121, which includes a dozen exciting examples) also is more disorganized, with greater emphasis on clarinet than Kansas City style allows. Neither Chicago nor New Orleans jazz particularly stresses a beat, which every musician of 1941 considers a vital part of *le hot*."[37] Oddly, Dexter's celebration of Kansas City Jazz in the liner notes concludes by pronouncing it lapsed into dotage—"Kansas City jazz had been born, had grown into maturity, and had slumped into senility."[38] Dexter's pronouncement proved a bit premature.

As DECCA RELEASED the *Kansas City Jazz* album in the spring of 1941, the last great big band to come out of Kansas City, the Jay McShann band, rose nationally, boosted by good fortune and a hit recording. After closing at Fairyland in September 1940, McShann returned to the Century Room and further refined the band's personnel, replacing alto saxophonist Earl Jackson with John Jackson. Slim and pensive, Jackson rivaled Parker as a soloist.[39] While based at the Century Room, the McShann band toured regionally, ranging north to Des Moines, Iowa, east to Paducah, Kentucky, and west to Wichita, Kansas. During a Thanksgiving weekend engagement in Wichita, a brash young college student and jazz fan, Fred Higginson, invited McShann and other band members for a couple of after-hours sessions at radio station KFBI, named after Kansas Farmer and Business. KFBI traced its lineage back to Dr. Brinkley, the goat gland doctor. McShann, figuring the band could use a little experience in the studio before the pending Decca sessions, took Higginson up on his offer.

The station's engineer recorded the sessions to acetate discs, capturing the unit jamming on the standards "I Found a New Baby," "Body and Soul," "Moten's Swing, "Coquette," "Lady Be Good," "Honeysuckle Rose," and on their theme song, listed as an untitled blues. While the band struggled to find its niche in the Kansas City jazz tradition, Charlie Parker had already transcended previous jazz conventions. Gene Ramey felt band members could not fully appreciate Parker's technique and ideas. "When I look back, it seems to me that Bird was at the time so advanced in jazz that I do not think we realized to what degree his ideas had become perfected." Ramey observed. "For instance, we used to jam 'Cherokee.' Bird had his own way of starting from a chord in B natural and B flat; then he would run a cycle against that; and, probably, it would only be two or three bars before we got to the channel [middle part] that he would come back to the basic changes. In those days, we used to call it 'running out of key.' Bird used to sit and try to tell us what he was doing. I am sure that at that time nobody else in the band could play, for example, even the channel to 'Cherokee.' So Bird used to play a series of 'Tea For Two' phrases against the channel, and, since this was a melody that could easily be remembered, it gave the guys something to play during those bars."[40]

Parker's innovative technique and wealth of ideas are evident in his solos on "Body and Soul" and "Moten's Swing." Parker maintains the ballad tempo of "Body and Soul" while running in and out of key. Taking a cue from Parker, the band and Buddy Anderson switch to double time, before returning to the ballad tempo in the last eight bars of the out chorus. After the piano introduction to "Moten's Swing," the band launches into the familiar riff pattern. Parker follows with a confident, articulate solo, highlighted by triplets in the second eight-bar section, and triplet flourishes toward the end of the bridge, first stating, on record, his musical signature.[41] Parker had matured into a fully realized improviser, already pioneering a new musical style critics later labeled bebop. He soon had company.

At the same time, band mate Buddy Anderson, John Birks "Dizzy" Gillespie, then a member of the Cab Calloway band, and other young players were headed in a similar musical direction. Anderson, a great admirer of Parker and Gillespie, brought the two together, during the 1940 Christmas season. Anderson clearly recalled the circumstances leading to Gillespie's introduction to Parker.

> I went out with a group of the fellas in Jay McShann's band to dig Cab's [Cab Calloway's] band. Orville Minor, a trumpet player who was with McShann then, and I went out to dig Cab and dug Dizzy. He knocked us out. . . . He was different from anything we'd seen. So at intermission we got to talking with him and told him about a jam session down on the street, you know, Nineteenth and Vine. It was called the Kentucky Club [Kentucky Bar-B-Q]. Sure 'nuff, Diz showed up and he was real different, every moment. So we talked with him a little bit after he got off the stand. I was telling him mainly about Charlie Parker, but Charlie didn't show that night for some reason. But that next day, everybody got up about twelve, as cats do, and we met again, right in front of that Kentucky Club; that is, Diz and I met. We were talking and Charlie showed up, just out of the clear, showed up with his horn. And we talked a little while, and Dizzy wanted to hear us play. So we went over to the Musician's Local 627. We went upstairs to the piano and Dizzy sat down at the piano; he played. He wanted to hear me play trumpet and Charlie play saxophone. So we went through several numbers with him, but Diz was really feeling his oats then; he was coming through. He really didn't dig Bird, or me either, at that time, but it was a fine meeting.[42]

Actually, Gillespie, quite taken by Parker, strongly felt he had found a musical soul mate. "I was astounded by what the guy could do," Gillespie declared. "These other guys that I had been playing with weren't my colleagues, really. But the moment I heard Charlie Parker, I said, there is my colleague. . . . I had never heard anything like that before. The way that he assembled notes together. That was one of the greatest thrills because I had been a Roy Eldridge fan up until then, but I was definitely moving on into myself. Charlie Parker and I were moving in practically the same direction too, but neither of us knew it."[43] Parker and Gillespie led the next generation of jazz musicians, whose personalities and music better suited small ensembles, freeing them to experiment with different harmonic and rhythmic approaches to improvisation. Constrained by the rhythmic rigidity and arrangements of big bands, they worked out new musical ideas in after-hours jam sessions. Cab Calloway discouraged extracurricular activities by band members. Gillespie, while serving in Calloway's band, had to sneak out to jam. "Cab frowned on the idea of guys going out blowing, but I went anyway," Gillespie disclosed. "In the different towns we'd visit, I'd go out and blow. People would say, 'He's with Cab Calloway,' Cab didn't like that. But I'd sneak out anyway. . . . I was thinking about my own development. When we were in New York, after the show, I'd go to Minton's and then to Monroe's Uptown House and jam until seven o'clock in the mornings."[44]

In contrast, Parker enjoyed a great deal of musical and personal freedom in the McShann band. Rather than discouraging after-hours woodshedding by band members, McShann, more often than not, joined in on the fun. Gene Ramey attributed McShann's laid-back temperament to the sense of one big happy family. "By his own personality McShann created a happy band. The guys were like family," Ramey asserted. "Often I'd pick up *all* the guys, and after work we'd go back home or to some restaurant in town. You knew he [McShann] was the boss, but you could sit down and talk to him or cuss him out. It was a real good feeling like that."[45] While Harlan Leonard refused to tolerate Parker's drug use and absenteeism, McShann bent over backward to keep the rising young star in his orbit. When Parker messed up, McShann simply advised him—"Go get yourself together, go crazy for three days, then come back sit down and cool it. Get it out of your system. He'd come back like there wasn't anything happening."[46] Other times, Ramey kept Parker in line and watched over him like a father.

The McShann band spent early spring 1941 working the territories, playing one-nighters in clubs, proms, and private dances across Missouri, Illinois, Nebraska, Kansas, Arkansas, and Iowa. Parker received his nickname, Yardbird, while on the road in Nebraska. McShann revealed: "Whenever he saw some chicken on the menu, he'd say, 'Give me some of the yardbird over there.' We were in two cars, and the car he was in drove over a chicken, and Bird put his hands on his head and said, 'No, stop! Go back and pick up that yardbird.'

He insisted on it and we went back and Bird got out of the car and carefully wrapped up the chicken and took it with him to the hotel where we were staying and made the cook there cook it for us. He told him we had to have this yardbird."[47] Tickled by Parker's insistence on turning a roadkill into an evening meal, band members began referring to him as Yardbird, later shortened to Bird.

In early April, the band returned home to regroup and prepare for the Decca recording session, scheduled for Dallas later that month. While rehearsing, the band suffered a setback when tenor saxophonist William Scott heeded the call of the newly activated military draft. The government had instituted the draft the previous fall in response to the war spreading across Europe and the Far East. Scott's departure, the first local musician to be inducted, brought home to band members the reality of events unfolding abroad. The loss of Scott, the music director and principal arranger, came at an inopportune time for the band, as it prepared for the Decca session. McShann promptly replaced Scott with Harry Ferguson, a reliable section player, as a stop-gap measure.

Hedging his bets going into the session, McShann then added Walter Brown, a popular local blues vocalist. Brown came to Kansas City during the summer of 1937 from a Civilian Conservation Corps camp in Oklahoma. Square-faced with a rough complexion and nasal vocal style, Brown opened at the Sunset Club. Like Joe Turner, he served double duty as a singing waiter. After Turner's departure for New York, local music fans crowned Brown the new king of the blues by popular vote in a contest staged on the *Vine Street Varieties*. Brown played the Gold Crown Tap Room, the Paseo Tap Room, and the Subway Club before joining Woody Walder's Swingsters at the Kentucky Bar-B-Q. Featuring spicy barbecue, a spacious dance floor, and a long bar surrounded by a balcony, the Kentucky Bar-B-Q quickly became the new hot spot for after-hours jam sessions. McShann, during a late-night visit to the Kentucky Bar-B-Q, on impulse, offered Brown a job. "I heard Walter singing the blues at 19th and Vine," McShann recalled. "I went in and told him I like that blues you did, do another blues. . . . And he did the blues, so I said we might be doing some recording. If you're not tied down with these cats here we might get some stuff together and start rehearsing."[48] Brown, keen to record his signature song, "Confessin' the Blues," eagerly joined the band for the upcoming Decca recording session.

McShann, adjusting to losing Scott and adding Brown, rehearsed the band for several weeks leading up to the session. Brown and McShann wrote lyrics for "Hootie Blues" and worked out an arrangement for "Confessin' the Blues." Leaving Kansas City in the early hours of April 28, the band drove straight through to Dallas. In the studio, McShann wanted to record the band's modern compositions, including Parker's "What Price Love," later known as "Yardbird Suite," but Jack Kapp's brother Dave, who produced the session, had other ideas. Dave wanted to record exclusively blues and boogie-woogie for Decca's newly launched sepia series, targeting the burgeoning race market. McShann recalled how Kapp kept requesting blues and boogie numbers, while the band was recording their record repertory on the sly. "We had a lot of modern stuff in the book. We got down there, and Dave Kapp said play the tunes you want to record," McShann related. "We played three or four tunes. Kapp told us, 'Personally I like all the stuff you got, but truthfully I can't sell it.' So he came out and said, 'Can you guys do any kind of boogie-woogie?' Play me a boogie-woogie.' He smiled because it was a take, but we didn't know it was a take. Then he said, 'play a blues,' and we played a blues. He smiled again, telling us, 'that's what I want.' He said, 'Do one more blues tune, and I'll take what you want to pick out.' So we picked out 'Swingmatism.'" [49]

Ironically, while Kapp only grudgingly allowed McShann to record "Swingmatism," it best represented the band's true sound, inspired by the hard-swinging style of the Basie band. Taken at a brisk tempo, the brass and reed sections introduce the theme, with heavily accented compound riffs. McShann's assured piano solo at the bridge leads to a gliding solo by Parker. In the conclusion, the sections forcefully restate the riff pattern established in the opening bars, before closing with a Basie style coda. Meeting Kapp halfway, McShann followed with two blues featuring the full band, "Hootie Blues" and "Dexter Blues." Based on the standard "Donkey Serenade," "Hootie Blues" eloquently expresses the blues in an orchestral context. McShann sets the mood with a staid four-bar introduction, shadowed by Gene Ramey's walking bass line. The trumpets answered by the saxophone section, then lazily state the twelve-bar blues theme with held notes. Parker follows with a cool, cleanly executed twelve-bar solo, switching to his signature double time in the ninth and tenth bars. Parker's confident solo neatly segues into Walter Brown's relaxed three-chorus vocal, embellished by Buddy Anderson's sensitive inventive obligato accompaniment. The lyrics fashioned by Brown and McShann perfectly fit the pensive mood of the arrangement. "Hello, little girl, don't you remember me. . . . [T]ime ain't been so long, but I had break you see, well I'm doing all right found me a kwepie doll. . . . [S]he lives two flights up and she sends me with a smile." The full band takes it out by restating the theme. Ramey explained the sections played behind the beat to enhance the blue feeling of Brown's delivery and the lyrics. "If you listen to 'Hootie Blues,' you'll notice how far behind the real tempo the horns come in. That gave it a lazy image and bluesy sound."[50] The band employs the same technique of held notes behind the beat, enhancing the blue mood of "Dexter Blues." Out of gratitude, McShann dedicated "Dexter Blues" to Dave Dexter, guaranteeing a review, or at least a mention, in *Down Beat*.

The rhythm section, better suited to the pure blues and boogie-woogie styles Kapp wanted to capture, carried the rest of the session recording "Vine

Street Boogie," "Hold 'Em, Hootie," and "Confessin' the Blues." Led by McShann's two-fisted boogie piano rollicking across the full range of the keyboard, the rhythm section romped through the two boogie-woogie numbers, "Vine Street Boogie" and "Hold 'Em, Hootie." Walter Brown's conversational vocal style on "Confessin' the Blues" underscores the intimacy of the lyrics: "Baby, here I stand before you, with my heart in my hand, I want you to read it, mama, hoping that you'll understand, well, baby, mama, please don't dog me around, I'd rather love you, baby, than anyone else I know in town." Delighted with the results of the session, Kapp rushed the masters for "Confessin' the Blues" and "Hootie Blues" to the pressing plant. Released in early June, "Confessin' the Blues" hit nationally. Musicians in the know flipped the disc over, where they first discovered Parker's genius.

The sudden success of "Confessin' the Blues" caught McShann totally by surprise. "We went out on the road for a couple of months." McShann recalled, "We came into Tulsa, Oklahoma, and ran into a guy who told us he just heard our record at Jenkins, so we went down to Jenkins and listened to it. We didn't know the records had been released."[51] Heavy play in record stores and jukeboxes swiftly broke "Confession' the Blues" nationally. Over the years, the American Federation of Musicians (AFM) fought the proliferation of jukeboxes tooth and nail to no avail. Club owners across the country switched from live music to jukeboxes. While musicians cost money, jukeboxes paid off like slot machines. The record industry, long at odds with the AFM, cultivated jukebox operators, gleaning feedback on the popularity of new releases. Manie Sacks of Columbia records attributed the phenomenal sales of records in 1941 to jukeboxes. "Coin-operated phonographs also have made records more popular," Sacks observed. "There's no doubt about it— the boxes have made the public record-conscious."[52] In mid-June, Dave Dexter recommended "Confessin' the Blues" as a sleeper destined to be a jukebox hit in his "Most Popular in the Coin Machines" column in *Down Beat*. Dexter let the recommendation stand in his column for several months, stoking demand by jukebox operators.

Rather than tour nationally on the crest of "Confessin' the Blues," McShann chose to honor a previous commitment to play a summer engagement at Fairyland Park. Out of loyalty to John Tumino, McShann spent the summer at Fairyland, which in the end turned out to time well invested. In gratitude, Tumino repaid McShann many times over. The popularity of "Confessin' the Blues" carried past the summer and sold more than 81,000 copies by fall, well on its way to becoming the biggest seller in the history of Decca's Sepia Series. After closing at Fairyland Park, the band embarked on a tour of ballrooms on the Gopher Meadowlark circuit in Texas, Missouri, and Oklahoma, outdrawing Earl Hines, Les Hite, and Lionel Hampton. Writing in *Down Beat*, Mike Morales marveled how the band's success came without the benefit of representation by a national agency. "McShann has no MCA, Glaser,

Rockwell or Charlie Green behind him. Just a young guy named Tumino, who has Jay's interests at heart and who seldom leaves McShann with an open date on tour."[53]

Tumino capitalized on the popularity of "Confessin' the Blues" by booking an ambitious tour, extending east to New York from Kansas City. Before hitting the road, McShann adjusted the personnel, replacing tenor saxophonist Harry Ferguson with Freddie Culliver. Lawrence "Frog" Anderson joined Joe Baird in the trombone section. McShann added a touch of sophistication for the uptown taste of New York audiences by engaging Albert "Al" Hibbler, a rich baritone who specialized in ballads. Hibbler first caught McShann's attention while sitting in with the band during a date in San Antonio the previous spring.

> We were doing one-nighters and got to San Antonio. First person I ran into when I got to the auditorium was Hibbler. He introduced himself and asked if he could sing a number with the band. So, to get rid of him I said, "yeah." He came up after the first intermission and sang "I Understand." Boy, the crowd went crazy, so then I said, "What else you do?" We did a couple of more tunes, and the crowd went crazy when he did "Trees." He really wanted to get away from the town and travel with the band. So I told him, "I'll be getting in touch with you and we will make arrangements for you to join the band in a couple or three weeks." I sent him a ticket and didn't hear anything from him, so I wondered what was happening. He called me and said, "Hey, man I been waiting for you to send for me." I told him, "I had already sent for him." He had a gal, and she intercepted the telegram and ticket because she didn't want him to go. He met me in Oklahoma, and we drove to Kansas City. That night Bird and all the cats carried him all over Kansas City singing. Bird playing, and Hibbler singing. They just had themselves a ball that night.[54]

Leaving Kansas City on September 28, the band worked its way across the South and up the Midwest before heading east. In Houston, the band packed the Civic Auditorium, breaking all attendance records. Moving across the South the band played a double bill with Milton Larkin's band at the Louisiana State Fair in Shreveport, before heading to Chicago for a second Decca recording session on November 18. Kapp and McShann, attempting to duplicate the phenomenal popularity of "Confessin' the Blues," almost exclusively featured Walter Brown accompanied by the rhythm section. The full band sat out the recording date, with only Bernard Anderson, Bob Mabane, and John Jackson joining in on "One Woman's Man." Outside of the Basie-inspired jump blues instrumental "So You Won't Jump" the rest of the selections recorded—"'Fore Day Rider," "Red River Blues," "Baby Heart Blues," "Cryin' Won't Make Me Stay," and the follow-up song, "New Confessin' the Blues"— were cast in the same stylistic vein as "Confessin' the Blues." Wrapping up the session for Decca in short order, the McShann band headed to New York.

During the band's journey east, the Japanese bombed Pearl Harbor. The next day the United States declared war. The outbreak of war hit the entertainment industry like a bombshell, particularly in California. Fearing another sneak attack by the Japanese, the government immediately shut down the entire West Coast. Frequent blackouts plunged nightspots into darkness. Radio stations curtailed band remotes and other nonessential broadcasting. Club and ballroom patrons stayed home, glued to their radios for the latest development on the war front. Ballroom owners, fearful of losing money, canceled one-night stands by bands with little notice. The cloud of uncertainty settling across the nation quickly dimmed opportunities for musicians.

Luckily, McShann managed to evade the immediate repercussions of the war and establish his band in New York, with the help of the Moe Gale Agency. During a Christmas Eve dance in Gary, Indiana, Moe Gale's brother Tim stopped by to have a first-hand look at the McShann band. Eager to cash in on the continued popularity of "Confessin' the Blues," Gale offered McShann a seven-year contract with the Gale agency. Realizing the Gale agency offered the most direct route to success in New York ahead of the spreading tide of war, McShann consulted with Tumino. McShann then accepted Gale's offer with the stipulations that Tumino be allowed to stay aboard as manager and the band be immediately booked into Gale's Savoy Ballroom in Harlem.

Pleased with the new addition to his agency's roster, Gale arranged for the McShann band's debut at the Savoy Ballroom pitted in a battle of the bands against the wildly popular Lucky Millinder band on Friday, February 13, 1942. Millinder, misjudging the strength of the McShann band, based on the Decca recordings featuring Walter Brown and the rhythm section, sent the band a postcard boasting, "We're going to send you hicks back to the sticks." McShann and crew pulled into New York ragged and tired after taking the wrong route to New York. "McShann had one of those big old long Buicks, and I was driving, with about five or six guys in it," Ramey related. "I took what I thought was the shortest route to New York, up and over the mountains, instead of taking the Pennsylvania Turnpike. We struggled and struggled, but we finally got to New York, raggedy and tired. When we got up on the bandstand, where the Savoy Sultans used to play, the people were looking at us like we were nothing. Lucky Millinder was on the main bandstand. Everything we had was shabby-looking, including our cardboard stands, and we only had one uniform—a blue coat and brown pants."[55] Taking one look at the ragtag McShann band, Millinder, the band's conductor and business manager, confidently repaired to the offices downstairs, leaving his band leaderless on the stand.

McShann, feeling a little intimidated by the Millinder band's reputation, held the band back until the last set. "Lucky had been blowing everybody out of there, so he was supposed to be the baddest thing around New York," McShann explained. "We decided to go in and lay low, play a few stocks. We were playing alternating sets of thirty minutes. Play a few stocks and fool

(10) Lincoln Gardens
459 E 31st

(13) Dreamland Cafe
3518-20 S. State
Dreamland Ballroom
3618-20 S. State

Grand Terrace (22)
3955 S. Parkway

Savoy Ballroom
(27) S. Parkway +
E. 47th

28) 4719 S. Parkway
Regal
Theatre

LAKE MICHIGAN

WASHINGTON PARK

around until the date was three-fourths over and then go into the book on
'em. So that's what we did; we fooled around and played a few stocks. Every
once in a while old Bird would say, 'Hootie, you better get in the books,
baby!' After 12 o'clock we began getting in the books a little bit. Lucky's band
guy went down and told Lucky he better come upstairs and see what these
guys were doing. Lucky replied, 'I ain't worried about those western dogs.'
The next set we got down in the books, so Lucky is raring to take his stand.
He ran out there and started doing a lot of show stuff. He had the audience
worked up, and they were swinging, doing the Lindy Hop. When he started
with all of his show stuff the band lost the beat. Soon as he finished his last
note, we hit right in on him. Pulled the crowd completely away from Lucky.
We got through that night, and Lucky came over and said, 'You son of a
bitches, you blew our ass out tonight—you did it.' That was our introduction
to New York."[56] The two bandleaders hit it off famously and spent the rest of
the evening together carousing in Harlem nightclubs.

Alternating between the Savoy Ballroom and the Apollo Theater, the
McShann band swiftly gained favor with New York audiences and critics. In
the March 1942 issue of *Metronome*, Barry Ulanov gushed about the band's
performance at the Savoy Ballroom. "Every once in a while it is a reviewer's
privilege to introduce a great new band to his readers. This is such an occasion. For not since Count Basie came out of Kansas City has so impressive a
jazz organization made its appearance in New York for the first time." Ironically, Ulanov's comparison reflected the Basie band's current status rather
than the reality of its shaky debut in New York. After commending the sections and the overall sound of the band, Ulanov singled out Parker's great
promise. "John Jackson's lead tone is pretty and the jazz set forth by the Parker
alto is superb. Parker's tone tends to rubberiness, and he has a tendency to
play too many notes, but his continual search for wild ideas, and the consis-
tency with which he finds them, compensate for weaknesses that should be
easily overcome." Ulanov further complimented vocalist Walter Brown and
Al Hibbler, who he rated "incomparable among male ballad singers." Ulanov
tempered his self-professed "rave" review by criticizing the roughness of the
sections caused by the lack of an inspired arranger to tighten the band's overall orchestration. In conclusion, Ulanov highly recommended the band, ob-
serving, "The spirit of the band seems wonderful. The material is first-rate.
Jay McShann can achieve musical greatness and commercial success."[57]

During the band's residency at the Savoy in spring 1942, Dizzy Gillespie
sat in with the trumpet section, hoping to earn a slot in the band. Having left
the Cab Calloway band the previous fall, after an ugly confrontation with
Cab, Gillespie freelanced around New York. He renewed acquaintances with
Parker and Buddy Anderson during the late-night sessions at Minton's Playhouse and Monroe's Uptown Inn. Finding kindred musical spirits in Parker,
Anderson, and the other members of the McShann band, Gillespie tried to

work his way into the band by showing up at the Savoy every night. "Diz came down and played with us every night," McShann stated. "So after about three weeks, Diz said I been here every night for about three weeks, when do I get on the payroll. I said we were so poor if somebody came in for free I wouldn't be able to make it. We were getting a little over scale at the Savoy."[58] Moe Gale, the owner of the Savoy, required the bands in his agency's roster to play regularly at the Savoy for little pay in exchange for national routing. Once on tour, bands soon found that outside of major venues like the Regal Theater in Chicago and the Paradise Ballroom in Detroit, the links in Gale's circuit were often tenuous, particularly in the South.

In late spring 1942, the Gale agency booked the McShann band on a tour of ballrooms, clubs, hotels, and theaters across the South and back up through the Midwest. During the southern leg of the tour, band members found themselves at the mercy of local promoters and police. "Then we went down South and had a lot of trouble," Ramey recalled. "In Augusta the operator left with the money at halftime, and the cops said we had to pay the rent of the hall, as well as the bouncers and people on the door, or go to jail. In Martinsville, Virginia, the same thing happened, and this time they were not only going to take us to jail but they were going to take our instruments and the bus as well. In Natchez, Mississippi, they put Walter Brown and Bird in jail for smoking cigarettes in a screened porch of the rooming house where they were staying. If they'd been smoking pot, they'd have been there forever, but John Tumino had to go and pay twenty-five dollars each to get them out. When they joined us in Little Rock, they had knots on their heads big enough to hang a hat on. They had really taken a beating."[59] Gladly leaving the South, the band played a string of one-nighters back to the Savoy Ballroom in mid-May.

WHILE McSHANN ESTABLISHED his band nationally, Harlan Leonard struggled to keep the Rockets together back in Kansas City. In April 1941, Jesse Price left Leonard and formed an eleven-piece group, subsidized by Eddie Spitz, the owner of the College Inn. Adding insult to injury, the new Price group replaced the Rockets as the house band at the College Inn. With Tumino concentrating on breaking the McShann band, work became slim for the Rockets in Kansas City and the Midwest. Frustrated, Leonard dropped his association with Tumino, switching to the McConkey Music Corporation. The change brought little improvement in the band's fortune. In June, the Rockets opened at Tootie's Mayfair, a roadhouse owned by Tootie Clarkin, a colorful former police officer who lovingly tended to the chickens scratching around the back yard. Located outside the city limits at 79th and Wornall, Tootie's stayed open all night, attracting hordes of late-night revelers. Tootie's gave the Rockets regular summer employment, but it was a step-down from the prestigious College Inn and a far cry from the Golden Gate Ballroom and other major venues the band played while affiliated with MCA.

Leonard, feeling unappreciated in his hometown, went public with his dissatisfaction in an article by Bob Locke published in the August 15 issue of *Down Beat*. "What's that old wheeze about a prophet being without honor in his own country? That's something which perplexes Harlan Leonard, leader of the Kansas City Rockets orchestra, whose band is one of the most popular in the Middle West except in his own home town, Kaycee. His orchestra consistently draws good biz for bookers in every terp [dance] temple in this area, but when he comes home, down go the b. o. [box office] receipts. . . . [I]n Kaycee itself, the crew goes unappreciated." After chronicling Leonard's accomplishments over the years, Locke summed up Leonard's dilemma. "Today, Leonard finds himself at the crossroads of his career. He has lost Jesse Price, the 'sparkplug' drummer, on the basis of whose presence in the band Music Corporation of America signed the crew to a contract. Yet musically his band has improved and is sharper than ever."[60]

Band members, sensing a lack of direction, deserted the Rockets. Star trombonist Fred Beckett joined the Nat Towles band, and was replaced by veteran trombonist Walter Monroe, doubling on trumpet. Henry Bridges left after inheriting a drugstore from his uncle. Out of loyalty, Myra Taylor stuck with Leonard, in the face of better offers. Jesse Price, fresh from a short stint with Ella Fitzgerald, raided the Leonard band again to form a new big band, adding to the turmoil in the ranks of the Rockets. Leonard managed to patch up the Rockets, drawing from the pool of talent in Kansas City and the Midwest. Orvella Moore, formerly with the all-woman band the Harlem Playgirls, brought a lively piano style to the group. Russell "Big Chief" Moore, a Native American from Phoenix, contributed a spirited style and broad range to the trombone section. Leonard, writing off 1941 as "just a bum year" in an interview in *Down Beat*, downplayed the recent changes in his band's personnel by explaining that the "band needed weeding out and also new blood."[61]

Facing diminished opportunities in Kansas City, Leonard launched an extended tour of one-nighters across Missouri, Nebraska, Kansas, and Oklahoma. In early June, Leonard abruptly canceled the rest of the tour, citing transportation problems. A shortage of gasoline and rubber combined with a government recall of charter buses made touring, particularly for one-night stands, increasingly difficult for bands across the country. Even big-name bands felt the effects of the transportation crunch. A month earlier, the Earl Hines band became stranded after the government claimed its bus. Trains, expensive and not suitable for the routing of one-night stands, were unreliable and often commandeered for the war effort. Furthermore, Jim Crow restrictions made train travel for bands difficult across the southern territories. The sum of the effects devastated the Rockets and other bands, relying as they did on a regional circuit of small towns. Unable to continue the tour, the Rockets returned to Kansas City.

Compounding Leonard's woes, the booking agent made off with the receipts from the tour. Myra Taylor described the band's long road trip as a "starvation tour." "We went on tour and played a different place every night," Taylor confided. "The dates weren't too far apart, and the ballrooms were packed. I thought we were making money. Harlan gave me an allowance of $1 a day, so I thought I would be in for a big payday at the end of the tour, but when we got back to Kansas City, Harlan told me I owed him $11. He ended up giving me $9, explaining the man [the booking agent] ran off with all the money."[62] Leonard's old friend Harry Duncan, back in charge of the dance pavilion at Fairyland Park, came to the band's rescue. Faced with a dwindling supply of traveling bands from the transportation shortage, Duncan engaged the Rockets for the summer at Fairyland Park, which gave Leonard a safe harbor from the winds of war wreaking havoc on the entertainment industry.

DURING THE SUMMER OF 1942, the war on the home front intensified, affecting all aspects of the entertainment industry. The Office of Defense Transportation banned orchestras from using buses after June 30, imposing an extreme hardship on already strapped African American bands. Frequent blackouts plunged clubs into darkness, and in the process sent patrons scurrying home. Record companies drastically cut production after being limited to 30 percent of their 1941 consumption of shellac, used in the production of records. The production of jukeboxes ceased in order to conserve metal. Musical instrument manufacturers switched to making shell casings for defense. The draft devastated the ranks of bands, and created a shortage of choice musicians.

The President of the American Federation of Musicians, James Petrillo, compounded matters by imposing a ban on recording sessions by union members. Convinced records, jukeboxes, and radio transcription services were robbing musicians of jobs, Petrillo threw down the gauntlet at the union's annual conference in mid-June and forbade members from recording after July 30, 1942. The ban hit musicians, already reeling from the effects of the war, the hardest. With touring opportunities trimmed, bandleaders increasingly relied on income from records. The record industry quickly adapted to the looming recording ban. Jukebox operators stocked up on previously released recordings, and the record labels rushed bands into the studio to "beat the ban."

Dave Kapp hurried the McShann band into the studio before the ban took effect. "Confessin' the Blues" and the band's other blues recordings sold well, but critics, who had seen the band live, felt Kapp held the band back by not recording the full group. In *Down Beat*, Bob Locke accused Kapp of selling the band short by favoring the rhythm section and Walter Brown on record. "Somebody, and I think it's Dave Kapp of Decca Records, has been fooling the public! I'm, sore, and so are a gob of other critics. And for good cause, since there's no reason on earth why the Jay McShann band, yeah, all sixteen pieces of it, shouldn't be on wax instead of hiding it behind the skirts of a blues singer, Walter Brown by name and the rhythm quartet."[63] In response, Kapp and McShann used the full band for the July 2 session in New York.

Not breaking entirely with their earlier formula, Kapp and McShann featured Walter Brown on two of the four selections recorded: "Lonely Boy Blues" and "The Jumpin' Blues." "Lonely Boy Blues," stylistically reminiscent of Brown's earlier recordings, features the entire band, which resulted in a fuller, more sophisticated sound. "The Jumpin' Blues," written by McShann, Parker, and Ramey, embodies the classic Kansas City style, with the relaxed drive of the rhythm section accented by pronounced riffs constructed around a head arrangement colored by an overall feeling of the blues, all coming together to create a strong focused sense of swing. "We sat down and started humming riffs that would fit," Ramey recounted. "I got the first eight bars and he [Parker] got the last four. Then Brown came in and sang, and as we rehearsed we fitted other riffs. Not a note was written on that, either, but it became McShann's theme song." In contrast, Archie "Skipper" Hall carefully crafted East Coast style arrangements for the instrumental "Sepian Stomp," and the popular ballad "Get Me on Your Mind," featuring Al Hibbler.[64] During the session, alto saxophonist John Jackson replaced Parker as the saxophone section's star soloist, even on Parker's composition "The Jumpin' Blues."

Just as the McShann band peaked in popularity, Parker drifted away in a narcotic and alcoholic haze. For years Parker had drunk heavily and dabbled in heroin but had managed to keep his habits in check. Living and working in Harlem, a distribution center for heroin, Parker began using heavily, feeding his growing habit by scamming money from friends and acquaintances. As with the Leonard band earlier, he began showing up late for jobs and disappearing without explanation. McShann noticed the change in Parker. "Bird was with me four years, but he changed in that time," McShann observed. "His heart wasn't like it was at the beginning of our big band. He had got into the habit of going to places like Monroe's in New York with his horn under his arm. There he might blow just a couple of tunes and then step off the stand for a taste. With me, too, his time had been going bad—showing up late, and so on."[65]

Parker's petty scams on fellow band members for money hit a discordant note in the group's harmony. Ramey recalled an incident one Sunday afternoon at the Savoy Ballroom, resulting in Parker's dismissal from the band. "Bird had gone over to Walter Brown's wife and gotten Brown's last five dollars!" Ramey reported. "Brown came over while Bird was on the bandstand and they got into a fight. Each of them was so high, they never made contact. It was like a slow motion picture of a fight. They'd swing at each other and fall down. As a result, a guy from Joe Glaser's [Moe Gale's] office demanded that Charlie Parker be fired immediately. McShann had to let him go, but after a couple of weeks we were getting so many complaints that we got him back."[66] As an insurance policy, McShann gave Ramey an additional stipend to keep Parker in line.

In early winter, the band left the comfort of the Savoy for a short tour down the East Coast and across the Midwest. At the Paradise Theater in Detroit, Parker overdosed and passed out while soloing, which led to another dismissal from the band. Trombonist Clyde Bernhardt, who joined the band the previous September, vividly recalled the circumstances: "The band played its first show that Friday night," Bernhardt detailed.

> After we did Mary Lou Williams' *Roll 'Em*, a hell of a band number, Walter Brown sang a blues. When we hit *Cherokee*, Parker walked down front as usual and began blowing real hot when all at once he just fell over. Down on the floor, out cold. People in the audience screamed. We kept playing but I was dumb-founded—thought he dropped dead. They pulled the curtain and the stage manager dragged Parker off, put him in a back room, and tried to revive him while we continued the show. After the set we all ran back and Parker was sitting there laughing. "What the hell happened, man?" He was saying. We were wondering the same thing. "Goddamn, must have had too much of that shit." Jay didn't say anything. He was easygoing. The next day some guys [narcotics agents] came up to where Parker and Brown was staying, a rooming house run by a big 250-pound feminine guy, out there on Adams Avenue. Tore the place apart, ripped carpets up, cut open mattresses. . . . Parker played the rest of that weekend, but on Monday he was high again. The owner of the theater told Jay to get rid of him, and the next day Parker was on his way back to New York.[67]

Parker briefly reunited with the band when it returned to New York, but soon left with other members to join Earl Hines. "Earl Hines got five or six guys out of the band. He tried to take all of my first chair cats. . . . Hines was so nice about it," McShann mused. "He said, 'look, I got the money. I'm going to get 'em whether you want me to have them or not. I want to straighten you out if they owe you money, so you'll get all your money back.' I never did think anything about it. He said he was 'going to make a man out of Bird.' Next time I saw Earl Hines, about four or five months later, he said, 'Come get this cat. Come get him away from me. He owes everybody in the band. He owes every loan shark. He owes everybody in New York! I bought him a brand new horn, and he doesn't know where the horn is. He doesn't know what he did with it.' I said, 'I thought you were going to make a man out of him.' He said: 'Hell no, come get this son of a bitch.'"[68] Glad to be rid of Parker, McShann declined Hines's offer. An eternal optimist, McShann rebuilt the band and continued touring ahead of the shock waves of war.

WHILE ENGAGEMENTS REMAINED SCARCE in the East, South, and Midwest, new opportunities, fueled by a thriving local defense industry, opened up in Los Angeles. With few consumer goods available, workers spent their dollars on entertainment, creating a demand for musicians in the clubs dotting Hollywood and lining Central Avenue from Little Tokyo to Watts.[69] In the fall of 1942, Harlan Leonard joined the legions of musicians and bands migrating to Los Angeles. After closing his summer engagement at Fairyland Park, Leonard found himself at a turning point of his career. Without a recording contract or affiliation with an agency and with only slim prospects in the Midwest, Leonard decided to try his hand in Los Angeles. Signing with the Frederick Brothers Music Corporation, based in Hollywood, Leonard moved his headquarters to Los Angeles and opened at Zucca's Terrace in Hermosa Beach in late October. After clicking with audiences at the Terrace, Leonard moved up to Zucca's Hollywood Casino in mid-November. In mid-December, the draft swept up a number of band members, which forced Leonard to abandon the engagement at the Casino and regroup. Adept at building new bands, Leonard sent for drummer Johnny Otis, who was working with the Lloyd Hunter band in Omaha. Born Johnny Veliotes to Greek immigrant parents, Otis so strongly identified with African American culture that he passed himself off as a light-skinned African American. After rebuilding the Rockets, Leonard began a long-term engagement at the Club Alabam', located next to the Hotel Dunbar in the heart of Central Avenue. Finding his niche in California, Leonard abandoned Kansas City and moved his family to Los Angeles.

Leonard dismantled the Rockets after finishing a year-long run at Club Alabam'. In the end, Leonard, a strong family man, opted for job security. "The war was taking all the good musicians big-paying bandleaders were not snatching," Leonard recounted. "I began to think. After 20 years of no family life, travel all the time, I decided to quit it—before I, so much in love with my music, got out there and couldn't get back." Taking a job with the IRS, Leonard rose steadily in the ranks and retired after twenty-six years of service. Looking back on his career as a bandleader later in life, Leonard wistfully observed, "If I had it to do all over again, I'd do it a little differently."[70]

NOT ONE TO SETTLE DOWN, McShann strove to keep his band together on the road. But by late winter 1943, the sum of travel difficulties, a turn of fortune with the Moe Gale agency, and the draft had taken its toll on the McShann band. Clyde Bernhardt well remembered the hardships traveling with the McShann band during the war years. "We were deep in wartime then, so it was almost impossible to charter a band bus because the Army was using them all," Bernhardt recollected.

We had no choice but to go as regular passengers on the train. Some of the guys never did get used to not having a private bus for themselves. . . . Trains was so damn crowded in those war years. We couldn't have gotten on the train at all if our road manager hadn't paid off some of the station masters. When we get on, there barely be room to stand in a corner. Many times I sat on my suitcase for three hundred miles—sleep on it too. Other riders, mostly soldiers, slept on the floor, and when the conductor came through he had to step over everybody. In the South many trains be segregated and the problems even worse. Food wasn't available, so most of the time we did without. Bring on sardines and crackers or maybe some bread and bologna, but the bologna didn't stay fresh for long. Sometimes we run outside for a candy bar when the train pulled in a station. But it pulled right out, so we hop back fast. We paid for our own food and accommodation—that was our expense. Schedules were always getting loused up due to late trains and midnight missed connections. When we got in town we search for a cab to take us to a hotel that was always filled up. Even my YMCA rooming houses were not always available. Man, it was rough.[71]

The capricious schedule of one-night stands booked by the Gale Agency compounded the band's hardships on the road. Despite the band's successful recordings and busy schedule, McShann ended up owing the Gale Agency money. "After we got to New York they [Gale Agency] wanted to squeeze John Tumino out, so they started sending us out without support, no placards or publicity, so we couldn't make any money," McShann disclosed. "They tried to get the band in debt. Well, they called me in the office and told me they weren't running a loan office. They told me how much money I owed them and said I might have to send John back to Kansas City. They said we were going to have to sign a contract and forget about everything else. They were trying to squeeze us to death. John went into action and booked enough jobs to pay back the Gale Brothers, and I went with GAC [General Amusement Corporation]."[72] In parting with the Gale Agency, McShann relinquished his regular engagements at the Savoy Ballroom, which paid little but earned the band considerable prestige and easy access to other venues on the East Coast.

Signing with GAC in Chicago, McShann joined a small, but impressive roster of top bands including Benny Carter, Louis Jordan, and Cab Calloway. Formerly the Rockwell-O'Keefe Agency, GAC maintained a strong network of ballrooms, theaters, and clubs stretching across the country. Touring under the GAC banner, the McShann band traveled widely, playing up to ninety consecutive one-nighters. As the band toured across the country, the draft and hard traveling eroded the band's lineup, until only a handful of original members remained.

The McShann band waxed its final session for Decca when James Petrillo partially lifted the ban on recordings in late fall 1943. The band recorded four selections in Decca's New York studio on December 1, 1943—"Wrong Neighborhood," featuring trumpeter Bob Merrill on vocals, and "Hometown Blues," with Walter Brown, echo the band's earlier hit blues recordings. McShann, hoping to cash in on the popularity of war songs, recorded "Say Forward I'll March," an instrumental rendered in the classic Kansas City style featuring the shouting brass section riffing over the saxophone section, highlighting McShann's rollicking piano and Paul Quinichette's powerful, Lester Young–inspired tenor saxophone solos. Decca assigned the first three selections to the long queue of recordings slated to be released over the next few years and rejected the fourth recording, "Save Me Some."

Ironically, as McShann expressed an eagerness to contribute to the war effort by recording "Say Forward I'll March," he managed to stay one step ahead of his induction notice. "I told the draft board here [Kansas City] I would let them know where to send my induction notice. They sent it to New York, and they missed me in New York," McShann confessed. "I told 'em to send it to California, and they missed me there." Returning from the West Coast, the band stopped in Kansas City for a one-night engagement at the Municipal Auditorium on May 21, 1944, where draft board officials inducted McShann on the stage. "We were getting ready to play at the Municipal Auditorium," McShann disclosed. "These two guys came up and said we've got some business to do with you Mr. McShann, so I told my band man to take 'em back to the band room and get them a taste. At intermission, these guys came over and showed me their credentials and my induction papers with two I's meaning immediate induction. Then I realized these guys were serious. George Salisbury finished out the engagement for me. I told John Tumino, 'When these guys get through take all the uniforms and put the uniforms up and take the music home with you tonight.' But he didn't take the music home with him that night. When he went down the next day the music was gone."[73] The officials whisked McShann away to Fort Leavenworth, Kansas, and immediately pressed him into service. Deprived of McShann's steady leadership, music, and uniforms, band members dispersed across the country, ending the last great African American big band to come out of Kansas City.

Basie, Kirk, and a host of other well-established bandleaders disbanded after the war, bringing to a close the big band era. Unfettered from big band conventions, Charlie Parker, Dizzy Gillespie, and other modernists regrouped, creating bebop, a musical revolution. Jay McShann, Big Joe Turner, and others took a different musical path pioneering rhythm and blues and rock 'n' roll. After suffering setbacks from the cleanup and World War II, Kansas City's music scene rebounded in the 1940s and 1950s, producing a string of soloists who followed the trail blazed by Kirk, Mary Lou Williams, Basie, McShann, and Parker into the national spotlight.

Epilogue
Parker's Mood

"Don't hang your head when you see those six pretty horses pullin' me.
Put a twenty-dollar silver piece on my watch chain,
Look at the smile on my face,
And sing a little song to let the world know I'm really free.
Don't cry for me, 'cause I'm going to Kansas City."

—Music by Charlie Parker and lyrics by King Pleasure,
"Parker's Mood," 1953

As PUNISHMENT FOR STAYING ONE STEP AHEAD of the draft, Jay McShann served in the regular army rather than touring with a military band like his contemporaries who promptly heeded the call of duty. Fortunately, considering the circumstances, he served only a short time. Plagued by flat feet and other minor health problems, McShann received a medical discharge from military service in early fall 1944. Eager to regroup, McShann returned to Kansas City, only to find band members scattered across the country. "Didn't have no big band to come back to. Didn't have nobody, and didn't have no book," McShann recounted.[1] His fortunes turned after a chance encounter with Dave Dexter.

While checking in with Local 627, McShann happened upon Dave Dexter, who was in town producing a recording session for Capitol Records, a new label founded by songwriters Buddy DeSylva and Johnny Mercer and Glen Wallichs, the owner of Wallichs' Music City, a pioneering mega-music store located on the corner of Sunset and Vine in Hollywood. Established in June 1942, just before James Petrillo's edict halting recordings by the rank and file, Capitol feverishly recorded to beat the ban, stockpiling enough potential hits to gain a foothold in the market. In early winter 1942, Wallichs brought Dexter aboard to handle publicity and help Johnny Mercer develop a hot jazz catalog. Dexter moved from New York to Los Angeles, where he published the *Capitol News*, a glossy newsletter distributed by record stores, and signed Nat King Cole, who became one of Capitol's brightest stars. Given free range, Dexter embarked on his most ambitious project to date: a four-album set chronicling the history of jazz.

In mid-October 1944, Dexter returned home to visit family and record Julia Lee fronting an all-star band featuring Walter Page, Oliver Todd, Baby Lovett, and Tommy Douglas for the Kansas City segment of the set. Delighted to find McShann available, Dexter gave him top billing, recording the ensemble as Jay McShann's Kansas City Stompers. Evoking the pure Kaycee style, the band led by McShann faithfully rendered the evergreen "Moten's Swing" and then traded solos on a loose laid-back version of the standard "On the Sunny Side of the Street." Lee delivered two spirited vocals, the blues standard "Trouble in Mind" and "Won't You Come Over to My House?" a risqué number she originally recorded fifteen years earlier with her brother George's band. Julia's playful, come hither vocal on "Won't You Come Over to My House?" hit with jukebox operators, eventually winning her a contract with Capitol.[2] Dexter, lost in the details of the session, missed the opportunity to sign McShann on the spot.

While in town, McShann reunited with Walter Brown, who was at the time headlining a revue at Gilmore's Chez Paree, a popular nightspot located on the site of the former Cherry Blossom Club. Brown, Walter Page, and other musicians, cut loose by the demise of the big bands, filtered back to Kansas City, joining those who stayed behind to spark a modest revival in the local club scene. The Chez Paree, operated by Alberta Gilmore, a civic-minded entrepreneur with an eye on the bottom line, showcased revues traveling on the fledgling chitlings circuit, a loose amalgamation of clubs descended from the old TOBA circuit. Contortionist "Puzzle Bone" Jackson, comedian Willie "Tickle Britches" Map, and other holdovers from the vaudeville tradition shared the bill with blues shouters, sweet balladeers, and exotic dancers. The Chez Paree offered two shows nightly, but closed promptly at 1:30 A.M., in keeping with Missouri liquor laws. Scott's Theatre-Restaurant, located a block east at 18th and Highland in the former Boone Theater, proclaimed to be the "1944 sensation . . . in the heart of the nation" and featured a fast-paced show accompanied by Tommy Douglas and His All-Stars.[3] Bandleader and businessman Chauncey Downs, back in town from Michigan, operated the Casa Loma Ballroom at 18th and Prospect, the site of numerous battles of the bands. Lincoln Hall at 18th and Vine remained a popular spot for the younger set. Downtown at the College Inn, trumpeter Oliver Todd led an eight-piece combo featuring pianist George Salisbury, Countess Margaret Johnson's brother Roy on bass, and Jay McShann's cousin Pete on drums. Tootie's Mayfair, the Sterling Club, and other after-hours roadhouses out in the county provided steady work for small ensembles. McShann, not inclined to settle back down in Kansas City, headed back to the national scene.

On the heels of the Capitol recording session, McShann returned to New York, intent on forming a new big band. "I was in Kansas City for a week, and then I went to New York," McShann recalled. "Gale [Moe Gale Agency] got in touch with me and told me, 'We can book you and you don't have to have a big band now. Why don't you use about four or five pieces and only have to pay about three or four people to play? We can book you and get the same money we got for the big band. Decide which singer you want to use and that's it.' I wanted to hear that big band sound. . . . It was a different thing because a lot of the dance halls were made into bowling alleys. During that little while I was in the army everything changed."[4]

Unwisely rebuffing Gale's offer and advice, McShann formed a full-size band and resumed his association with the General Amusement Corporation. Finding former band members otherwise engaged, McShann hastily drew together a band of less-than-stellar players. Robbed of his band book at the Municipal Auditorium in Kansas City earlier in the year, McShann threw together a new library of head arrangements drawn from the original band's Decca hits and jazz standards. The ill-equipped band lurched off to a rough start.

In January 1945, the unseasoned McShann big band followed Art Tatum into Club Downbeat on 52nd Street for an eight-week stand. The Downbeat, like other clubs on the street, usually featured a small combo and an intermission pianist to entertain between sets. Seeking to pull crowds away from its principal 52nd Street competitors—the Three Deuces, Onyx, and Spotlite Clubs—the Downbeat booked McShann's big band as a change of pace. Barry Ulanov, who had greeted the original McShann band's arrival at the Savoy years earlier with a rave review, gave the new band a generous plug in *Metronome*: "It's an uncommon pleasure to sit back and listen to Jay take a couple of choruses, before and after his other able soloists, who need more rehearsing together and alone, but still, even in a ragged ensemble, produce great kicks."[5] The novelty of the big band soon wore off. *Metronome*'s competitor *Down Beat* reported the experiment "failed badly," causing the Downbeat to return to its former entertainment policy.[6] McShann, disregarding the ill omen, steered the band to the West Coast.

Once on the road, McShann found the big band to be financially untenable. "By the time I got to California, I decided that I was through with trying to have a big band because it was too expensive," McShann confided.[7] In the summer of 1945, McShann pared down the big band to a small ensemble and opened for an extended engagement at Little Joe's, a cozy club in Los Angeles. The blossoming African American community focused around Central Avenue warmly welcomed McShann's urbane style of blues. In the next few years, the changes wrought by World War II brought a majority of the big bands of the 1930s to a grinding halt. Andy Kirk and Count Basie, no exceptions to the rule, disbanded in the post–World War II period.

THE DECLINE OF THE CLOUDS OF JOY began with the departure of Mary Lou Williams in July 1942. Kirk replaced Williams with Kenny Kersey, a lanky pianist and composer from Canada, then forged ahead, expanding the band to eighteen pieces. Attempting to remain current with Earl Hines, who recruited Charlie Parker and Dizzy Gillespie and other young lions of the bop generation, Kirk added modern players including Howard McGhee and Fats Navarro, with little success. "During the war I had to enlarge my band because the style then called for it," Kirk explained. "I had to meet the competition then, even though it was a fad. I had seven and eight brass . . . it was loud and wrong. . . . Towards the end of the war things started to fall apart."[8] Kirk persevered through the early 1950s, despite a high turnover rate and steadily diminishing opportunities. In the mid-1950s, Kirk disbanded the Clouds of Joy, which by that time bore little resemblance to the band he brought east from Kansas City. Only the ever-faithful Harry Lawson remained from the original band. From time to time, Kirk raised the banner of the Clouds of Joy, using pickup musicians, but he eventually left music altogether to manage the Hotel Theresa in Harlem. Ironically, had Mary Lou Williams stayed on, a streamlined version of the Clouds of Joy might have successfully made the transition to the modern era. Kirk, never fully appreciating Williams's contribution to the band, unwisely let her walk away. In the end, Williams fared better than her former boss.

MARY LOU WILLIAMS left the Kirk band with few regrets. "For twelve years with the band I'd known swell times and bad ones, but barnstorming and the 'New System' of management were bringing me down," Williams recalled. "Looking back I can smile at our life on the road. Towards the end, though, there was no more brotherly love. I had lost so much through thefts that for a solid year I had to sleep with everything I owned. When someone broke in my trunk and took earrings, Indian-head pennies and silver dollars which I cherished, I decided to leave. Dragging my trunk off the bus, I drove to Pittsburgh."[9] Recognizing the end of an era, Williams formed a progressive six-piece ensemble featuring drummer Art Blakey and her soon-to-be-husband, Harold "Shorty" Baker on trumpet. In September 1942, Williams's new band opened at Kelly's Stable on New York's booming 52nd Street, establishing her career as a leader.

Moving to the Cecil Hotel on 118th Street next to Minton's Playhouse, Williams musically adopted Thelonious Monk, Bud Powell, and other leaders of the bop movement. "During that period, Monk and the other kids would come by my apartment every morning around four or pick me up at Café [Café Society] after I'd finished my last show, and we'd play and swap ideas until noon or later," Williams reminisced. "Monk, Tadd Dameron, Kenny

Dorham, Bud Powell, Aaron Bridges, Billy Strayhorn, plus various disc jockeys and newspapermen, would be in and out of my place at all hours, and we'd really ball."[10] Ardently working in the midst of the musical marathon occurring nightly in her apartment, she crafted arrangements for Duke Ellington and orchestrated her own ambitious projects. In June 1946, Williams performed three movements of her *Zodiac Suite*, accompanied by the Carnegie Pop Orchestra at Carnegie Hall, in a rare marriage of orchestral music and jazz on the broad stage of that stately venue. Unfortunately, Williams's critical acclaim from concerts and recordings failed to garner financial compensation equal to her brilliance. After living in Europe during the early 1950s, Williams retired from music altogether to seek spiritual renewal. Returning to music in 1957, Williams resumed club and concert work throughout the 1970s, finding time to teach and compose sacred works for orchestra. All the while, she continued blossoming musically, like the hardy morning glory. Embracing innovations by ensuing generations of musicians, Mary Lou Williams remained at the forefront of new movements from bebop to free jazz throughout her long illustrious career.

LIKE WILLIAMS, Count Basie endured musically, becoming a respected elder of jazz. Basie managed to keep his band together during the course of the war, despite a continual turnover of personnel. Lester Young drifted in and out of the group before being drafted into a tragic tour of military duty that ended with his incarceration in the detention barracks. In late 1949, Basie abandoned the remnants of the hard-swinging band he led out of Kansas City, following a fallow stretch of dates. "That turned out to be the last year for the band that I brought east from Kansas City.... Things were drying up for big bands, and finally I just got tired of being out there on the road just catching those dates as we could catch them," Basie revealed. "So when we got to Memphis on the way back east from Mississippi and the West, I decided to lay off for a while. So that was it. I didn't tell anybody anything about what I was going to do until I did it. I didn't even talk to Jimmy Rushing about it beforehand."[11] Rushing, capitalizing on his well-established reputation, launched his solo career. The two suddenly ended a partnership stretching back to their days in the territories with the Blue Devils.

The next month Basie formed a combo and opened at the Brass Rail in Chicago. With ballrooms closing across the country, he concentrated on club work for the next several years. Unceremoniously dropped by Columbia Records at the end of 1951, Basie signed with Norman Granz's Clef label and rebuilt his big band. With members of the original band scattered, Basie drew from the next generation of soloists and created a new style of orchestral expression. While remaining rhythmically anchored in the Kansas City tradition, Basie modernized the band by adding advanced arrangements and soloists. Arranger and alto saxophonist Ernie Wilkins articulated the band's new style, by orchestrating fresh voicings and extending the dynamic range of the sections.[12]

During the summer of 1952, the band opened at Birdland, "the Jazz Corner of the World" in Manhattan at 1678 Broadway, named in honor of Charlie Parker. Using Birdland as a base of operation for the rest of the decade, the band toured extensively, playing concert halls in the United States and Europe. During the Christmas season of 1954 Joe Williams joined, giving the band the strong vocalist lacking since Basie's split with Jimmy Rushing five years earlier. Williams's rendition of the rhythm and blues standard "Everyday I Have the Blues" gave the band its first big hit in years. A hard-swinging arrangement of the popular standard "April in Paris" by Wild Bill Davis followed, establishing the band's new orchestral style of tightly voiced sections balanced by cleanly executed solos. In 1957, Neal Hefti succeeded Ernie Wilkins as principal arranger, further expanding the band's musical palette. Switching to the Roulette label, an offshoot of Birdland, the band documented the new collaboration with the recording *Basie!* in the fall of 1957. Throughout his long and distinguished career, Basie collaborated with top young arrangers such as Quincy Jones, Thad Jones, and Sammy Nestico. While continually refining the band's sound, Basie retained the distinctive strains of Kansas City style. Becoming an institution, Basie made hundreds of records and garnered a wealth of awards while traveling the globe spreading the gospel of Kansas City Jazz.

SIMILARLY, Jay McShann endured, withstanding career ups and downs to become a revered elder statesmen of jazz and blues. Free of the big band, Jay McShann moved easily into the crowded rhythm and blues circuit, traveling the California coast with a small group playing nightclubs and dances. At a date in Vallejo, California, Jimmy Witherspoon joined the vocal lineup, replacing Walter Brown. Witherspoon, a beefy handsome stylist with a husky alto, provided a fitting counterpoint to Crown Prince Waterford's frantic style of preaching the blues. Much to McShann's surprise, fans crowding the bandstand kept requesting "Confessin' the Blues." In short order, McShann recut "Confessin' the Blues" for the Philo label. Recasting the standard in the popular blues style of the day, the band riffs behind Witherspoon's impassioned vocal accented by the vamping rhythm section. The new version of "Confessin' the Blues," along with the other blues and boogie numbers McShann recorded for Philo, sold well in African American neighborhoods, giving his career a boost.

For the next five years, McShann rode the crest of the post-war urban blues craze, touring the country and recording for a series of independent labels. In November 1947, McShann entered the studio for the Supreme label while under contract to Mercury. To avoid a legal conflict with Mercury, McShann gave Jimmy Witherspoon top billing and took a back seat in the rhythm section. The band's cover of the chestnut "Ain't Nobody's Business," released in spring 1949, hit big, quickly rising to number one on the *Billboard* Race Chart and remaining there for a better part of the year. During that time *Billboard* formally christened the new style of urban blues, renaming its Race Chart as the Rhythm and Blues Chart. The immense popularity of "Ain't Nobody's Business" established Witherspoon's career nationally. Cashing in on his newfound fame, Witherspoon struck out on his own as a leader. The two parted on good terms with McShann graciously continuing to accompany Witherspoon on recording sessions while leading his own group.

In 1950, McShann left the road and settled down in Kansas City with his family. "I had three daughters to raise by then. . . . I knew the time was comin' when they'd have to be in school. . . . I did a southern tour, checked out the schools all the way along. When I got to Kansas City, I bought a home."[13] McShann joined forces with Ben Webster and other musicians who had returned to Kansas City, creating a revival in the club scene. *Down Beat* noted the rebound of the entertainment scene in Kansas City: "Music biz is still booming here to a fever-pitch that has rival agents calling each other for talent. Local spots are doubling up on bands and combos, using the continuous entertainment policy which has just begun to click here and is definitely paying off."[14] McShann formed a six-piece combo for what would turn out to be a seven-year engagement at Baker & Louie's Club No. 2, widely known as Johnny Baker's, a popular gathering spot for the college dance set at 55th and Troost, Kansas City's racial dividing line.

SEGREGATION REMAINED the rule in Kansas City, but the African American community grew steadily by establishing a strong foothold in the northernmost stretch of Troost Avenue and shouldering south past 27th Street. Eighteenth and Vine survived as an entertainment center, but the business district followed the migration of the community and gradually shifted south along Troost and Prospect Avenues. Local 627 remained at the center of musical activity. Freed from William Shaw's heavy hand in 1949, the union doubled as a social club where members could check on gigs and have a drink and a quick game of dominos, while checking on gigs. The union, hoping to recapture the spirit of the golden days, fostered rehearsal bands led by Jimmy Keith and pianist Willie Rice. Unable to breech the color barrier still surrounding downtown hotels, the bands played mainly social engagements and dances in the 18th and Vine area.

THE WARREN DURRETT ORCHESTRA, John Coon, Les Copley, and several other top white big bands from Local 34 kept the Pla-Mor ballroom and downtown hotels hopping. Warren Durrett, a multi-instrumentalist fluent on trumpet, alto and tenor saxophones, and piano, hailed from Lebanon, Kansas, located 290 miles northwest of Kansas City. Tall, lean, bespectacled, and ambitious, he apprenticed with college and territorial bands from 1939 to 1942. A talented arranger, Durrett decided late in 1942 to try his luck in Kansas City. He quickly found his niche playing in trios, commercial hotel bands, and occasional jazz combos. In 1945, bandleader Johnny Coon, son of legendary Carleton Coon of Coon-Sanders Night Hawks fame, persuaded Durrett to take a job leading a ten-piece band at the Hotel Continental. Combining danceable music with swing originals, the Durrett band featured trumpeters Wayne Ruppenthal and Sherman Gibson, trombonist Arch Martin, and Marilyn Maye, a talented entertainer and engaging vocalist with a wide range. Trombonist Bob Brookmeyer, a gifted arranger with a shy broad grin, impeccably groomed wavy brown hair, and wry sense of humor, developed the band's book before moving on to Chicago to work with Orrin Tucker. Durrett, an astute businessman and bandleader, remained based in Kansas City, playing the Pla-Mor, downtown hotels, and college dances with occasional jaunts into what remained of the territories.[15]

RACIAL BARRIERS came down in the sundry clubs still dotting 12th Street and scattered from 40 Highway on the eastside of town to out in the county just past 85th Street, the southern city limit. "Besides the Durrett Orchestra, I played in a lot of black bands," Arch Martin confessed.

> I guess because they were playing a lot of jazz. I'd sit in with Lucky Enois at the Half-A-Hill on 40 Highway, just east of Tootie's Mayfair. The Scamps used to play there too. There were always good players to sit in with at The Paradise and Ducey's on 40 Highway. The Playhouse was also in the County, out on Blue Ridge Boulevard. They didn't start to swing until after the joints in town closed, then they'd go till 5 or 6 in the morning. Ben Webster played the Zombie Club on 103rd just east of state line. He'd play sitting down in a rocking chair. Irene McLauren was the vocalist with him. Myra Taylor was playing around town then, too. The "Spider and the Fly" was her big hit. Tex Johnson a great tenor player, and I used to go to the Blue Room and sit in with Charles Kynard, one hell of an organ player. The Jungle Club downtown on the south side of 12th between Grand and McGee featured strippers backed by local musicians. The Tropicana on 12th Street for a short while, was a big Latin club. After hours all of the musicians used to hang out at Richard Dickert's Venture Inn on 14th Street just west of Pennsylvania. Close the blinds and turn up the jukebox. Or, Milton Morris' club, Milton's on Main. Both had great jazz on their jukeboxes. The Cuban Room on Linwood just west of Main on the south side of the street featured Julia Lee and Baby Lovett. Chris Connor who was just getting her start then played there too. South of Linwood Boulevard on Troost the glittering Jewel Box featured pianist Sammy Tucker, a few doors south the Golden Horseshoe featured pianist Bettye Miller and Milt Abel on bass.[16]

Twelfth Street remained a center of musical activity. On either side of 12th Street near Paseo, the Boulevard and Orchid rooms featured Billie Holiday, Sarah Vaughan, Dizzy Gillespie, and other national artists on tour ably backed by local house bands led respectively by pianist George Salisbury and trumpeter Orestie "Rusty" Tucker.

CHARLIE PARKER, TRAVELING BETWEEN THE COASTS, occasionally stopped in Kansas City to visit his mother, renew old acquaintances on 18th Street, and play an odd gig at Tootie's Mayfair. Although Parker never arrived on time and usually brought trouble, the affable owner Tootie Clarkin took him back time and time again. "In the later days he [Parker] would work for me for $30 a night. In 1953 he came out to the club one night in an open convertible with some white girl he'd picked up in town," Clarkin confided. "We got word somehow that she was trying to frame him on a narcotics charge for the government. He only had time to play eight bars of 'How High the Moon' when we motioned him off the bandstand and helped him skip town. I got up and said, 'the Bird goofed,' and the audience understood." According to Clarkin, the girl later framed two other musicians.[17] Parker's truncated appearance in Kansas City became the rule rather than the exception late in his career. After leaving McShann, Parker's career careened like a roller coaster, lifted to new heights by his charisma and brilliance as an improviser, only to derail and crash from alcohol and drug abuse.

Joining the Earl Hines band in December 1942, Parker found a soul mate in Dizzy Gillespie. Woodshedding after hours in hotel rooms and on buses between engagements, Parker and Gillespie polished the new mode of expression, which later became known as bebop. While Gillespie's onstage antics belied his conventional lifestyle, Parker's cool dispassionate stage presence masked his tumultuous life marked by drug abuse and outrageous behavior. "I think they really complemented one another," Trummy Young, a trombonist with the group, observed. "I think Diz got some things from Bird, and Bird got some things from Diz. But, every time they got on the stand, it was competitive. The two of them. They had blood in their eyes every time. They loved one another. But they would try to extend each other to make a move."[18] Parker, Gillespie, and the other modernists clashed with the traditionalists in the Hines band. Gillespie in short order left the band to return to the freedom of late-night jam sessions in New York. Parker stayed on through the steamy summer of 1943, playing army bases across the Midwest. Leaving the band that fall, Parker moved back to his mother's house in Kansas City where he joined a small ensemble led by bassist Winston Williams at Tootie's Mayfair.

In 1944, Parker and Gillespie briefly reunited in vocalist Billy Eckstine's band. A tall suave baritone with perfect diction, Eckstine launched his career with the Earl Hines band before stepping out on his own on 52nd Street in New York City. Shortly after arriving on the street, Eckstine formed a modern big band directed by Gillespie. An unlikely champion of the new music, Eckstine, known as Mr. B, specialized in romantic ballads. In the summer of 1944, the Eckstine band embarked on a tour across the South, swinging back through the Midwest. Buddy Anderson and John Jackson, formerly with the McShann band, joined in Kansas City. Parker came aboard in St. Louis from the staid Noble Sissle band. However, more at home with a small group, Parker left the Eckstine band when it returned to New York in September.

On convergent musical paths since first meeting at the corner of 19th and Vine five years earlier, Parker and Gillespie finally joined forces in the spring of 1945 at the Three Deuces on 52nd Street. Leading a small combo, the two defined and set the standard for the still-emerging style. "The height of the perfection of our music occurred in the Three Deuces with Charlie Parker," Gillespie revealed.

> He'd gotten in touch with me, played in the [Eckstine] big band, and finally we'd assembled in a setting ideal for our music, the quintet. With Yard and Max Roach, Bud Powell and Curley Russell, aw, man it was on fire all the time. . . . Bud Powell was the definitive pianist of the bebop era. . . . Yard and I were like two peas. . . . His contribution and mine just happened to go together, like putting salt in rice. Before I met Charlie Parker my style had already developed, but he was a great influence on my whole musical life. The same thing goes for him too because there was never anybody who played any closer than we did. . . . Sometimes I couldn't tell whether I was playing or not because the notes were so close together. . . . The enunciation of the notes, I think, belonged to Charlie Parker because the way he'd get from one note to another, I could never. . . . What I did was very much an extension of what Roy Eldridge had done—Charlie Parker definitely set the standard for phrasing our music, the enunciation of notes.[19]

In the same succinct manner that distinguished his style, Parker explained, "It's just music. . . . It's trying to play clean and looking for the pretty notes."[20]

The quintet abruptly disbanded after closing at the Three Deuces in early July. Later that month, Parker returned to the Deuces leading his own quintet on a double bill with the Erroll Garner Trio. Covering the group's premier, *Down Beat* noted Parker's new stature in the jazz community, "Altoman Charlie Parker, Dizzy Gillespie sidekick who is credited among musicians as being as much responsible for the amazing Gillespie style as Dizzy himself, went into the Three Deuces recently."[21] That fall Parker made his first recordings as a leader for the Savoy label. Opening on the street and recording with his own group, Parker had truly arrived in New York.

In December 1945, Gillespie and Parker bore the banner of bebop to the West Coast for a six-week engagement at Billy Berg's, a supper club on Vine Street between Sunset and Hollywood Boulevards. Met by indifferent audiences, Gillespie and other band members gladly returned to New York at the close of the run. Parker, going his own way, cashed in his airline ticket and stayed in Los Angeles. Just scraping by, Parker played for tips up and down Central Avenue before settling down to a regular engagement at the Finale

Club, an after-hours joint with a low ceiling near the corner of 1st and San Pedro in Little Tokyo. While in Los Angeles, Parker recorded for Dial Records, a fledgling label established by Ross Russell, a gangly former merchant seaman with a ruddy complexion, who owned the Tempo Music Shop.

Ostentatiously looking out for his best and only client's interest, Russell set up a publishing company for Parker's compositions and drafted a contract that paid him 2 cents per side for his original compositions. Parker readily signed the royalty contract but, true to form, failed to follow through on the publishing agreement, and so left his compositions in limbo. The next week, Parker signed over half the royalties for all contracts with Dial to his drug connection Emery Byrd, known as Moose the Mooche, in exchange for heroin. Byrd, picked up in a narcotics sweep, notified Russell of the agreement from his cell at San Quentin. Caught up in the panic from the crackdown on Central Avenue, Parker holed up in an unheated garage and drowned his habit in gallons of wine. Oddly, Parker tolerated heroin better than alcohol.

In the throes of alcohol abuse, Parker's health declined rapidly, manifested by mental disorientation and sudden jerky movements of his limbs. Alerted to Parker's rapidly deteriorating condition, Russell rushed him back into the recording studio on June 29, 1946. A hefty dose of Phenobarbital administered at the start of the session rendered Parker incoherent. Escorted back to his hotel, Parker turned up at the courtesy desk, stark naked, quarter in hand, looking for change for the phone. After being helped back to his room several more times, Parker passed out with a lit cigarette and set his mattress on fire. The police officers who arrived with the fire department had little sympathy for the still-naked and indignant Parker, who vigorously protested the invasion of his privacy. With no inclination or time to argue, the officers slapped Parker down with a blackjack, handcuffed him, rolled him up in a blanket, and tossed him in the back of a squad car. Fortunately, a liberal judge sentenced Parker to a minimum of six months in Camarillo State Hospital, a "country club" mental institution, located seventy miles north of Los Angeles, overlooking the Pacific Ocean.[22] Safe from his own excesses, Parker slowly regained his health.

A few months after his discharge from Camarillo in January 1947, Parker returned to New York and entered the most productive period of his career. From 1947 to 1951, he recorded prolifically while performing in a wide variety of venues, ranging from nightclubs to Carnegie Hall. Starting with the Influence of the Year award in *Metronome* for 1947, Parker won a trophy case of awards, dominating the competition for best alto in *Metronome* and *Down Beat*. He toured Europe in 1949 and 1950, delighting fans with his musical bag of tricks. Years of abuse caught up with Parker during the 1950 tour, when bleeding ulcers forced him to return prematurely to the United States. In July 1951, at the urging of the narcotics squad, local authorities revoked Parker's cabaret card that enabled him to work in New York. The loss of his card forced Parker to tour constantly, traveling great distances for little pay. Able to make more money as a single, Parker abandoned his regular group in favor of local pickup bands, becoming essentially a soloist for hire.

Left to his own devices, Parker careened across the country from one misadventure to another, alienating club owners along the way. When local authorities reinstated Parker's cabaret card in 1953, he resumed working in New York. Plagued by declining physical health and bouts with mental illness, Parker worked irregularly during the last two years of his career. Parker died March 12, 1955, in the suite of his friend, the Baroness Pannonica de Koenigswarter, a noted patron of jazz. After a public memorial service in New York, Parker's mother Addie and his third wife, Doris, brought his body back to Kansas City for burial in Lincoln Cemetery, located in an unincorporated area between Kansas City and Independence. Addie buried her boy on the crest of a hill underneath a tree so he would always be cool in the shade.

IN KANSAS CITY, Parker's death came as no surprise to those who knew him well. Jay McShann philosophically observed, "I knew it was gonna happen sooner or later. The way he was goin' with that dope and all. He could only last so long."[23] While Parker rocketed to the pinnacle of jazz only to plummet from his own excesses, McShann maintained an even keel, raising a family and playing in Kansas City. Working outside the musical mainstream, McShann had little opportunity to record or tour.[24] His luck changed near the end of 1955 when he hit the national charts once again with "Hands Off Him," featuring Priscilla Bowman, a tall brassy young vocalist from Kansas City, Kansas. Recorded for the Vee-Jay label in early September 1955, "Hands Off Him" climbed to number one on the *Billboard* Rhythm and Blues Chart, remaining there for sixteen weeks. Taking a break from his regular stand at Johnny Baker's in early 1956, McShann launched a tour to the East, stopping along the way in Chicago to record again for the Vee-Jay label. On the road, McShann quickly discovered much had changed in the music industry during his hiatus from the national scene.

ROCK 'N' ROLL, a new musical rebel, had arrived, eclipsing rhythm and blues in popularity with the Baby Boom Generation, conceived during the war and just coming of age. Former territorial bandleader Jesse Stone and Big Joe Turner inadvertently sparked the rock 'n' roll revolution with their smash hit "Shake, Rattle and Roll," recorded for the Atlantic label in February 1954. After fronting a series of bands during the 1930s and mid-1940s, Stone concentrated on arranging and composing, acting as artist and repertoire director for various rhythm and blues labels before joining Atlantic records in 1949. Ironically, Atlantic's other staff arranger, tenor saxophonist Budd Johnson, cut his musical teeth with Stone in the Midwestern territories and Kansas City with the T Holder and George E. Lee bands. An up-and-coming label specializing in rhythm and blues, Atlantic aggressively exploited new talent and signed established rhythm and blues artists, including Big Joe Turner.

Turner's affiliation with Atlantic came at an opportune time. Dropped by Decca in 1945, Turner recorded for Savoy and a number of other small labels with modest success. In early May 1951, Ahmet Ertegun, the founder of Atlantic, signed Turner on the heels of his disastrous appearance with Count Basie at the Apollo Theater. Unable to read music, Turner clashed with the band's intricate arrangements and so drew the wrath of the unforgiving audience at the Apollo. After the show, Ertegun, who had previously recorded Turner for the National label, followed the discouraged vocalist to a bar around the corner and consoled him with an Atlantic contract.

Ertegun astutely paired Turner with Stone. Familiar with Turner's style from their days in Kansas City, Stone crafted simple arrangements of his own catchy compositions for the recording sessions. Working easily together in the studio they produced a number of respectable hits for Atlantic. "Shake, Rattle and Roll," spiced with earthy sexual references focused around the sly double entendre of a "one-eyed cat peeping in a sea food store," hit with pubescent white males and African American record buyers. Released in May 1954, "Shake, Rattle and Roll" remained on the *Billboard* Rhythm and Blues Chart for thirty-two weeks, peaking at number one on three different occasions. The pronounced beat of the rhythm section and stripped-down instrumentation, combined with Turner's lusty delivery, charted a new direction in music.

Realizing the major breakthrough scored by Stone and Turner, Atlantic executives searched for a term for the new music. "Jerry [Wexler] wanted to call this new departure 'cat music,' but of course the term 'rock 'n' roll' took hold as the popular description for this music," Ertegun explained. "For Joe Turner it was just another record, and he didn't care what they called it."[25] Bill Haley, a chubby country artist with a genial grin and spit curl plastered across his forehead, covered "Shake, Rattle and Roll" for the Decca label, sanitizing the lyrics and swapping a guitar for the saxophone as the lead instrument. Haley's version sold well over a million copies, largely due to its use in the 1955 film "The Blackboard Jungle." Inspired by Haley, other young white musicians defied convention, picked up guitars, and rock and rolled. Older African American musicians like Turner and Jay McShann soon found themselves out of fashion with the young style-conscious rock 'n' roll generation.

Jay McShann and Priscilla Bowman arrived in New York during early spring 1956, sharing a bill at the Apollo Theater with Bo Diddley, Big Maybelle, Screamin' Jay Hawkins, Don and Dewey, the Drifters, the Dells, and the Moonglows. The management of the Apollo gave Priscilla Bowman star billing on the marquee. The teenagers crowding the Apollo barely noticed the diminutive bandleader behind the piano. Next, McShann and company swept across the South headed for the western leg of the tour. En route, the band learned of the turmoil in the aftermath of the vicious murder of Emmett Till, a fourteen-year-old Chicago youth visiting relatives in Mississippi, a year earlier. Approaching the Mississippi border, bassist Oscar "Lucky" Wesley balked at crossing the state line for fear of being mistaken as an outside agitator. "I told them, you all go on," Wesley said. "If you're not back in two days, I'll take the trailer and meet you back in Kansas City."[26] Reconsidering, McShann and band members beat it back to the safety of Kansas City, resuming their regular engagement at Johnny Baker's.

In 1957, McShann reunited with Jimmy Witherspoon to record an album of Kansas City standards, "Goin' to Kansas City Blues," for the RCA Victor label. The LP sold well, but failed to reestablish McShann's career nationally. Sticking close to home, McShann played the sundry clubs dotting the city and social affairs for the country club set. Although the Kansas City style had become passé to national taste, local audiences still hungered for the old sound, preferably with a side of barbecue ribs served up in an intimate club. Playing nightly for an eager public, veterans of the tradition happily dispensed ample portions of riffs and hot solos fired by the rhythm section. Bandleader Tommy Douglas worked his trade in and around the Kansas City area, punctuated by long stretches spent in the territories. Jimmy Keith fronted a series of small combos, working steadily in supper clubs and black-and-tan taverns. Claude Williams gigged regularly around town with his trio, alternating between guitar and his beloved violin. Drummer Baby Lovett, Julia Lee's long-time partner, teamed up with barrelhouse pianist Everett Johnson to dish up boogie-woogie at the Crossroads, situated north of the Missouri River, within shouting distance of the old Riverside municipal racetrack, put out to pasture by the Kaycee cleanup. After being dropped by Capitol, Julia Lee played for tips at the Hi-Ball Lounge on 12th Street.

As work became scarce locally during the mid-1960s, new markets opened up in Europe for McShann and other Kaycee jazz legends. These new opportunities came about largely due to the emerging international record industry led by Dave Dexter and Capitol Records. On a lark, while vacationing in California during the summer of 1966, McShann contacted Dexter, then the international artist and repertoire director for Capitol Records, a subsidiary of EMI, England. Dexter, having acquired the Beatles for Capitol a few years earlier, enjoyed the luxury of picking and choosing his projects. The wild success of the Beatles and the subsequent invasion of the Rolling Stones and other English rockers created a trans-Atlantic record industry that soon engulfed the globe. Dexter, tired of dealing with the Beatles, particularly John Lennon, whom he detested as much as Charlie Parker, ushered McShann into the studio once again, more for old times sake than record sales. The album "McShann's Piano," rendered in the pure Kansas City boogie-woogie and blues style he played thirty years earlier at the Monroe Inn, revitalized McShann's career, particularly with young white audiences in Europe.

McShann's follow-up recordings for the Sackville and Atlantic labels in the 1970s cemented his reputation internationally. McShann spent much of the next thirty years touring Europe.

Bruce Ricker's 1979 film *The Last of the Blue Devils* furthered the cause of Kansas City Jazz, spotlighting Jay McShann, Joe Turner, Count Basie, Claude Williams, Jesse Price, Eddie Durham, and others who created the tradition. The *Goin' to Kansas City Exhibit*, a multi-media exhibit and concert produced in 1980 by Howard Litwak and Nathan Pearson in conjunction with the Kansas City Museum, further celebrated Kansas City's rich musical heritage, reuniting Joe Turner, Jay McShann, Claude Williams, and other Kansas City greats. Most recently, director Clint Eastwood and producer Bruce Ricker prominently featured McShann in the documentary *Piano Blues*. Unaffected by celebrity, McShann maintains his home base in Kansas City, where he first launched his career, although he rarely plays locally.

TODAY, KANSAS CITY IS LIKE A GENTEEL ELDERLY LADY of former ill repute reluctant to discuss her notorious past. Unlike the other cradles of jazz—New Orleans, Chicago, and New York—Kansas City does little to celebrate the colorful history that spawned its distinctive jazz tradition. While Storyville and Mahogany Hall live in infamy, Annie Chambers, the grand madam converted to virtue in her old age, and the bustling red-light district centered around 14th Street have largely been forgotten. The frequently vandalized statue of Alderman Jim Pendergast, which once perched on the rim of Mulkey Park overlooking his beloved West Bottoms, has been restored and tucked away in a safer corner of the city. No memorials to Boss Tom Pendergast exist outside of those of his own creation, the magnificent art deco courthouse, city hall, and municipal auditorium. Even the smallest gesture recognizing Boss Tom's role in transforming Kansas City from a dusty cow town into the Paris of the Plains meets with howls of indignant protest from political puritans who trot out examples of the machine's excesses. Notwithstanding the best efforts of generations of civic crusaders, strains of the intemperate spirit of old Kaycee fostered by the Pendergast Machine still survive.

Riverboat casinos dot the banks of the Missouri River from North Kansas City to Riverside, not far from the old municipal track. Policemen who once busted backroom gamblers freelance for the boats, escorting suckers to rows of whirling slot machines. Women still loiter on street corners in unofficially designated areas of town, not waiting for the bus. Unregulated, they spill over into the surrounding neighborhoods, brazenly plying their trade wherever they can. Jackson County remains a major drug-trafficking center, with crack cocaine and methamphetamine replacing heroin and morphine. Green Mexican marijuana remains a staple, supplanted by a fierce homegrown Indica strain after the fall harvest. Clubs peppering the city from downtown to out in the county past 85th Street feature jazz and blues nightly. With the relaxation of the restriction on closing time a decade ago, many clubs stay open until 3 A.M. A few reopen at 6 A.M. to greet the third shift. The clubs, along with casual engagements for the country club set, provide regular work for a host of musicians.

After years of holding out, in 1970, Local 627 finally merged with Local 34, the white musicians union, to become the American Federation of Musicians Local 34-627. The combined unions include 700 members. Over the years, leading Kansas City musicians followed the trail blazed by Bennie Moten and moved to New York or California. Others stayed behind, raising families and eking out a living playing society gigs and club dates. Recently, many top players have returned to Kansas City and revitalized the jazz scene. Unfortunately, Kansas City's vibrant jazz scene receives little ink in the national press. A bright spot, the Jazz Ambassadors, a local jazz advocacy group, has picked up the slack, publishing the *JAM* magazine. Oddly, Kansas City style is seldom performed where it originated. In New Orleans, any musician worth his or her salt can on the spot muster an impression of Louis Armstrong. However, most Kansas City groups prefer hard bop, Latin, and other modern styles to "Moten's Swing" or the other classics of the pure Kaycee style. Similarly, few landmarks of the golden age of Kansas City Jazz survive.

Twelfth Street, a one-time neon riot of bars, gambling dens, and taxi dance halls, fell victim to urban renewal and the freeway that choked the life from the city core during the 1960s. The wise guys who lorded over the strip packed up and moved years ago to sunnier venues in Las Vegas. An untidy surface parking lot for the adjacent police department occupies the hallowed site of the Reno Club, where Charlie Parker witnessed Lester Young and Count Basie making jazz history. No plaque marks the spot. The ravages of time and elements wiped out the glory of Fairyland Park and Winnwood Beach, leaving no trace of the romance and gaiety of summer nights in Old Kaycee, during a time when the Great Depression cast a pall over much of the country. The Pla-Mor's expansive entertainment complex featuring the million-dollar ballroom gave way to progress in the early 1970s and was torn down for a car dealership. The El Torreon survived, serving as a roller rink, then a rock palace called the Cowtown Ballroom in the early 1970s. It has now been converted into storage and performance space for alternative rock bands.

Eighteenth and Vine miraculously escaped the urban renewal wrecking ball that leveled surrounding neighborhoods during the 1960s. A multi-million-dollar redevelopment effort, launched in 1997, featuring the American Jazz and Negro Leagues Baseball Museums, has sparked a minor renaissance in the historic district. New housing units have been erected, and two new restaurants anchor the stretch of 18th Street between Paseo and Highland. The renovated Gem Theater has reopened as a performing arts venue. The jazz museum, situated on the corner of 18th and Vine, showcases the legacies of Ella Fitzgerald, Louis Armstrong, Duke Ellington, and Charlie Parker. Around the corner at 1823 Highland stands the headquarters of Local 627, now known as the Mutual Musicians Foundation, a monument to the glory of Kansas City Jazz. Local and visiting musicians still gather at the foundation in the wee hours to test each other's mettle, jamming until the people go home the next morning, conjuring the spirit of old Kaycee.

Notes

1. TALES FROM TOM'S TOWN

1. Westbrook Pegler, "In Spite of All, Mr. Pendergast Runs a Good Town," *Kansas City Journal-Post*, February 21, 1938, 13.
2. Edward Morrow, quoted in Maurice Milligan, *Missouri Waltz* (New York: Charles Scribner's Sons, 1948),12.
3. Mary Lou Williams, quoted by Max Jones in *Talkin' Jazz* (New York: W. W. Norton, 1988), 187.
4. Dave E. Dexter, Jr., "Moten and Lee Are Patron Saints of Kansas City Jazz. . . . Town Hits Its Peak in the 1930's As Spawning Ground for Musicians," *Down Beat*, February 1, 1941, 8.
5. Club owner Milton Morris related the story during numerous conversations with Haddix.
6. Jay McShann, interview by Chuck Haddix, June 27, 1997, Kansas City, Missouri.
7. John Albertson, "Stories of Uncle Milty Live On," *Jazz Ambassador Magazine* (October/November 1992): 17.
8. Nathan Pearson, *Goin' to Kansas City* (Urbana: University of Illinois Press, 1987), 97–98.
9. An advertisement for horse races at Riverside Park in the *Kansas City Call* proudly touted the opening day as the "Judge H. F. McElroy Inaugural Opening." *Kansas City Call*, May 20, 1932, 7A.
10. James C. Fitzpatrick, "Horse Racing Sometimes Slow Getting out of the Gate," *Kansas City Times*, January 2, 1985, A-1, A-8.
11. C. C. Nicolet, "National Crime Capital," *Columbia Missourian*, July 15, 1933. Article from vertical clipping file on crime in Special Collection, Downtown Kansas City Public Library.
12. Milligan, *Missouri Waltz*, 12.
13. Westbrook Pegler, "Columnist Makes the Rounds of Kansas City's Night Spots," *Kansas City Journal-Post*, February 19, 1938, 18.

14. Harry Wohl, "Rise and Fall of 'Boss Tom,'" *St. Louis Star-Times*, February 7, 1945. Article from vertical clipping file on crime in Special Collection, Downtown Kansas City Public Library.

15. This was one of Morris's favorite stories, repeated often. The conversation probably occurred when Morris accompanied Julia Lee to the White House for the annual White House Correspondents dinner on March 5, 1949.

16. "John Lazia Is Exonerated," *Kansas City American*, September 24, 1931, 1.

17. John Cameron Swayze, liner notes to *K.C. in the 30s*, Capitol Records, T1057.

18. "Bad Advertising for Kansas City," *Kansas City Star*, August 14, 1933. Article from vertical clipping file on crime in Special Collections, Downtown Kansas City Public Library.

19. "Kansas Town Company Records" (KC352). Native Sons Archives, Western Historical Manuscripts Collection—Kansas City.

20. William Reddig, *Tom's Town: Kansas City and the Pendergast Legend* (Philadelphia and New York: J. B. Lippincott, 1947), 19.

21. Brian Burnes, "Border War Episode of 1863 to be Re-enacted," *Kansas City Star*, August 23, 2003, p. B-1, 4. Understandably, the observances of the event differs on either side of the border.

22. Reddig, *Tom's Town*, 24.

23. Ibid.

24. W. G. Secrest, "Colorful Figure in Red Light District for Half Century Relates Her Story Nightly," *Kansas City Journal-Post*, May 15, 1932, 6B.

25. From a 1913 report on prostitution by the Church Federation of Kansas City, included in the vertical clipping file on prostitution located in Special Collections at the Downtown Kansas City Public Library.

26. See Lawrence H. Larsen and Nancy J. Hulston, *Pendergast!* (Columbia: University of Missouri Press, 1997), 15–17.

27. Reddig, *Tom's Town*, 25–26.

28. Ibid., 28.

29. Ibid., 34.

30. Larsen and Hulston, *Pendergast!*, 61–62.

31. Quoted in Reddig, *Tom's Town*, 88.

32. See Dory DeAngelo, *Voices Across Time: Profiles of Kansas City's Early Residents* (Kansas City: Tapestry Publications, 1987).

33. *1920 Kansas City Directory and Business Catalog* (Kansas City: Gate City Directory Company), 2448.

34. Woodbury used the familiar of her first name, with her middle name as her pseudonym.

35. Edward A. Berlin, *King of Ragtime: Scott Joplin and His Era* (New York: Oxford University Press, 1994), 48–56.

36. See Peter A. Munstedt, "Kansas City Music Publishing: The First Fifty Years," *American Music* (winter 1991): 357–68.

37. Cy Dewar, interview by Frank Driggs, August 29, 1975, Kansas City, Missouri.

38. "Automobiles Valued at $250,00 Will Be Shown at February Exposition." Undated article from Loren McMurray scrapbook in the Frank Driggs collection.

39. Dance announcement for Eddie Kuhn's Dance Specialists at Braney's Auditorium, Point Marion, Pennsylvania, 1920. Loren McMurray scrapbook in the Frank Driggs Collection.

40. Throughout 1922 Conn featured McMurray, along with F. Pike, L. Canfield, L. Reynolds, W. Markwith, and P. Biese, endorsing the Conn saxophones as "The

World's Best" saxophones. Loren McMurray scrapbook in the Frank Driggs collection.

41. Floyd Estep, interview by Frank Driggs, November 12, 1974, Los Angeles, California.

42. Cliff Halliburton, interview by Frank Driggs, November 1, 1974, Kansas City, Missouri.

43. Estep, interview.

44. Armistice had just been declared on November 11, 1918.

45. Joe Sanders, "The Coon-Sanders Story (Part II)," *Jazznotes* (Indianapolis Jazz Club) 6, 1(1961): 3.

46. See Joe Popper, "America's Band," *Star Magazine*, July 9, 1989, 8–23, 26–27.

47. Fred Edmiston, *The Coon-Sanders Nighthawks: The Band That Made Radio Famous* (Jefferson, NC: McFarland, 2003), 7–8.

48. Sanders, "The Coon-Sanders Story (Part II)," 4.

49. Ibid., 5.

50. The personnel included Harry Silvertone, violin; Clyde Hendrix, cornet; Carl Norberg, trombone; Harley McLane and Harold Theill, saxophones; Robert Norfleet, banjo; Joe Sanders, piano; and Carleton Coon, drums.

51. The band had previously made a guest appearance on WRW, operated by the *Kansas City Post*.

52. Popper, "America's Band," 23.

53. "Nighthawks Defy Sleep," *Kansas City Star*, December 10, 1922, 6B.

54. "Joe Sanders Is Dead," *Kansas City Times*, May 15, 1965, 1-D.

55. Edmiston, *Coon-Sanders Nighthawks*, 124.

56. Rex Downing, quoted by Bob Harrington in "Tales of Coon-Sanders," *The Mississippi Rag*, April 1991, 12.

57. The Night Hawks spent the winter season at the Blackhawk in 1926, 1928, 1929, and 1930. During the winter of 1927 the Blackhawk featured the Ben Pollock Orchestra, forcing the Night Hawks to tour regionally. Edmiston, *Coon-Sanders Nighthawks*, 204–5.

58. Florence Stout, quoted by Harrington in "Tales of Coon-Sanders," 11.

59. Edmiston, *Coon-Sanders Nighthawks*, 266.

60. Ibid., 283.

61. Sanders attempted to keep the band together with little success. The Night Hawks disbanded on Easter Sunday 1933. Sanders relocated to Hollywood in 1934, writing music for movies with Gus Kahn. In 1935, he formed a new group, the Ole Left-Hander and His Orchestra, and returned to the Blackhawk. Sanders's fortunes declined when the Auburn Motor Car Company went bankrupt. He had invested heavily in Auburn stock at the urging of Mr. Cord, who owned the company. Sanders remained popular in the Midwest and toured nationally, but he never enjoyed the national prominence that he achieved as co-leader of the Night Hawks. John Coon, Carleton's son and a bandleader in his own right, explained: "Joe was difficult to get along with. He could be a real pain in the ass, just get mad and walk off the stage. Dad always dealt with the club owners, and if Dad wasn't there, they didn't want anything to do with Joe." Ending his career as a bandleader in 1953, Sanders returned to Kansas City, where he died in 1965.

62. Dave E. Dexter, Jr., "Kaycee Strictly a Colored Town," *Down Beat*, January 1, 1941, 8.

63. "Some Ofays from Kansas City," *Down Beat*, January 15, 1941, 8.

2. CARRIE'S GONE TO KANSAS CITY

1. Buck O'Neil, interview by Chuck Haddix, December 15, 1994, Kansas City, Missouri.

2. Andy Kirk, *Twenty Years on Wheels* (Ann Arbor: University of Michigan Press, 1989), 68–69.

3. United States Department of the Interior, National Park Service. "National Register Of Historic Places Continuation Sheet," 18th and Vine Historic District, Kansas City, Jackson County, Missouri, Section 7, 1.

4. Ibid., 15.

5. "A Crowd Heard Negro Tenor," *The Kansas City Sun*, December 16, 1917, 1.

6. D. A. Holmes, "Street's Big Opening May 15th," *Kansas City Call*, May 11, 1923, 4.

7. Buck O'Neil, interview.

8. See Janet Bruce, *The Kansas City Monarchs: Champions of Black Baseball* (Lawrence: University Press of Kansas, 1985).

9. The State Historical Society of Missouri, Newspaper Collection.

10. Robert Trussell, "Journalism Wars of KC's Jazz Age," *Kansas City Star*, February 20, 1990, 1-C, 4-C.

11. "Lincoln Theatre Opens," *Kansas City Sun*, February 21, 1920, 3.

12. See Henry T. Sampson, *Blacks in Blackface: A Source Book on Early Black Musical Shows* (Metuchen, NJ: Scarecrow Press, 1980).

13. Clarence E. Muse, "T. O. B. A. Victims," *Kansas City American*, August 9, 1928, 3.

14. Terry Waldo, *This Is Ragtime* (New York: Hawthorn Books, 1976), 72.

15. Dr. O. H. Simpson, "The Truth About Blind Boone," *Kansas City Call*, March 2, 1923, 4B.

16. Jack A. Batterson, *Blind Boone: Missouri's Ragtime Pioneer* (Columbia: University of Missouri Press, 1998), 23–24.

17. Batterson, *Blind Boone*, 44–45.

18. "Boogie Woogie," *New Grove Dictionary of Jazz* (London: Macmillan Press, 1989), 135.

19. Landon Laird, "About Town," *Kansas City Times*, October 23, 1942, 2.

20. Edward Berlin, *Ragtime* (Los Angeles: University of California Press, 1980), 149.

21. See William H. Kenney, "James Scott and the Culture of Classic Ragtime," *American Music* (summer 1991): 172.

22. David A. Jasen and Trebor Jay Tichenor, *Rags and Ragtime: A Musical History* (New York: The Seabury Press, 1978), 112, and Waldo, *This Is Ragtime*, 72.

23. Rudi Blesh and Harriet Janis, *They All Played Ragtime* (New York: Knopf, 1959), 115.

24. See Jasen and Tichenor, *Rags and Ragtime: A Musical History*, 111–21.

25. Sandra R. Lieb, *Mother of the Blues: A Study of Ma Rainey* (Amherst: University of Massachusetts Press, 1981), 3.

26. "Langston Hughes an Interesting Visitor in Kansas City This Week," *Kansas City Call*, April 7, 1939, 1.

27. Whitney Balliett, *American Singers: Twenty-Seven Portraits in Song* (New York: Oxford University Press, 1988), 46.

28. John Randolph, "A Pioneer Race Recorder," *Record Researcher*, unknown date or volume.

29. "They Liked the Band," *Kansas City Call*, July 29, 1932, 1–2.

30. Nathan W. Pearson, Jr., *Goin' to Kansas City* (Chicago: University of Illinois Press, 1987), 20.

31. Ross Russell, *Jazz Style in Kansas City and the Southwest* (Berkeley: University of California Press, 1971), 172.

32. Pearson, *Goin' to Kansas City*, 21–22.

33. At the time youth bands were often referred to as pickaninny bands after the pejorative term pickaninny, referring to African American babies and children.

34. Reginald T. Buckner, "Rediscovering Major N. Clark Smith," *Music Educators Journal* (February 1985): 36–42.

35. Quoted in E. Diane Lyle-Smith, "Nathaniel Clark Smith (1877–1934): African-American Music Educator and Composer," *The Bulletin of Historical Research in Music Education* (Lawrence: The Division of Music Education and Music Therapy, The University of Kansas) 17, 2 (January 1996): 104–6.

36. Walter Page as told to Frank Driggs, "About My Life in Music," *The Jazz Review* (November 1958): 12.

37. Jasper Allen as told to John Beaman, "Memories of Kansas City Early Jazz," *jazz report* 6, 10 (December 1958): 3.

38. Raymond Williams, "Music," *The Lincolnian*, 1919, 34.

39. "Thousands Pay Tribute to Late Lieut. Europe," *Kansas City Call*, June 10, 1922, 6.

40. Smith moved to Chicago in 1922, organizing Pullman Porter singing groups and teaching at Wendell Phillips High School, where his students included Lionel Hampton. Relocating to St. Louis in 1931, Smith joined the faculty at Sumner High School. In 1932, Smith won the Wannamaker Prize for his composition "Negro Folk Suite," which was performed by the St. Louis Symphony in 1933. The CBS network broadcast Smith's "St. Louis Blues" radio program, originating from KMOX, for three years. In June 1935, Smith returned to Kansas City to concentrate on his publishing business. After walking from his home to the Musicians Protective Union 627 at 1823 Highland, Smith suffered a stroke and died on October 8, 1935.

3. GET LOW-DOWN BLUES

1. Bands from traveling shows commonly played ballyhoo, a teaser from the show, in the street to attract patrons for the show's evening performance.

2. Charles A. Starks, "Negro Bands in Rivalry," *Kansas City Sun*, July 28, 1917, 3.

3. Paul Banks, interview by Frank Driggs, October 11, 1957, Kansas City, Kansas.

4. Born George Ewing Lee in Boonville, Missouri, 1896.

5. Clarence Love quoted by John Wooley's "Love's Labor Found," *Tulsa* (April 1985): 69.

6. Herman Walder quoted in Nathan Pearson's *Goin' to Kansas City* (Chicago: University of Illinois Press, 1987), 151.

7. Jesse Stone quoted in *Goin' to Kansas City*, 127.

8. Born Benjamin Moten on November 13, 1894.

9. See Dave E. Dexter, Jr., liner notes to *Kansas City Jazz* (1941), Decca 214.

10. Dude Langford quoted in Pearson, *Goin' to Kansas City*, 122.

11. Ibid., 122–23.

12. Ad for Bennie Moten's Jazz Orchestra, *Kansas City Call*, May 6, 1922.

13. Charles A. Starks, "Radio Bugs Hear Jazz Fit by Moten's Orchestra," *Kansas City Sun*, March 24, 1923, 6.

14. "Famous Trixie Smith Engagement Flivvers After Third Performance," *Kansas City Call*, December 8, 1922, 8.

15. Sheldon Harris, *Blues Who's Who* (New York: DaCapo Press, Inc., 1979), 70.
16. All of the songs recorded by Brown and Bradford were written by Kansas City composers: Paul Banks, Hattie Pearson, Sylvester Kimbrough, and Ada Brown's sister, Ruth Wise.
17. Ada Brown, "Evil Mama Blues," OKeh 8101, October 1923.
18. "Kansas City's Record Making Orchestra," *Kansas City Sun*, November 30, 1923, 9.
19. "Kansas City's Own Race Artists," *Kansas City Call*, November 23, 1923, 2.
20. "Local Artists Entertain OKeh Record Dealers," *Kansas City Call*, February 8, 1924, 1.
21. Different dates have been given for Leonard's birthday date, but according to his daughter, JoAnn Leonard, the correct date is July 2, 1905.
22. See Ray Batt's liner notes to *Bennie Moten's Kansas City Orchestra 1923–25*, Retrieval FJ-120.
23. See Ross Russell, *Jazz Style in Kansas City and the South-West* (Berkeley: University of California Press, 1971), 95.
24. "Winston Holmes Sues Columbia Record Co.," *Kansas City Call*, December 10, 1926, 5.
25. J. Godrich and R. M. Dixon in *Blues and Gospel Records 1902–1942* (New York: Oxford University Press, 1997) assert that Lena Kimbrough and Lottie Beaman were the same woman, with Beaman using her married name Kimbrough for the Meritt session. The source of this mix-up is an interview with Doug Jystrup transcribed by John Godrich in *Blues Unlimited* 48 (January 1968). Jystrup asserts that Lena Kimbrough's sister Estella was featured in the publicity photo Holmes used to publicize "The City of the Dead" and the two women were the same person. However, this is not the case. Coverage of their recordings and concerts in the local press between 1925 and 1926 indicate they were two different women working in Kansas City at the same time.
26. "Winston Holmes Makes First Record," *Kansas City Call*, December 12, 1924, 2.
27. "Morrison Orchestra Coming to This City," *Kansas City Call*, April 3, 1925, 1.
28. A copy of the McDaniels Meritt recording is yet to surface, but Holmes advertised it locally along with the two previous releases in the *Kansas City Call* on May 28, 1926. Billed as a "'Meritt Recording' Star," McDaniels did an in-store performance at Holmes's shop in June 1926 while she was in town playing at downtown theater on the Pantages circuit.
29. Holmes recorded a number of other selections with Lee that he never released, including: "There Ain't No Maybe in My Baby's Eyes," "Won't You Come Over," "California," and "It Made You Happy When You Made Me Cry." Holmes retained the masters, which, according to Mrs. Holmes, were stolen during the 1950s.
30. "Orchestra Furnishes Number on Midnite Bill," *Kansas City Call*, November 19, 1926, 6.
31. "Orchestras Play to Tie in Newman Contest," *Kansas City Call*, December 3, 1926, 7.
32. Banks, interview.
33. "Bennie Moten Makes Records for Victor," *Kansas City Call*, December 17, 1927, 4.
34. Published correspondence in article, "Moten Orchestra Commended by Victor Music Director," *Kansas City Call*, January 28, 1927, 2.
35. Roy Wilkins, Editorial, *Kansas City Call*, March 9, 1928, 4-B.
36. Ed Lewis as told to Frank Driggs, "Kansas City Brass," *The Jazz Review* (May 1959): 17.

37. Jasper Allen as told to John Beaman, "Memories of Kansas City Early Jazz," *Jazz report* (December 1958): 3.

38. "Lammar Wright Going Big in New York," *Kansas City Call*, October 14, 1927, 7.

39. "'Africana' Sets Record in K.C.," *Kansas City Call*, April 13, 1928, 8.

40. "Bennie Moten's Orchestra has Returned Home," *Kansas City American*, September 13, 1928, 4.

41. "Bennie Moten Home in September," *Kansas City Call*, July 20, 1928, 7.

42. Jasper Allen, interview by Frank Driggs, September 21, 1974, Charlotte, North Carolina.

43. Ed Lewis as told to Frank Driggs, "Ed Lewis' Story," *The Jazz Review* (June 1959): 23–24.

44. Ibid., 23.

45. "Moten's Band Draws Crowd at Paseo Hall," *Kansas City Call*, September 14, 1928, 4.

46. See Lon A. Gault, *Ballroom Echoes* (Andrew Corbet Press, 1989).

47. Article on opening of the Pla-Mor in *Kansas City Times*, November 25, 1927, from the Pla-Mor clipping file in Special Collections at the Downtown Branch of the Kansas City Public Library.

48. Carmichael recorded "Stardust" for the Gennett label with the Emil Seidel Orchestra on October 31, 1927, before joining the Goldkette band at the Pla-Mor. Carmichael originally composed "Star Dust" as an up-tempo foxtrot. A few years later Mitchell Parish supplied the lyric, turning it into a ballad.

49. Floyd Estep, interview by Frank Driggs, Los Angeles, November 12, 1974.

50. "3,000 at Opening of El Torreon," *Journal Post*, December 16, 1927, 5.

4. THE TERRITORIES

1. Ed Lewis as told to Frank Driggs, "Ed Lewis' Story," *The Jazz Review* (June 1959): 23.

2. Walter Page as told to Frank Driggs, "About My Life in Music," *The Jazz Review* (November 1958): 14.

3. Nathan W. Pearson, Jr., *Goin' to Kansas City* (Chicago: University of Illinois Press, 1987), 39.

4. Pearson, *Goin' to Kansas City*, 39.

5. Ibid., 67.

6. Jimmy Rushing as told to Helen McNamara, "Pack My Bags and Make My Getaway: Jimmy Rushing Details His Life-Long Odyssey as a Blues Singer," *Down Beat*, April 8, 1955, 22.

7. Count Basie, *Good Morning Blues* (New York: Random House, 1985), 5.

8. The article "300 Members are in Union of Musicians," *Kansas City Call*, September 14, 1928, 4 reported 87 members by 1927. The article "Six Bands to Battle for Honors," *Kansas City Call*, May 2, 1930, cited the membership as 347 members. Williams Shaw, who became president in 1928, deserves much of the credit for the phenomenal growth of the union.

9. The Blue Devils actually arrived in Kansas City first, performing with a stage show at the downtown Grand Theater in November 1922, but the Morrison band became the first to play for African Americans in the 18th and Vine area.

10. Andy Kirk as told to Frank Driggs, "My Story," *The Jazz Review* (February 1959): 12.

11. Born George Morrison, 1892.
12. The personnel of the band included: George Morrison, violin; Mrs. Desdemona Weaver-Davis, piano; Mrs. Hattie McDaniels-Langford, comedienne and vocals; Leo Davis, saxophone and clarinet; Alvin Wall, saxophone and clarinet; Theodore Morris, trombone; Joseph Miller, cornet; Andrew Kirk, tuba and bass saxophone; John Sailes, drums and baritone horn; and William Dirvin, banjo.
13. In 1940, McDaniels became the first African American to win an Oscar, awarded for best supporting actress as Mammy in *Gone with the Wind*.
14. Born Andrew Dewey Kirk, May 28, 1898.
15. Kirk, "My Story," 12.
16. Born Terrence Holder, 1898.
17. Snub Mosely, interview by Frank Driggs, February 1980, New York City.
18. Kirk, "My Story," 12.
19. Ibid., 13.
20. The personnel of the band included: T Holder and Harry "Big Jim" Lawson, trumpets; Allen Durham or Flip Benson, trombone; Alvin "Fats" Wall and Lawrence Freeman, reeds; Marion Jackson, piano; William Dirvin, banjo; Andy Kirk, tuba; and Harry "Stumpy" Jones, drums.
21. Jack Kapp added the middle name Lou on her first solo piano recording to make her name more unique. According to Rust (*Jazz Records*,1720), Williams recorded "Night Life" and "Drag 'Em" (Brunswick 7178) on April 24, 1930.
22. Born Mary Elfrieda Scruggs, May 8, 1910. Williams gave this as her birth date, but in Linda Dahl, *Morning Glory: A Biography of Mary Lou Williams* (New York: Pantheon Books, 1999), 14–15, Dahl theorized she might have been born earlier.
23. Dahl, *Morning Glory*, 8–24.
24. Mary Lou Williams quoted in Max Jones, *Talking Jazz* (New York: W. W. Norton, 1988), 184.
25. After reuniting with Jeanette, Mary and the Synco Jazzers made their first recordings, accompanying Jeanette and as a unit. See Brian Rust, *Jazz Records: 1897–1942*, (New York: Arlington House, 1978), 820, 1718.
26. Williams in Jones, *Talking Jazz*, 186.
27. Mary Lou Williams, "Mary Lou on the Clouds of Joy," *Melody Maker*, April 17, 1954, 5.
28. Andy Kirk, interview by Frank Driggs, January 24, 1958, New York City.
29. Andy Klein, "Another Helping of Liver and Onions and Jazz: An Interview with George James and John Williams Transcribed," *International Association of Jazz Record Collectors Journal* (Summer 1997): 35.
30. Advertisement for Decoration Day Dance, *Kansas City Call*, May 24, 1929, 7.
31. Pearson, *Goin' to Kansas City*, 50.
32. Born Jesse Stone, November 16, 1901.
33. Pearson, *Goin' to Kansas City*, 10–11.
34. Ibid., 11.
35. Jesse Stone, interview by Nathan Pearson and Howard Litwak, June 15, 1977, Long Island, New York. Western Historical Manuscripts Collection, University of Missouri–Kansas City.
36. Pearson, *Goin' to Kansas City*, 48–49.
37. Ibid., 49.
38. Ibid.
39. "Blues Serenaders and George E. Lee Orchestra Contest, December 30," *Kansas City Call*, December 24, 1926, 6.
40. Ibid.

41. "Lee's Orchestra Wins Contest," *Kansas City Call*, January 7, 1927, 4.
42. "Hundreds Turned Away at Orchestra Contest," *Kansas City Call*, February 11, 1927, 5.
43. The Blues Serenaders recorded four selections for the OKeh label in St. Louis on April 27, 1927, marking the first step in establishing the group nationally. See Brian Rust *Jazz Records: 1897–1942*, 1507.
44. See Gunther Schuller, *Early Jazz* (New York: Oxford University Press, 1968), 288–91.
45. See Fredrick R. Swischer, *Kansas City Jazz, 1923–1937: The Music*, unpublished dissertation (D.M.A.), Special Collections, Miller Nichols Library, University of Missouri–Kansas City, 38–39.
46. Jesse Stone, interview by Pearson and Litwak.
47. Pearson, *Goin' to Kansas City*, 50.
48. Ibid., 67.
49. Ibid., 68.
50. Born Walter Sylvester Page, February 9, 1900.
51. Page, "About My Life in Music," 12.
52. Stanley Dance, *The World of Count Basie* (New York: DaCapo, 1980), 63.
53. Quoted in Derek John, *A Solid Foundation: Walter Page's Early Musical Journey*, Senior Thesis, University of Kansas, 2000, Lawrence, Kansas, 1.
54. Advertisement for the Grand Theater, *Kansas City Sun*, November 25, 1922, 8.
55. "Trixie Smith and the Byrd Ewing Company at the Auditorium," *Kansas City Sun*, November 25, 1922, 8.
56. The Blue Devils included: Ermir Coleman, leader and trombone; William Blue, clarinet; Lawrence Williams, cornet; Edward "Crackshot" McNeill, drums; Page, bass; and Willie Lewis, piano.
57. Page, "About My Life in Music," 13.
58. Born Henry Smith, August 24, 1904.
59. Don Gazzaway, "Conversations with Buster Smith, Part One," *The Jazz Review* (December 1959): 18.
60. Page, "About My Life in Music," 13.
61. Born Oran Thaddeus Page in Dallas, Texas, on January 27, 1908.
62. Born James Rushing, August 26, 1903.
63. Jimmy Rushing as told to Helen McNamara, "Pack My Bags and Make My Getaway," 22.
64. Born William Basie, August 21, 1904.
65. Basie, *Good Morning Blues*, 57.
66. Ibid., 64–65.
67. Ibid., 86.
68. Advertisement for "Big Street Fair and Carnival," *Kansas City Sun*, April 12, 1919.
69. Basie, *Good Morning Blues*, 86.
70. Ibid., 98.
71. Uncredited theatrical revue, *Kansas City Call*, July 8, 1927, 5.
72. Basie, *Good Morning Blues*, 101–2.
73. Ibid., 5.
74. Stanley Dance, *World of Count Basie*, 20.
75. Jasper Allen as told to John Beaman, "Memories of Kansas City Early Jazz," *jazz report* 6, 10 (December 1958).
76. Page, "About My Life in Music," 14.
77. Advertisement for dance at Paseo Hall, *Kansas City Call*, October 26, 1928, 9.
78. "Blue Devils a Riot at Halloween Dance," *Kansas City Call*, November 2, 1928, 10.

5. BLUE DEVIL BLUES

1. Andy Kirk, *Twenty Years on Wheels* (Ann Arbor: University of Michigan Press, 1989), 61.
2. Ibid., 62.
3. Mary Lou Williams interview in Max Jones, *Talking Jazz* (New York: W. W. Norton, 1988), 189.
4. Kirk, *Twenty Years*, 64.
5. Andy Kirk as told to Frank Driggs, "My Story," *The Jazz Review* (February 1959): 13–14.
6. Kirk, *Twenty Years*, 66–67.
7. Earl Wilkins, "Dance Gossip," *Kansas City Call*, September 20, 1929, 2.
8. Williams interview in Jones, *Talking Jazz*, 188.
9. At the time, the Coon-Sanders Night Hawk Orchestra, Phil Baxter, and Bennie Moten were under contract to Victor.
10. Williams interview in Jones, *Talking Jazz*, 188
11. See Fredrick R. Swischer, *Kansas City Jazz, 1923–1937: The Music*, unpublished dissertation (D.M.A.), Special Collections, Miller Nichols Library, University of Missouri–Kansas City.
12. Ibid.
13. See Amy Bauer, *Mary Lou Williams and Kansas City Style*, presented at the annual meeting of the Sonneck Society for American Music, February 19, 1998, in Kansas City, Missouri.
14. Druie Bess, interview by Frank Driggs, St. Louis, Missouri, 1985.
15. See Swischer, *Kansas City Jazz*, 81–83.
16. See Gunther Schuller, *Early Jazz: Its Roots and Musical Development* (New York: Oxford University Press, 1968), 298.
17. "Public Demand Makes Heavy Sales for George Lee Records," *Kansas City Call*, January 25, 1930, 7.
18. Roland Gelatt, *The Fabulous Phonograph* (New York: Collier Books, 1977), 255.
19. The Little Billies and Southern Troubadours were relatively short lived, disbanding in 1931. The Little Billies suffered from disorganization and lackluster musicianship. Unable to truly compete with Moten, Kirk, Lee, and other top-shelf bands, the Little Billies found its niche in club work, playing regularly at the Black and Tan Cotton Club on Independence Avenue. The Southern Troubadours served as a training ground for up-and-coming musicians, including: James "Big Daddy" Walker, guitar; Clyde Hart, piano; Alton "Ellis" Moore, trombone; Joe Keyes, trumpet; Ben Webster, tenor saxophone; and Joe [Jo] Jones, drums. Greatly influenced by Duke Ellington, the Southern Troubadours, variously known as the Southern Serenaders and Cotton Club Orchestra, toured regionally before disbanding in May 1931, as the result of a raid by Blanche Calloway.
20. Members discussed buying a building for their headquarters as early as 1920.
21. "First Annual Musicians Ball Draws Great Crowd," *Kansas City Call*, December 6, 1929, 9.
22. "Beats Bennie Moten," *Kansas City Call*, May 10, 1929, 10.
23. "Bennie Moten Takes Over Blue Devil Orchestra," *Kansas City Call*, June 21, 1929, 8.
24. Don Gazzaway, "Conversations with Buster Smith," *The Jazz Review* (December 1960): 12.
25. Interview with Bus Moten, *Coda* (undated).

26. Born Edward Durham, San Marcos, Texas, August 19, 1906.

27. Stanley Dance, *The World of Count Basie* (New York: C. Scribner's Sons, 1985), 61.

28. George Hoeffer, "Held Notes Eddie Durham," *Down Beat*, July 19, 1962, 54.

29. Count Basie, *Good Morning Blues* (New York: Random House, 1985), 113–14.

30. Ibid., 114.

31. Ibid., 122.

32. Ibid., 116.

33. Nat Hentoff, "Jimmy Rushing," *Down Beat*, March 6, 1957, 20, 66.

34. "George Lee and Bennie Moten in Contest Next Monday Night," *Kansas City Call*, December 27, 1929, 10.

35. Earl Wilkins, "Dance Gossip," *Kansas City Call*, April 11, 1930, 10.

36. Earl Wilkins, "Dance Gossip," *Kansas City Call*, July 25, 1930, 9.

37. "Cotton Pickers Band, Finest of Negro Orchestra, Are Here," *Kansas City Call*, January 10, 1930, 2.

38. "Kansas City Falls on Face Before Onslaught of New York Jungle Band," August 1, 1930, 9.

39. Brian Rust's *Jazz Records 1897–1942* (New Rochelle, NY: Arlington House, 1978) lists Oran "Hot Lips" Page as a member of the group. However, this was not the case. According to reports and personnel listings in the *Kansas City Call*, Page did not join the group until February 1931.

40. According to coverage of the recording session in the *Kansas City Call* on November 7, the band recorded five more selections than what are listed in Rust's book, including: "Baby Mine," "High and Dry," "Elsie," "Long Introduction," and "Zella Mae," written by Basie and Durham for Moten's daughter. Evidently, these wax masters were held back and never submitted to Victor.

41. Earl Wilkins, "Dance Gossip," *Kansas City Call*, January 16, 1931, 7.

42. Earl Wilkins, "Dance Gossip," *Kansas City Call*, March 13, 1931, 7.

43. Kirk, "My Story," 16.

44. Ibid., 14.

45. Earl Wilkins, "Dance Gossip," *Kansas City Call*, April 3, 1931, 10.

46. "At the Lafayette Theatre," *New York Age*, April 11, 1931, 6.

47. "Lafayette Theatre," *New York Age*, April 25, 1931, 6.

48. Williams in Jones, *Talking Jazz*, 188.

49. "Post-Midnight Stomp is Set for Tomorrow," *Kansas City Call*, May 22, 1931, 10.

50. Dance, *World of Count Basie*, 62–63.

51. "Greatest Band Battle Yet Staged," *Kansas City Call*, June 26, 1931, 7.

52. Earl Wilkins, "Dance Gossip," *Kansas City Call*, July 3, 1931, 8.

53. Basie, *Good Morning*, 132–33.

54. Ed Lewis as told to Frank Driggs, "Ed Lewis' Story," *The Jazz Review* (June 1959): 24.

55. Earl Wilkins, "Dance Gossip," *Kansas City Call*, January 15, 1932, 7B.

6. MOTEN'S SWING

1. The personnel of the revamped Moten band included: Bennie Moten and Bill Basie, piano; Buster Moten, director and accordion; Buster Berry, banjo; Jack Washington, baritone saxophone; Ben Webster, tenor saxophone; Eddie Barefield, alto saxophone and clarinet; Walter Page, string bass and sousaphone; James Rushing, vocals; Elmer Crumbley, trombone; Eddie Durham, trombone and guitar; Willie McWashington, drums; and Oran Page, Joe Smith, and Joe Keyes, trumpets.

2. Hot Lips Page as told to Kay C. Thompson, "Kansas City Man," *Record Changer* (December 1949): 18.

3. Walter Page as told to Frank Driggs, "About My Life in Music," *The Jazz Review* (November 1958): 14.

4. Stanley Dance, *The World of Count Basie* (New York: C. Scribner's Sons, 1985), 63.

5. "The Band in Two Parties Before Going," *Kansas City Call*, February 19, 1932, 7B.

6. "Hayes Organizes New Band with Men from Moten, Lee," *Kansas City Call*, February 19, 1932, 1B.

7. Nathan W. Pearson, Jr., *Goin' to Kansas City* (Chicago: University of Illinois Press, 1987), 152.

8. The union staged the ball to support modifying the Volstead Act to make beer and wine legal.

9. Advertisement for Musicians Ball, *Kansas City Call*, March 4, 1932, 7B.

10. Pearson, *Goin' to Kansas City*, 156.

11. Ibid., 157.

12. "Nine Crack Bands to Play for Musicians Ball on Monday," *Kansas City Call*, March 4, 1932, 7B.

13. Earl Wilkins, "Dance Gossip," *Kansas City Call*, March 11, 1932, 7B.

14. Count Basie, *Good Morning Blues* (New York: Random House, 1985), 137–38.

15. Pearson, *Goin' to Kansas City*, 157.

16. Earl Wilkins, "Dance Gossip," *Kansas City Call*, March 11, 1932, 7B.

17. Earl Wilkins, "Dance Gossip," *Kansas City Call*, April 1, 1932, 7B.

18. Earl Wilkins, "Dance Gossip," *Kansas City Call*, April 29, 1932, 10B.

19. Andy Kirk as told to Frank Driggs, "My Story," *The Jazz Review* (February 1959): 15.

20. "Uncle Sam's Padlock Sends Musicians Club Down and Out," *Kansas City Call*, July 4, 1930, 9.

21. "New Night Club, Hawaiian Gardens Opens Tomorrow," *Kansas City Call*, July 15, 1932, 5B.

22. Whitney Balliett, *American Singers: Twenty-Seven Portraits in Song* (New York: Oxford University Press, 1988), 47–48.

23. Johnson was born March, 24, 1904, and Turner, May 18, 1911.

24. Pete Johnson as told to Jonny Simmen, "My Life My Music," *Jazz Journal* (August 1959): 8.

25. Murl Johnson interview in *The Pete Johnson Story* (New York–Frankfurt, 1965), 33. Publisher is Blues Unlimited Magazine, compiled and edited by Hans J. Mauerer.

26. Balliett, *American Singers*, 46.

27. Ibid., 47–48.

28. Andy Kirk, "My Story," 16.

29. Basie, *Good Morning*, 141.

30. Dance, *World of Count Basie*. 320.

31. Ibid., 319, 321.

32. See Gunther Schuller, *Early Jazz: Its Roots and Musical Development* (New York: Oxford University Press, 1968), 313.

33. See Fredrick R. Swischer, *Kansas City Jazz, 1923-1937: The Music*, unpublished dissertation (D.M.A.), Special Collections, Miller Nichols Library, University of Missouri–Kansas City, 118–26.

34. Basie, *Good Morning*, 144.

35. "Bennie Moten in Home Coming Dance Friday," *Kansas City American*, December 29, 1932, 7.
36. Pearson, *Goin' to Kansas City*, 71.
37. "Gala Opening for Cherry Blossom Soon," *Kansas City Call*, March 17, 1933, 3B.
38. "1,176 Attend Opening of New Cherry Blossom Club," *Kansas City Call*, April 14, 1933, 3B.
39. Basie, *Good Morning*, 145–46.
40. "Count Basie Now Owner of Bennie Moten's Band," *Kansas City Call*, September 15, 1933, 3B.
41. The personnel of the Basie band included: Joe Keyes, first trumpet; Dee Stewart, second trumpet; Oran Page, third trumpet; Dan Minor, first trombone; Eddie Durham, second trombone; Henry Smith, first saxophone; Herschel Evans, second saxophone; Jack Washington, third saxophone; Willie McWashington, drums; Clifford McTier, guitar; Walter Page, bass violin; William "Count" Basie, piano; and James Rushing, vocalist.
42. The personnel of the Moten band included: Tommy Douglas, first saxophone; Jesse Washington, second saxophone; Robert L Mabane, third saxophone; Rozelle Claxton, piano; Joe Smith, first trumpet; Clarence Davis, second trumpet; Charles Rousseau, third trumpet, guitar, and violin; Eddie Morant, first trombone; Eddie Durham, second trombone, guitar, and violin; Jap Allen, bass violin and sousaphone; Jesse M. Price, drums; Buster Moten, accordion and director; and James Phillips, guitar and violin. "Bennie Moten Announces Formation of New Band," *Kansas City Call*, September 29, 1933, 3B.
43. "Night Club Notes," *Kansas City Journal-Post*, October 28, 1933, 7.
44. The Labor Temple, a standby for local bands, could not accommodate the crowds attracted by national bands such as Duke Ellington, Louis Armstrong, Claude Hopkins, and the immensely popular Cab Calloway. The previous June, Calloway had attracted 6,000 fans to Convention Hall.
45. "Roseland Ballroom to Have Negro Patronage," *Kansas City Call*, October 27, 1933, 13.
46. "Crowd of Five Hundred Hears Fletcher Henderson," *Kansas City Call*, December 22, 1933, 11.
47. Basie, *Good Morning*, 148–49.
48. Mary Lou Williams interview in Max Jones, *Talking Jazz* (New York: W.W. Norton, 1988), 192.
49. Dance, *World of Count Basie*, 266–67.
50. Ibid., 268.
51. "Mrs. Vivian Winn Basie Asks Divorce," *Kansas City Call*, January 26, 1934, 1.
52. Pearson, *Goin' to Kansas City*, 158.
53. Ibid.
54. Ibid., 159.
55. Advertisement for the Eastside Musicians Club, *Kansas City Call*, November 9, 1934, 13.
56. Dave Dexter, Jr., "Kaycee Local 627 Prospered During 1930 Boom Days," *Down Beat*, January 15, 1941, 8.
57. Pearson, *Goin' to Kansas City*, 97–98.
58. There were two Piney Browns. Thomas was known as Big Piney, while the wiry Walter was known as Little Piney. Their nicknames were drawn from their hometown, Pine Bluff, Arkansas. After moving to Kansas City in 1917, the two went to work for Felix Payne, running smoke shops and shine parlors on 12th Street that served as fronts for gambling. Reuben Benton, secretary-treasurer of the

Kansas City Call, summed up the difference between the two brothers. "Now, Big Piney was the important one, but Little Piney was the popular one, the notorious one." A noted athlete, Big Piney competed in national tennis tournaments and led his semi-pro baseball team, the Kansas City Royals, to several city championships. His legitimate business interests included the first metered African American taxicab company in Kansas City, the Panama Taxi Company. After selling his taxi company, Big Piney wisely invested his money in the Homer Roberts Automobile Company, installing himself as vice president. Well established in Kansas City, the company expanded to Chicago, with plans to open another showroom in Cleveland, Ohio. In 1929, Piney moved to Chicago, where he died suddenly from stomach ulcers in August 1932. Little Piney escorted his brother's body back to Kansas City, where it lay in state at the home of his good friend and tennis partner, Felix Payne. After Big Piney's death, Little Piney became known simply as Piney.

59. Pearson, *Goin' to Kansas City*, 98.
60. Andy Kirk, *Twenty Years on Wheels* (Ann Arbor: University of Michigan Press, 1989), 68.
61. Early in the morning on May 26, 1930, while traveling with her brother George's band, Lee survived an accident that killed saxophonist Clarence "Tweedy" Taylor. Years later the group's trumpeter Sam Utterback related the misfortune to Kip Lornell:

> We had finished an engagement in Topeka Kansas. We were on our way back to Kansas City. We were supposed to get paid in Kansas City and George E. Lee had the money, so we were in a hurry to get home. . . . He [Johnny Thomas] had been driving at over a hundred miles per hour; he owned the car and was married to Julia Lee. . . . He had a brand-new Auburn convertible, a six passenger with leather seats and a canvas top. It must have been about four o'clock in the morning. The car did a dipsy-doodle, and turned over in the highway. It landed in the ditch, tore off the cover of the car, and threw Julia half-way from the front seat to the back seat, one leg was pinned down in the dirt. That's when "Tweedy" . . . got a puncture in the skull. They took him right away; when they came to pick him up, he was already dead. He'd been saying, "there's something pressing in my head, pressing in my head!" He didn't realize he was already dying. I was a lucky man, nothing but a cut finger. The car was still running like mad, and Johnny was in there pinned behind the steering wheel, and he was cursing. His wife [Julia Lee] said, "Stop that cursing, cut that motor off, and pray!"

> The tragic incident ended Julia Lee's desire to travel. From then on, she declined opportunities to tour, simply stating she would travel if she could "keep one foot on the ground." Sam Utterback's quote is taken from Kip Lornell, "From Panama's Cabaret to Small's Paradise: Samuel Utterbach's [*sic*] Jazz Odyssey," *Storyville* 125 (June-July 1986): 178–79.

62. "Record Crowd Celebrates at Musicians Annual Ball," *Kansas City Call*, March 15, 1935, 11.
63. Ed Lewis as told to Frank Driggs, "Ed Lewis' Story," *The Jazz Review* (June 1959): 24.
64. Herbert L. Henegan, "Thousands at Funeral for Bennie Moten," *Kansas City Call*, April 12, 1935, 1.
65. Pearson, *Goin' to Kansas City*, 129.

7. UNTIL THE REAL THING COMES ALONG

1. Count Basie as told to Albert Murray, *Good Morning Blues* (New York: Random House, 1985), 156.
2. Nathan W. Pearson, Jr., *Goin' to Kansas City* (Chicago: University of Illinois Press, 1987), 132.
3. Advertisement for Club Reno, *Kansas City Journal-Post*, October 26, 1935, 7.
4. Basie, *Good Morning*, 162.
5. Richard J. Smith, "Jazz Festival Tonight: The Reno Club Reunion," *Star Sunday Magazine of the Kansas City Star*, April 29, 1973, 10–14.
6. Vertna Saunders, interview by Frank Driggs, St. Louis, Missouri, September 26, 1978.
7. Buddy Tate as told to Frank Driggs, "My Story," *The Jazz Review* (December 1958): 19–20.
8. Max Jones, *Talking Jazz* (New York: W.W. Norton, 1988), 194.
9. Jones, *Talking Jazz*, 195.
10. Andy Kirk as told to Frank Driggs, "My Story," *The Jazz Review* (February 1959): 15–16.
11. "(It Will Have To Do) Until the Real Thing Comes Along," words and music by Sammy Cahn, Saul Chaplin, L. E. Freeman, Mann Holiner, and Alberta Nichols, Chappell & Co., Inc., 1936.
12. "Crowd Hears Lunceford and Kirk at Paseo," *Kansas City Call*, May 22, 1936, 9.
13. According to the Missouri State Climatologist F. Adan Akyur, Ph.D., the temperature exceeded 100 degrees for five days in June, twenty-one days in July, and eighteen days in August.
14. "Basie's Fine Music from One of Town's Worst Dives," *Down Beat*, July 1936, 2, 5. *Down Beat* was published monthly at this time. Shortly after Dexter joined *Down Beat*, he convinced the owners to go bi-monthly.
15. John Hammond, *John Hammond on Record* (New York: Ridge Press-Summit Books, 1977), 168, 170.
16. John Hammond, "Kansas City a Hot-Bed for Fine Swing Musicians," *Down Beat*, September 1936, 1, 9.
17. Don Gazzaway, "Buster and Bird: Conversations with Buster Smith Part III," *The Jazz Review* (February 1960): 13.
18. Basie, *Good Morning*, 170.
19. Ibid.
20. "Over 2,000 Jam Paseo Hall to Hear Ellington and Well Known Band," *Kansas City Call*, November 11, 1936, 14.
21. Chuck Haddix, "The Fiddler's Triumph," *Down Beat*, March 1999, 34.
22. Basie, *Good Morning*, 177.
23. Stanley Dance, *World of Count Basie* (New York: DaCapo Press, 1985), 42.
24. George Simon, "Dance Band Revues," *Metronome* (January 1937): 26.
25. "Count Basie Is Big Hit in Chicago," *Kansas City Call*, December 4, 1936, 9.
26. Count Basie quoted in the liner notes to "The Lester Young Story Volume 1," Columbia CG 33502, 1976.
27. See Fredrick R. Swischer, *Kansas City Jazz, 1923–1937: The Music*, unpublished dissertation (D.M.A.), Special Collections, Miller Nichols Library, University of Missouri–Kansas City, 170–75.
28. George Simon, "Dance Band Revues," *Metronome* (February 1937): 24.
29. Basie, *Good Morning*, 200.
30. Ibid., 199.

31. See Swischer, *Kansas City Jazz*, 202–8.
32. Benny Goodman, *The Kingdom of Swing* (New York: Stackpole Sons, 1939), 236.
33. Kirk, "My Story," 17.
34. Ibid., 15, 16.
35. Leon Hardwick, "Another Hit Tune Is Made by Andy Kirk," *Kansas City Call*, March 26, 1937, 13.
36. Simon, "Dance Band Revues," 26.
37. Kirk, "My Story," 16.
38. Andy Kirk, *Twenty Years on Wheels* (Ann Arbor: University of Michigan Press, 1989), 89.
39. Mary Lou Williams quotes in Max Jones, *Talking Jazz* (New York: W. W. Norton, 1988), 1960.
40. "H. Leonard Now Leader of New Band," *Kansas City Call*, February 5, 1937, 11.
41. Pearson, *Goin' to Kansas City*, 159–60.
42. The personnel of the new Kansas City Rockets included: Darwin Jones, Freddie Culliver, and James Keith, saxophones; James Ross, Edward Johnson, and Sidney Miller, trumpets; Richmond Henderson, trombone; Ben Curtis, bass; Robert Wilson, piano and vocals; and Edward "Lil Phil" Phillips, drums.

8. ROLL 'EM, PETE

1. Jay McShann, interview by Chuck Haddix, June 26, 1997, Kansas City, Missouri.
2. Various sources cite James Columbus McShann's year of birth as 1909, but according to McShann, January 12, 1916, is the correct date. The date is confirmed by early coverage of his career in the *Kansas City Call* and *Down Beat*.
3. McShann, interview.
4. Jay McShann as told to Frank Driggs, "Jay McShann Relates His Musical Career," *Jazz Monthly* 4, 1 (1958): 5.
5. Stanley Dance, *The World of Count Basie* (New York: DaCapo Press, 1985), 250.
6. According to a January 6, 1958, telegram from Jay McShann to Frank Driggs the personnel included: Henry Gray and Howard McGhee, trumpets; Hunter Gray, alto saxophone; Pal Tillman, tenor saxophone; Homer Woods, bass; Oscar Clark, drums; and Bill Powell, baton.
7. See Robert Smith Bader, *Prohibition in Kansas: A History* (Lawrence: University Press of Kansas, 1986), 227–29.
8. McShann, interview.
9. Dave E. Dexter, Jr., "Kansas City," *Metronome* (March 1937): 45.
10. McShann, interview.
11. Born Charles Parker, August 29, 1920.
12. Mrs. Parker is first listed in *Polk's Kansas City Directory* in 1934.
13. See Gary Giddins, *Celebrating Bird: The Triumph of Charlie Parker* (New York: Beech Tree Books, 1987), 28.
14. Robert Reisner, *Bird: The Legend of Charlie Parker* (New York: DaCapo Press, 1962), 158.
15. Reisner, *Bird*, 78.
16. Dave E. Dexter, Jr., *The Jazz Story: From the '90s to the '60s* (Englewood Cliffs, NJ: Prentice-Hall, 1964): 146.
17. Stan Britt, "The First Lady of Jazz," *Jazz Journal International* 34, 9 (1981): 11–12.

18. Reisner, *Bird*, 129.

19. "Young Orchestra Rapidly Increasing in Popularity," *Kansas City Call*, September 20, 1935, 9, lists the personnel: Keyes, pianist and arranger; Vernon Walker, Charles Parker, and Milton Chapman, saxophones; Wendell Oliver, Ed McDowell, and William Smith, trumpets; Robert Simpson, trombone; Ernest Daniels, drums; Wilfred Berry, guitar; Charles Forrester, bass; Elmer Brown, conductor; and Bernard Jackson, business manager.

20. According to records supplied by Richard Albrecht, secretary, treasurer, and CEO of American Federation of Musicians Union Local 34-627, Parker joined the union on October 31, 1935. Parker maintained his affiliation until July 5, 1945, when he was suspended for nonpayment of dues.

21. Reisner, *Bird*, 185.

22. Ibid., 185–86.

23. "Auto Mishap Is Fatal to G. W. Wilkerson," *Kansas City Call*, December 4, 1936, 1, 15.

24. Reisner, *Bird*, 76.

25. Dance, *World of Count Basie*, 274.

26. The lineup of Stewart's band included: Dee Stewart and Bob Hall, trumpets; Buster Smith, Ed Hale, and Odell West, reeds; Jesse Price, drums; and Billy Hadnott, bass.

27. McShann, interview.

28. Jay McShann as told to John Anthony Brisbin, "I Always Thought Blues and Jazz Went Together," *Living Blues* (January/February 2000): 19.

29. Don Gazzaway, "Buster and Bird: Conversations with Buster Smith Part III," *The Jazz Review* (February 1960): 14.

30. Gazzaway, "Buster and Bird," 13.

31. "Basie Plays for 3,100 Dance Fans," *Kansas City Call*, April 15, 1938, 14.

32. William M. Reddig, *Tom's Town: Kansas City and the Pendergast Legend* (New York: J. B. Lippincott Company, 1947), 279–80.

33. C. C. Nicolet, "National Crime Capital," article from vertical clipping file in Special Collections, Downtown Branch, Kansas City Public Library, July 15, 1933.

34. See Reddig, *Tom's Town*, 295–96.

35. Westbrook Pegler, "Westbrook Pegler Says—," *Kansas City Journal-Post*," February 19, 1938, 18.

36. McShann, interview.

37. Born Eugene Glasco Ramey, April 4, 1913.

38. Dance, *World of Count Basie*, 267–68.

39. E. LeRoy Brown, Jr., "These Names Make the News," *Kansas City Call*, May 6, 1938, 14.

40. "Down Beat in Tribute to the 'Countess,'" *Kansas City Call*, August 11, 1939, 17.

41. Dance, *World of Count Basie*, 267.

42. "International Sweethearts of Rhythm Gain Prominence with Their Unique Band," *Kansas City Call*, September 1, 1939, 16.

43. Dance, *World of Count Basie*, 271.

44. Dave E. Dexter, Jr., "Notes From the Night Clubs," *Kansas City Journal-Post*, May 28, 1938, 5.

45. Mary Lee Hester, *Going to Kansas City* (Sherman, TX: Early Bird Press, 1980), 138.

46. Marge Johnson, "My Man . . . Pete Johnson," *The Pete Johnson Story* (U.S. and Europe Fund Raising Project for Pete Johnson: New York-Frankfurt, 1965),

14–15. Publisher is Blues Unlimited Magazine, compiled and edited by Hans J. Mauerer.

47. The band included: Robert Wilson, piano; Ben Curtis, bass; Burney Cobb, guitar; Edward Phillips, drums; Harlan Leonard, Freddie Culliver, Darwin Jones, and James Keith, reeds; James Ross, Sidney Miller, and Edward Johnson, trumpets; and Richmond Henderson, trombone.

48. E. Leroy Brown, Jr., "These Names Make the News," *Kansas City Call*, October 1, 1937, 8.

49. E. Leroy Brown, Jr., "These Names Make the News," *Kansas City Call*, June 24, 1938, 5.

50. E. Leroy Brown, Jr., "'Hot Bed' of Swing May Send Another Sensation Out Soon," *Kansas City Call*, August 19, 1938, 16.

51. "M. C. A. Executive Comes Here to Hear Leonard's Kansas City Rockets," *Kansas City Call*, October 21, 1938, 9.

52. E. Leroy Brown, Jr., "These Names Make the News," *Kansas City Call*, October 28, 1938, 17.

53. See Giddins, *Celebrating Bird*, 46–50.

54. Dave E. Dexter, Jr., "Entertainment News from Night Clubs," *Kansas City Journal-Post*, August 6, 1938, 5.

55. Advertisement for Gold Crown Tap Room, *Kansas City Call*, November 11, 1938, 13.

56. JoAnn Leonard, *Harlan Leonard and His Rockets*, a compilation from his scrapbooks.

57. E. Leroy Brown, Jr., "These Names Make the News," *Kansas City Call*, December 9, 1938, 8.

58. The band included: Jesse Price, drums; Rozelle Claxton, piano; Winston Williams, bass; Odell West, tenor saxophone; Charlie Parker, alto saxophone; and William "Sleepy" Tomlin, trumpet.

59. Parker played the show's premiere the previous May, with the Buster Smith band, but did not merit special mention in the publicity.

60. "Prince Zulong In Return to V.S.V.," *Kansas City Call*, December 16, 1938, 9.

61. Ad for Harlan Leonard Band, *Kansas City Call*, December 23, 1938, 9.

62. Local legend has it Parker gave Dexter a hot foot at Local 627.

63. Dave E. Dexter, Jr., *The Jazz Story* (Englewood Cliffs, NJ: Prentice-Hall, Inc., 1964), 145, 155.

64. Bill Lane, "Harlan Leonard Recalls," *Los Angeles Sentinel Entertainment*, April 9, 1970, B-1.

65. John Hammond, *John Hammond on Record* (New York: Ridge Press-Summit Books, 1977), 210.

66. Howard H. Taubman, "Negro Music Given at Carnegie Hall," *New York Times*, December 24, 1938, 13.

67. Hammond, *John Hammond on Record*, 203.

68. Lloyd Stark, "The Governor's Call for Law Enforcement," *Kansas City Star*, December 23, 1938, 1.

69. E. Leroy Brown, "These Names Make the News," *Kansas City Call*, February 10, 1939, 16.

70. Redding, *Tom's Town*, 323–31.

71. Ibid., 327.

72. Bill Bagby, "Famed Singer Becomes Pawn in Agreement," *Kansas City Call*, January 10, 1941, 1–2.

73. Milton Morris recounted the incident to Haddix during the course of many conversations at his club, Milton's Tap Room, during the late 1970s.

9. HOOTIE'S BLUES

1. Dave E. Dexter, Jr., *Playback* (New York: Billboard Publications, 1976), 40.
2. Dave E. Dexter, Jr., "Sensation in 'Windy City,'" *Kansas City Call*, February 24, 1938, 16.
3. Dexter, "Sensation."
4. Considering the band's amateurish performance on the discs, it is surprising Bluebird signed the band sight unseen. After locating the discs in California, collector and historian Ken Poston supplied copies to Driggs. Much to Driggs's surprise, the discs contain lackluster performances of standards.
5. E. LeRoy Brown, Jr., "These Names Make News," *Kansas City Call*, May 12, 1939, 16.
6. "The New Records," *Down Beat*, April 1, 1940, 14.
7. Myra Taylor, interview by Chuck Haddix, Kansas City, Missouri, July 18, 2000.
8. Ibid.
9. Sharon A. Pease, "Swing Piano Styles," *Down Beat*, July 1939, 22.
10. The band at the time included: Earl Jackson, alto saxophone; William Scott, tenor saxophone; Bob Mabane, tenor saxophone; Orville "Piggy" Minor, a one-man trumpet section specializing in playing two trumpets at once; Gene Ramey, bass; Gus Johnson, drums; and Joe Coleman, vocals.
11. Jay McShann, interview by Chuck Haddix, Kansas City, Missouri, July 3, 1997.
12. Jay McShann interview, June 26, 1997.
13. Don Gazzaway, "Buster and Bird: Conversations with Buster Smith Part III," *The Jazz Review* (February 1960): 14.
14. Nat Shapiro and Nat Hentoff, *Hear Me Talkin' To Ya* (New York: Rinehart & Company, 1955), 354.
15. M. Levin and J. S. Wilson, "No Bop Roots in Jazz," *Down Beat*, September 9, 1949, 12.
16. Carl Woideck, *Charlie Parker: His Music and Life* (Ann Arbor: University of Michigan Press, 1996), 18.
17. Robert Reisner, *Bird: The Legend of Charlie Parker* (New York: DaCapo Press, 1962), 162.
18. McShann initially recalled Parker joining his band after a battle with the Leonard band on Easter, but the two bands never battled in Kansas City. When prompted by coverage of the event in the *Kansas City Call*, McShann remembered that it was the Keyes band. In an interview by Reisner, Keyes clearly identified Parker as a member of the Deans of Swing.
19. Jay McShann as told to Frank Driggs, "Jay McShann Relates His Musical Career," *Jazz Monthly* (January 1958): 6.
20. McShann, interview, June 26, 1997.
21. Bob Locke, "Scab Bandsmen Laugh Up Their Sleeves in K.C.," *Down Beat*, July 15, 1940, 20.
22. "Rockets Popular in East: To Make More Recordings, Two Musicians are Added," *Kansas City Call*, April 15, 1940, 17.
23. "Top Swing Vocalist in Entire Midwest," *Kansas City Call*, May 31, 1940, 15.
24. Bob Locke, "11,300 Dance to Miller in Kansas City," *Down Beat*, August 15, 1940, 21.
25. McShann interview, June 26, 1997.
26. Eric Barnouw, *The Golden Web: A History of Broadcasting in the United States, Volume II–1933 to 1953* (New York: Oxford University Press, 1966), 110.
27. "Leonard Ork Sunday Night Dates Set," *Kansas City Call*, January 10, 1941, 7.

28. "New Song Written Years Ago," *Kansas City Call*, October 3, 1941, 13.

29. Landon Laird, "K.C. Reunion in New York," reprinted from *Kansas City Times* by the *Kansas City Call*, January 3, 1941, 13.

30. Dave E. Dexter, Jr., liner notes from *Kansas City Jazz*, Decca Album No. 214, 6.

31. Ibid., 7.

32. Dexter, *Playback*, 60.

33. Dexter, *Kansas City Jazz*, 10–11.

34. Ibid., 13.

35. Ibid., 7.

36. Ibid., 8.

37. Ibid., 11.

38. Ibid., 5.

39. Minor and Anderson insisted that Jackson was superior to Parker as an improvisor, according to numerous unrecorded conversations with Chuck Haddix.

40. Reisener, *Bird*, 187–88.

41. Lawrence O. Koch, *Yardbird Suite: A Compendium of the Music and Life of Charlie Parker* (Bowling Green, OH: Bowling Green State University Press, 1988), 25–26.

42. Dizzy Gillespie, *To Be or Not to Bop* (Garden City, NY: Doubleday & Company, 1979), 117–18.

43. Ibid., 117.

44. Ibid., 110.

45. Stanley Dance, *The World of Count Basie* (New York: DaCapo Press, 1985), 271.

46. McShann, interview, July 3, 1997.

47. Reisener, *Bird*, 150.

48. McShann, interview, July 3, 1997.

49. Ibid.

50. Dance, *World of Count Basie*, 275.

51. McShann interview, July 3, 1997.

52. "1941 Record Sales to Hit 120 Million—Sacks," *Down Beat*, December 1, 1941, 15.

53. Mike Morales, "Kaycee Ork Outsells Big Names on Wax, Outdraws at Proms," *Down Beat*, November 4, 1941, 4.

54. McShann, interview, July 3, 1997.

55. Dance, *World of Count Basie*, 276.

56. McShann, interview, July 3, 1997.

57. Barry Ulanov, "Band Reviews," *Metronome* (March 1942): 12, 22.

58. McShann, interview, July 3, 1997.

59. Dance, *World of Count Basie*, 277.

60. Bob Locke, "Leonard is Sensation (But Not in Kaycee)," *Down Beat*, August 15, 1941, 16.

61. "Harlan Leonard Hires Flashy Girl Pianist," *Down Beat*, December 15, 1941, 28.

62. Myra Taylor, interview by Chuck Haddix, September 18, 2000.

63. Bob Locke, "Put Full McShann Ork on Wax," *Down Beat*, July 1, 1942, 4.

64. "Sepian Bounce" was originally released on the 78 rpm disc as "Sepian Stomp," but listed as "Sepian Bounce" on subsequent reissues.

65. Dance, *World of Count Basie*, 253.

66. Ibid., 277.

67. Clyde Bernhardt, *I Remember: Eighty Years of Black Entertainment, Big Bands, and the Blues* (Philadelphia: University of Pennsylvania Press, 1986), 154–55.

68. McShann, interview, June 26, 1987.

69. See liner notes for *Central Avenue Sounds: Jazz in Los Angeles (1921–1956)* (Los Angeles: Rhino Records).

70. Bill Lane, "Harlan Leonard Recalls: Regrets Missing Top," *Los Angeles Sentinel Entertainment*, April 9, 1970, B-1-A.

71. Bernhardt, *I Remember*, 156.

72. McShann, interview, July 3, 1997.

73. McShann, interview, June 26, 1997.

EPILOGUE

1. Jay McShann interviewed by John Anthony Brisbin, "Music Was a Good Life: Part Two of a Two Part Interview," *Living Blues* (May-April 2000): 51.

2. For the next fourteen years, Lee churned out risqué hits, becoming one of Capitol's best-selling artists. One of her first big hits, "Snatch and Grab It," went on to sell over 500,000 copies, without the benefit of any radio play. Unfortunately, Julia did not capitalize on the popularity of her recordings because of her fear of traveling. Refusing to tour in support of her recordings, Julia continued working at Milton Morris's taproom and other joints in Kansas City for tips throughout the twilight of her career, ending with her death in December 1958.

3. Advertisement for Scott's Theatre-Restaurant in the *Kansas City Call*, October 6, 1944, 8.

4. Jay McShann, interview by Chuck Haddix, Kansas City, Missouri, July 3, 1997.

5. Barry Ulanov, "New York Roundup," *Metronome* (February 1945): 13.

6. "Names Change But Street Still Jumps," *Down Beat*, February 15, 1945, 3.

7. McShann, interview, July 3, 1997.

8. Andy Kirk as told to Frank Driggs, "My Story," *The Jazz Review* (February 1959).

9. Max Jones, *Talking Jazz* (New York: W. W. Norton, 1988), 198.

10. Ibid., 201.

11. Count Basie, *Good Morning Blues* (New York: Random House, 1985), 282.

12. Chris Sheridan, *Count Basie: A Bio-Discography* (New York: Greenwood Press, 1986), 325–26.

13. Jay McShann, "Music Was a Good Life."

14. Joe Zammer, "Kaycee Club Biz 'At Fever Pitch,'" *Down Beat*, July 28, 1950, 5.

15. Durrett remained active as a bandleader until 1986.

16. Arch Martin, interview by Chuck Haddix, Kansas City, Missouri, December 16, 2003.

17. Robert Reisner, *Bird: The Legend of Charlie Parker* (New York: DaCapo Press, 1962), 68.

18. Ira Gitler, *Swing to Bop* (New York: Oxford University Press, 1985), 148.

19. Dizzy Gillespie, *To Be or Not to Bop* (Garden City, NY: Doubleday & Company, Inc., 1979), 231–32.

20. M. Levin and J. S. Wilson, "No Bop Roots in Jazz," *Down Beat*, September 9, 1949, 1.

21. "Apple Combats Hot Weather with Hot Jazz," *Down Beat*, August 1, 1945, 3.

22. Ross Russell, *Bird Lives: The High Life and Hard Times of Charlie (Yardbird) Parker* (New York: Charterhouse, 1973), 224–30.

23. Jay McShann as told to John Anthony Brisbin, "Music Was a Good Life!," *Living Blues* (March/April 2000): 54.

24. McShann recorded "The Duke and the Brute" and "You Got Me Begging" for the Mercury label with Ben Webster in Kansas City on October 27, 1951. Walter Bruyninckx, *60 Years of Recorded Jazz, 1917–1977* (Mechelen, Belgium: Bruyninckx, 1979), M175.

25. Ahmet Ertegun, *"What'd I Say": The Atlantic Story—50 Years of Music* (New York: Welcome Rain Press, 2001), 56–57, 69, 528.

26. Oscar "Lucky" Wesley, interview by Chuck Haddix, Kansas City, Missouri, April 28, 2002.

Acknowledgments

My PARTICULAR THANKS go to the subjects of the interviews who provided details that filled out the history of Kansas City's musical growth and development and eventual decline: Mr. and Mrs. Richard Smith, Jay McShann, Ed Lewis, Buddy Tate, Andy and Mary Kirk, Clarence Love, Paul Banks, Baby Lovett, Eddie Barefield, Budd Johnson, Ben Smith, Jesse Stone, Tommy Douglas, Thamon Hayes, Murl Johnson, Marshall W. Stearns, Eddie Durham, Ben Webster, Kenny Rickman, Elmer Payne, Buddy Anderson, Orville Minor, Dan Minor, Buster Smith, Curtyse Foster, Bill Saunders, Herman Walder, Girard T. Bryant, Bill Martin, Paul King, Bill Searcy, Lowell Pointer, Charles Goodwin, Booker Washington, Cliff Haliburton, Roy Hatfield, Thurman Rotroff, Floyd Estep, Bud Calvert, Pee Wee Erwin, and Warren Durrett. I also thank Jean-Pierre Battestini and Ken Poston. A special bow of gratitude to Margaret M. Maley, former film director of KMBC-TV. And thanks especially to Sheldon Meyer, and to Kim Robinson, Joellyn Ausanka, and Anne Holmes at Oxford University Press.

Frank Driggs

THANKS FIRST AND FOREMOST to Sheldon Meyer, an editor with the patience of Penelope and wisdom of Socrates. Kudos to Bob Porter, Bruce Ricker, and Russ Dantzler for helping introduce me to Frank and vice versa. Special thanks to Frederick R. Swischer for sharing his unpublished dissertation, a pioneering musical analysis of Kansas City Jazz and major contribution to the musical analyses in this history. Many thanks go as well to Gaylord Marr, Bill Tuttle, Joan Dean, Scott O'Kelley, Scott Roley Dude, Margaret Pushcheck, Dory DeAngelo, and E. C. Boldridge, the unofficial editors of the manuscript, for their guidance and good counsel; Stuart Hinds, regional reference coordinator of the Johnson County Library in Kansas, for his faith, encouragement, and help from the beginning; Bill Osment and the staffs of Special Collections and Document Delivery at the downtown branch of the Kansas City Public Library for service above and beyond the call of duty; Denise Morrison, archivist for the Kansas City Museum and Union Station, for her generous spirit and outstanding stewardship of Kansas City's rich history; and the staff at Western Historical Manuscripts Collection in Kansas City. I am grateful to Dick, Davey, Marjie, and the rest of the family of Dave E. Dexter, Jr., for their support of this project, in particular, Dave's brother Dick for his close reading of the early manuscript, unwavering friendship, and mastery of punctuation. Thanks as well to JoAnn Leonard and family for their help in telling Harlan Leonard's story, and to Ted Sheldon, Helen Spalding, Marilyn Carbonell, Charlie Stout, Rob Ray, Barb Croft, Pat Payne, Kevin McCarrison, and the rest of the staff of the Miller Nichols Library at UMKC for their steadfast support of this project. Likewise, I thank Norm Saks for his enthusiasm, goodwill, and invaluable insight into Charlie Parker. I give tribute to Annie Chambers, Felix Payne, and Winston Holmes, three hustlers, who contributed greatly to the character and color of Kansas City. These flowers are for Myra Taylor, Jay McShann, Claude Williams, Arch Martin, Arthur Jackson, Tim Whitmer, Rusty Tucker, Luqman Hamza, Lucky Wesley, Monte Nash, Eddie Saunders, and the other Kaycee cats keeping the tradition alive. Thanks to Zola Gordy, Mikey Randall, Preston Dunham, and David Conn for their good humor, steady friendship, and inspiration. I am grateful to my father, Jack Haddix, who always believed in me; my uncles, Robert Haddix and Sam McDowell, who first inspired me to be a writer; my mother, Betty, and stepfather, Tom Schnell; my brother, David, sister Gail, and brother-in-law Mel Cox, along with my sister Pamela. Thanks as well to my extended family, Joan and Dick Henges, along with Victoria and Brent Menninger for love and therapy. And lastly, but always first in my heart, Terri Mac, the love of my life, and our children, Will, Mimi, Sam, dear Lola, and the best boy in the whole world, Bex.

Chuck Haddix

Index